Ayu
Watanabe

L♥DK

エルディーケー

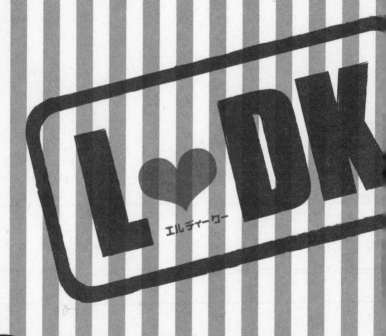

2

L♥DK

Ayu Watanabe

2

c o n t e n t s

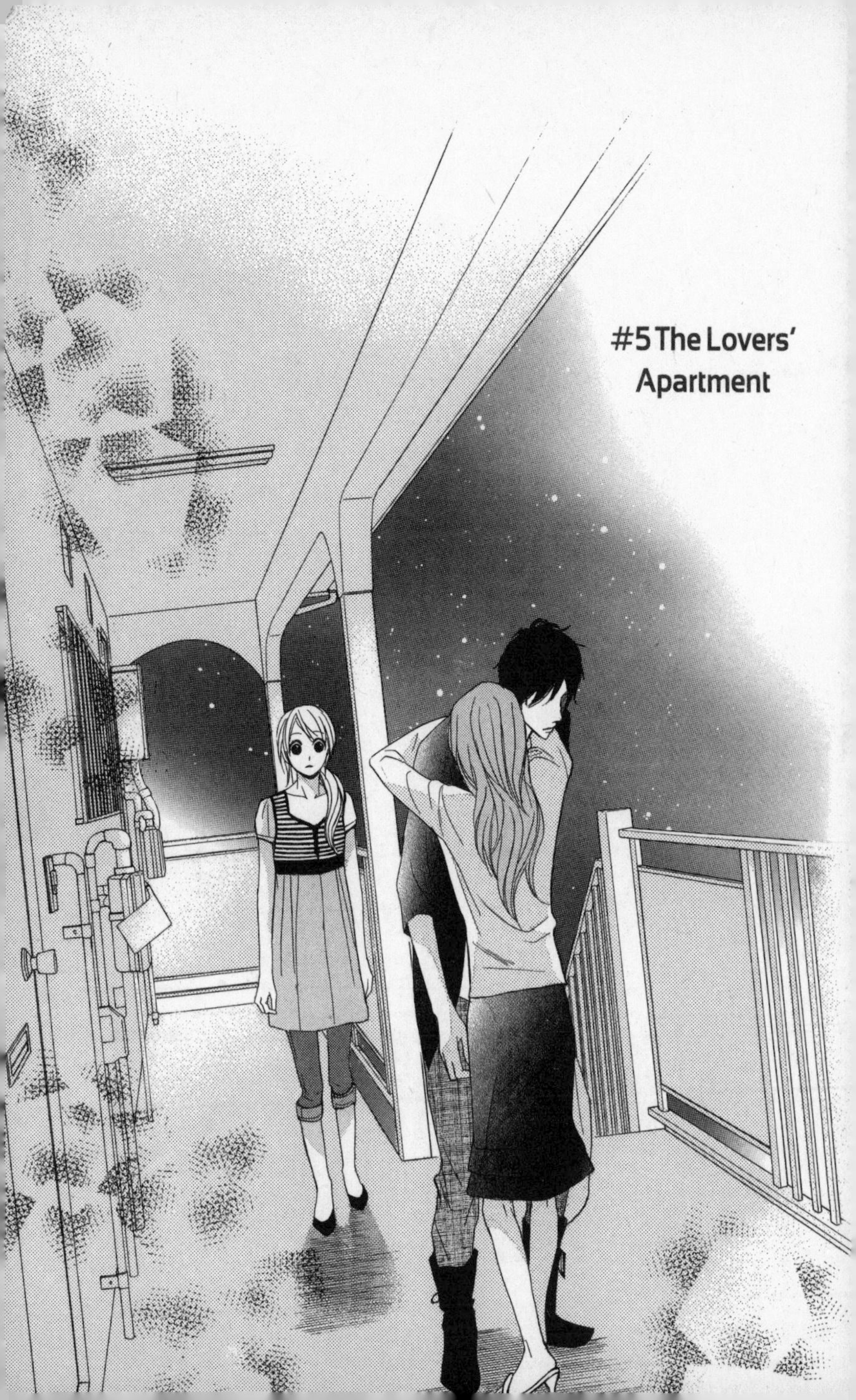
#5 The Lovers' Apartment

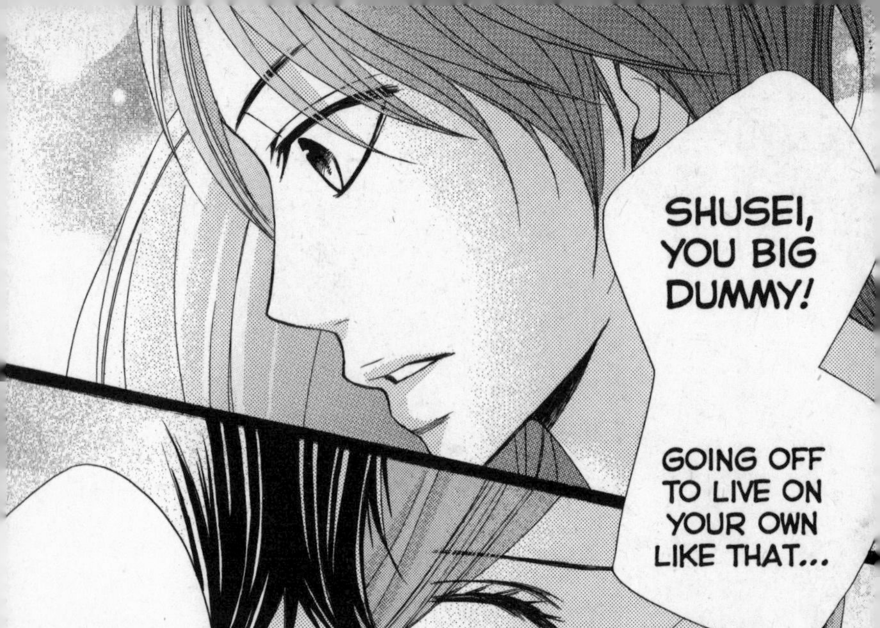
SHUSEI, YOU BIG DUMMY!
GOING OFF TO LIVE ON YOUR OWN LIKE THAT...
I'VE MISSED YOUUUUU!

THE STORY SO FAR

L♥DK

エルディーケー

Story

Aoi is a high school student living on her own who, through a curious turn of events, ends up living together in secret with the gorgeous Shusei, the "prince" of her school. At first, Aoi hates Shusei, but after experiencing a series of heart-racing moments, slowly but surely, Shusei becomes someone whom she can't get out of her mind. But just as Aoi realizes all this, she suddenly finds Shusei being embraced by a mysterious and beautiful woman!

Cast

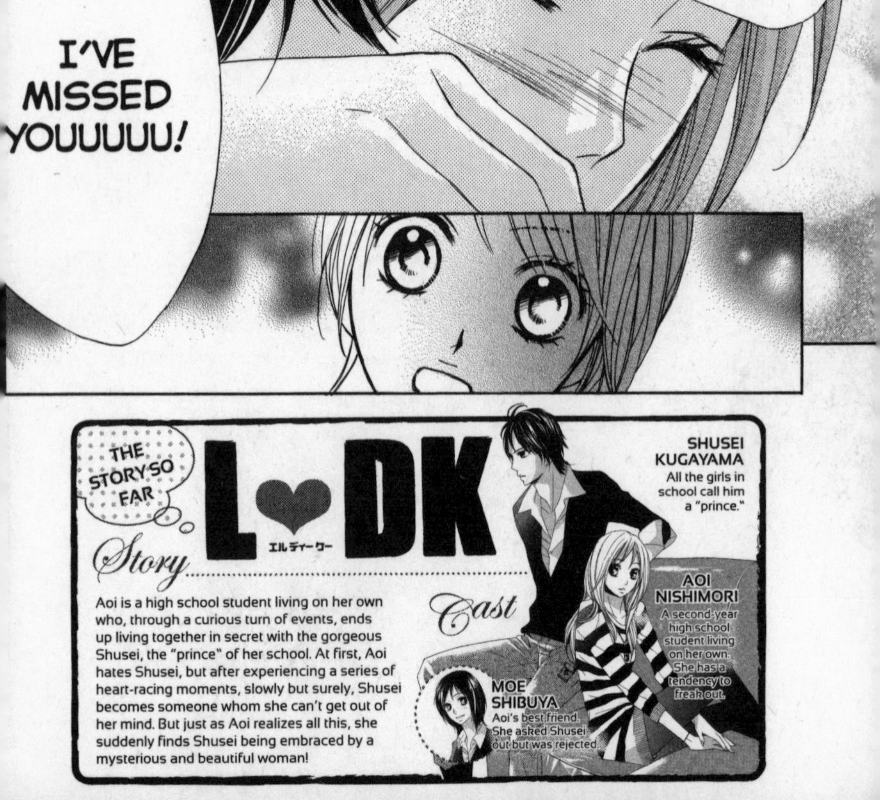

SHUSEI KUGAYAMA
All the girls in school call him a "prince."

AOI NISHIMORI
A second-year high school student living on her own. She has a tendency to freak out.

MOE SHIBUYA
Aoi's best friend. She asked Shusei out but was rejected.

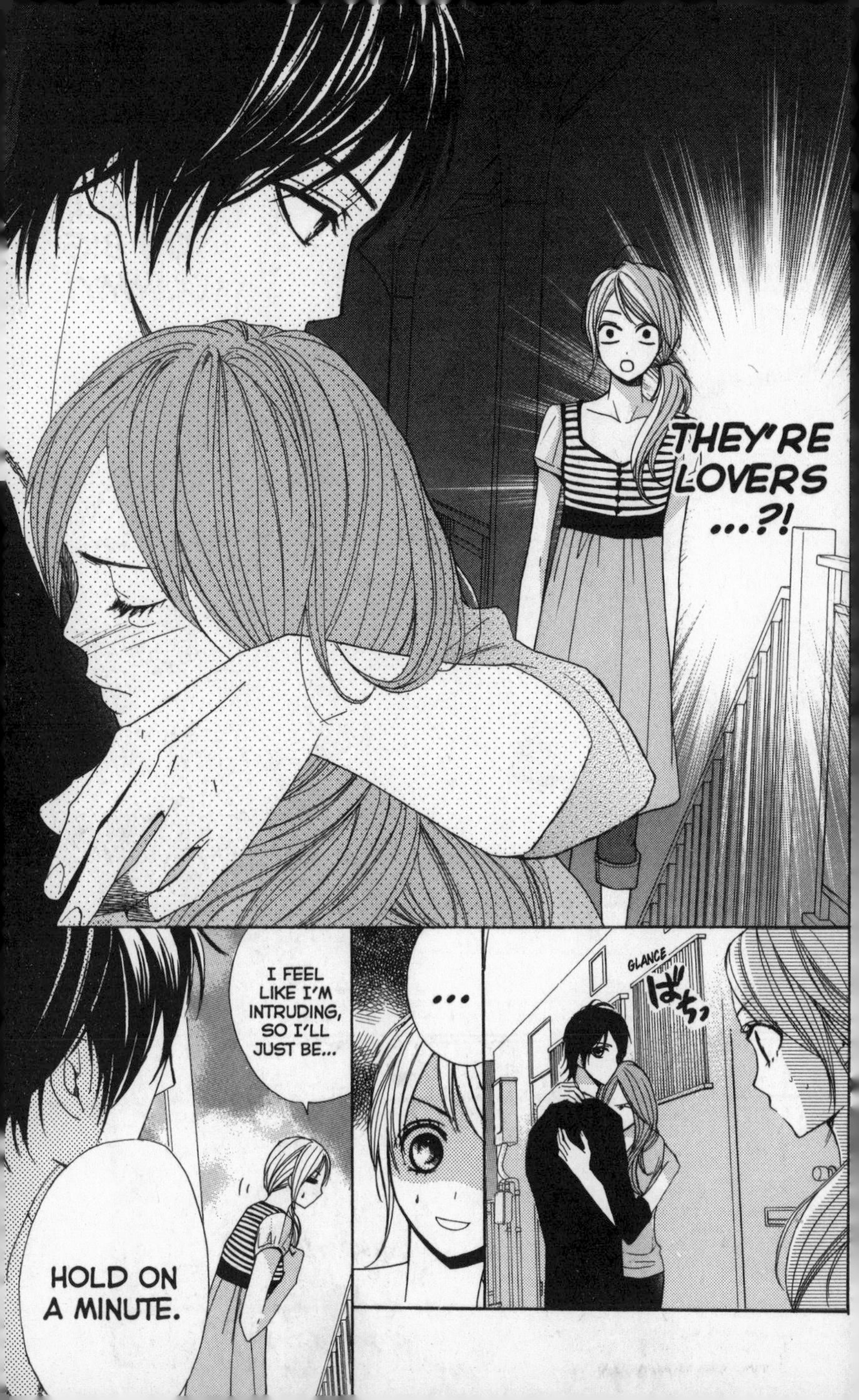
THEY'RE LOVERS ...?!
GLANCE
ぱちっ
...
I FEEL LIKE I'M INTRUDING, SO I'LL JUST BE...
HOLD ON A MINUTE.

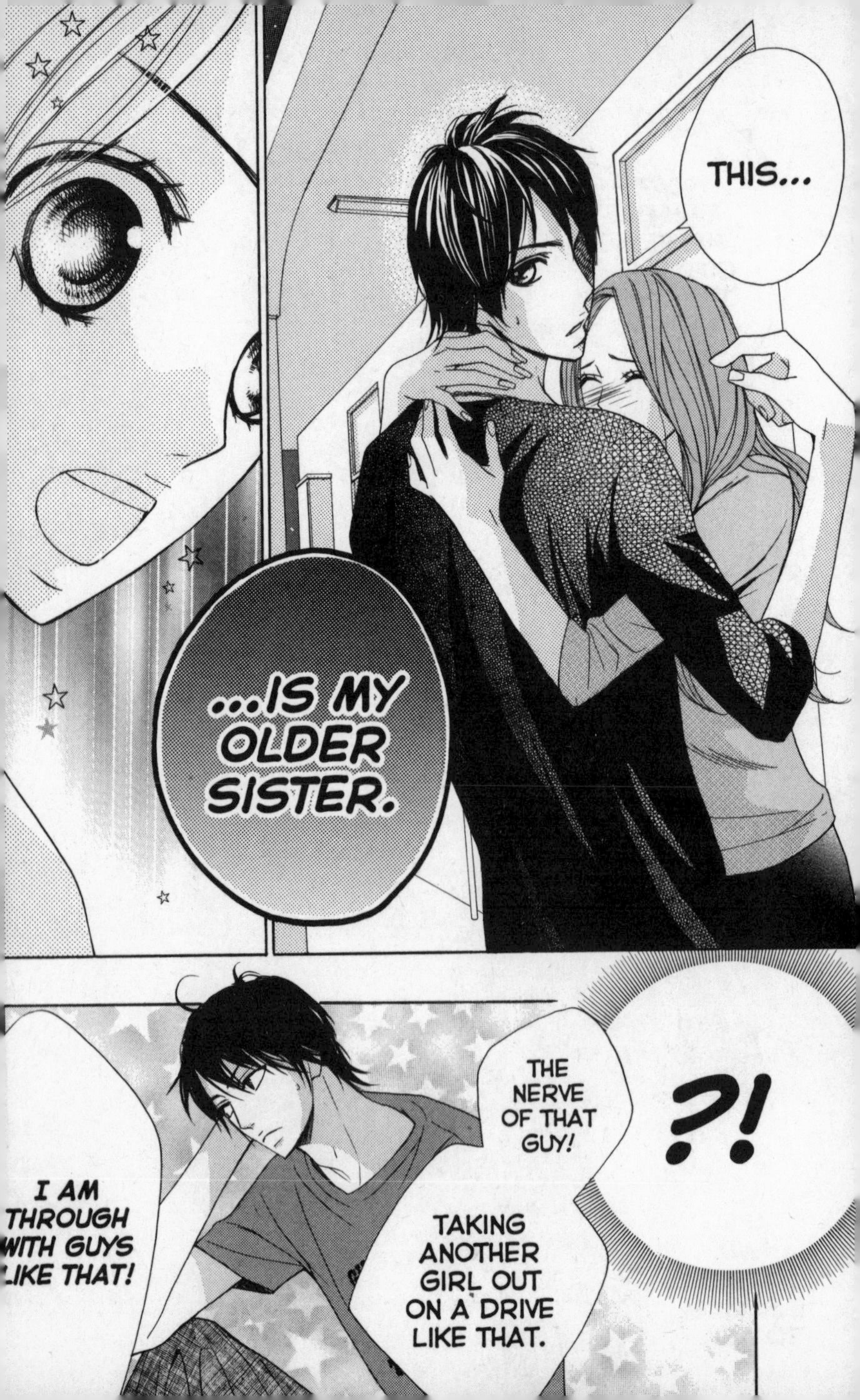
THIS...
...IS MY OLDER SISTER.
?!
THE NERVE OF THAT GUY!
TAKING ANOTHER GIRL OUT ON A DRIVE LIKE THAT.
I AM THROUGH WITH GUYS LIKE THAT!

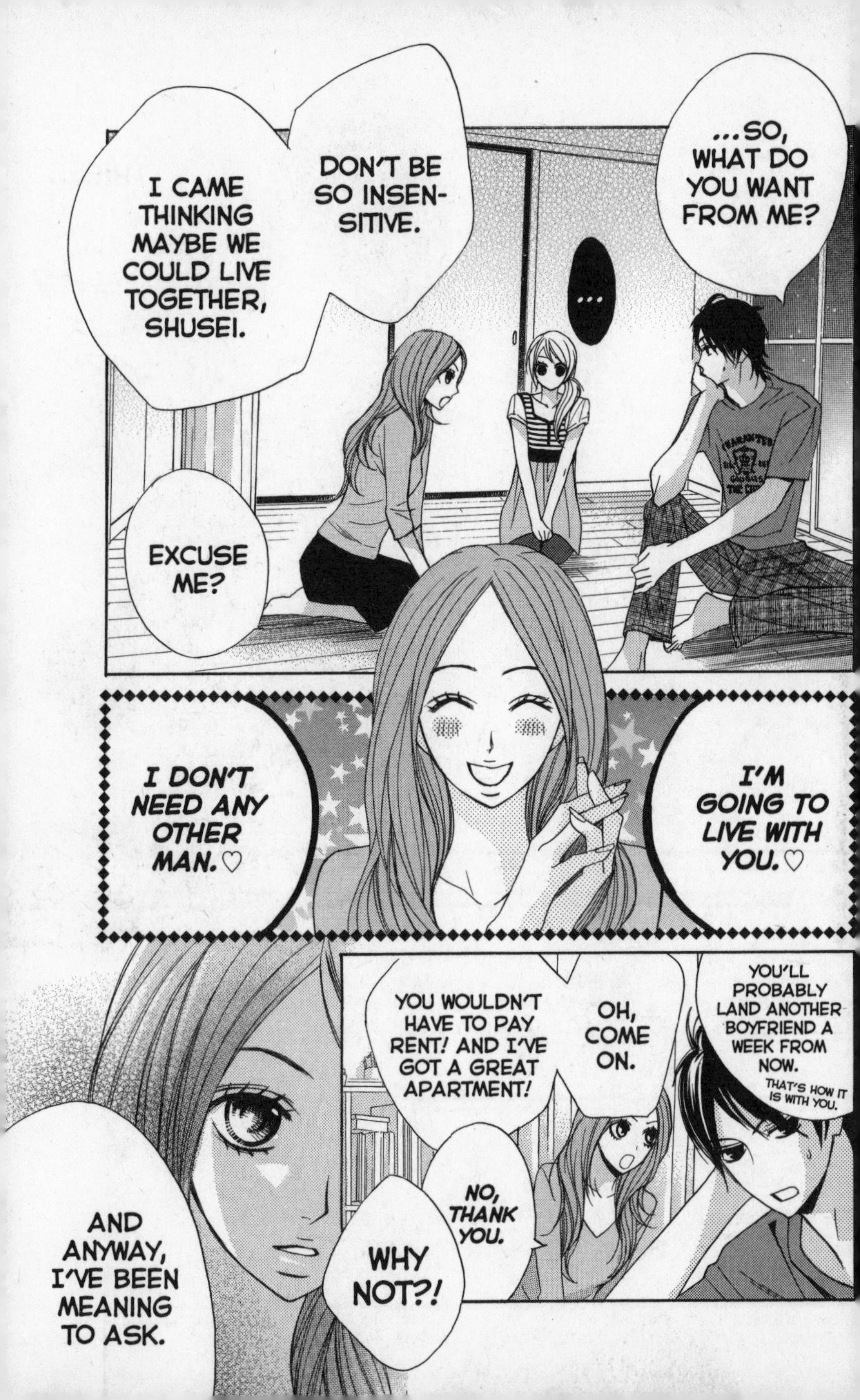
...SO, WHAT DO YOU WANT FROM ME?
...
DON'T BE SO INSEN-SITIVE.
I CAME THINKING MAYBE WE COULD LIVE TOGETHER, SHUSEI.
EXCUSE ME?
I'M GOING TO LIVE WITH YOU.♡
I DON'T NEED ANY OTHER MAN.♡
YOU'LL PROBABLY LAND ANOTHER BOYFRIEND A WEEK FROM NOW.
THAT'S HOW IT IS WITH YOU.
OH, COME ON.
YOU WOULDN'T HAVE TO PAY RENT! AND I'VE GOT A GREAT APARTMENT!
NO, THANK YOU.
WHY NOT?!
AND ANYWAY, I'VE BEEN MEANING TO ASK.

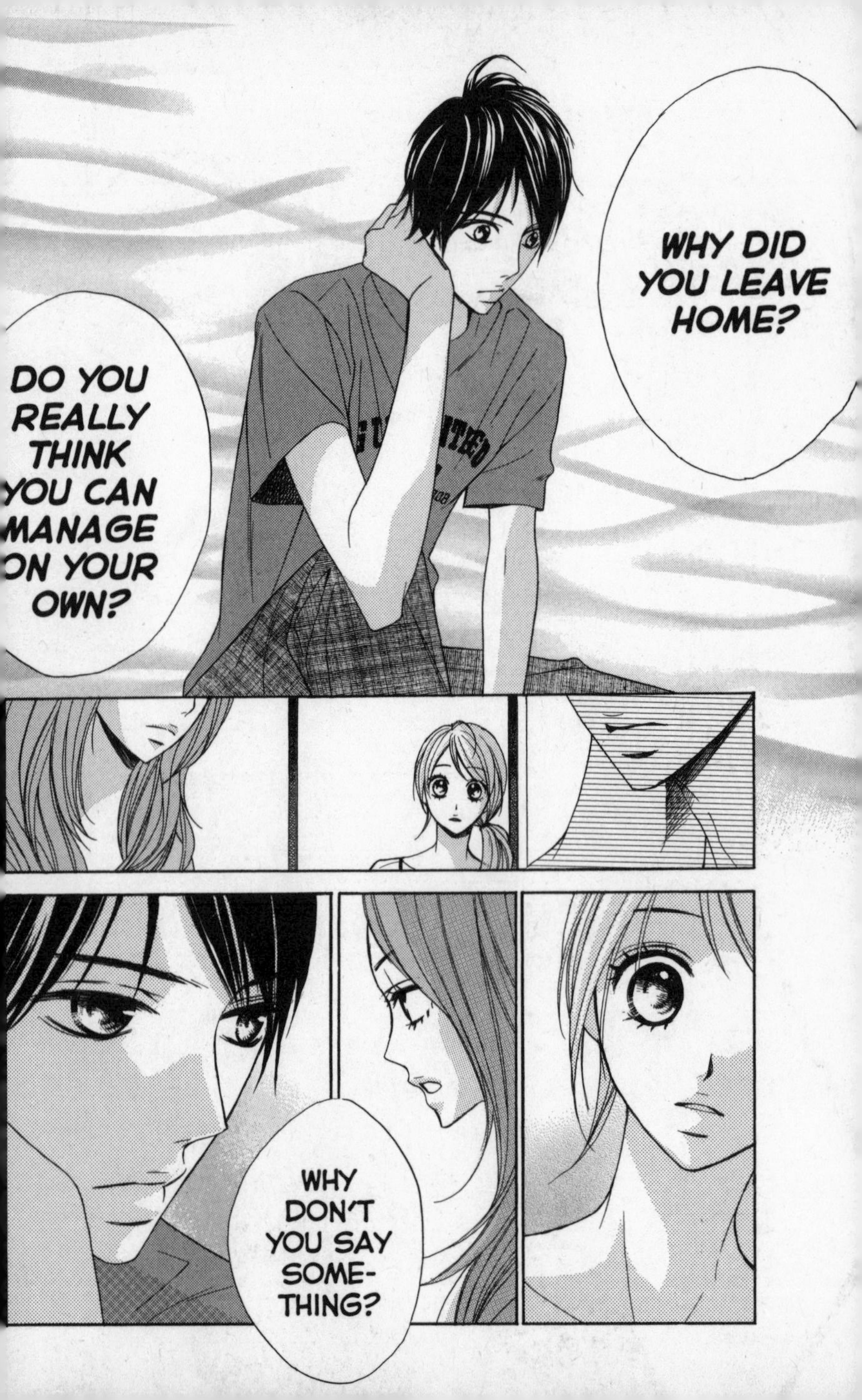
WHY DID YOU LEAVE HOME?
DO YOU REALLY THINK YOU CAN MANAGE ON YOUR OWN?
WHY DON'T YOU SAY SOME-THING?

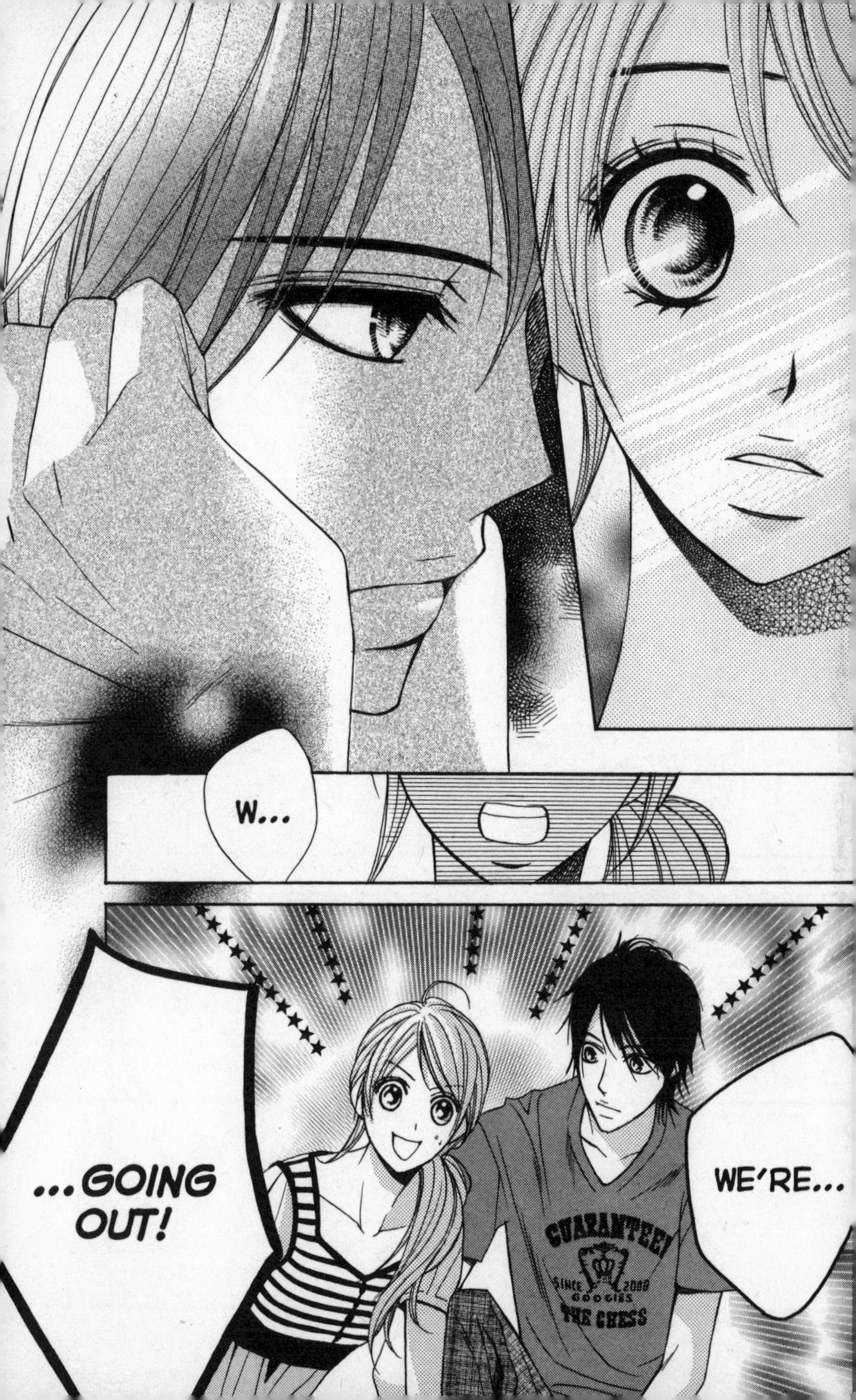
W...
WE'RE...
...GOING OUT!

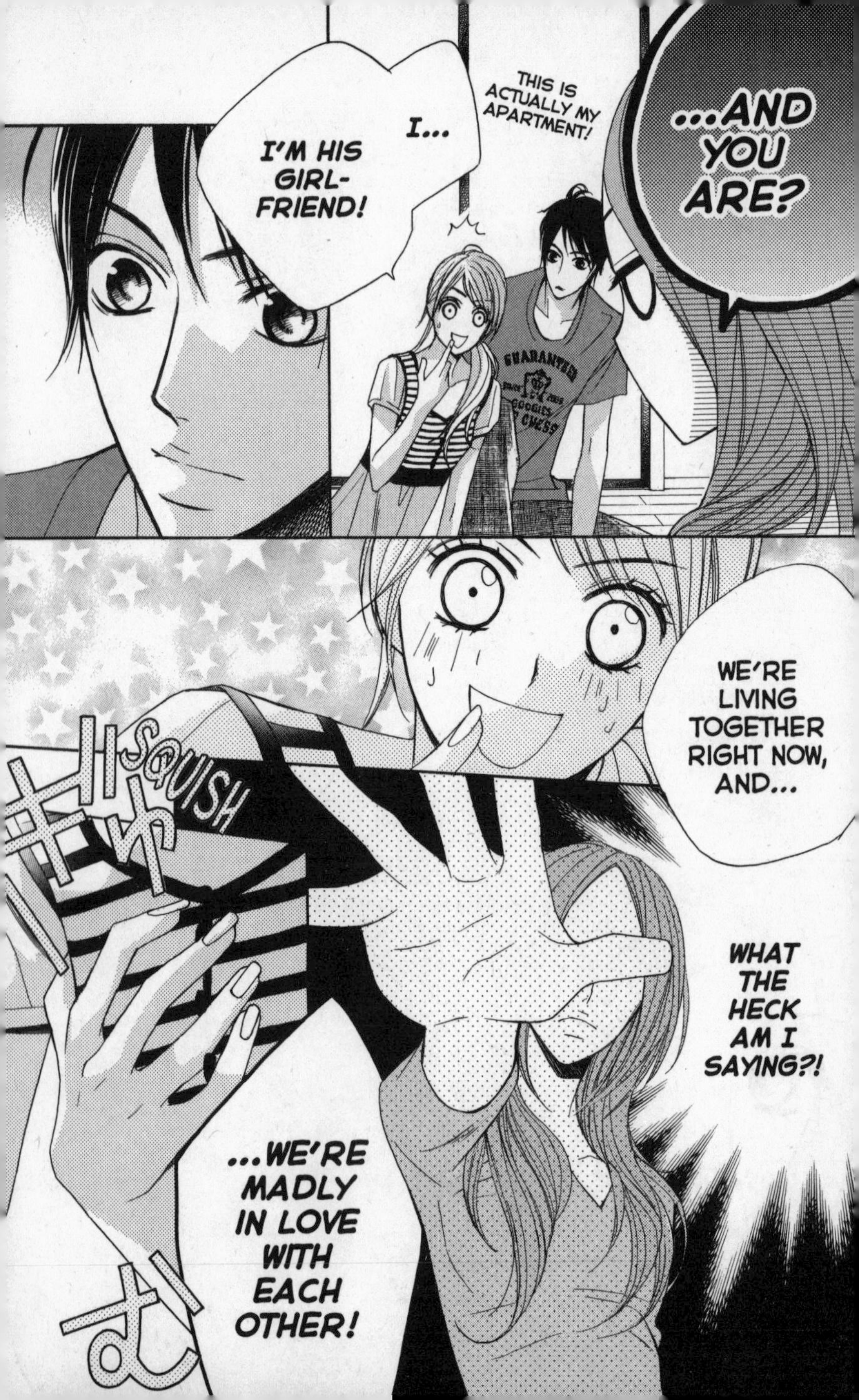
...AND YOU ARE?
THIS IS ACTUALLY MY APARTMENT!
I...
I'M HIS GIRL-FRIEND!
WE'RE LIVING TOGETHER RIGHT NOW, AND...
WHAT THE HECK AM I SAYING?!
SQUISH
...WE'RE MADLY IN LOVE WITH EACH OTHER!

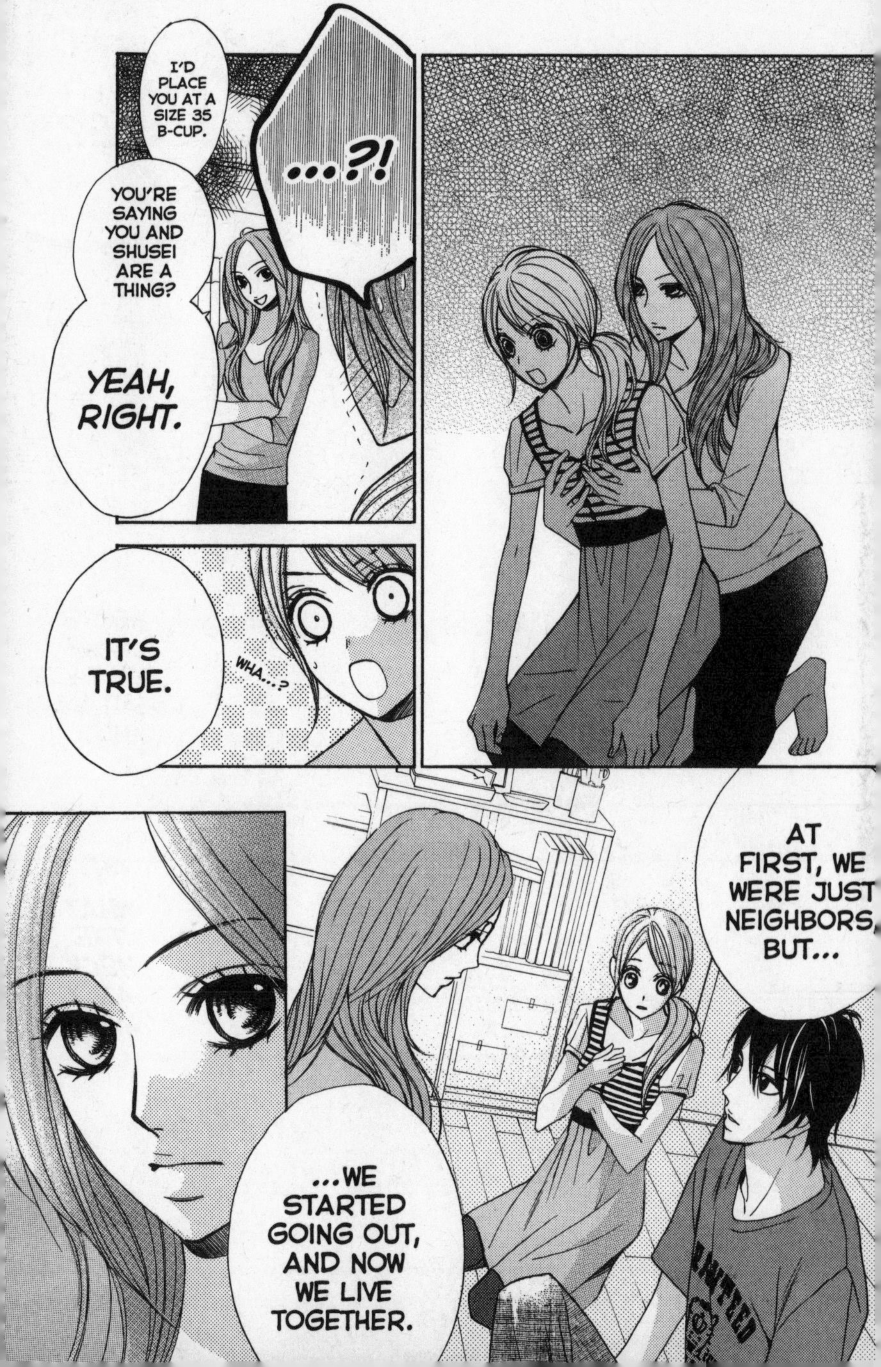
I'D PLACE YOU AT A SIZE 35 B-CUP.
...?!
YOU'RE SAYING YOU AND SHUSEI ARE A THING?
YEAH, RIGHT.
IT'S TRUE.
WHA...?
AT FIRST, WE WERE JUST NEIGHBORS, BUT...
...WE STARTED GOING OUT, AND NOW WE LIVE TOGETHER.

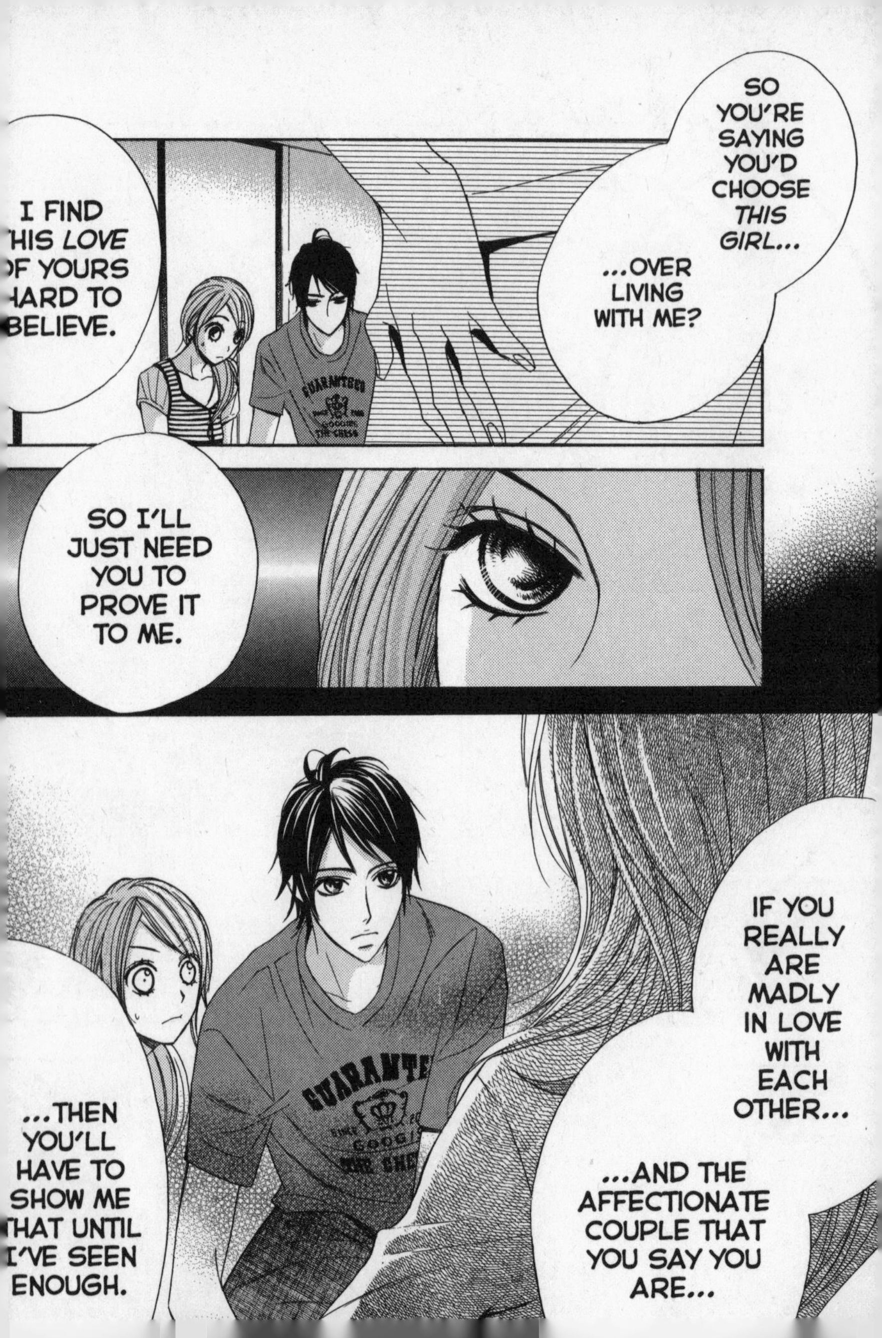
SO YOU'RE SAYING YOU'D CHOOSE *THIS* GIRL...
...OVER LIVING WITH ME?
I FIND THIS *LOVE* OF YOURS HARD TO BELIEVE.
SO I'LL JUST NEED YOU TO PROVE IT TO ME.
IF YOU REALLY ARE MADLY IN LOVE WITH EACH OTHER...
...AND THE AFFECTIONATE COUPLE THAT YOU SAY YOU ARE...
...THEN YOU'LL HAVE TO SHOW ME THAT UNTIL I'VE SEEN ENOUGH.

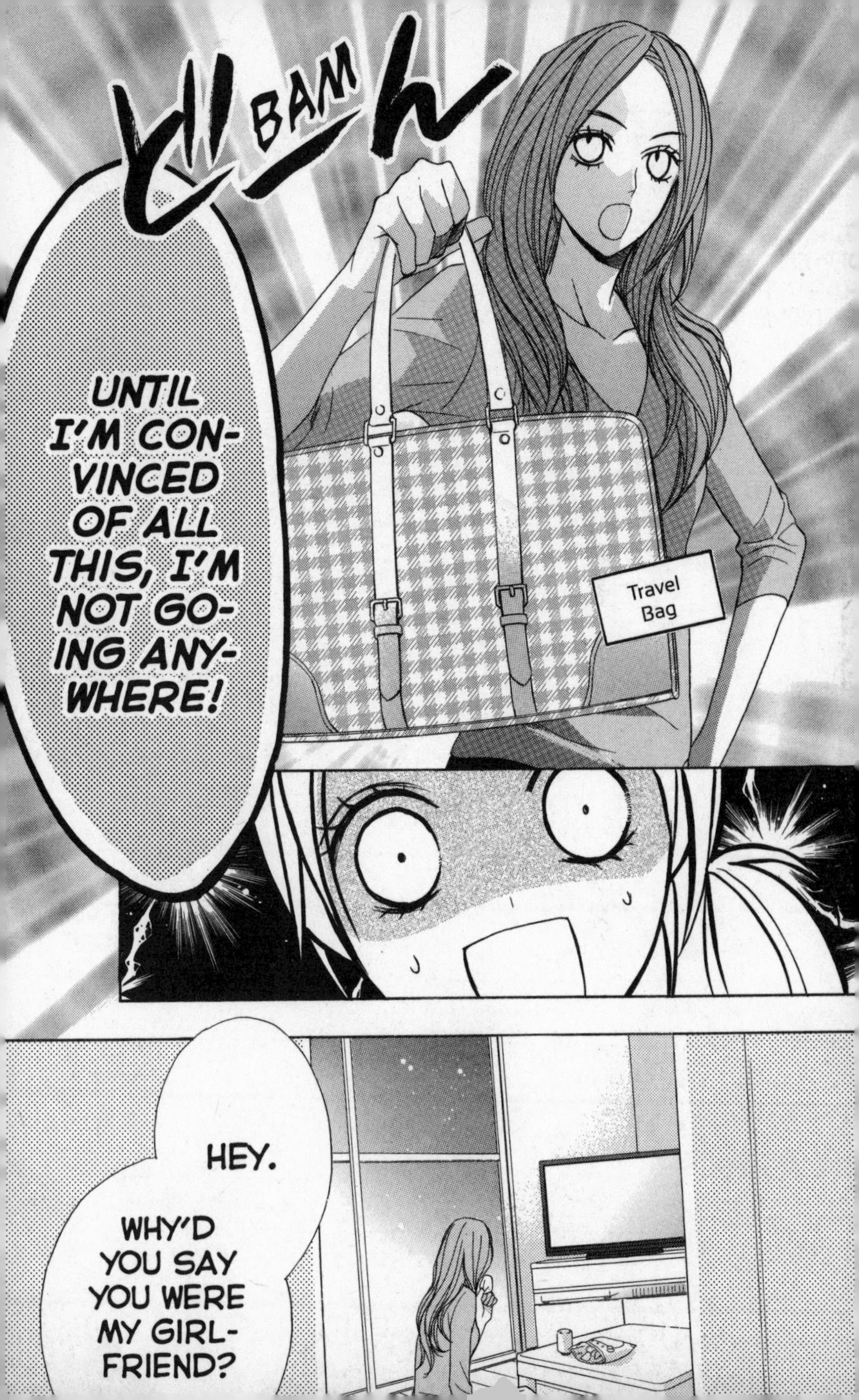

BAM
UNTIL I'M CONVINCED OF ALL THIS, I'M NOT GOING ANYWHERE!
Travel Bag
HEY.
WHY'D YOU SAY YOU WERE MY GIRLFRIEND?

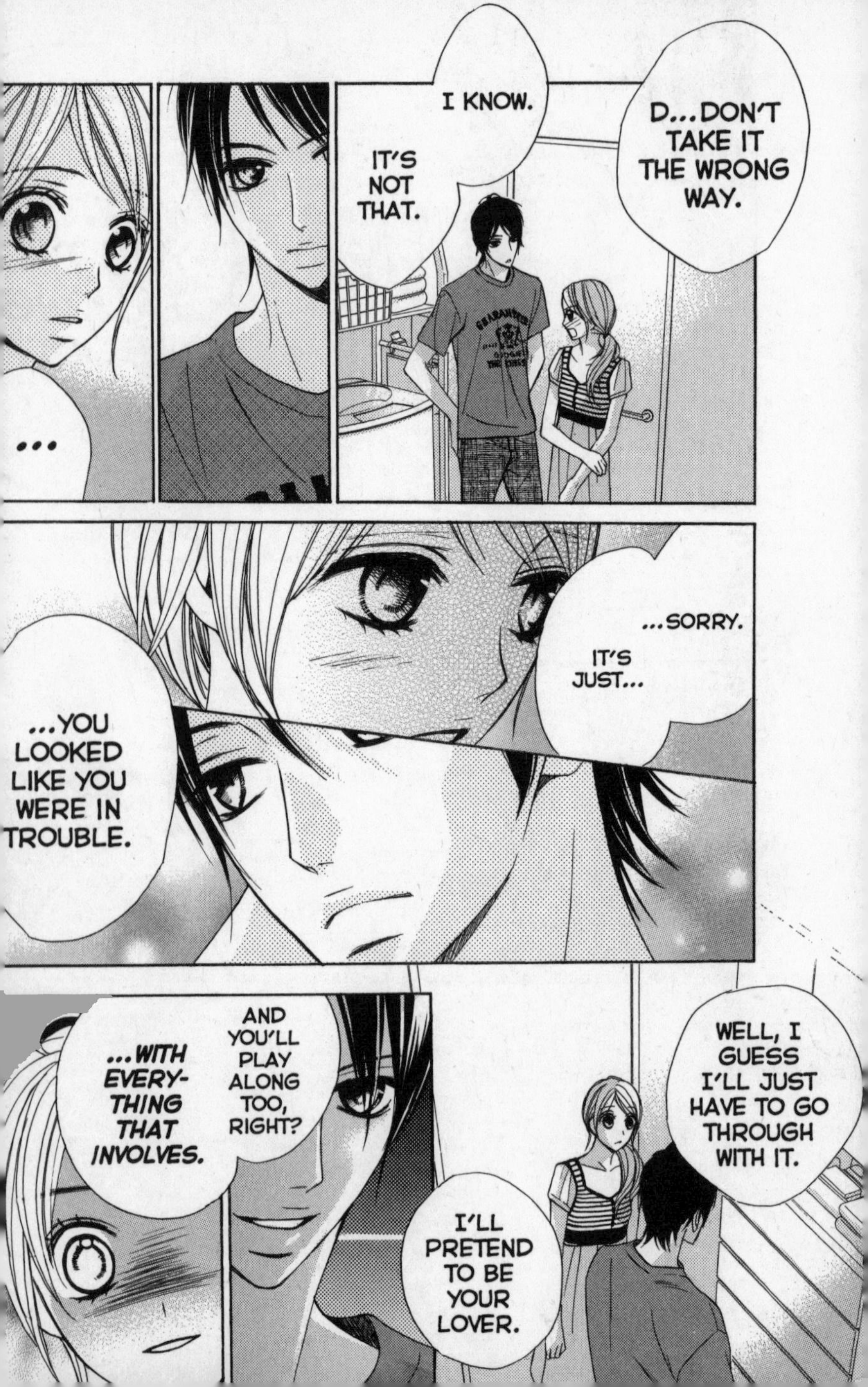
D...DON'T TAKE IT THE WRONG WAY.
I KNOW.
IT'S NOT THAT.
...
...SORRY.
IT'S JUST...
...YOU LOOKED LIKE YOU WERE IN TROUBLE.
WELL, I GUESS I'LL JUST HAVE TO GO THROUGH WITH IT.
I'LL PRETEND TO BE YOUR LOVER.
AND YOU'LL PLAY ALONG TOO, RIGHT?
...WITH EVERYTHING THAT INVOLVES.

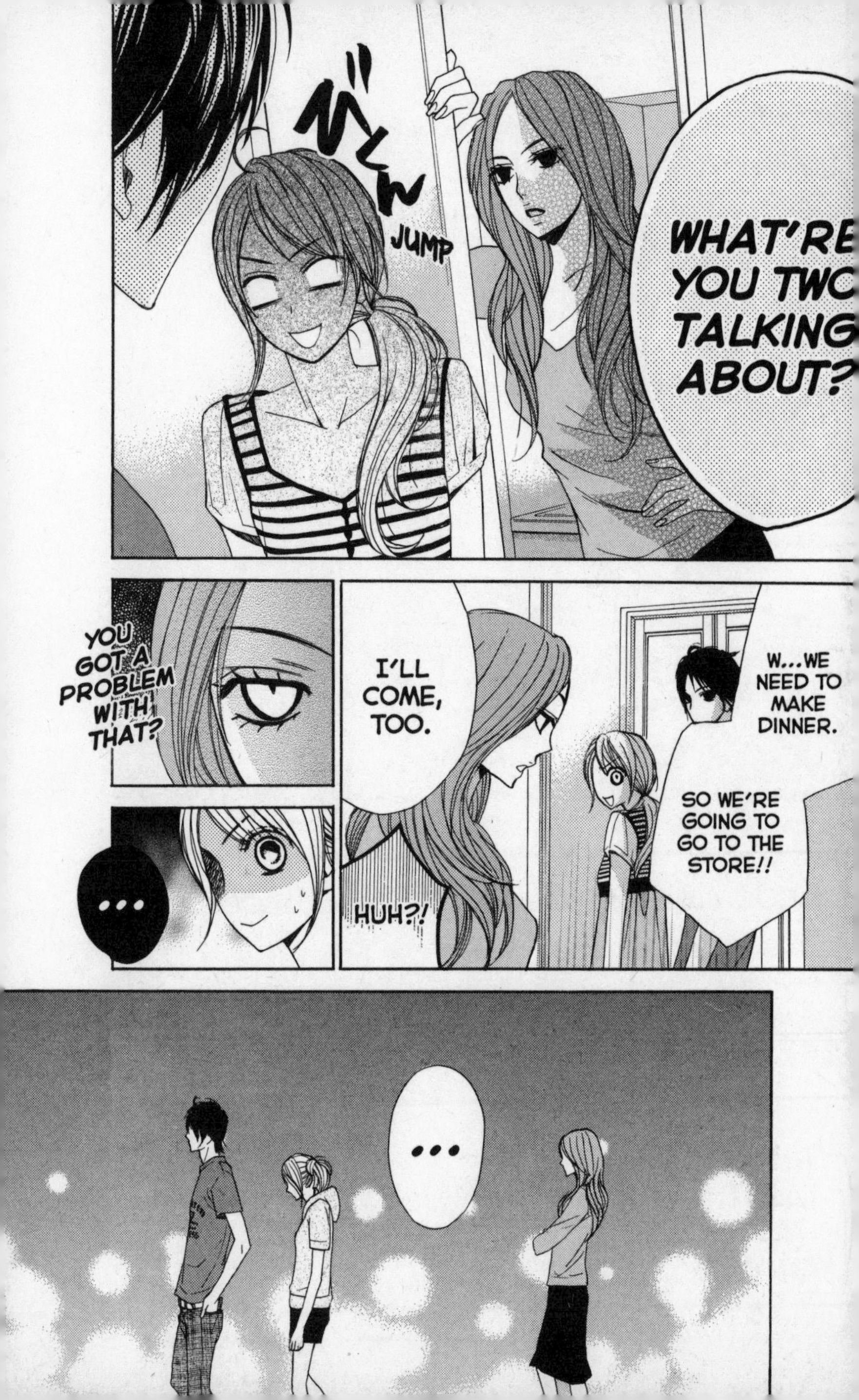
WHAT'RE YOU TWO TALKING ABOUT?
JUMP
W...WE NEED TO MAKE DINNER.
SO WE'RE GOING TO GO TO THE STORE!!
I'LL COME, TOO.
HUH?!
YOU GOT A PROBLEM WITH THAT?
...
...

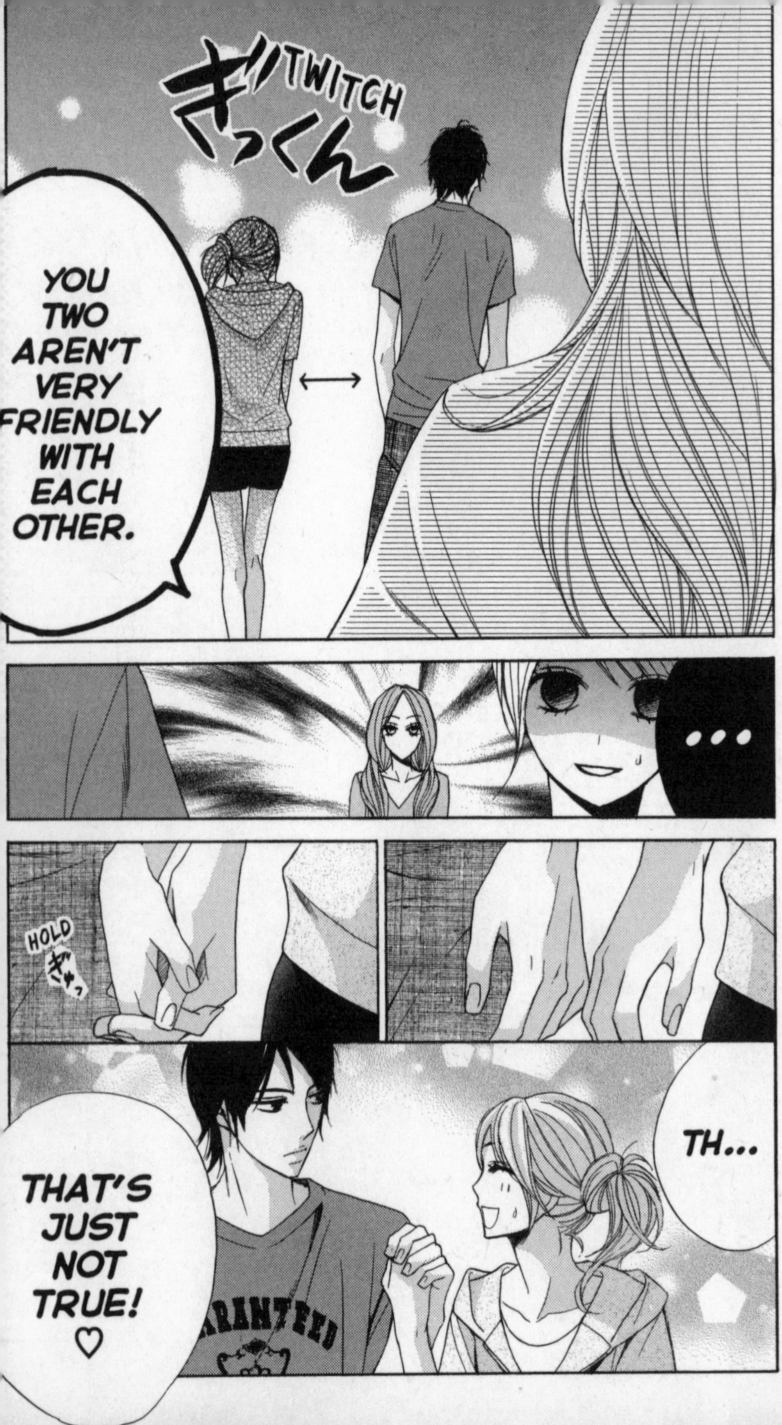
ぎっくん TWITCH
YOU TWO AREN'T VERY FRIENDLY WITH EACH OTHER.
...
HOLD ぎゅっ
TH...
THAT'S JUST NOT TRUE! ♡

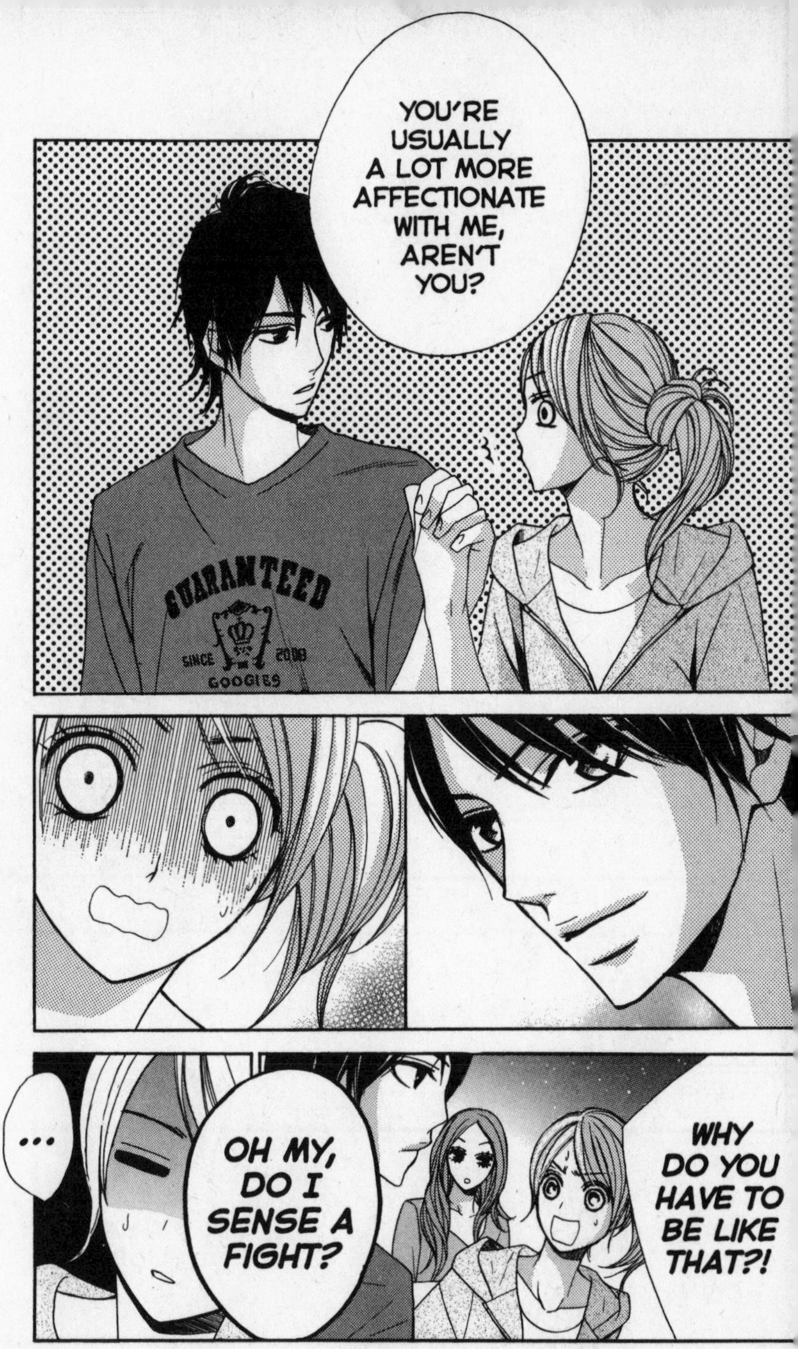
YOU'RE USUALLY A LOT MORE AFFECTIONATE WITH ME, AREN'T YOU?
WHY DO YOU HAVE TO BE LIKE THAT?!
OH MY, DO I SENSE A FIGHT?
...

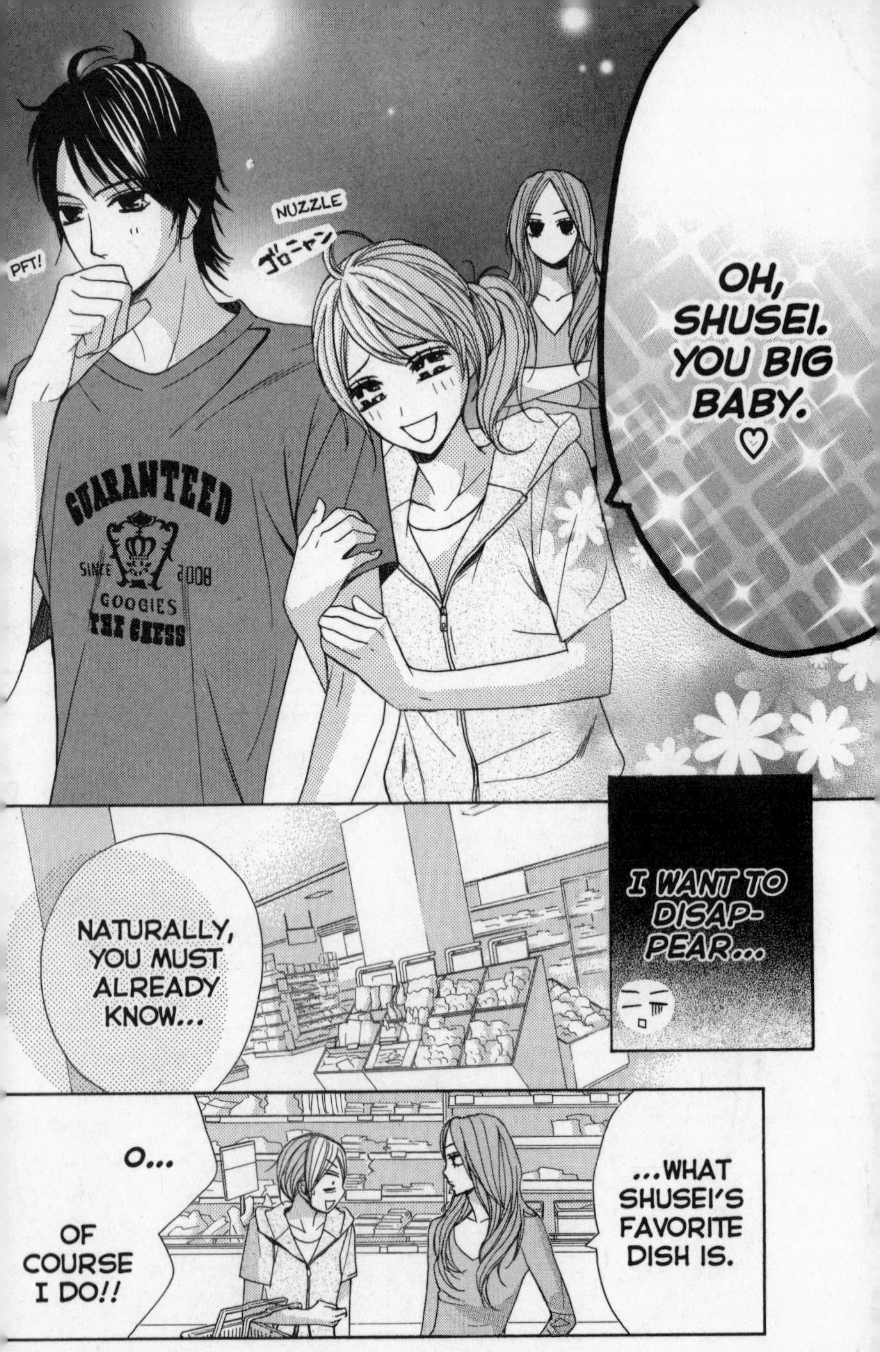
OH, SHUSEI. YOU BIG BABY. ♡
NUZZLE
ゴロニャン
PFT!
I WANT TO DISAP-PEAR...
NATURALLY, YOU MUST ALREADY KNOW...
...WHAT SHUSEI'S FAVORITE DISH IS.
O...
OF COURSE I DO!!

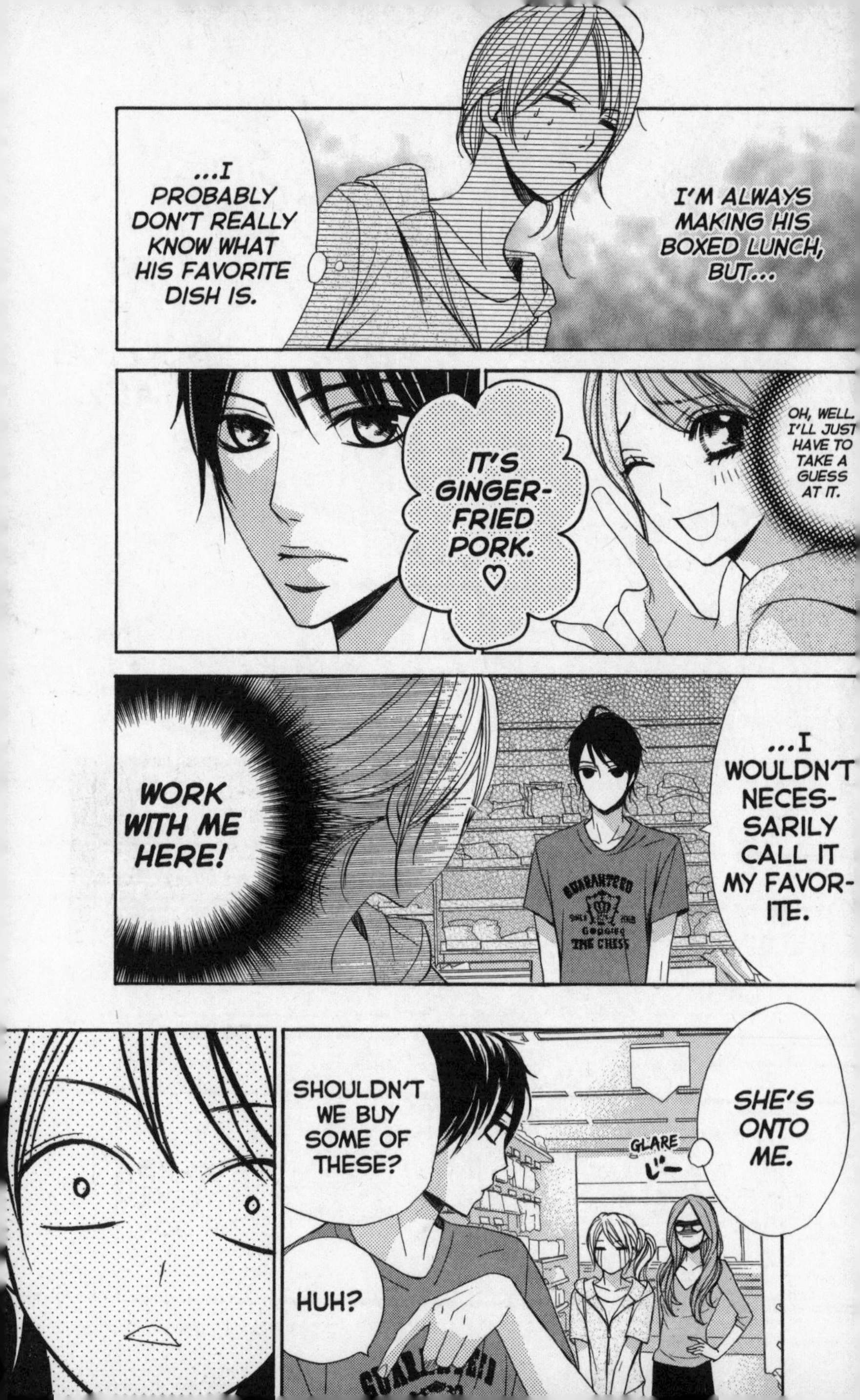
I'M ALWAYS MAKING HIS BOXED LUNCH, BUT...
...I PROBABLY DON'T REALLY KNOW WHAT HIS FAVORITE DISH IS.
OH, WELL. I'LL JUST HAVE TO TAKE A GUESS AT IT.
IT'S GINGER-FRIED PORK. ♡
...I WOULDN'T NECES-SARILY CALL IT MY FAVOR-ITE.
WORK WITH ME HERE!
SHE'S ONTO ME.
GLARE
じー
SHOULDN'T WE BUY SOME OF THESE?
HUH?

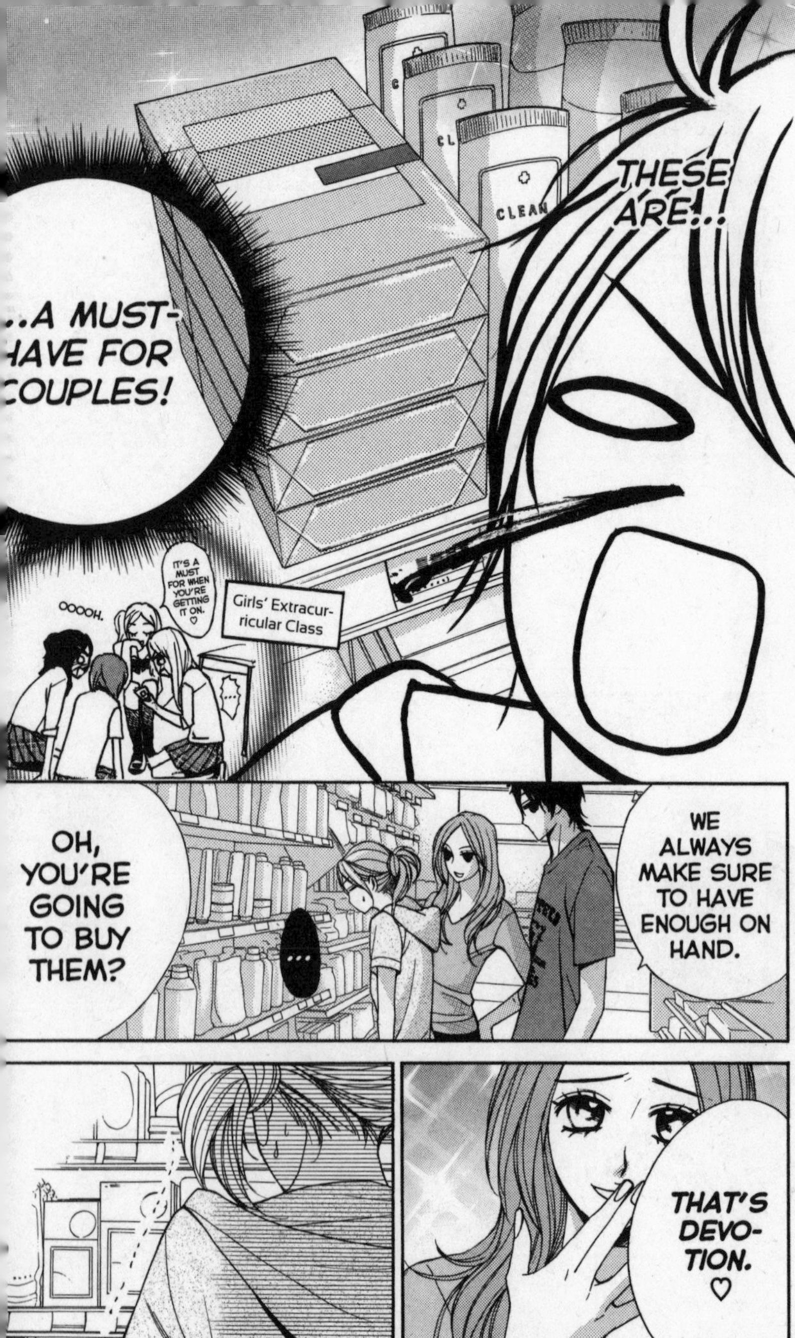
THESE ARE...
..A MUST-HAVE FOR COUPLES!
Girls' Extracurricular Class
IT'S A MUST FOR WHEN YOU'RE GETTING IT ON. ♡
OOOOH.
WE ALWAYS MAKE SURE TO HAVE ENOUGH ON HAND.
....
OH, YOU'RE GOING TO BUY THEM?
THAT'S DEVOTION. ♡

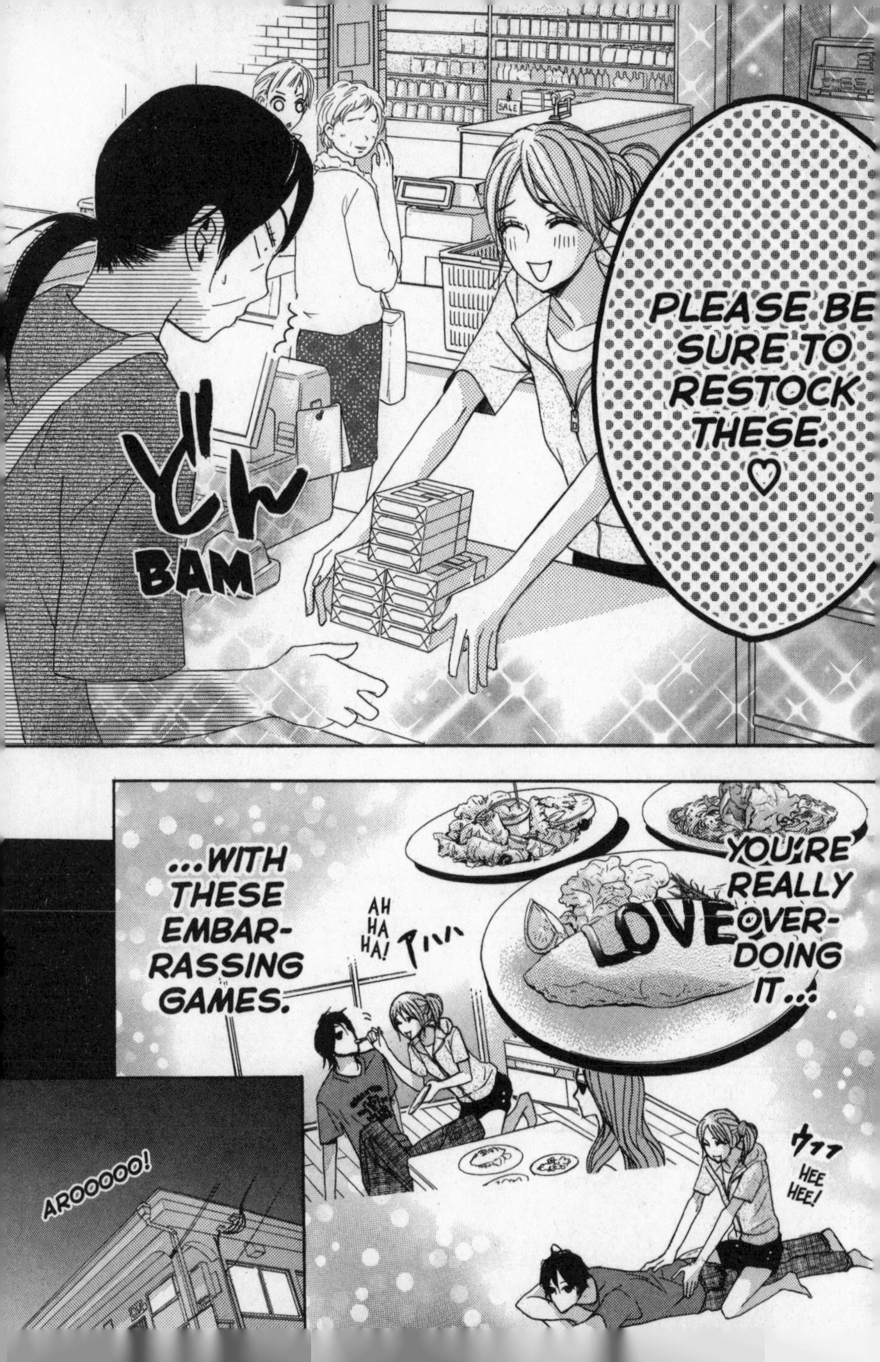
PLEASE BE SURE TO RESTOCK THESE. ♡
どん
BAM
YOU'RE REALLY OVER-DOING IT...
LOVE
AH HA HA!
アハハ
...WITH THESE EMBAR-RASSING GAMES.
ウフフ
HEE HEE!
AROOOOO!

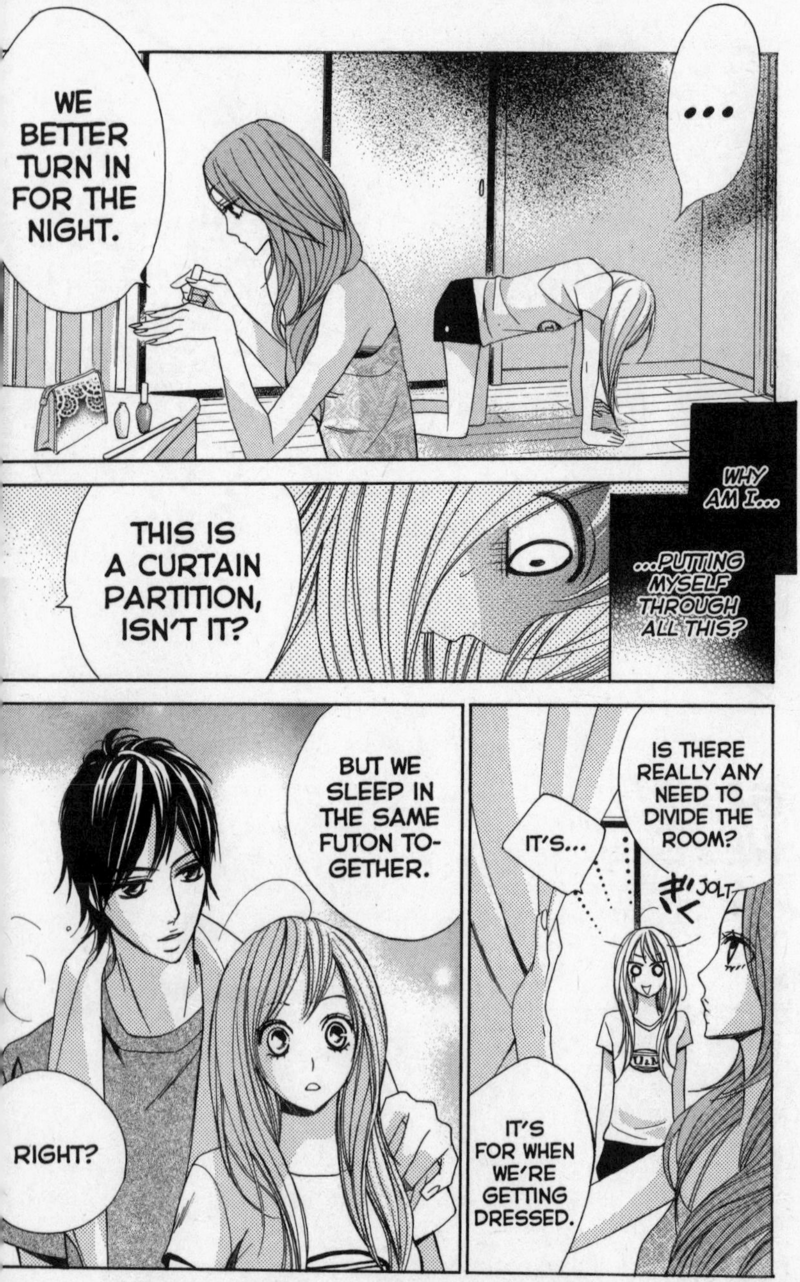
...
WE BETTER TURN IN FOR THE NIGHT.
WHY AM I...
...PUTTING MYSELF THROUGH ALL THIS?
THIS IS A CURTAIN PARTITION, ISN'T IT?
IS THERE REALLY ANY NEED TO DIVIDE THE ROOM?
JOLT
IT'S...
IT'S FOR WHEN WE'RE GETTING DRESSED.
BUT WE SLEEP IN THE SAME FUTON TO-GETHER.
RIGHT?

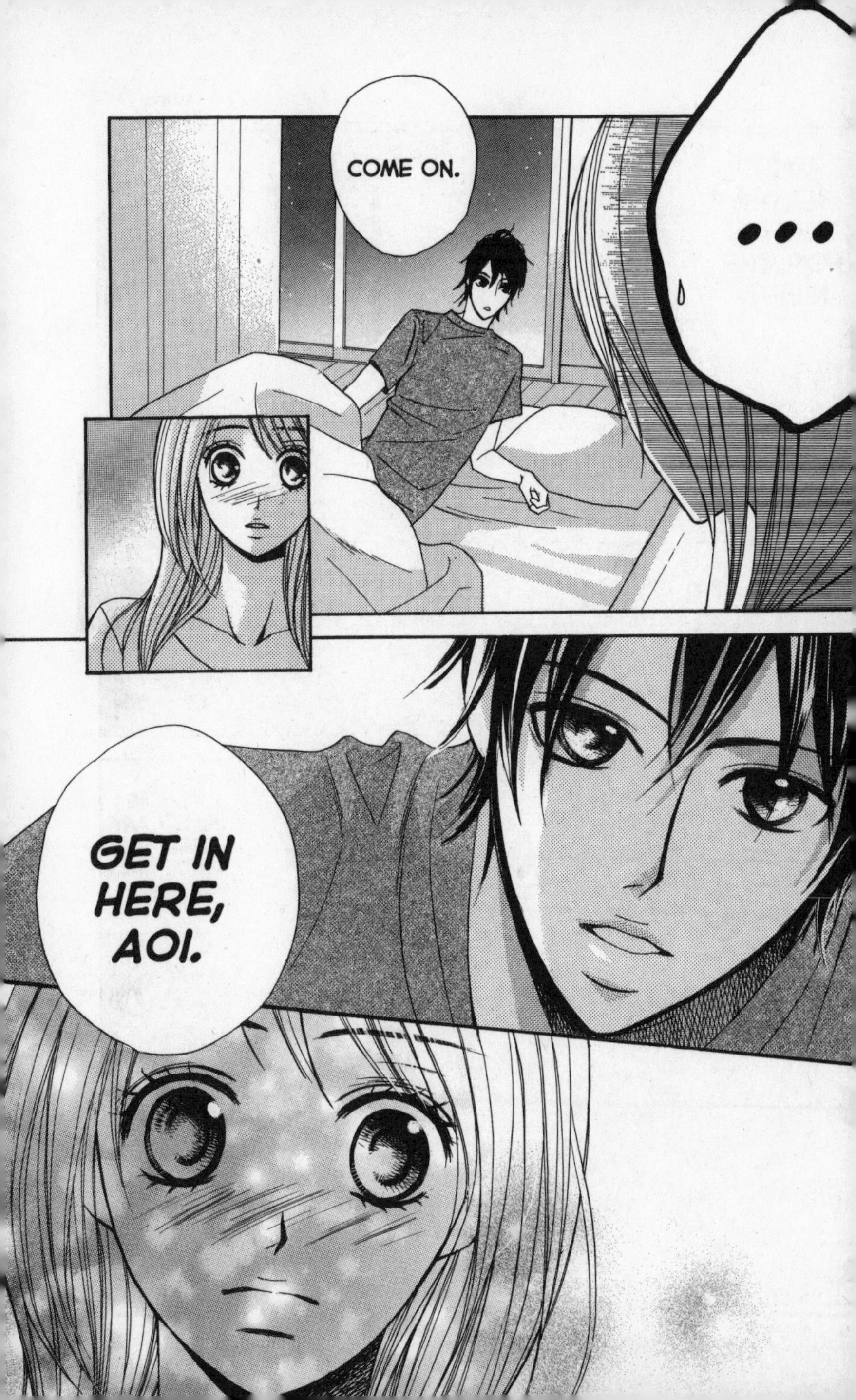
...
COME ON.
GET IN HERE, AOI.

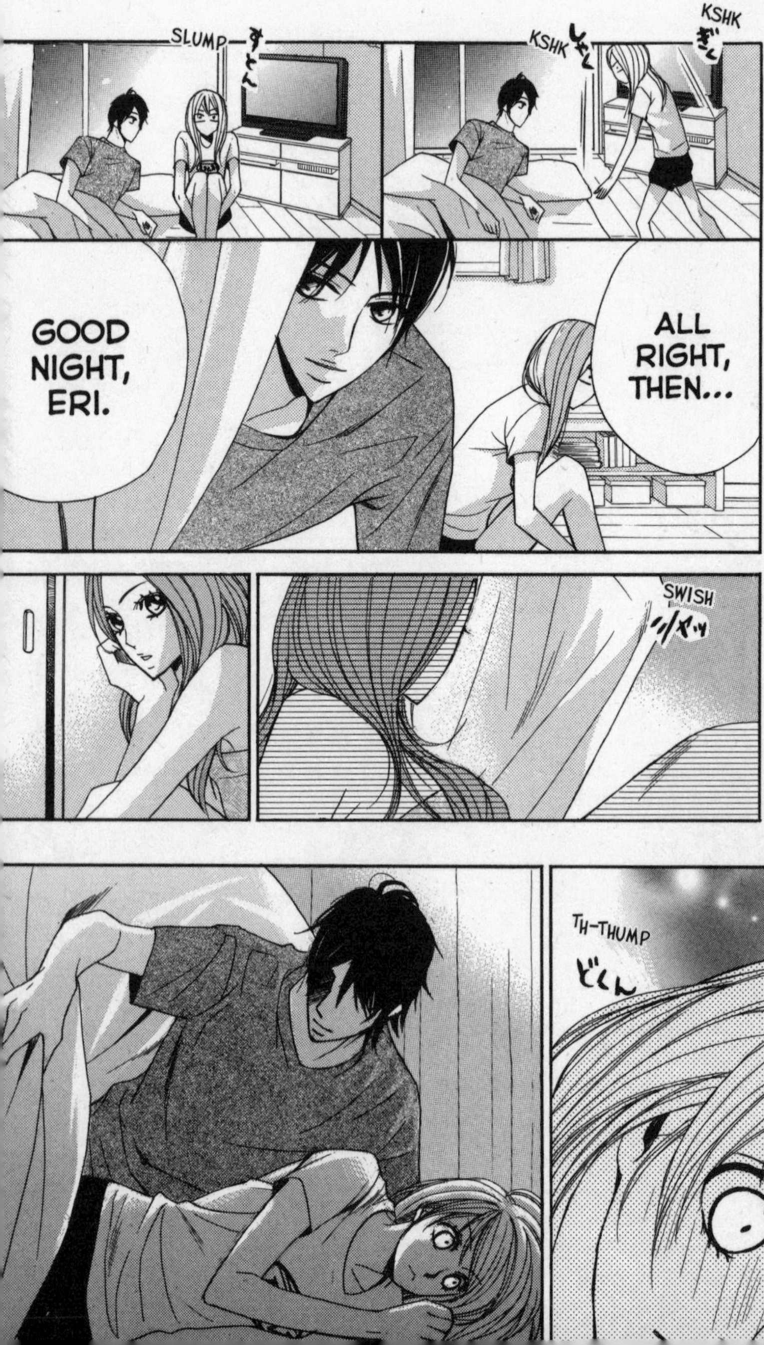
KSHK
KSHK
SLUMP
すとん
ALL RIGHT, THEN...
GOOD NIGHT, ERI.
SWISH
TH-THUMP
どくん

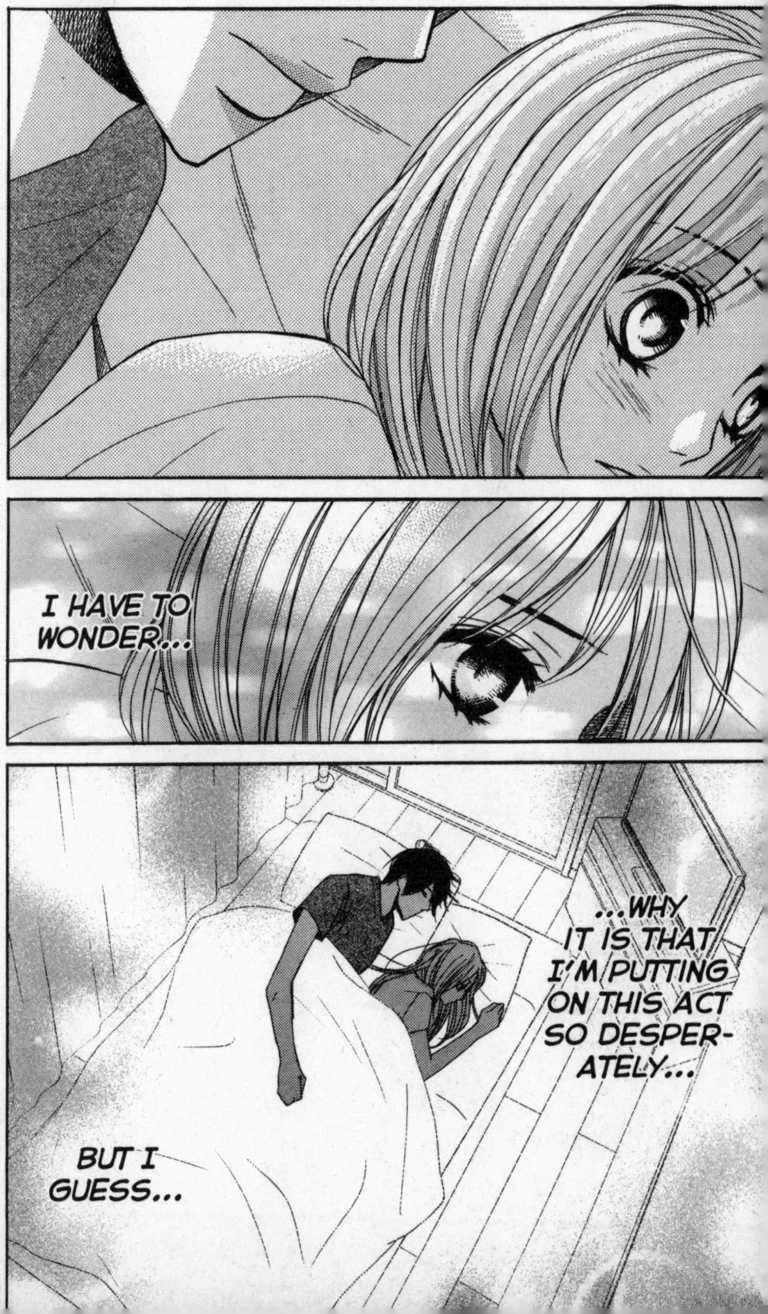
I HAVE TO WONDER...
...WHY IT IS THAT I'M PUTTING ON THIS ACT SO DESPER-ATELY...
BUT I GUESS...

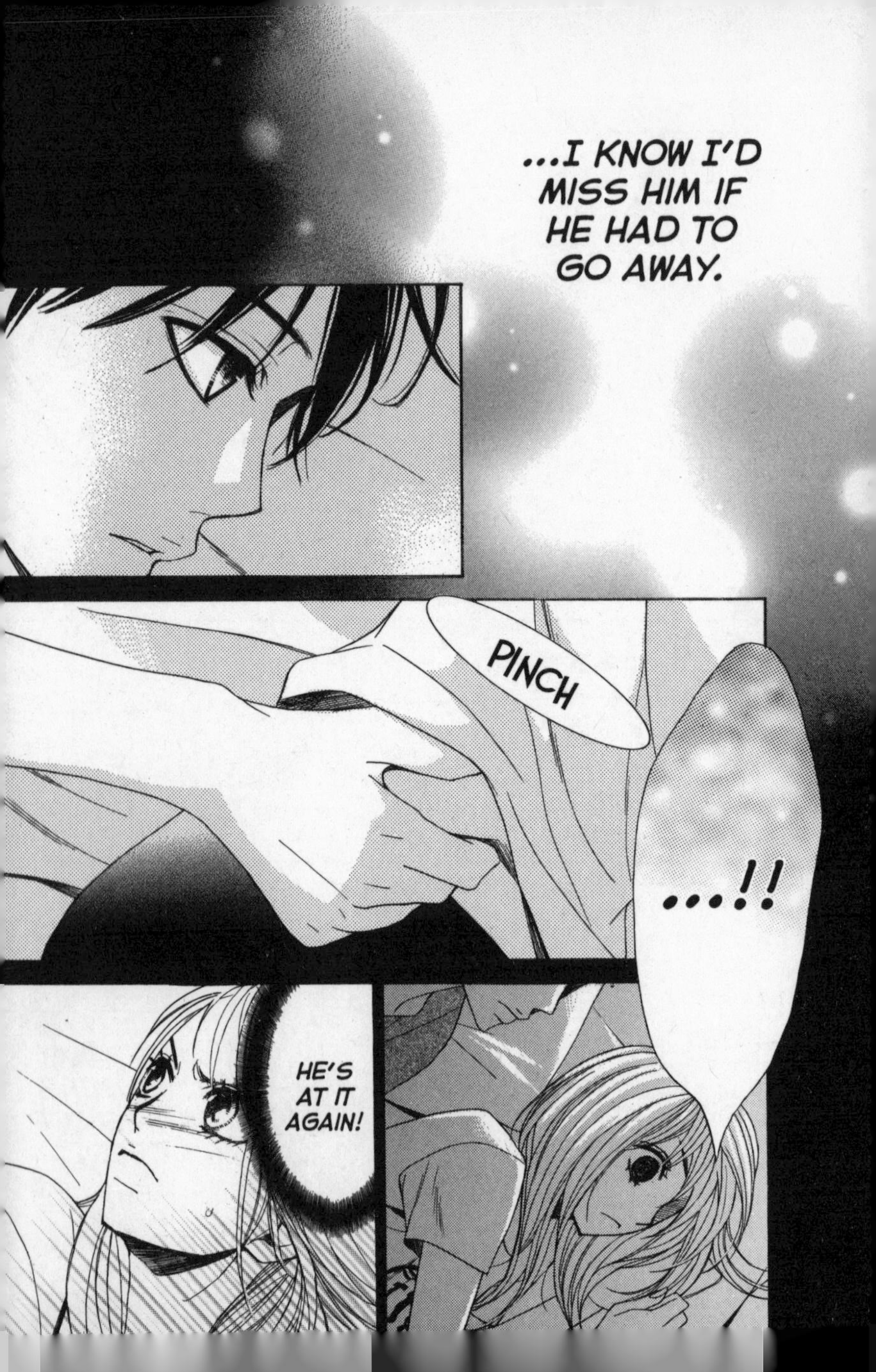
...I KNOW I'D MISS HIM IF HE HAD TO GO AWAY.
PINCH
...!!
HE'S AT IT AGAIN!

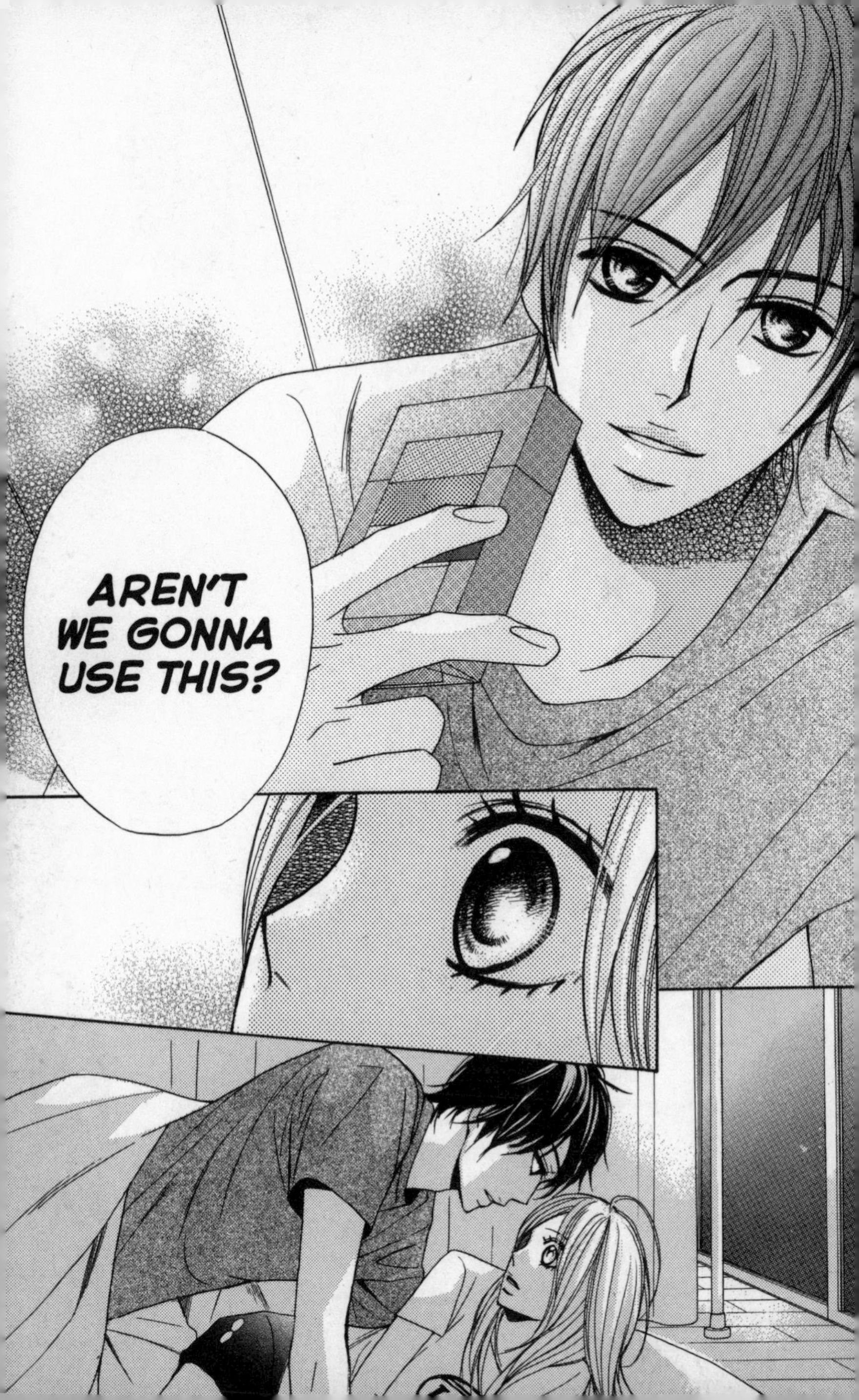
AREN'T WE GONNA USE THIS?

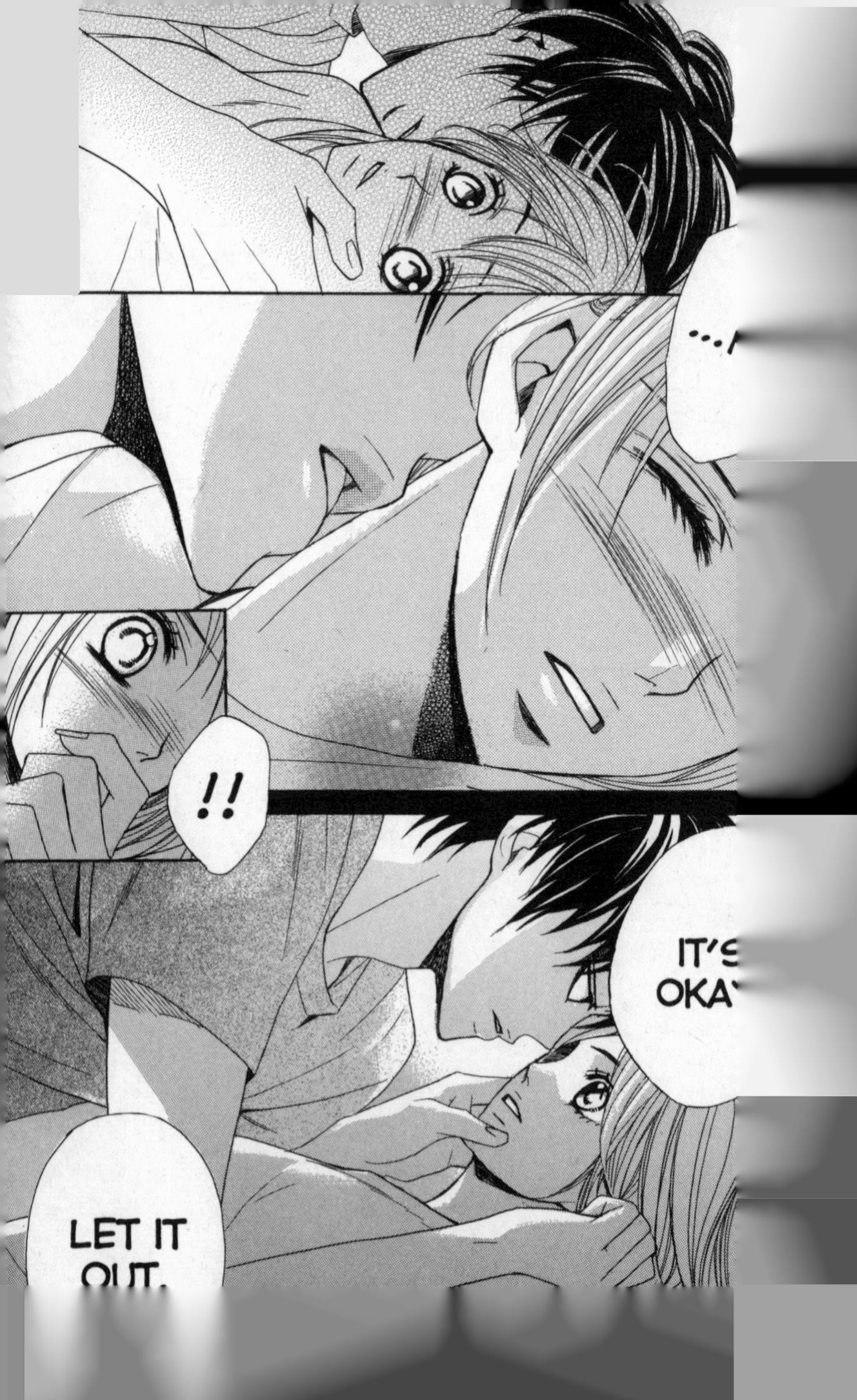
...!
!!
IT'S OKA
LET IT OUT.

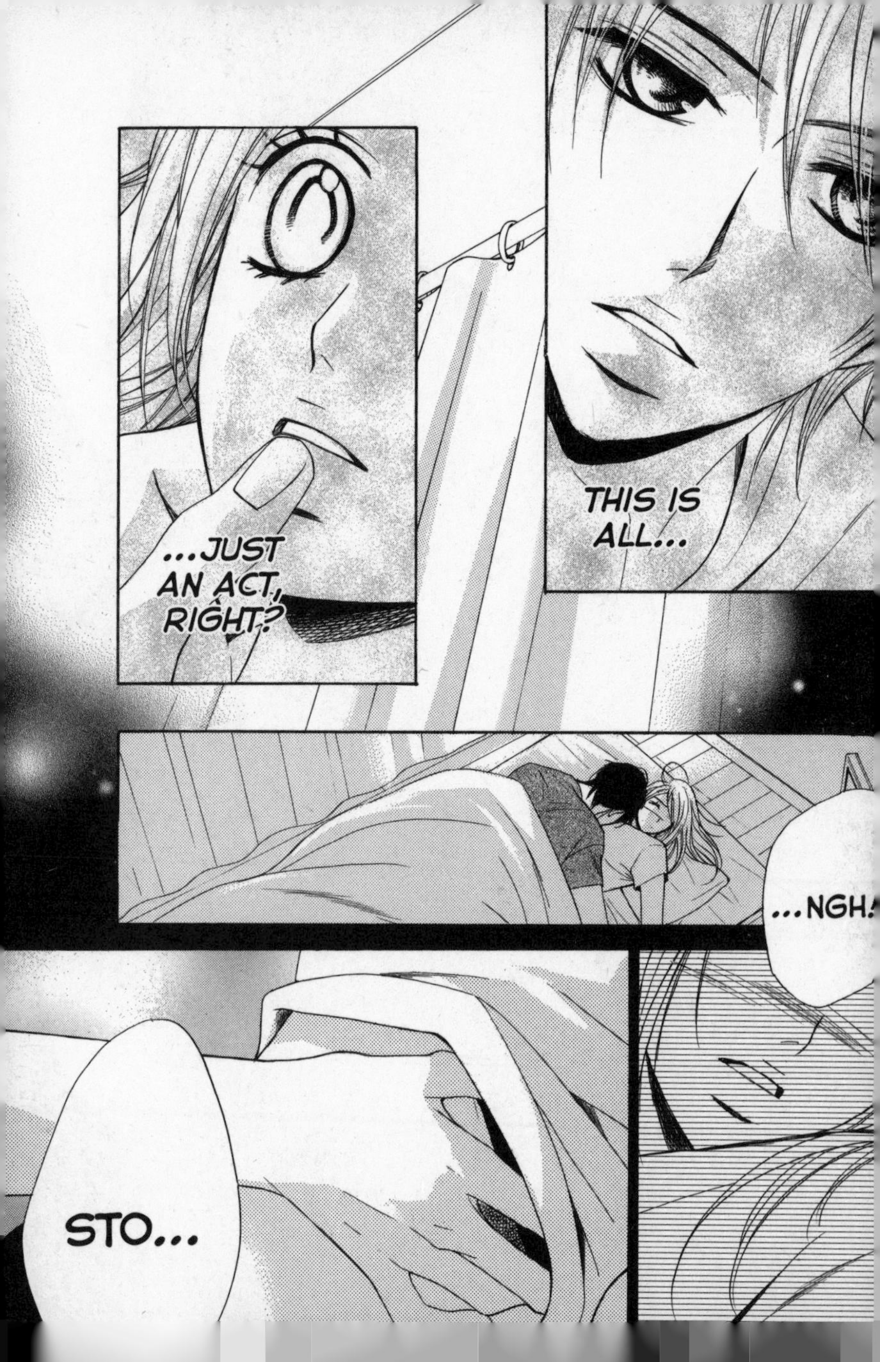
THIS IS ALL...
...JUST AN ACT, RIGHT?
...NGH!
STO...

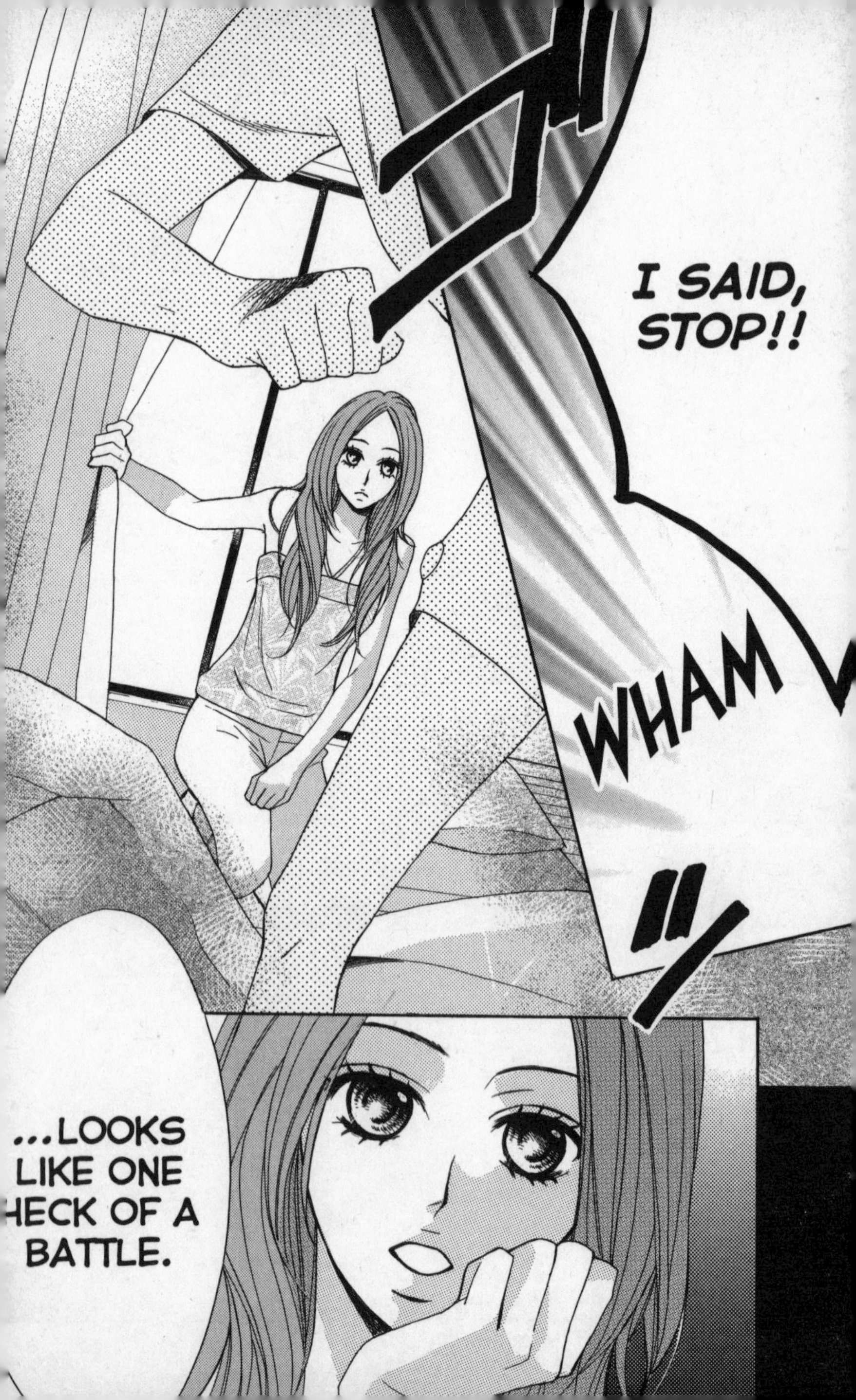
I SAID, STOP!!
WHAM
...LOOKS LIKE ONE HECK OF A BATTLE.

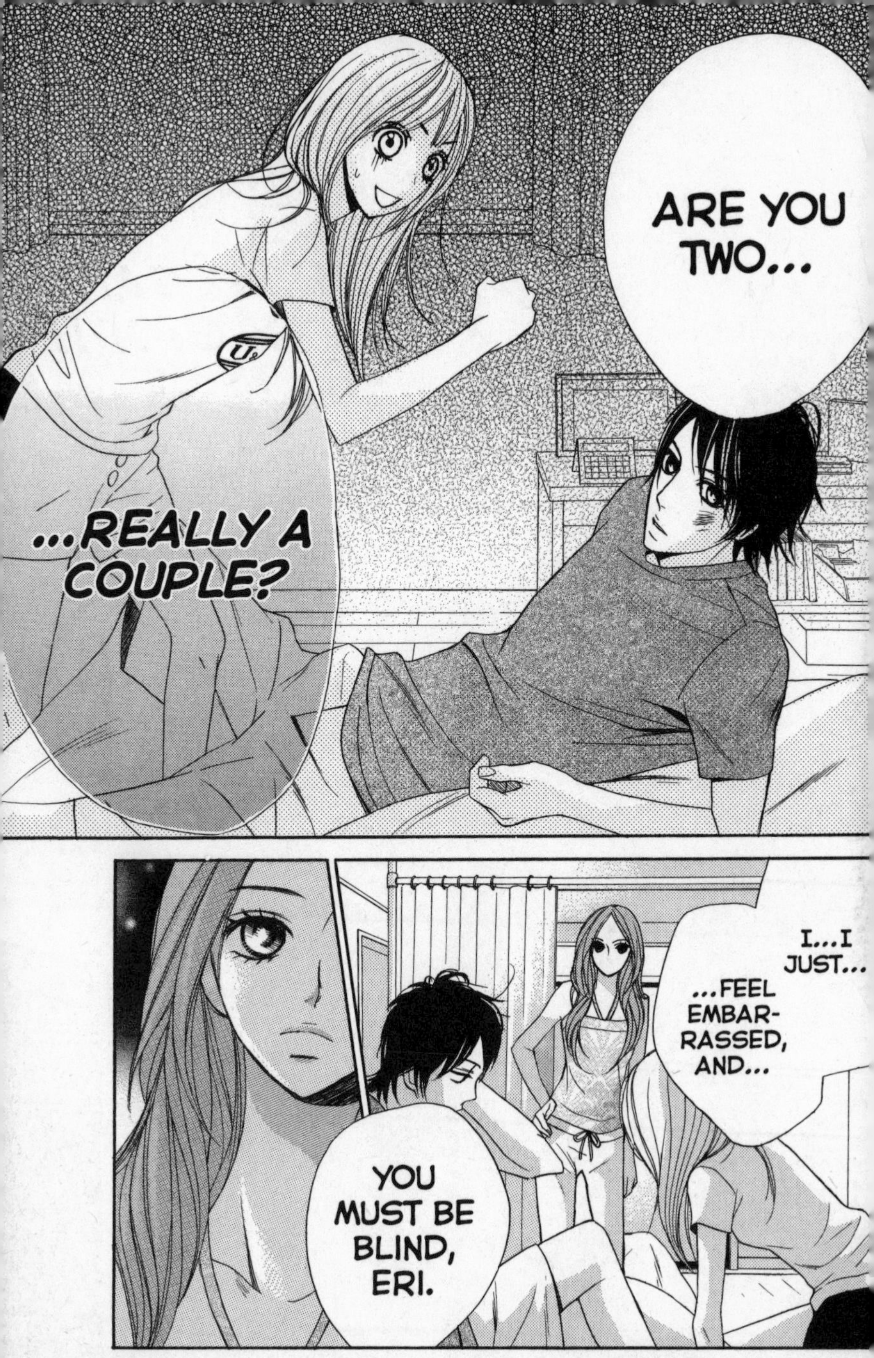
ARE YOU TWO...
...REALLY A COUPLE?
I...I JUST...
...FEEL EMBAR-RASSED, AND...
YOU MUST BE BLIND, ERI.

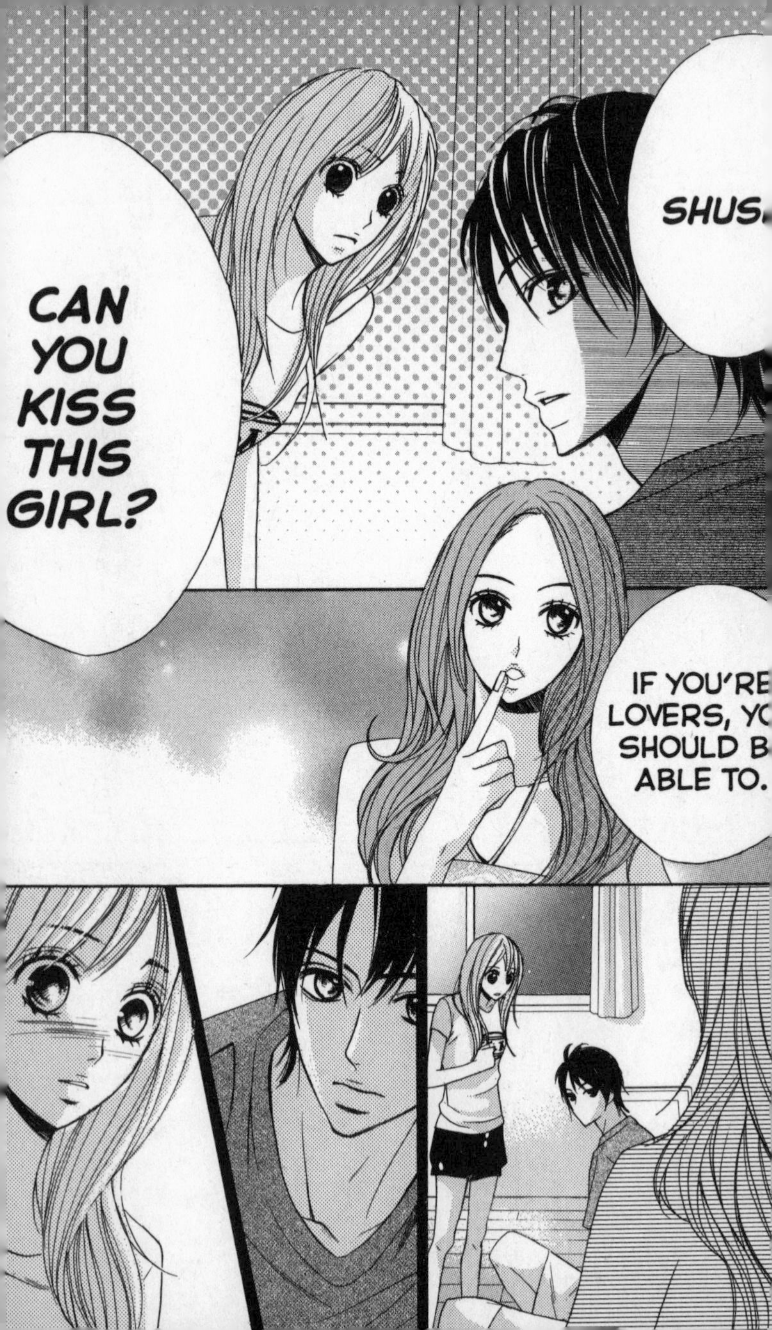
SHUS
CAN YOU KISS THIS GIRL?
IF YOU'RE LOVERS, YO SHOULD B ABLE TO.

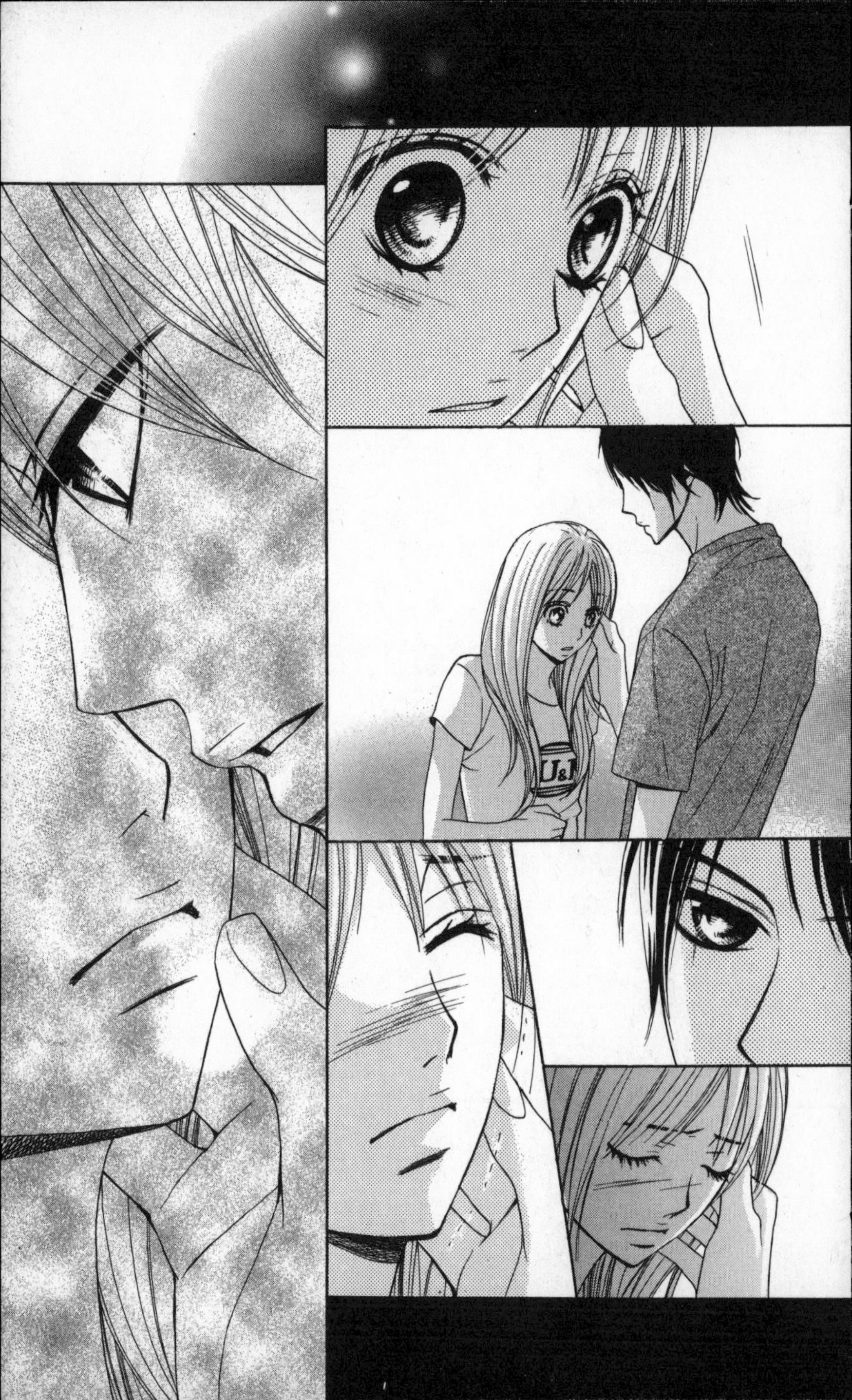

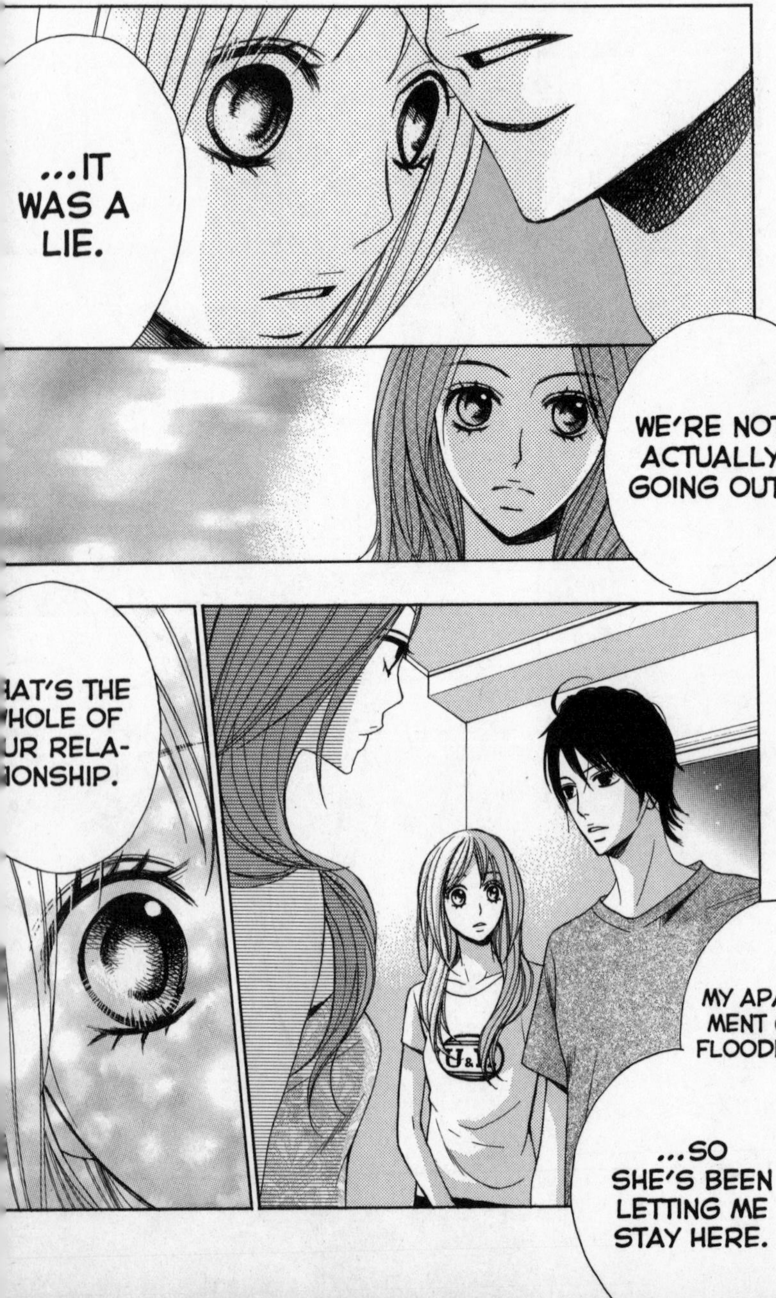
...IT WAS A LIE.
WE'RE NOT ACTUALLY GOING OUT.
MY APART-MENT GOT FLOODED...
...SO SHE'S BEEN LETTING ME STAY HERE.
HAT'S THE HOLE OF UR RELA-IONSHIP.

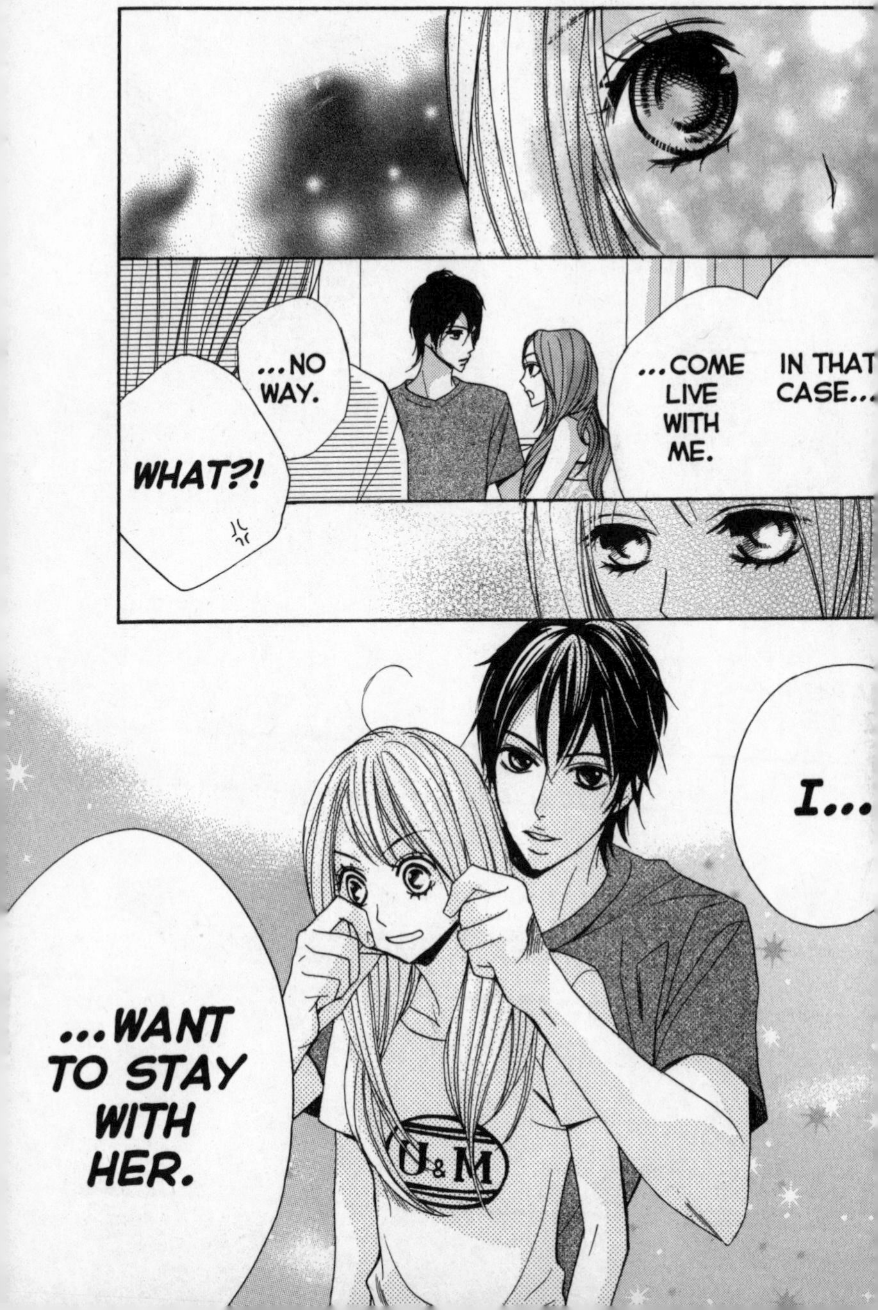
IN THAT CASE...
...COME LIVE WITH ME.
...NO WAY.
WHAT?!
I...
...WANT TO STAY WITH HER.

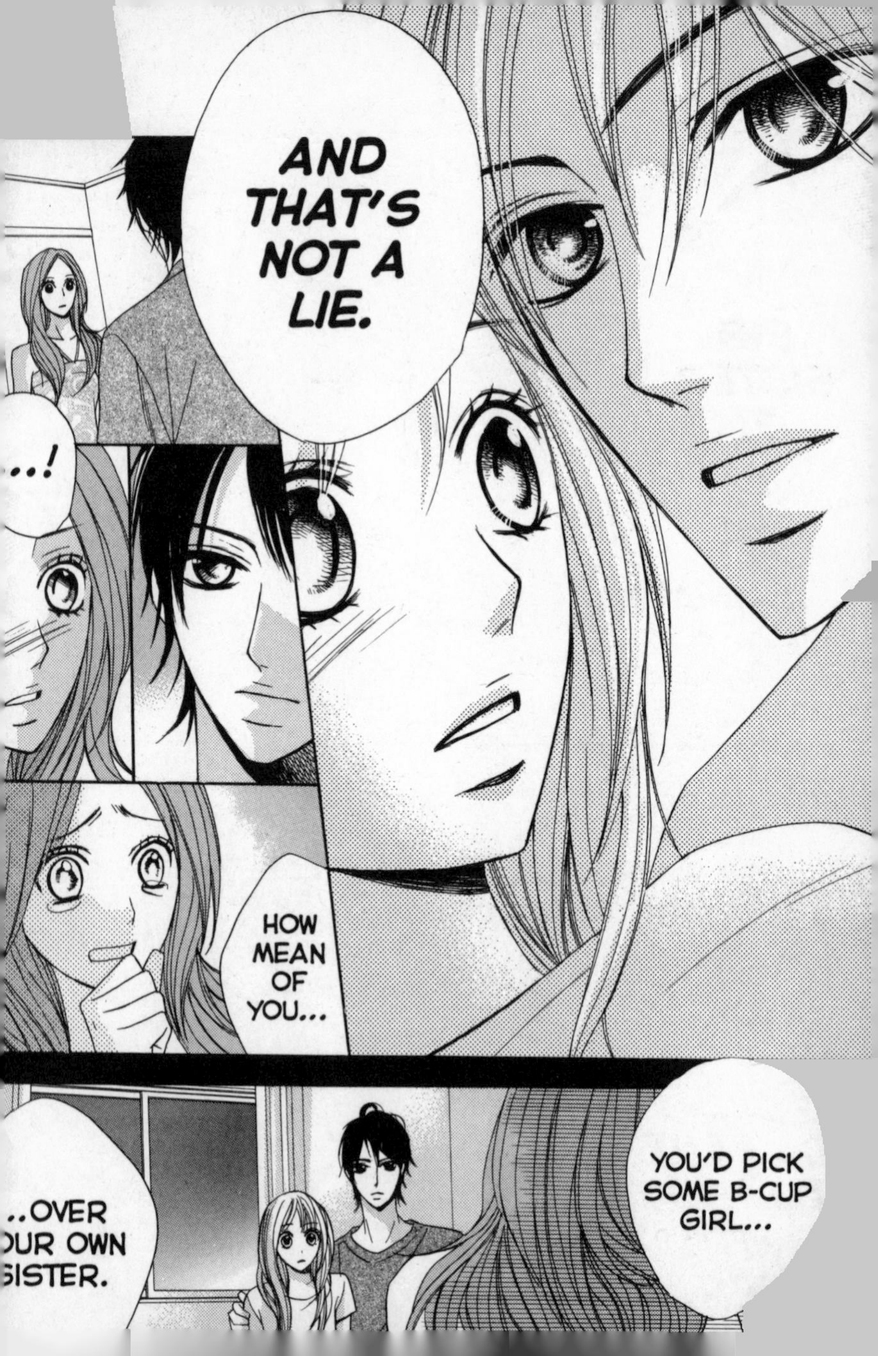
AND THAT'S NOT A LIE.
..!
HOW MEAN OF YOU...
YOU'D PICK SOME B-CUP GIRL...
..OVER OUR OWN SISTER.

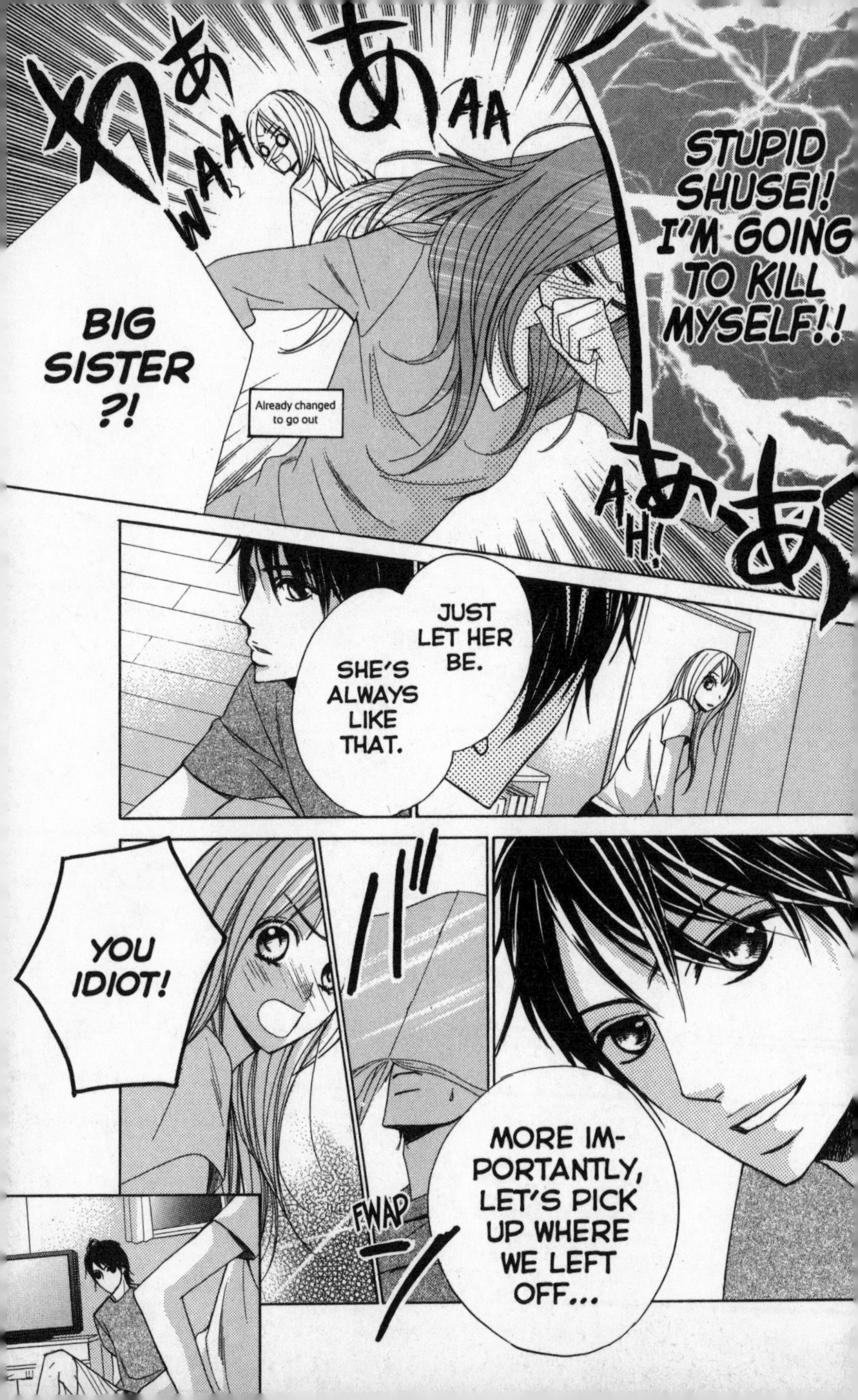
STUPID SHUSEI! I'M GOING TO KILL MYSELF!!
AH!
WAAAA
AA
BIG SISTER ?!
Already changed to go out
JUST LET HER BE.
SHE'S ALWAYS LIKE THAT.
MORE IM-PORTANTLY, LET'S PICK UP WHERE WE LEFT OFF...
FWAP
YOU IDIOT!

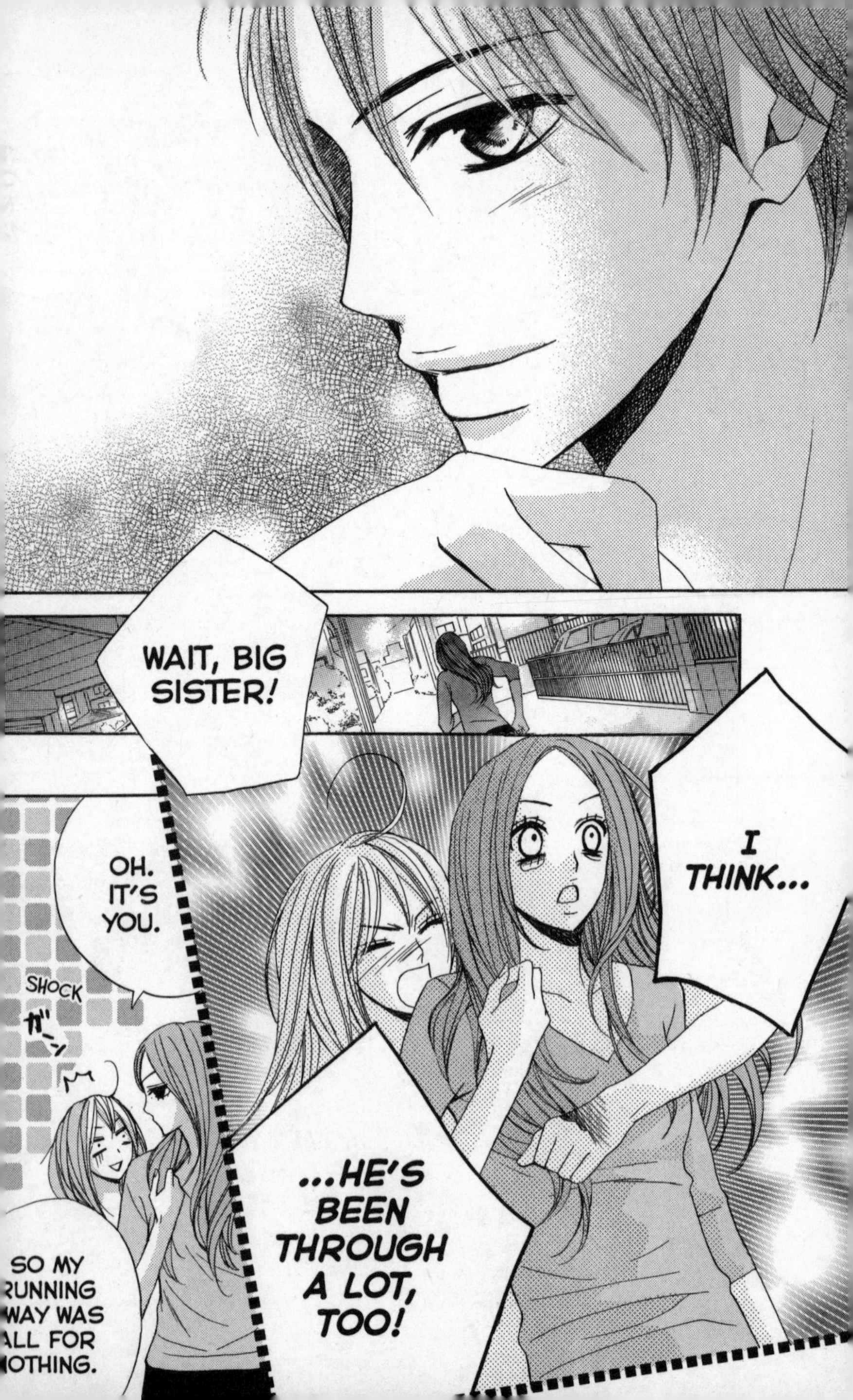

WAIT, BIG SISTER!
I THINK...
...HE'S BEEN THROUGH A LOT, TOO!
OH. IT'S YOU.
SHOCK
ガーン
SO MY RUNNING AWAY WAS ALL FOR NOTHING.

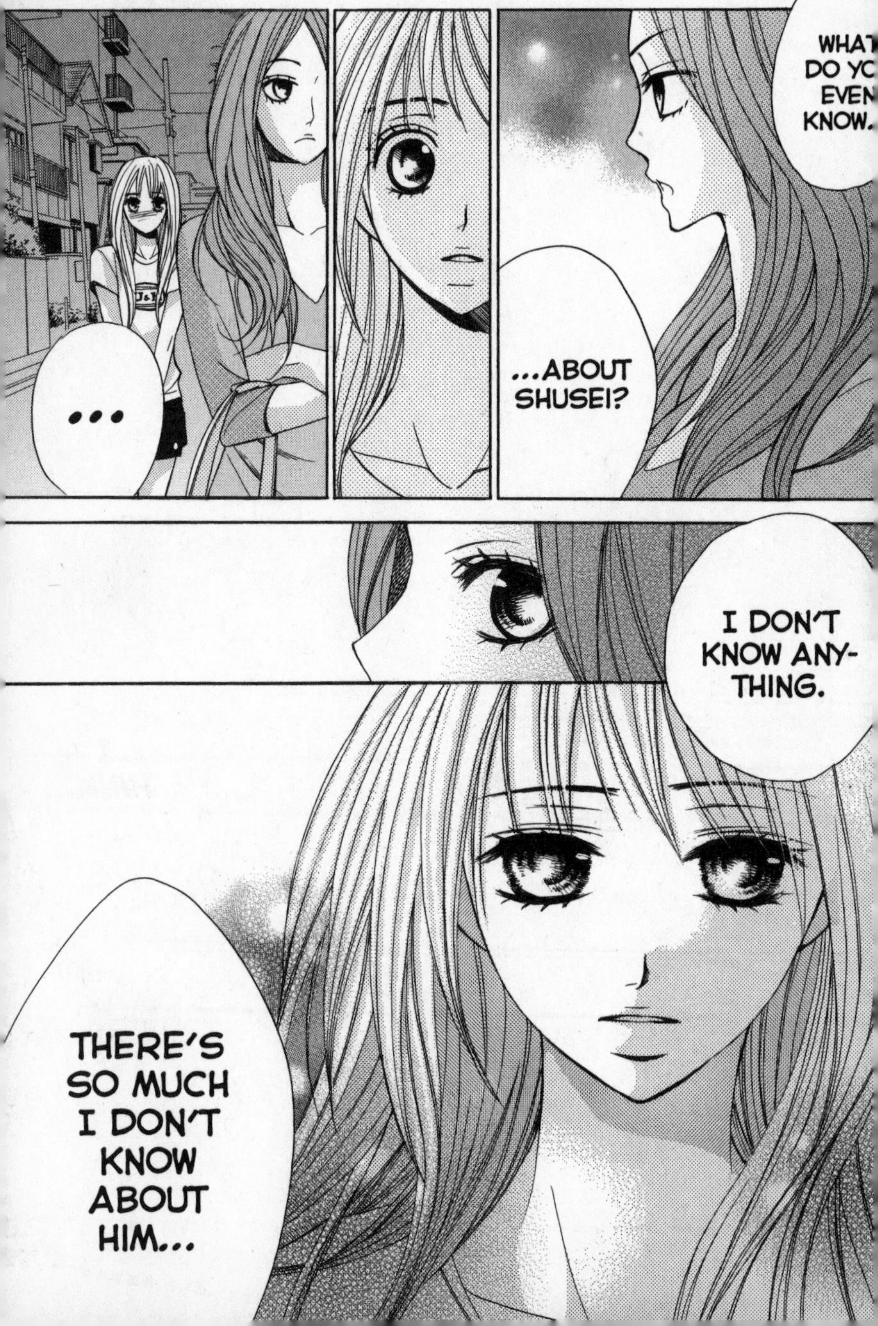
WHAT DO YO EVEN KNOW.
...ABOUT SHUSEI?
...
I DON'T KNOW ANY-THING.
THERE'S SO MUCH I DON'T KNOW ABOUT HIM...

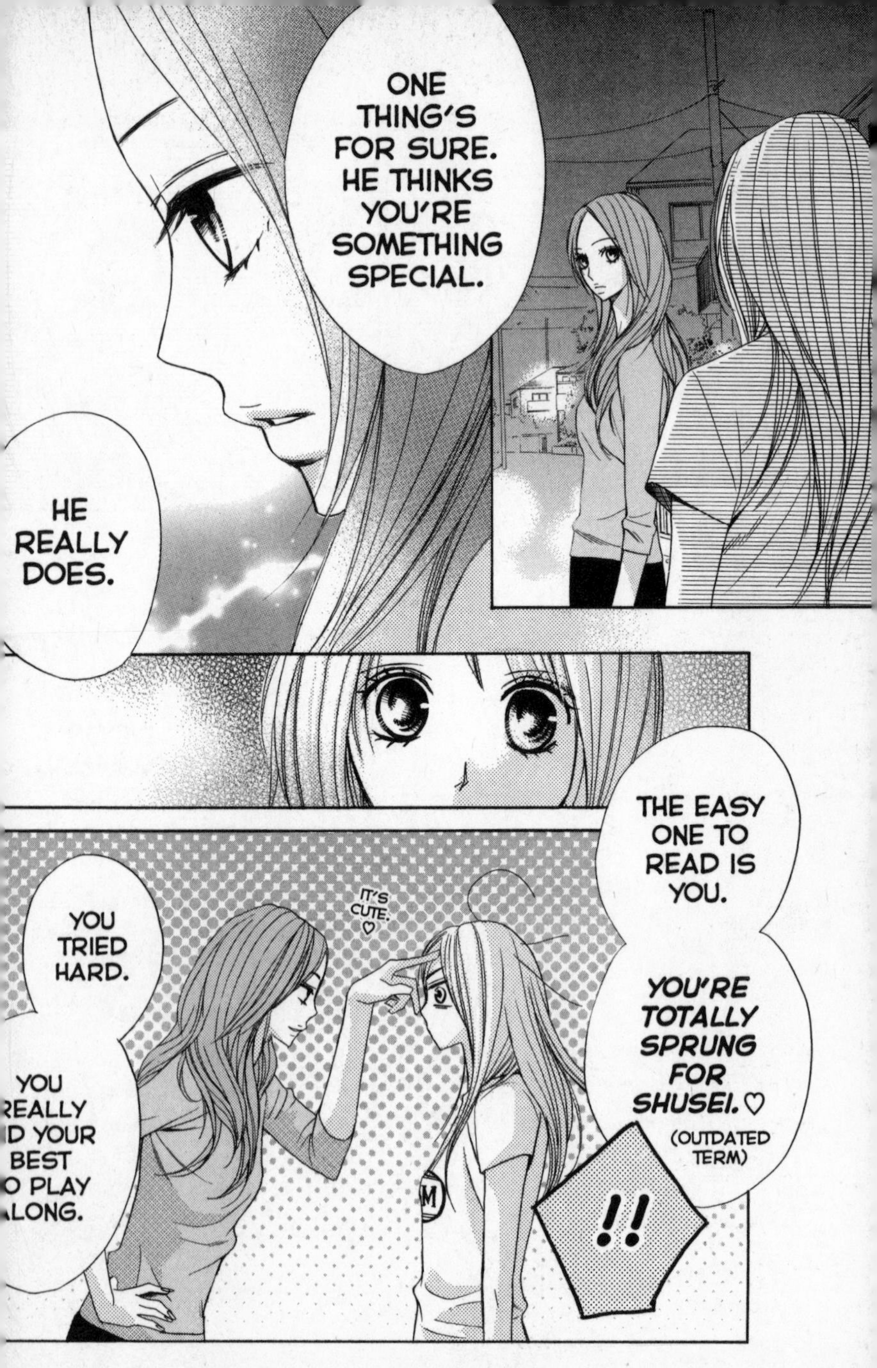
ONE THING'S FOR SURE. HE THINKS YOU'RE SOMETHING SPECIAL.
HE REALLY DOES.
THE EASY ONE TO READ IS YOU.
YOU'RE TOTALLY SPRUNG FOR SHUSEI.♡
(OUTDATED TERM)
IT'S CUTE.♡
YOU TRIED HARD.
YOU EALLY D YOUR BEST O PLAY LONG.
!!

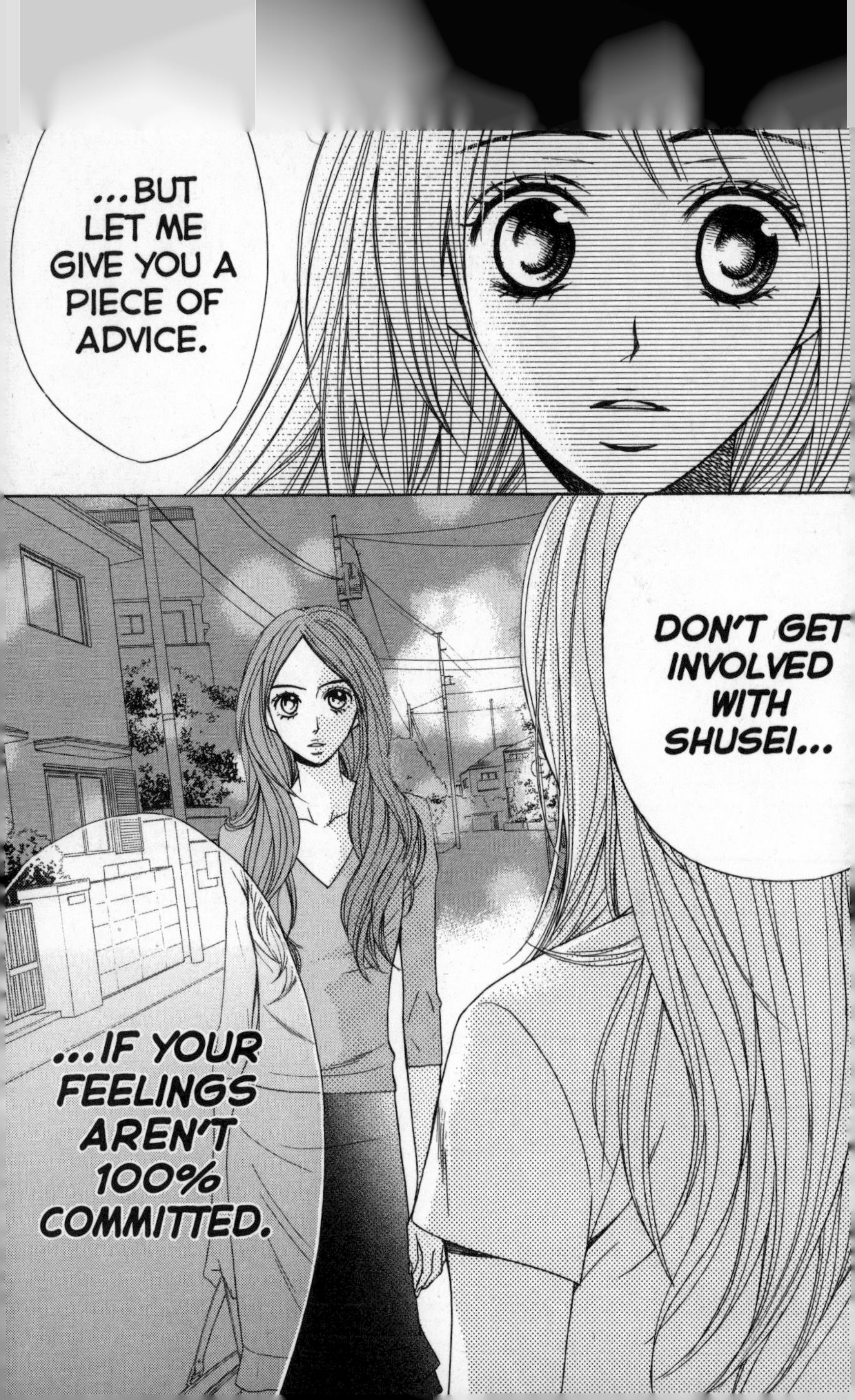
...BUT LET ME GIVE YOU A PIECE OF ADVICE.
DON'T GET INVOLVED WITH SHUSEI...
...IF YOUR FEELINGS AREN'T 100% COMMITTED.

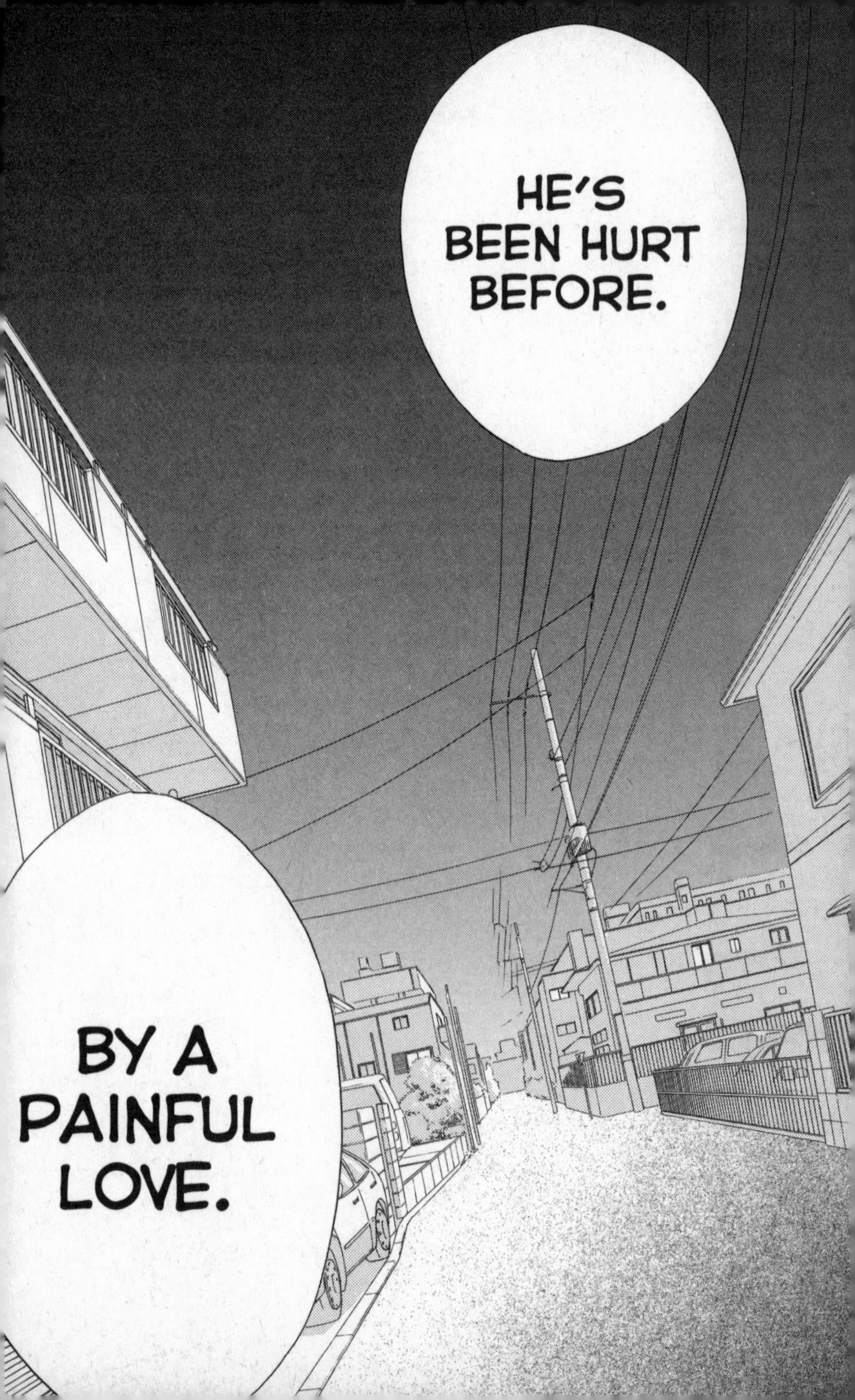
HE'S BEEN HURT BEFORE.
BY A PAINFUL LOVE.

L♥DK
エルディーケー

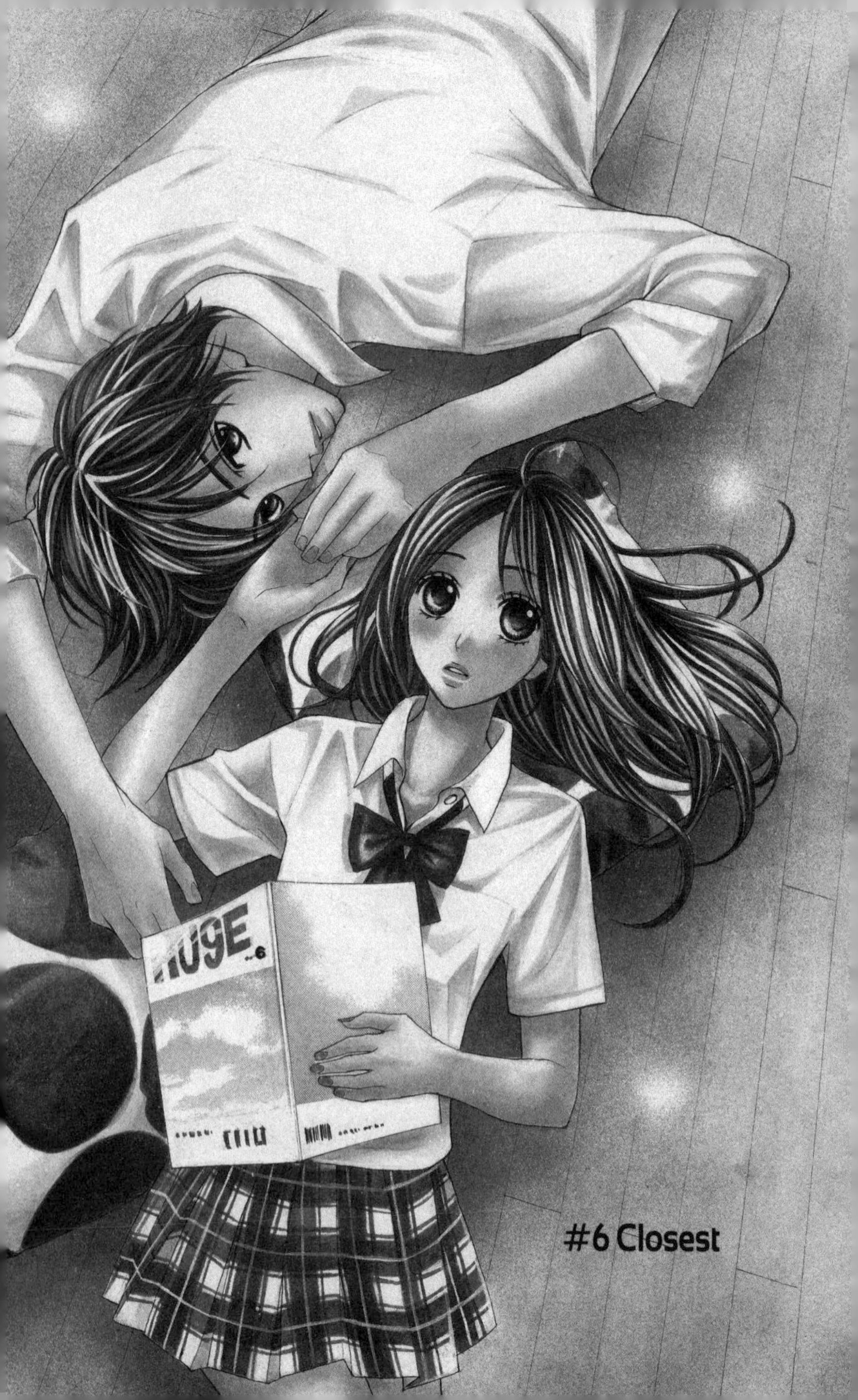
HUGE

#6 Closest

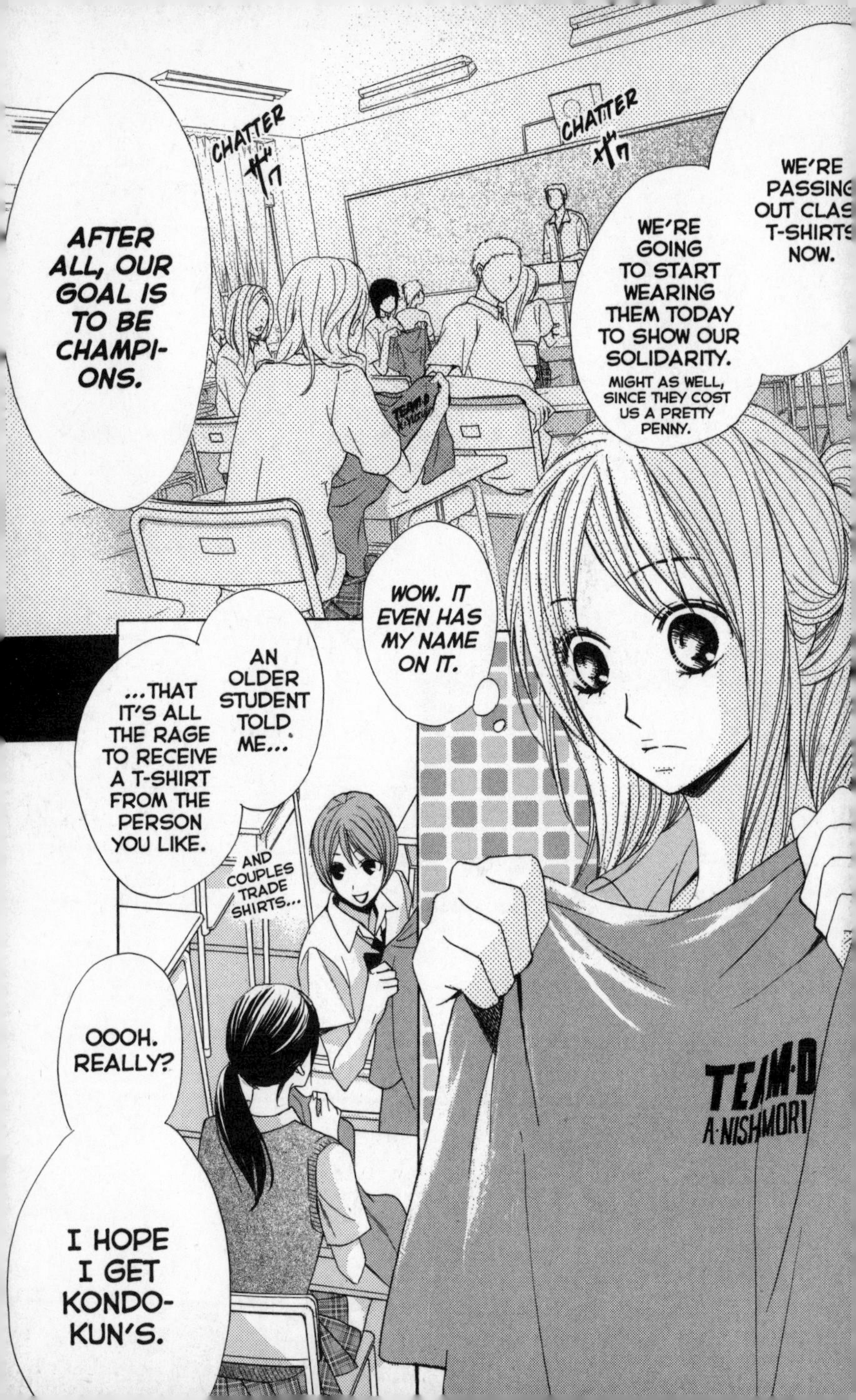

WE'RE PASSING OUT CLAS T-SHIRTS NOW.
WE'RE GOING TO START WEARING THEM TODAY TO SHOW OUR SOLIDARITY.
MIGHT AS WELL, SINCE THEY COST US A PRETTY PENNY.
CHATTER
CHATTER
AFTER ALL, OUR GOAL IS TO BE CHAMPIONS.
WOW. IT EVEN HAS MY NAME ON IT.
TEAM·D A·NISHMORI
AN OLDER STUDENT TOLD ME...
...THAT IT'S ALL THE RAGE TO RECEIVE A T-SHIRT FROM THE PERSON YOU LIKE.
AND COUPLES TRADE SHIRTS...
OOOH. REALLY?
I HOPE I GET KONDO-KUN'S.

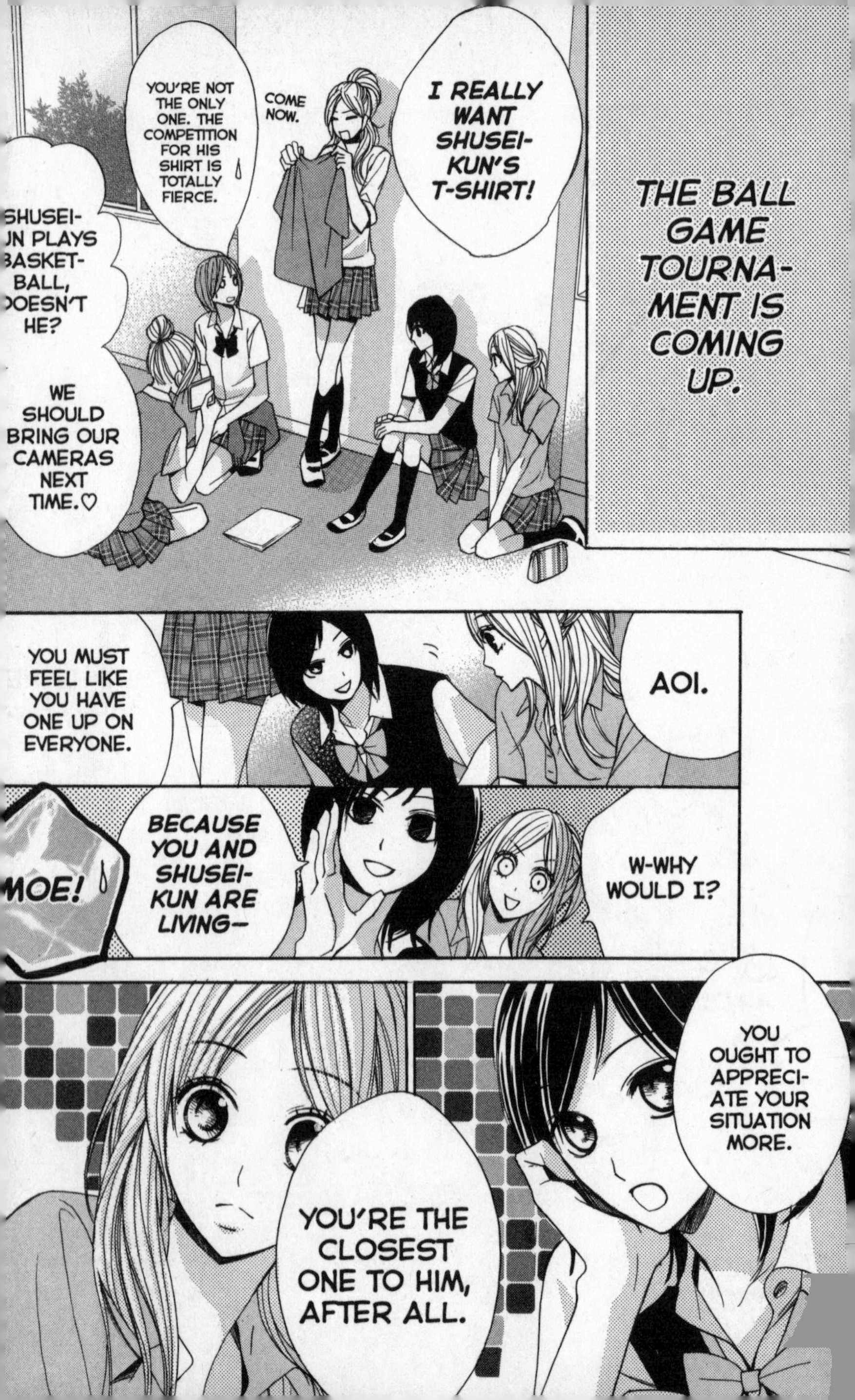
THE BALL GAME TOURNAMENT IS COMING UP.
I REALLY WANT SHUSEI-KUN'S T-SHIRT!
COME NOW.
YOU'RE NOT THE ONLY ONE. THE COMPETITION FOR HIS SHIRT IS TOTALLY FIERCE.
SHUSEI- JN PLAYS BASKETBALL, OESN'T HE?
WE SHOULD BRING OUR CAMERAS NEXT TIME.♡
AOI.
YOU MUST FEEL LIKE YOU HAVE ONE UP ON EVERYONE.
W-WHY WOULD I?
BECAUSE YOU AND SHUSEI-KUN ARE LIVING—
MOE!
YOU OUGHT TO APPRECIATE YOUR SITUATION MORE.
YOU'RE THE CLOSEST ONE TO HIM, AFTER ALL.

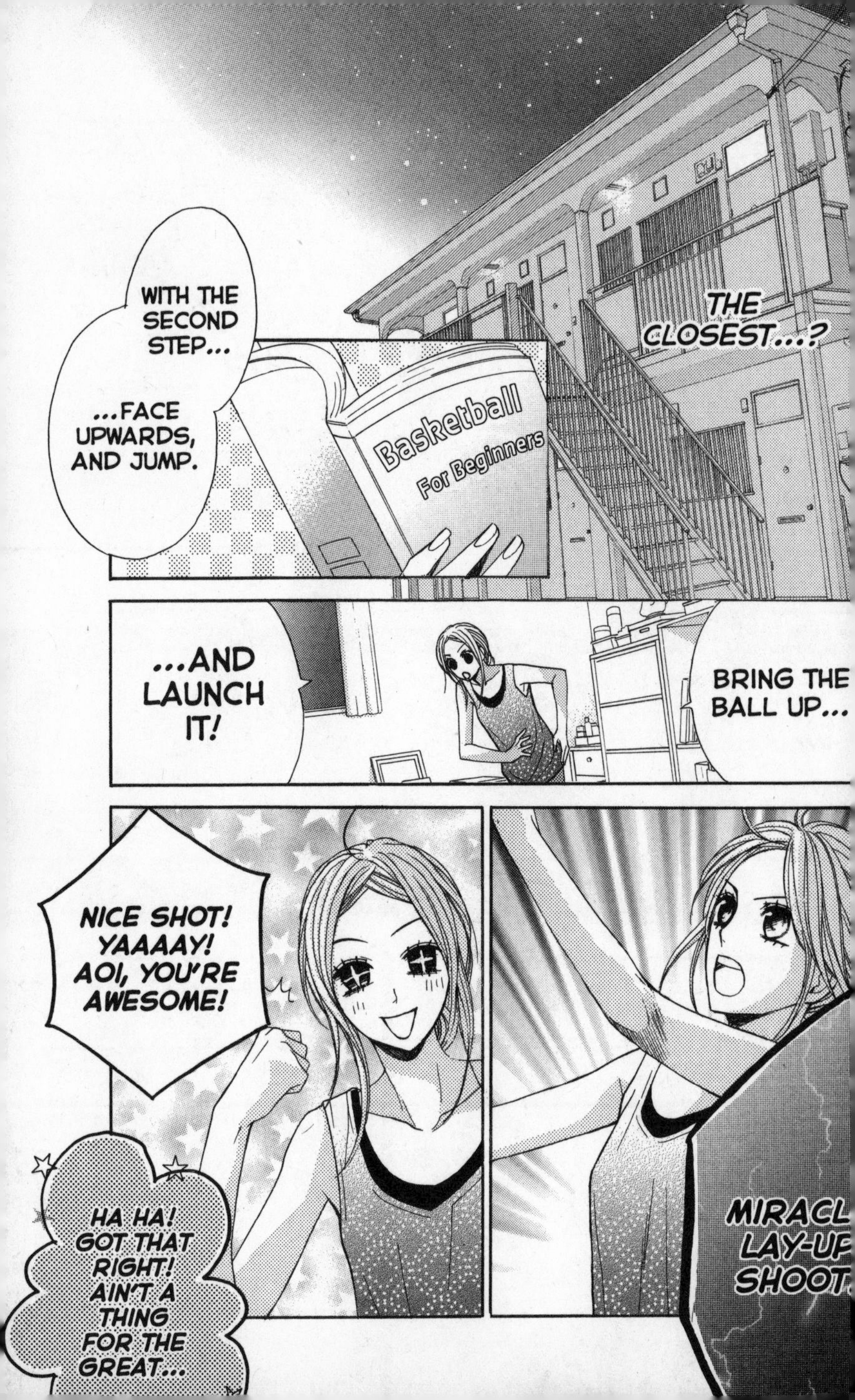
THE CLOSEST...?
WITH THE SECOND STEP... ...FACE UPWARDS, AND JUMP.
Basketball For Beginners
BRING THE BALL UP...
...AND LAUNCH IT!
MIRACL LAY-UP SHOOT
NICE SHOT! YAAAAY! AOI, YOU'RE AWESOME!
HA HA! GOT THAT RIGHT! AIN'T A THING FOR THE GREAT...

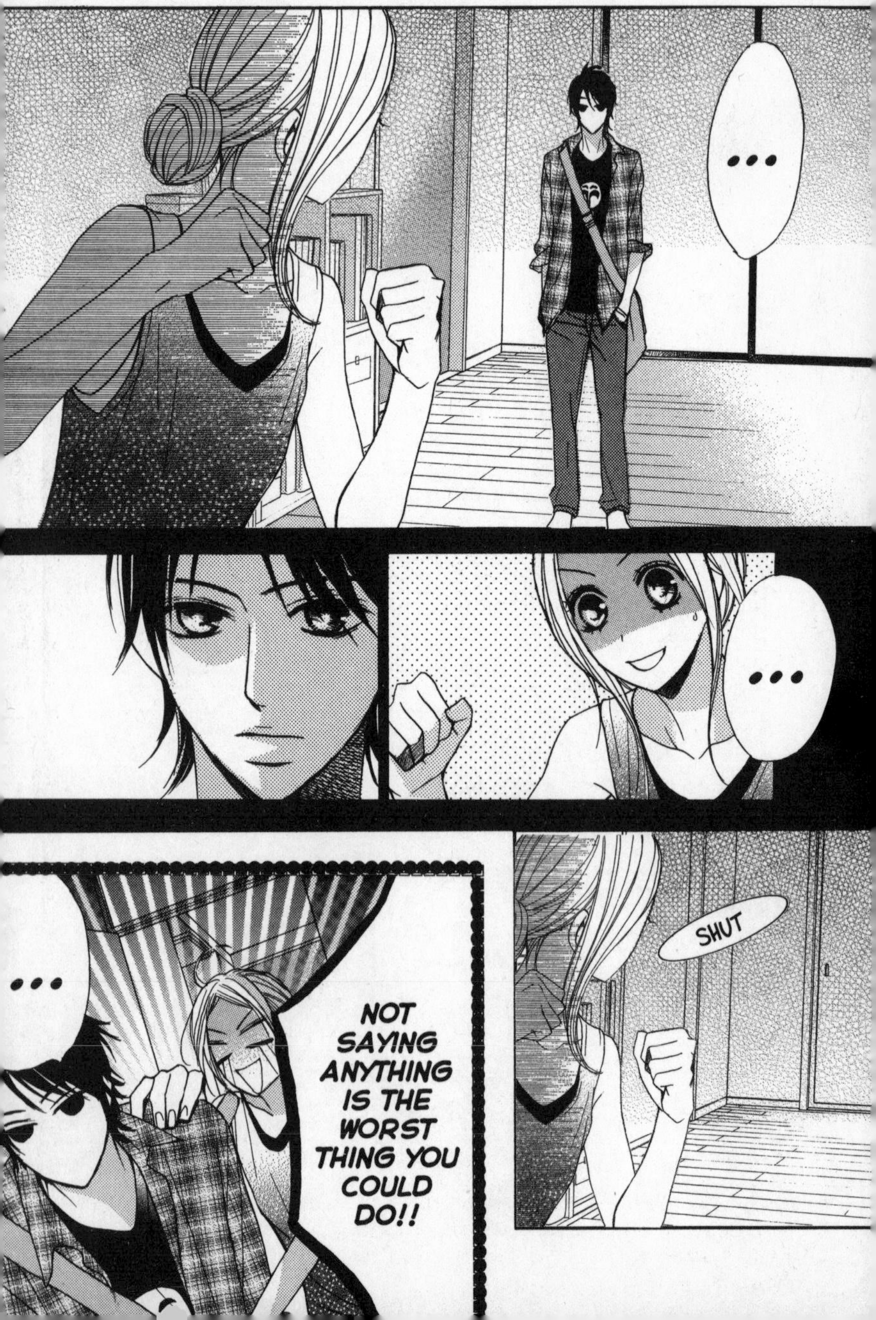
...
...
SHUT
NOT SAYING ANYTHING IS THE WORST THING YOU COULD DO!!
...

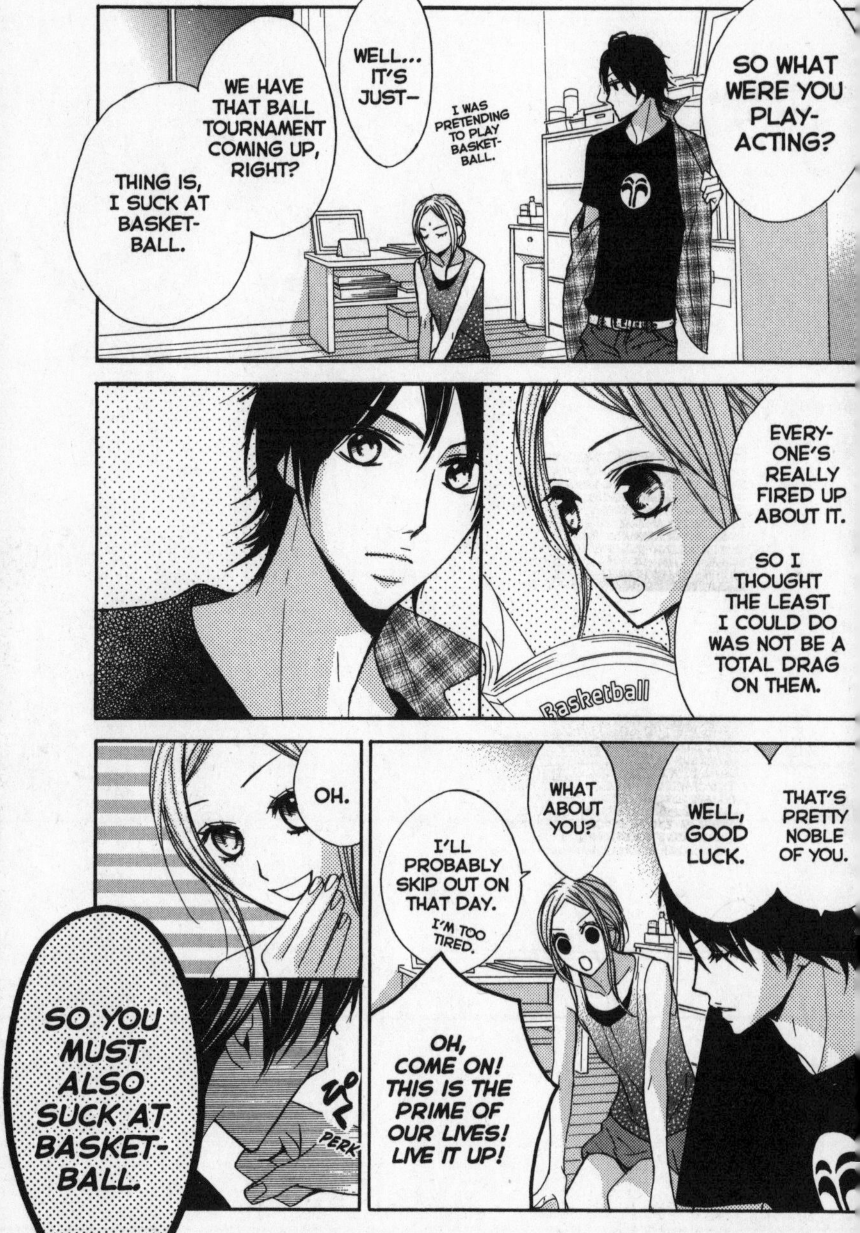
SO WHAT WERE YOU PLAY-ACTING?
WELL... IT'S JUST—
I WAS PRETENDING TO PLAY BASKET-BALL.
WE HAVE THAT BALL TOURNAMENT COMING UP, RIGHT?
THING IS, I SUCK AT BASKET-BALL.
EVERY-ONE'S REALLY FIRED UP ABOUT IT.
SO I THOUGHT THE LEAST I COULD DO WAS NOT BE A TOTAL DRAG ON THEM.
Basketball
THAT'S PRETTY NOBLE OF YOU.
WELL, GOOD LUCK.
WHAT ABOUT YOU?
I'LL PROBABLY SKIP OUT ON THAT DAY.
I'M TOO TIRED.
OH, COME ON! THIS IS THE PRIME OF OUR LIVES! LIVE IT UP!
OH.
PERK
SO YOU MUST ALSO SUCK AT BASKET-BALL.

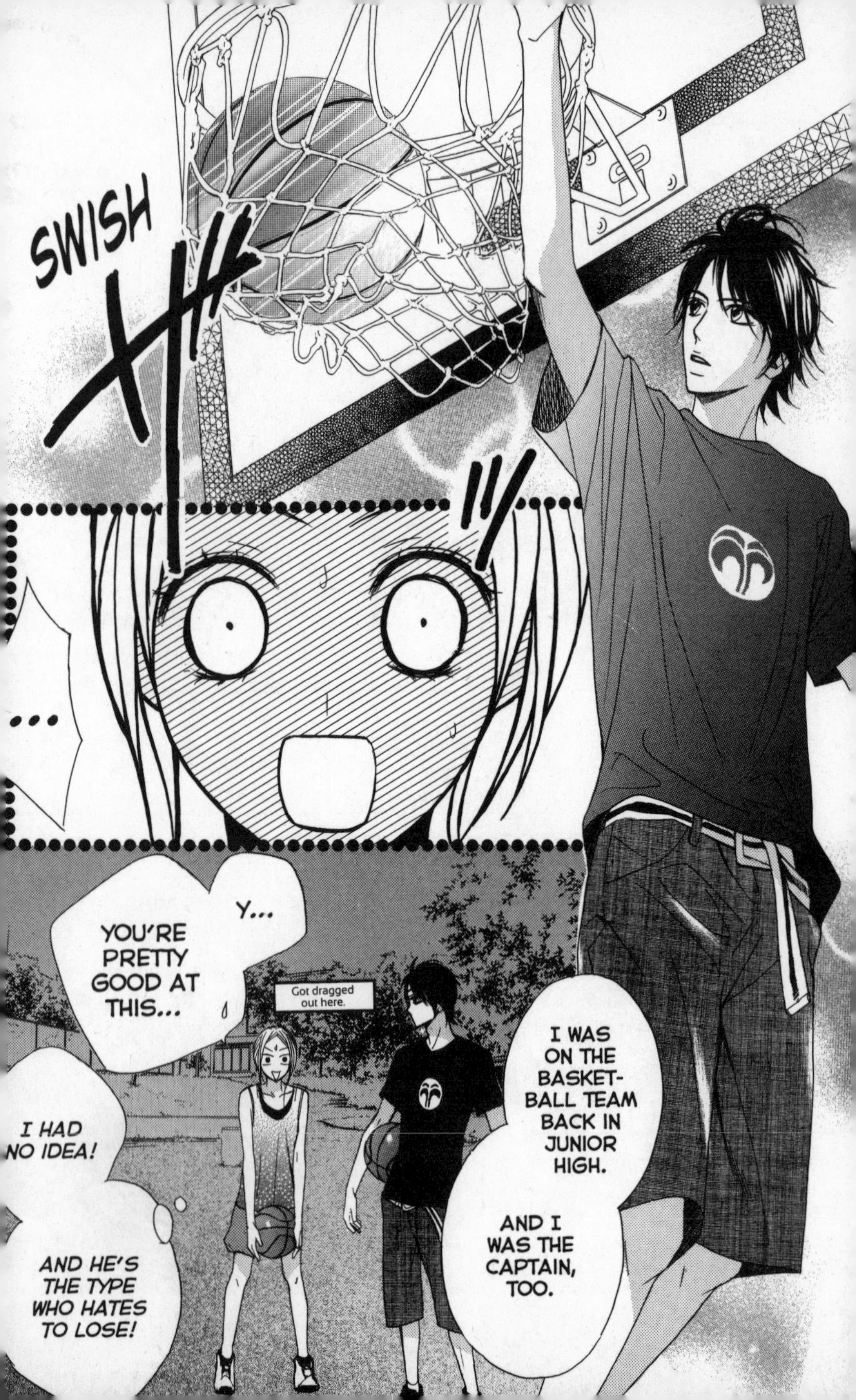

SWISH
...
Y... YOU'RE PRETTY GOOD AT THIS...
Got dragged out here.
I WAS ON THE BASKET-BALL TEAM BACK IN JUNIOR HIGH.
AND I WAS THE CAPTAIN, TOO.
I HAD NO IDEA!
AND HE'S THE TYPE WHO HATES TO LOSE!

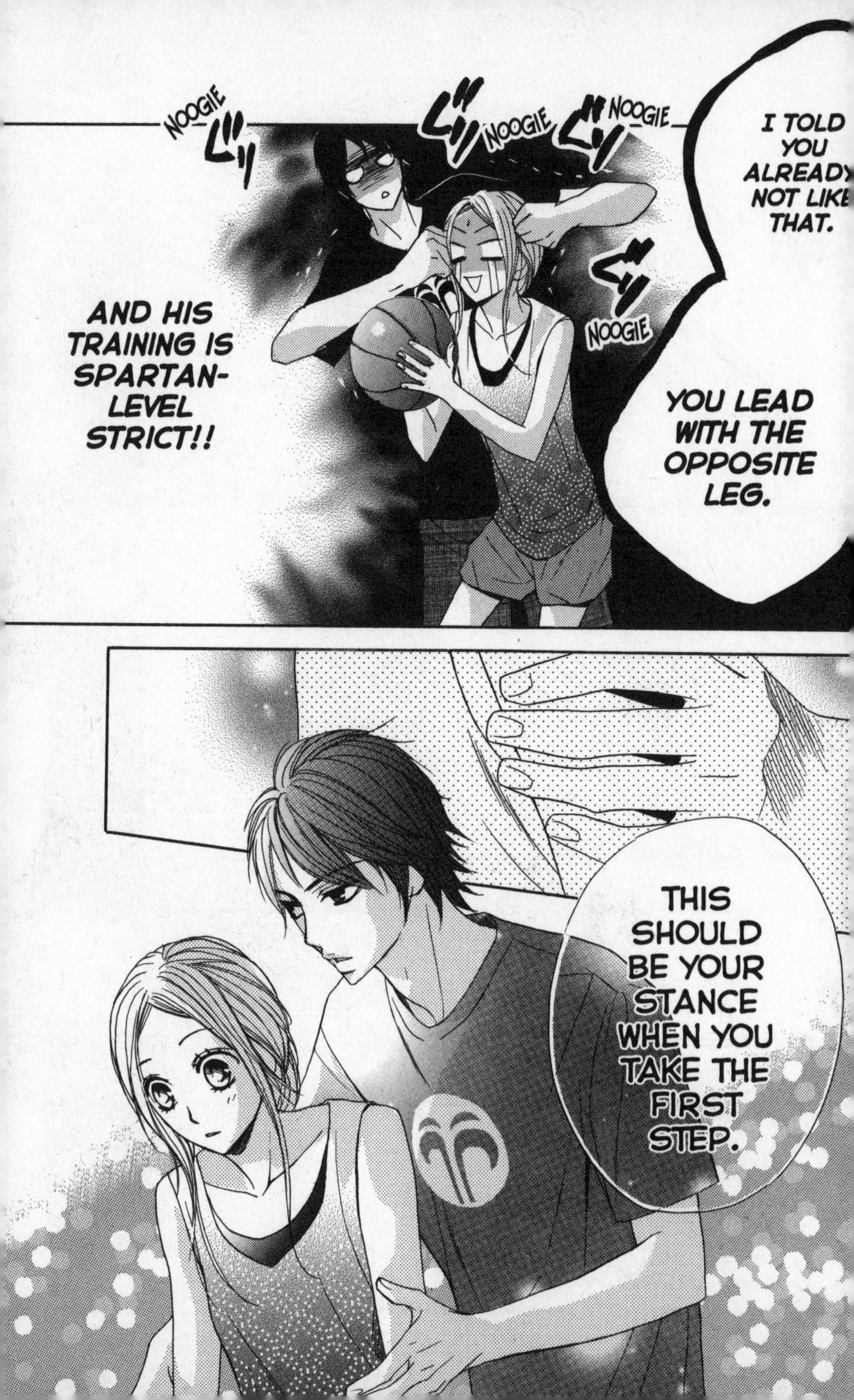
I TOLD YOU ALREADY NOT LIKE THAT.
YOU LEAD WITH THE OPPOSITE LEG.
NOOGIE
NOOGIE
NOOGIE
NOOGIE
AND HIS TRAINING IS SPARTAN-LEVEL STRICT!!
THIS SHOULD BE YOUR STANCE WHEN YOU TAKE THE FIRST STEP.

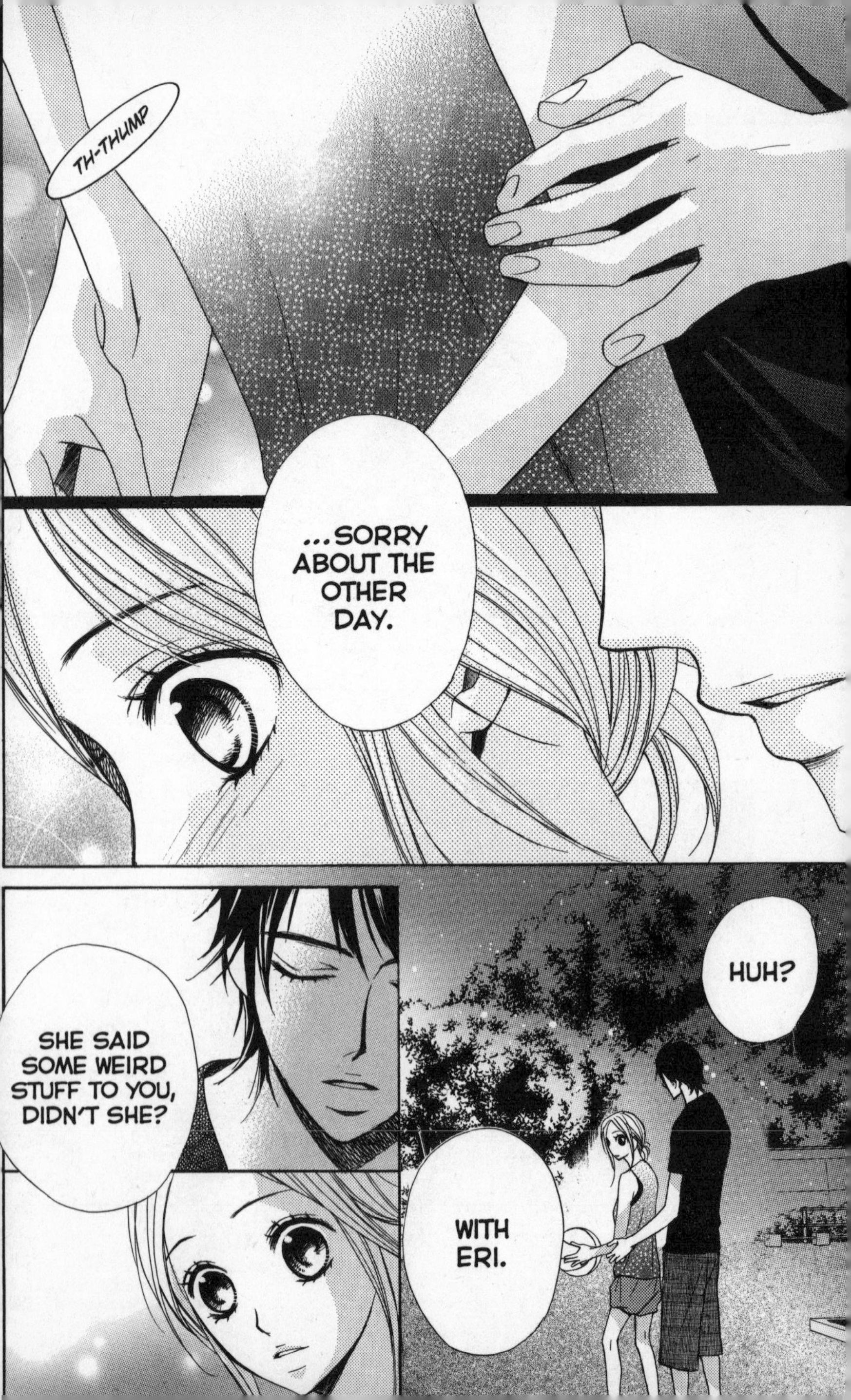
TH-THUMP
...SORRY ABOUT THE OTHER DAY.
HUH?
WITH ERI.
SHE SAID SOME WEIRD STUFF TO YOU, DIDN'T SHE?

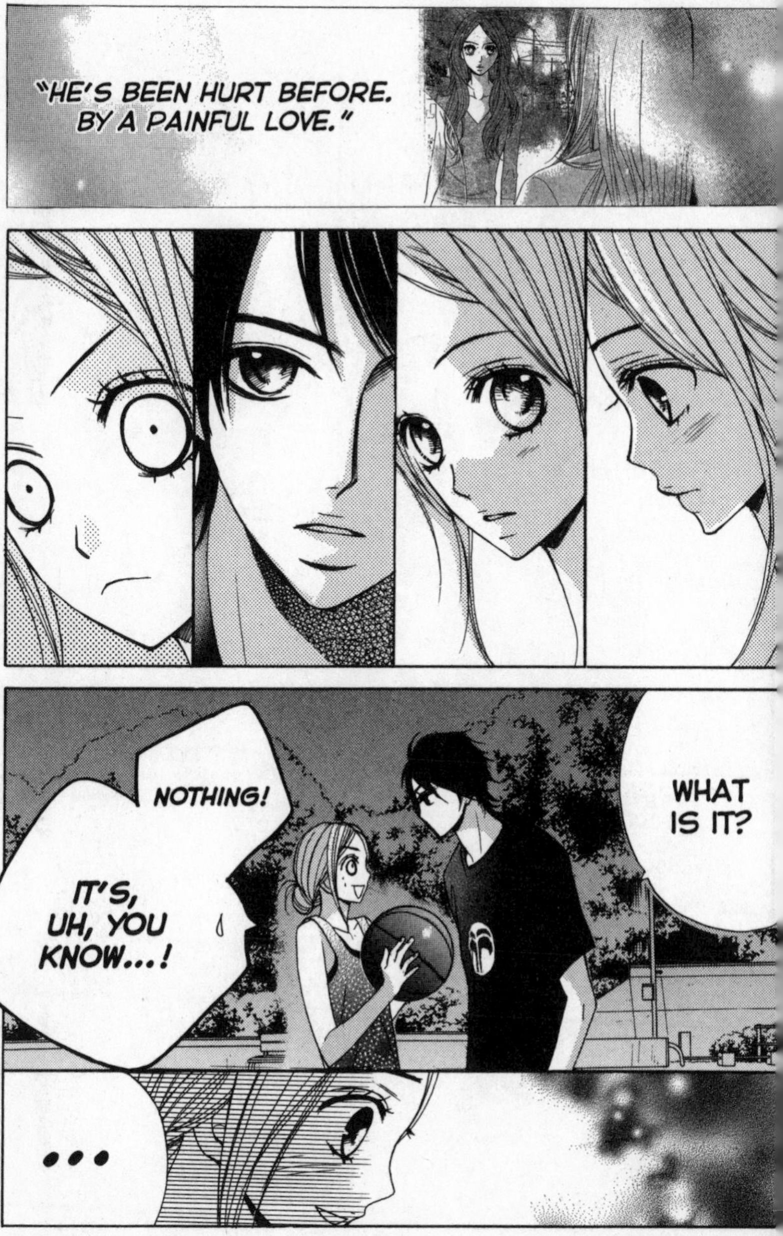
"HE'S BEEN HURT BEFORE. BY A PAINFUL LOVE."
WHAT IS IT?
NOTHING!
IT'S, UH, YOU KNOW...!
...

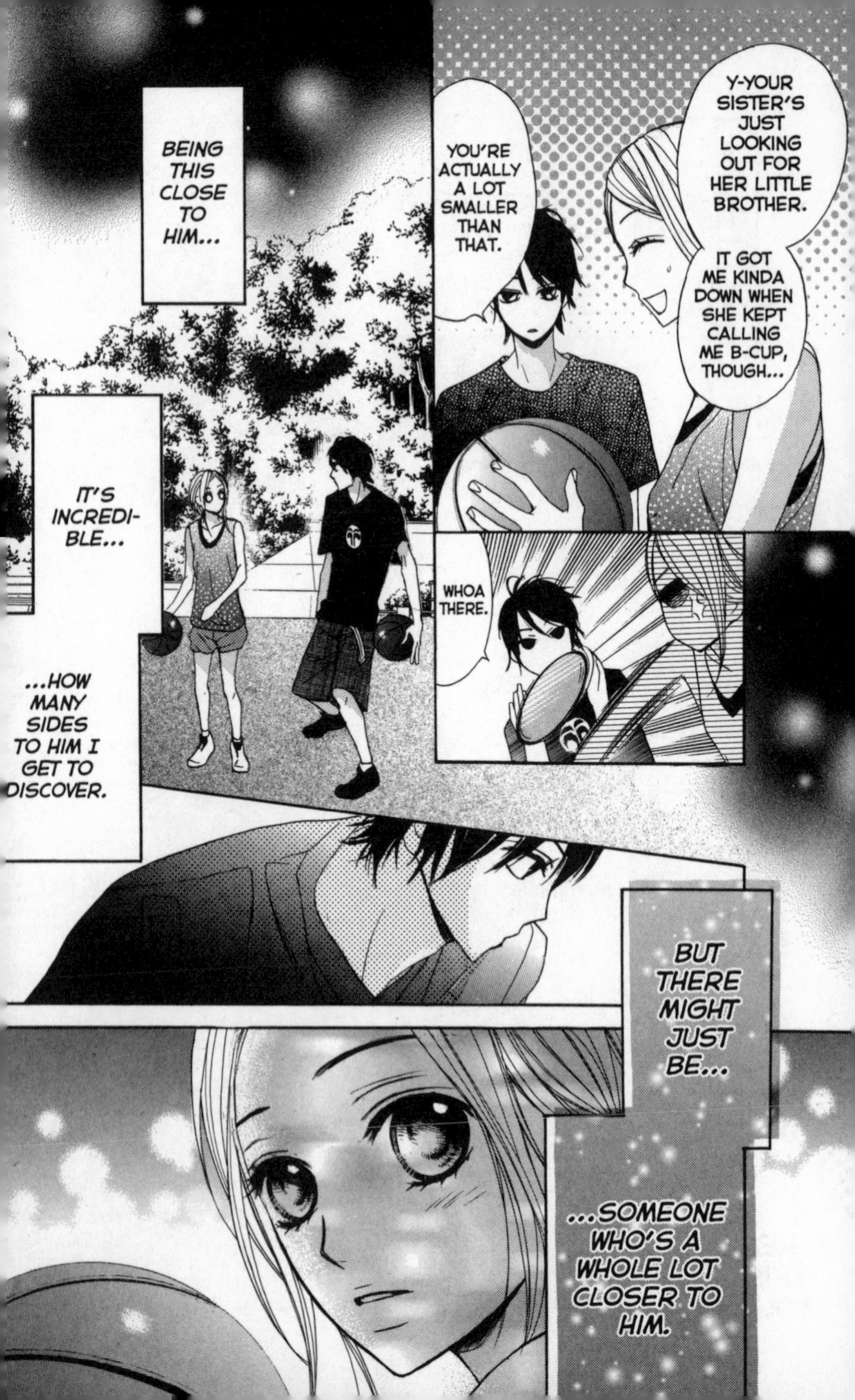
Y-YOUR SISTER'S JUST LOOKING OUT FOR HER LITTLE BROTHER.
IT GOT ME KINDA DOWN WHEN SHE KEPT CALLING ME B-CUP, THOUGH...
YOU'RE ACTUALLY A LOT SMALLER THAN THAT.
WHOA THERE.
BEING THIS CLOSE TO HIM...
IT'S INCREDI-BLE...
...HOW MANY SIDES TO HIM I GET TO DISCOVER.
BUT THERE MIGHT JUST BE...
...SOMEONE WHO'S A WHOLE LOT CLOSER TO HIM.

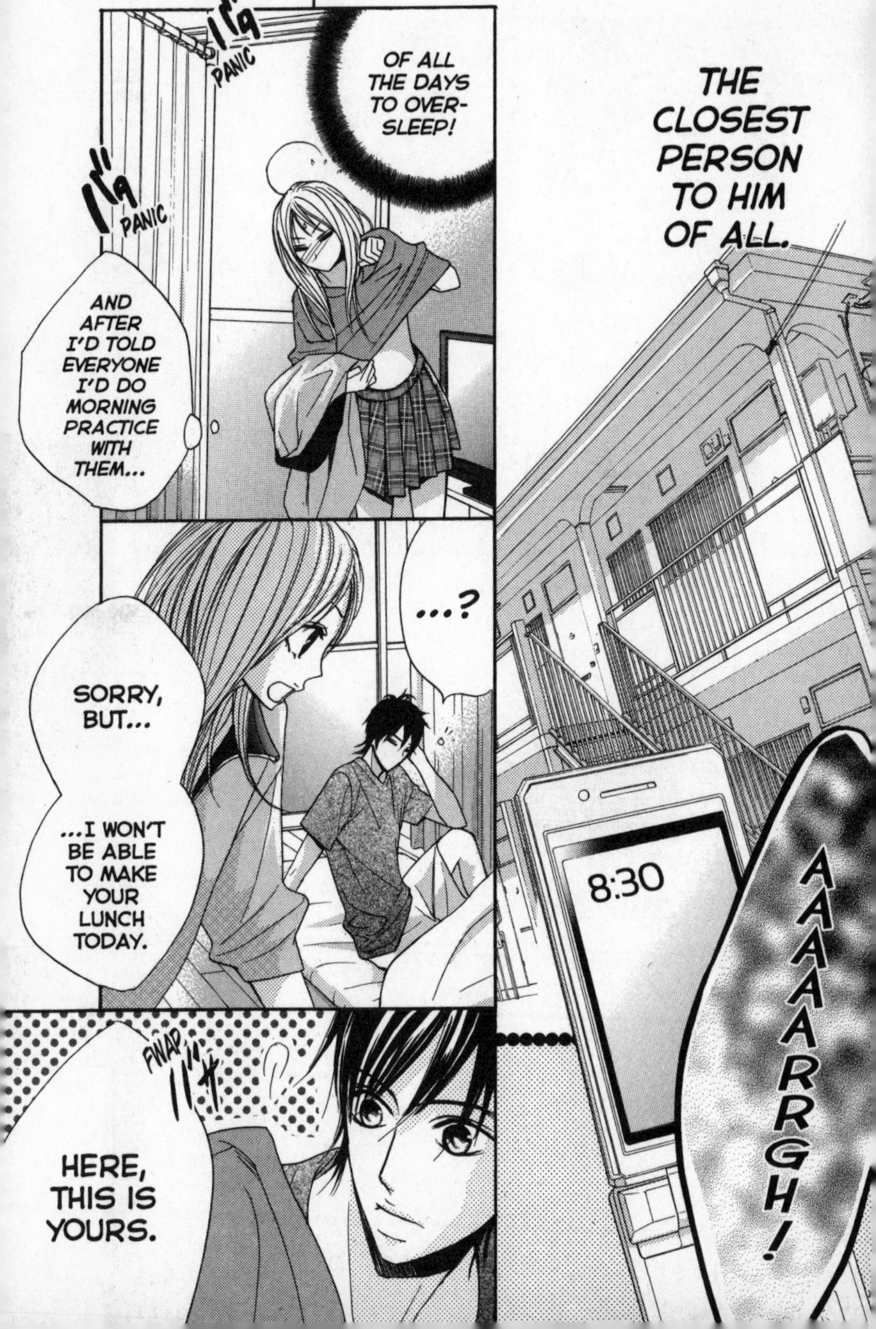
THE CLOSEST PERSON TO HIM OF ALL.
8:30
AAAAARRGH!
OF ALL THE DAYS TO OVER-SLEEP!
PANIC
PANIC
AND AFTER I'D TOLD EVERYONE I'D DO MORNING PRACTICE WITH THEM...
...?
SORRY, BUT...
...I WON'T BE ABLE TO MAKE YOUR LUNCH TODAY.
FWAP
HERE, THIS IS YOURS.

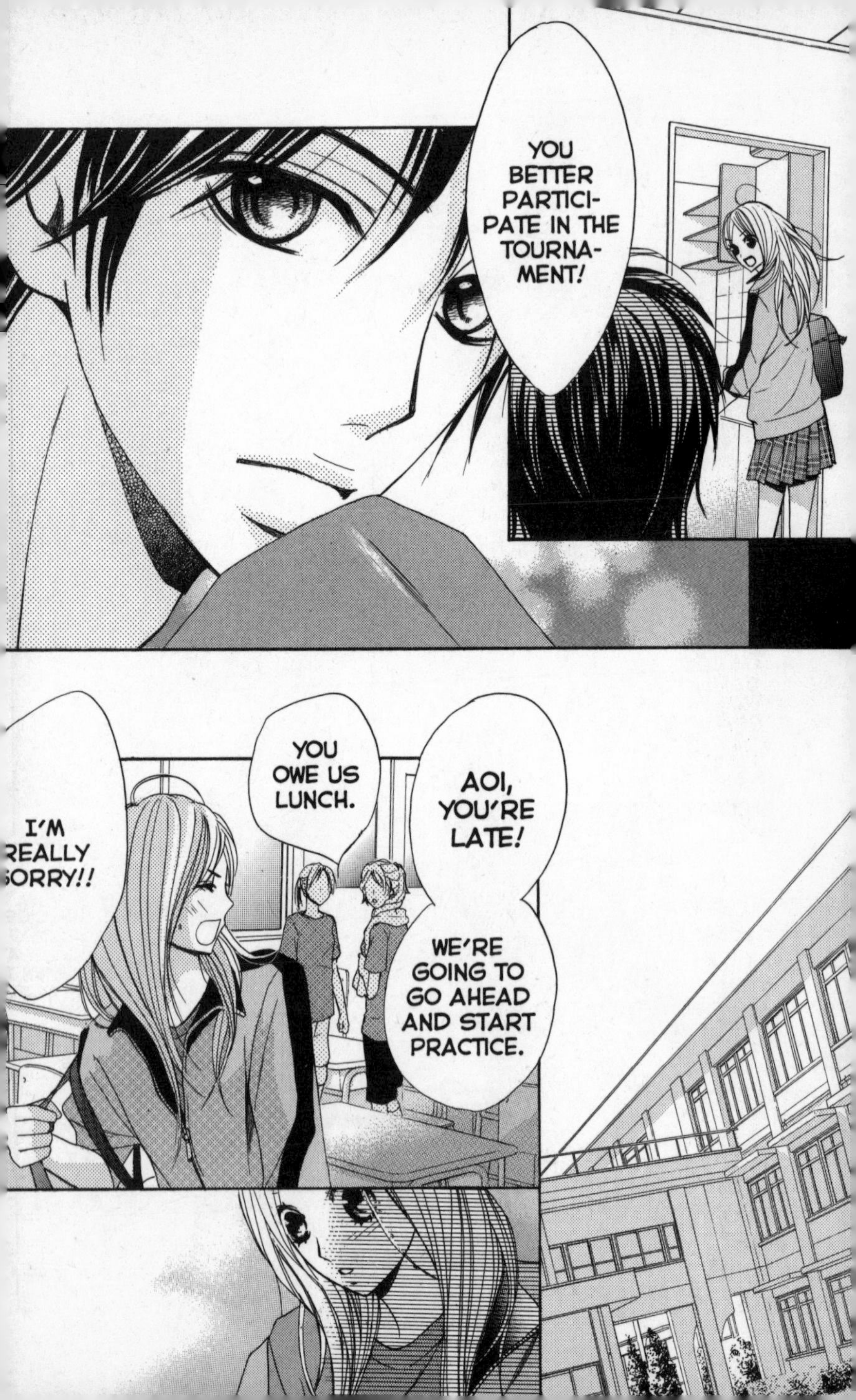
YOU BETTER PARTICIPATE IN THE TOURNAMENT!
AOI, YOU'RE LATE!
WE'RE GOING TO GO AHEAD AND START PRACTICE.
YOU OWE US LUNCH.
I'M REALLY SORRY!!

TEAM:1
S·KUGAYAM

...

"KUGA-YAMA."

HEY, YUMI, YOU'RE GOING FOR THA AREN'T YOU?

GOING FOR WHAT?

SHUSEI-KUN'S T-SHIRT.

YOU BET I AM.

I SPENT TWO HOURS DOING MY MAKE-UP THIS MORN-ING.

ZIP

TEAM:1
S·KUGAYAM

AH HA HA!

YOU'RE SILLY.

...

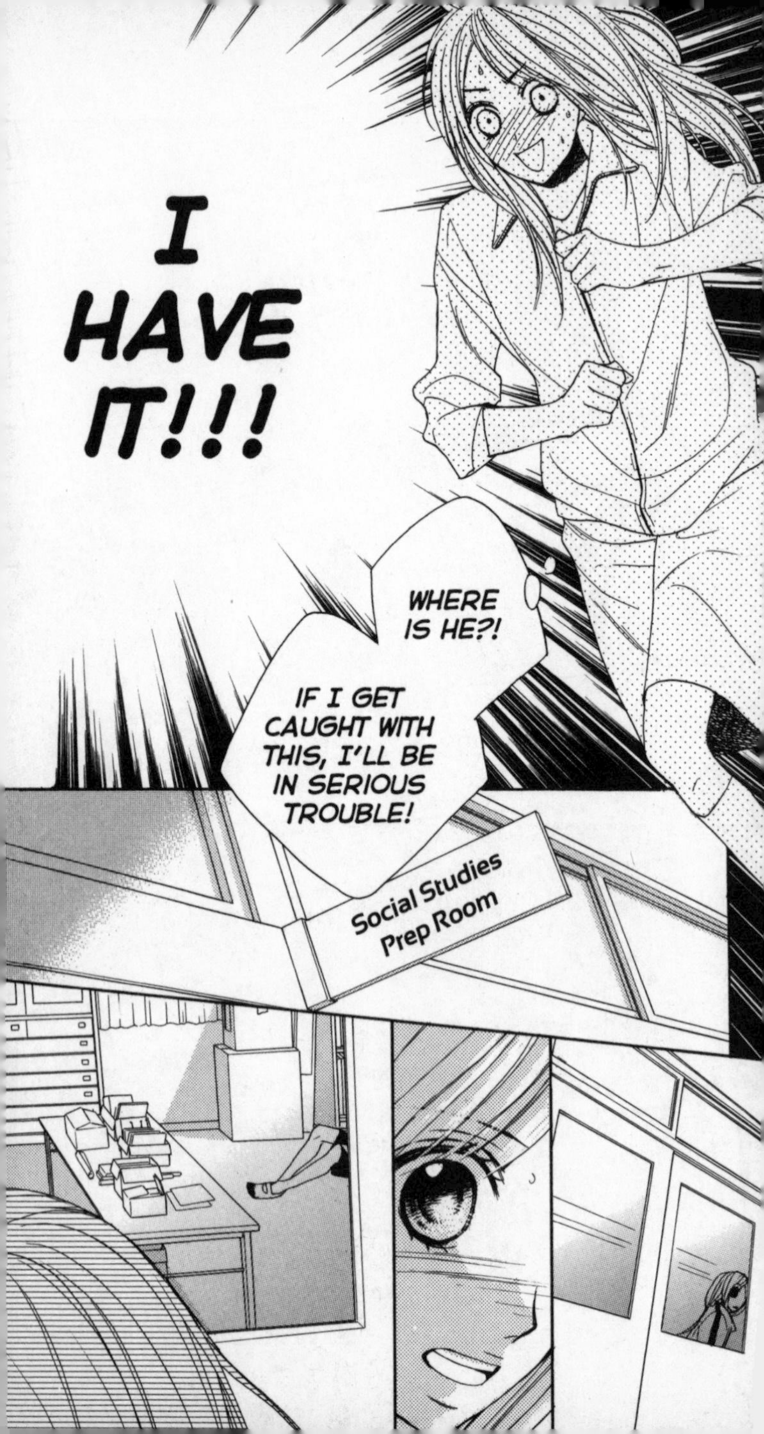
I HAVE IT!!!
WHERE IS HE?!
IF I GET CAUGHT WITH THIS, I'LL BE IN SERIOUS TROUBLE!
Social Studies Prep Room

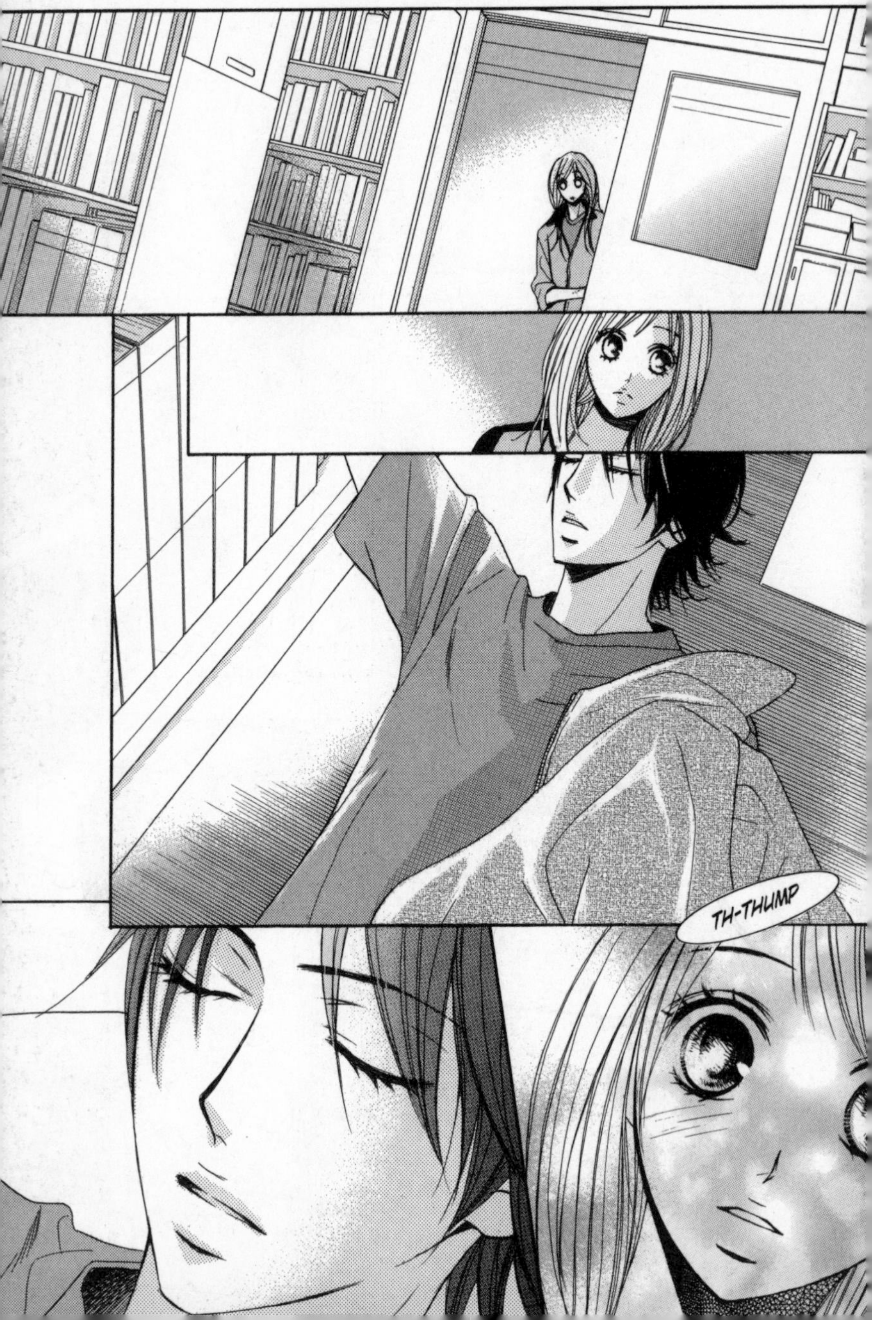
TH-THUMP

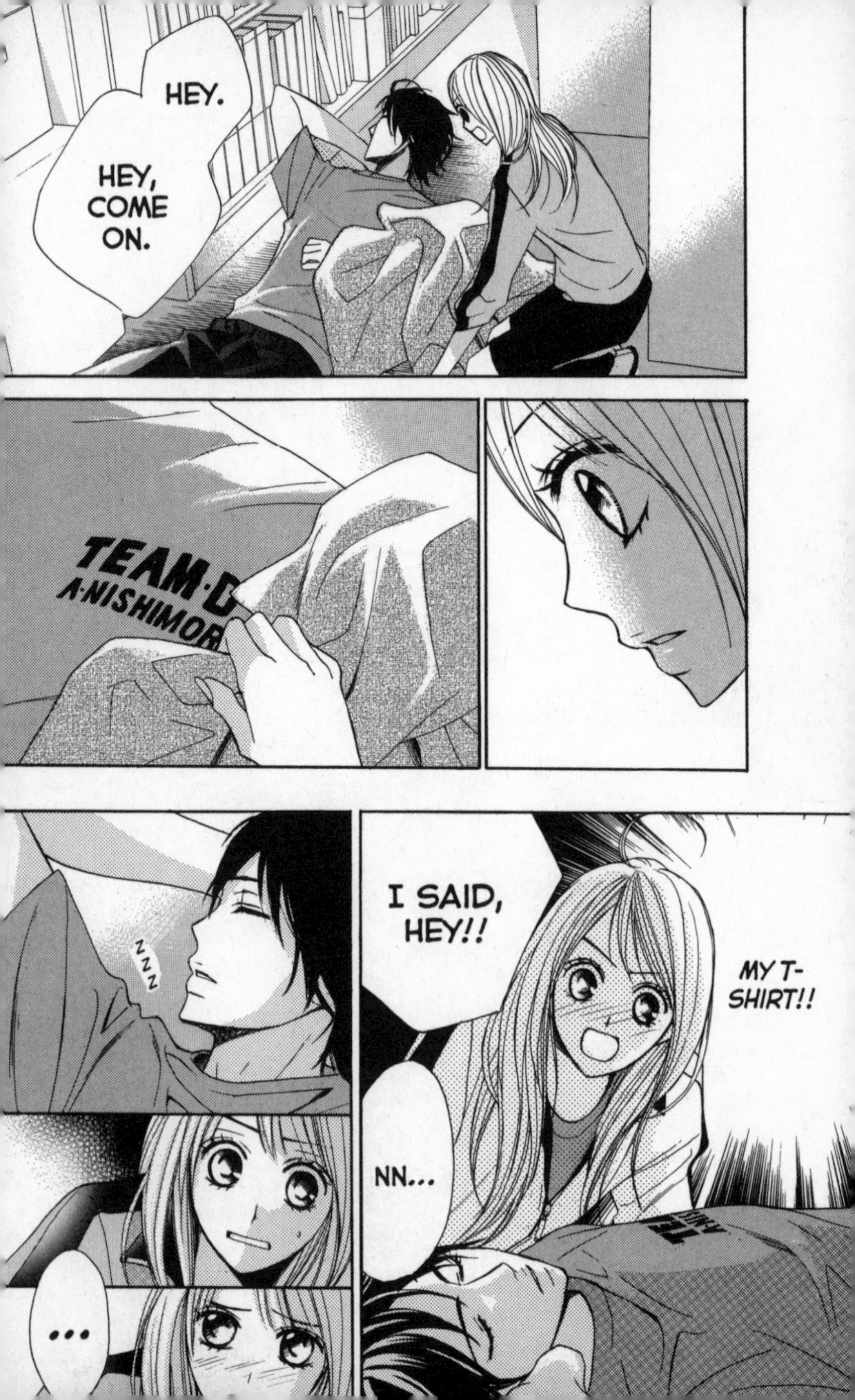
HEY.
HEY, COME ON.
TEAM·D
A·NISHIMOR
MY T-SHIRT!!
I SAID, HEY!!
NN...
ZZZ
...

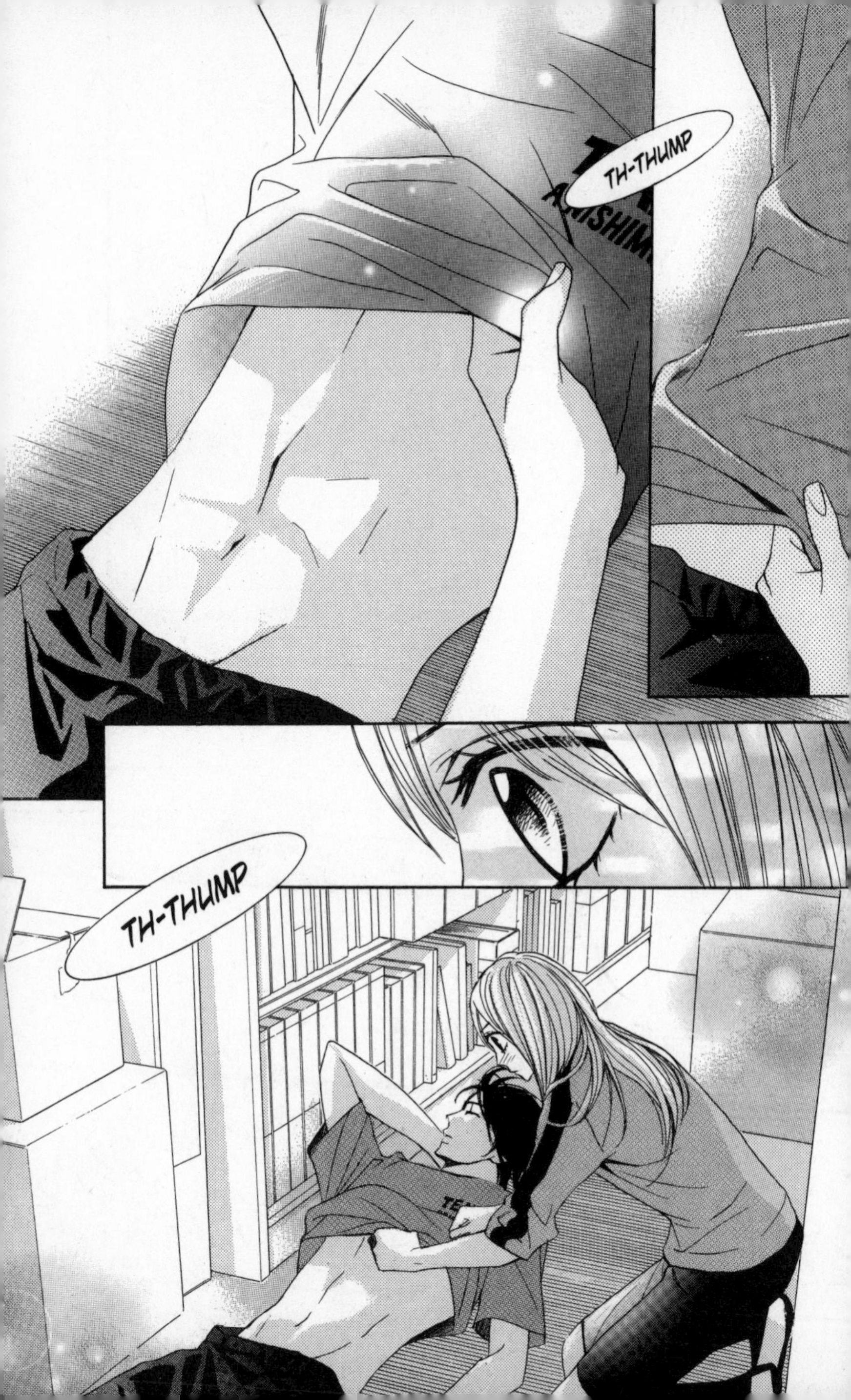
TH-THUMP
TH-THUMP

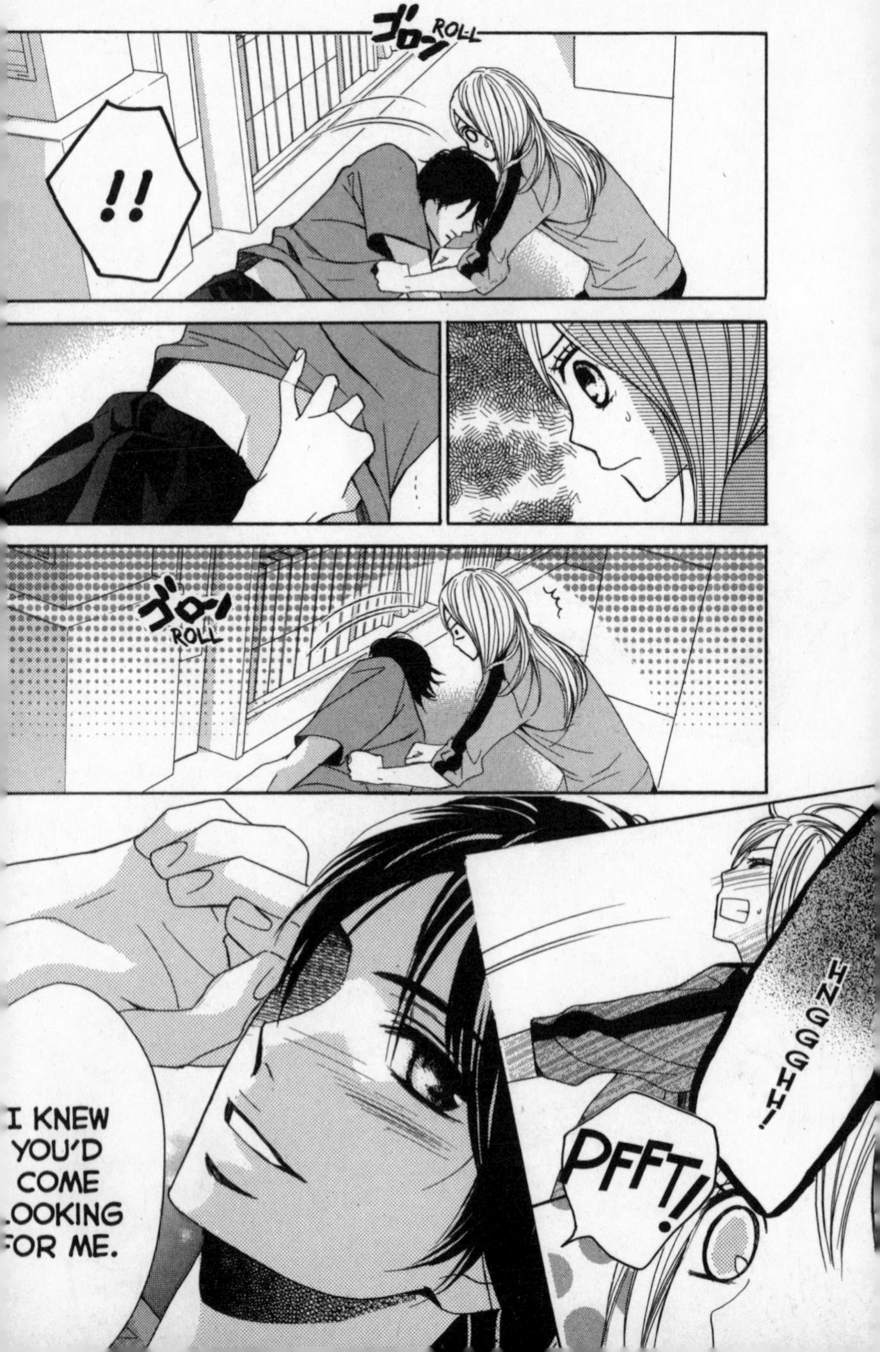
ゴロン
ROLL
!!
ゴロン
ROLL
HNGGGHH!
PFFT!!
I KNEW YOU'D COME LOOKING FOR ME.

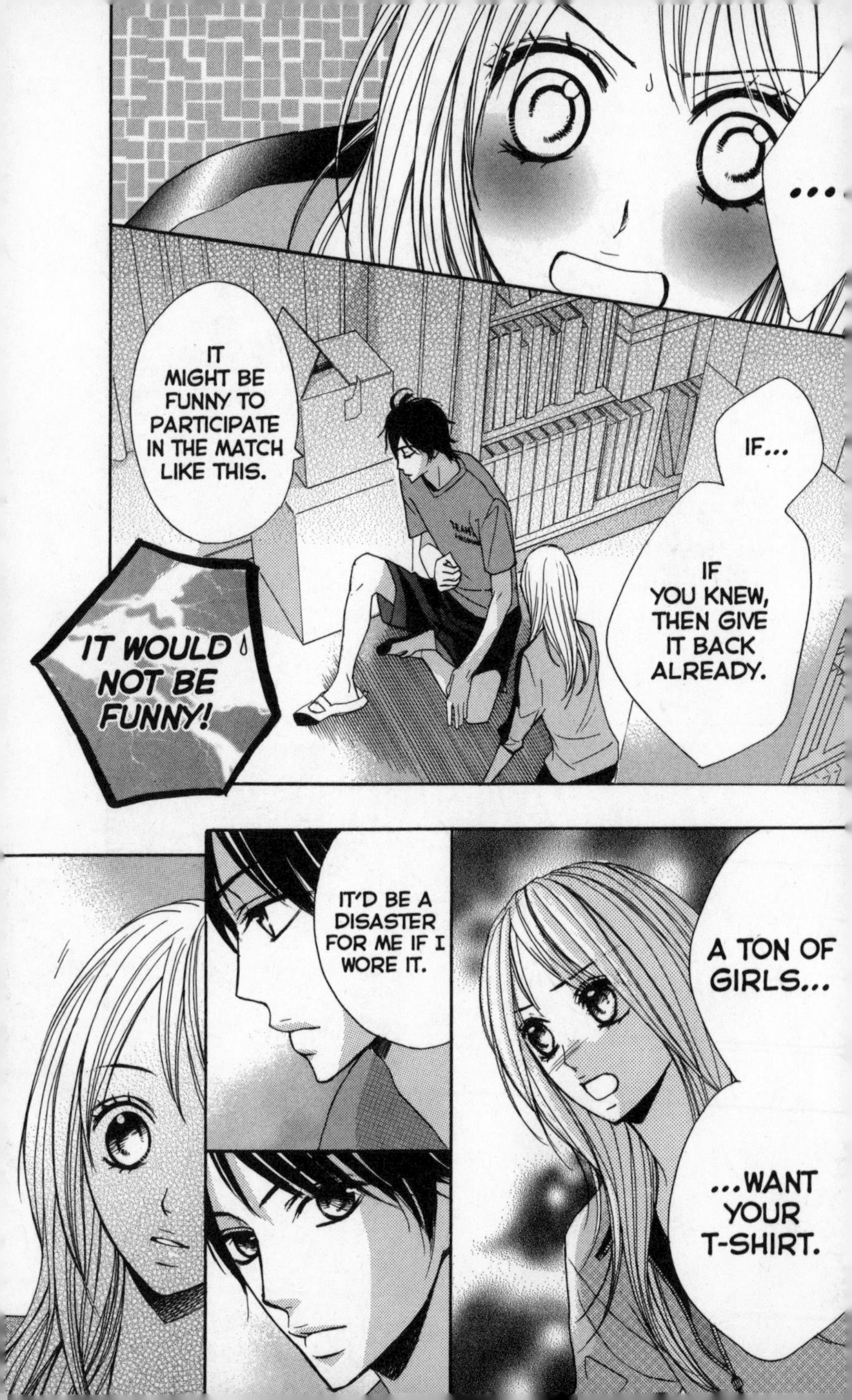
...
IF...
IF YOU KNEW, THEN GIVE IT BACK ALREADY.
IT MIGHT BE FUNNY TO PARTICIPATE IN THE MATCH LIKE THIS.
IT WOULD NOT BE FUNNY!
A TON OF GIRLS...
...WANT YOUR T-SHIRT.
IT'D BE A DISASTER FOR ME IF I WORE IT.

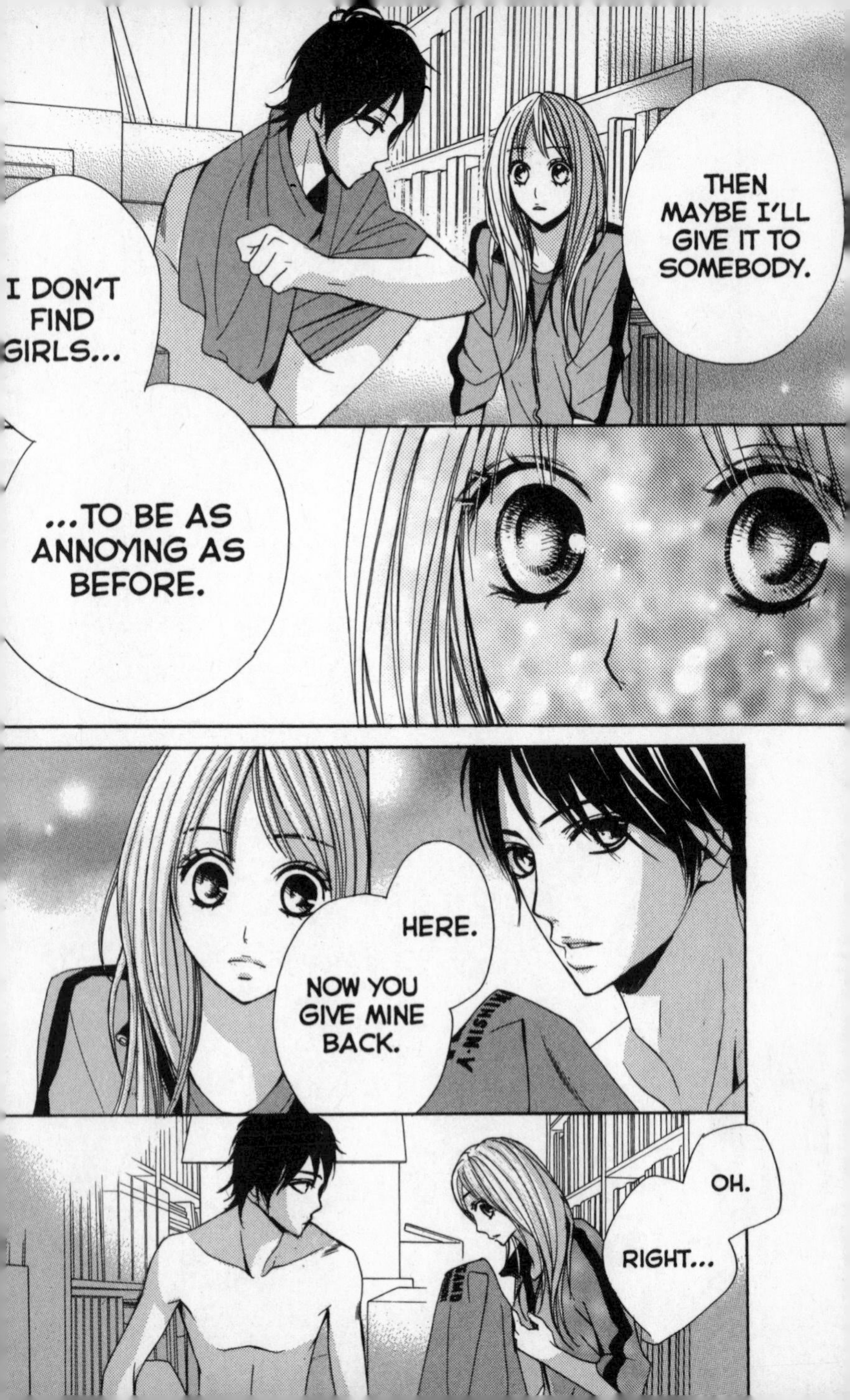
THEN MAYBE I'LL GIVE IT TO SOMEBODY.
I DON'T FIND GIRLS...
...TO BE AS ANNOYING AS BEFORE.
HERE.
NOW YOU GIVE MINE BACK.
OH.
RIGHT...

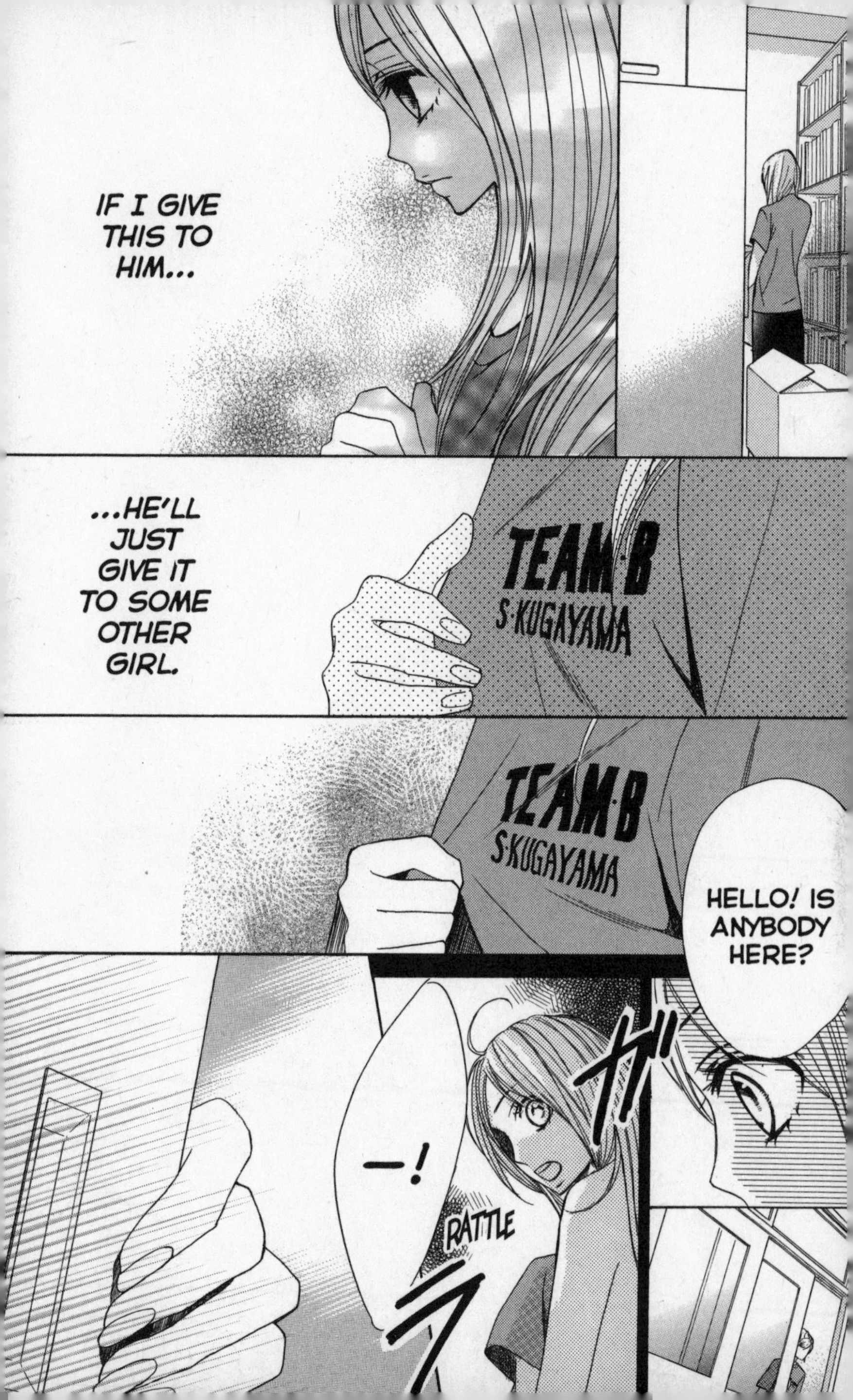
IF I GIVE THIS TO HIM...
...HE'LL JUST GIVE IT TO SOME OTHER GIRL.
TEAM·B
S·KUGAYAMA
TEAM·B
S·KUGAYAMA
HELLO! IS ANYBODY HERE?
—!
RATTLE

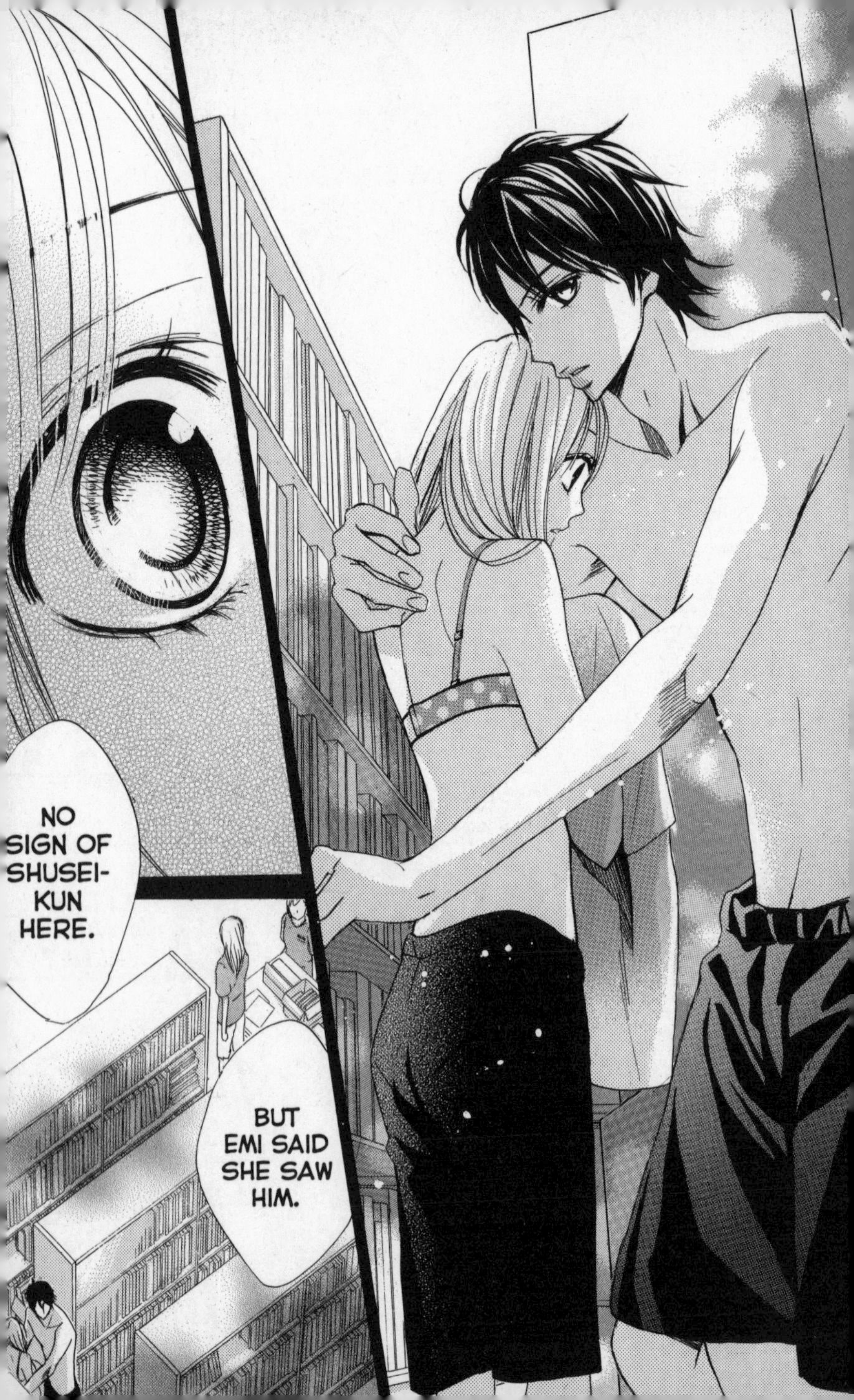
NO SIGN OF SHUSEI-KUN HERE.
BUT EMI SAID SHE SAW HIM.

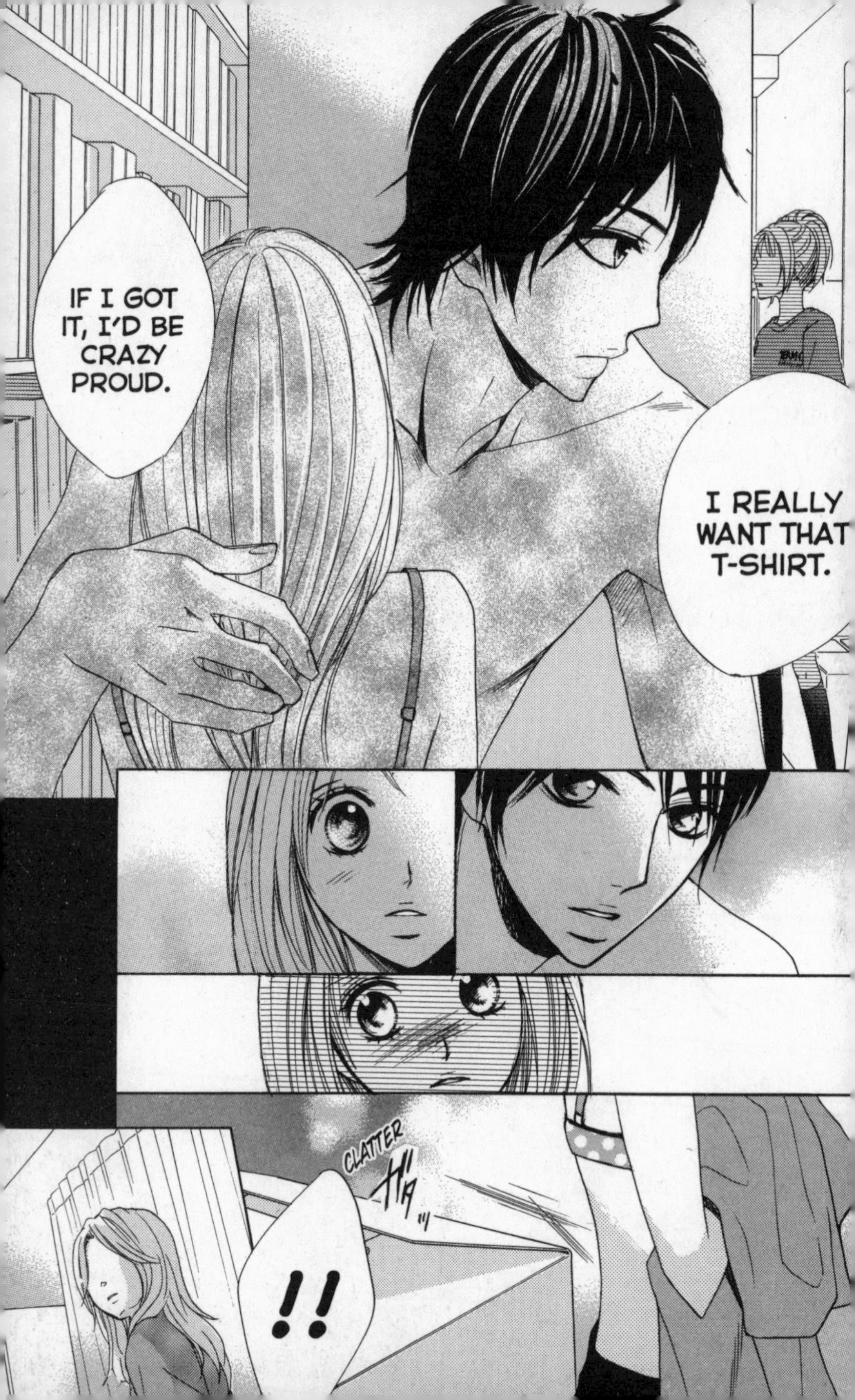
I REALLY WANT THAT T-SHIRT.
IF I GOT IT, I'D BE CRAZY PROUD.
CLATTER
!!

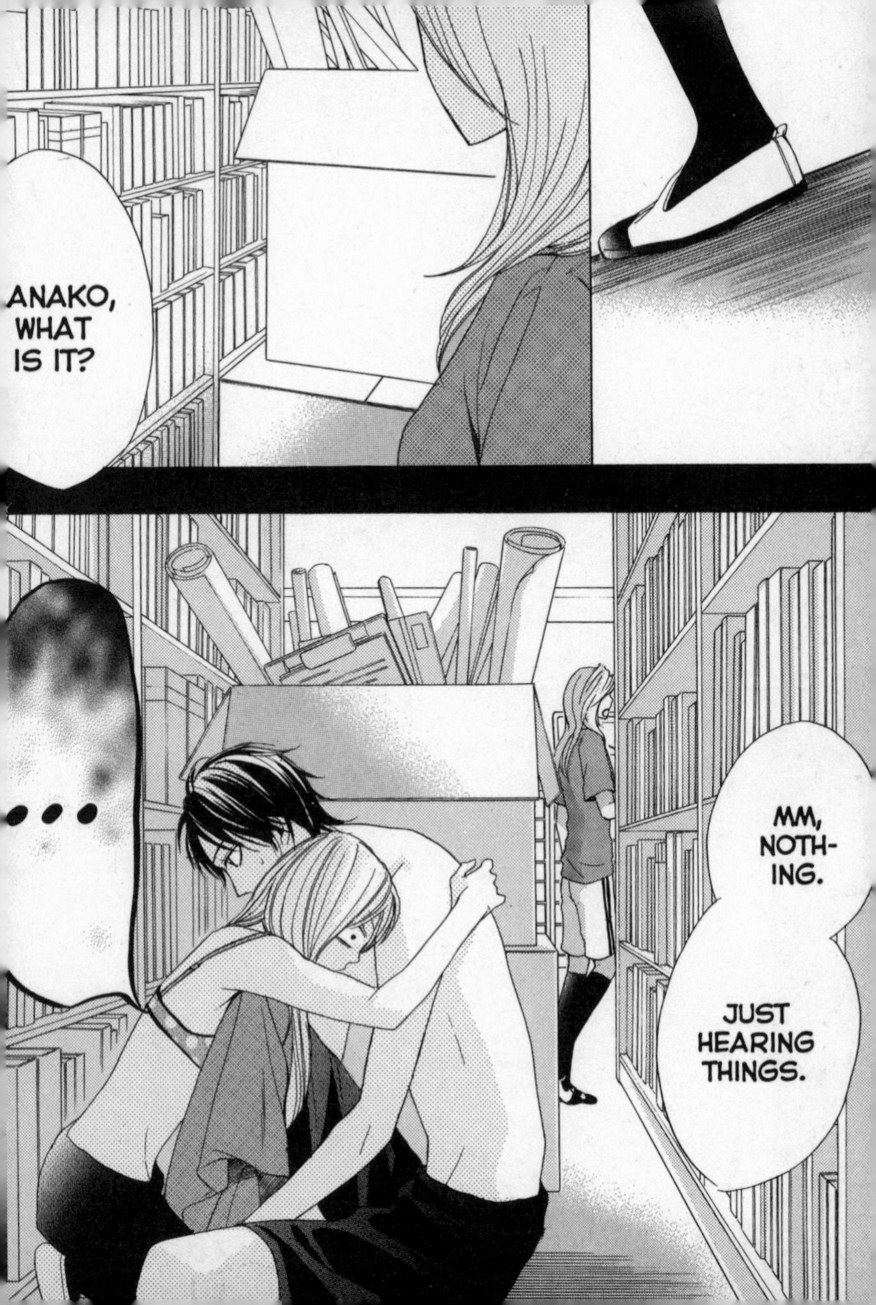
ANAKO, WHAT IS IT?
...
MM, NOTH-ING.
JUST HEARING THINGS.

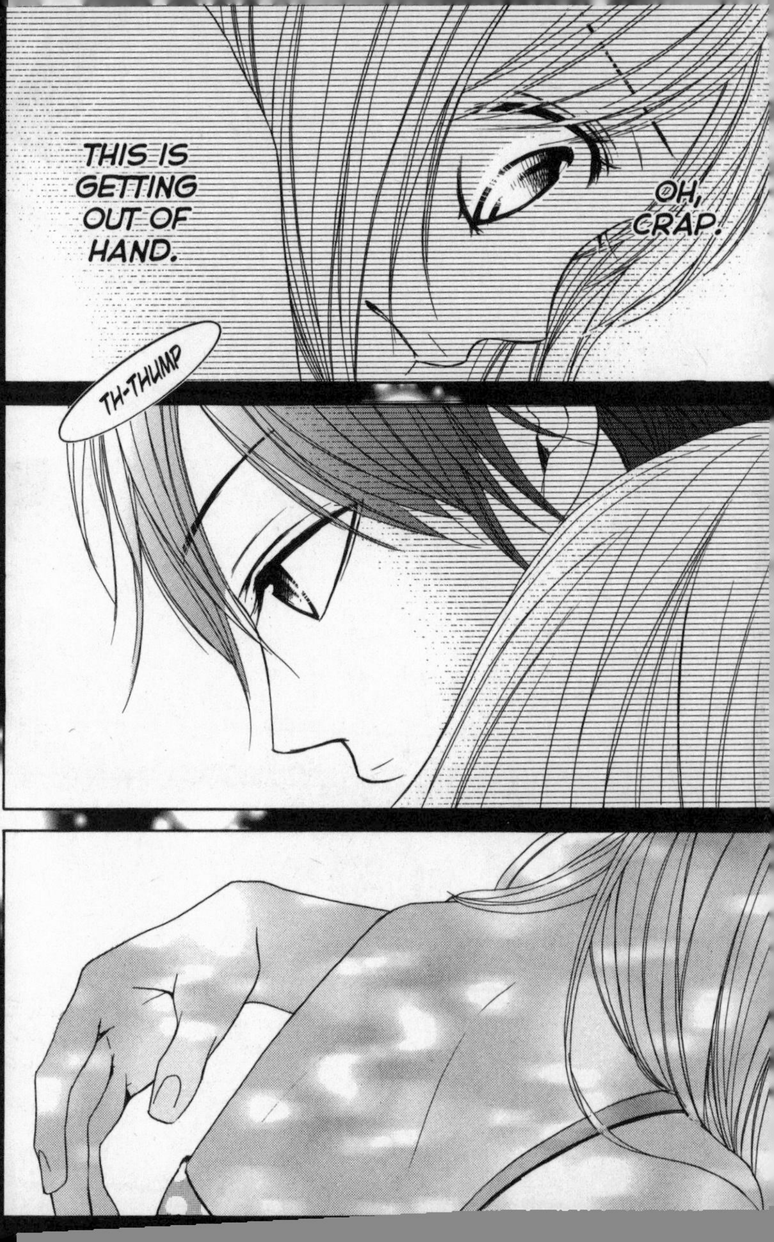
OH, CRAP.
THIS IS GETTING OUT OF HAND.
TH-THUMP

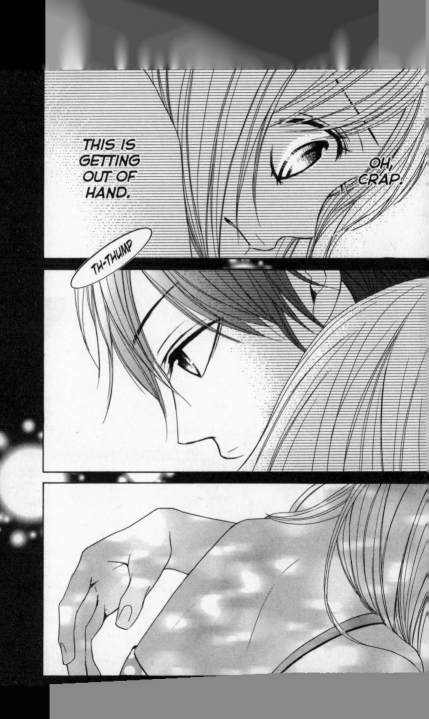

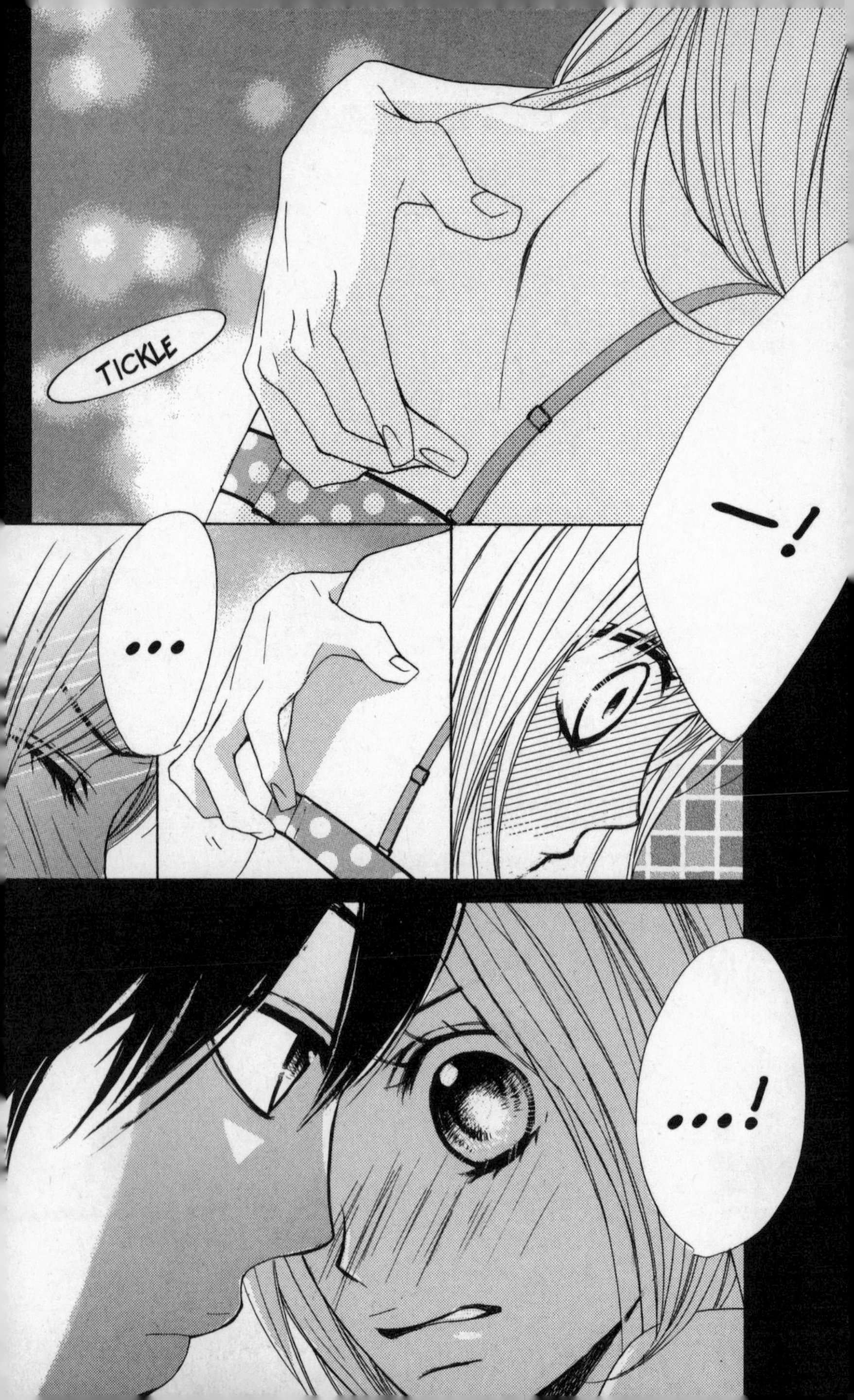
TICKLE
—!
...
...!

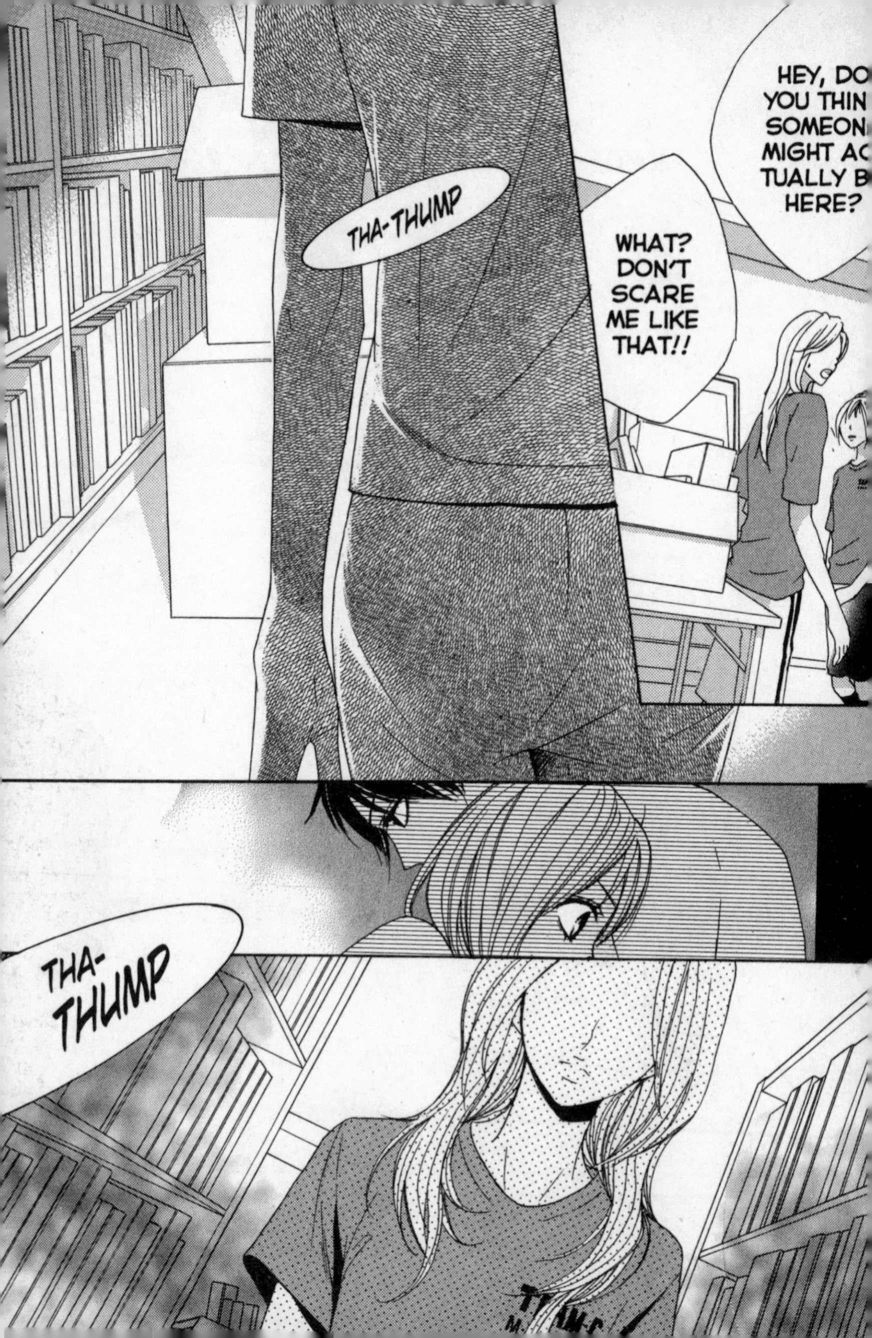
HEY, DO YOU THIN SOMEON MIGHT AC TUALLY B HERE?
WHAT? DON'T SCARE ME LIKE THAT!!
THA-THUMP
THA-THUMP

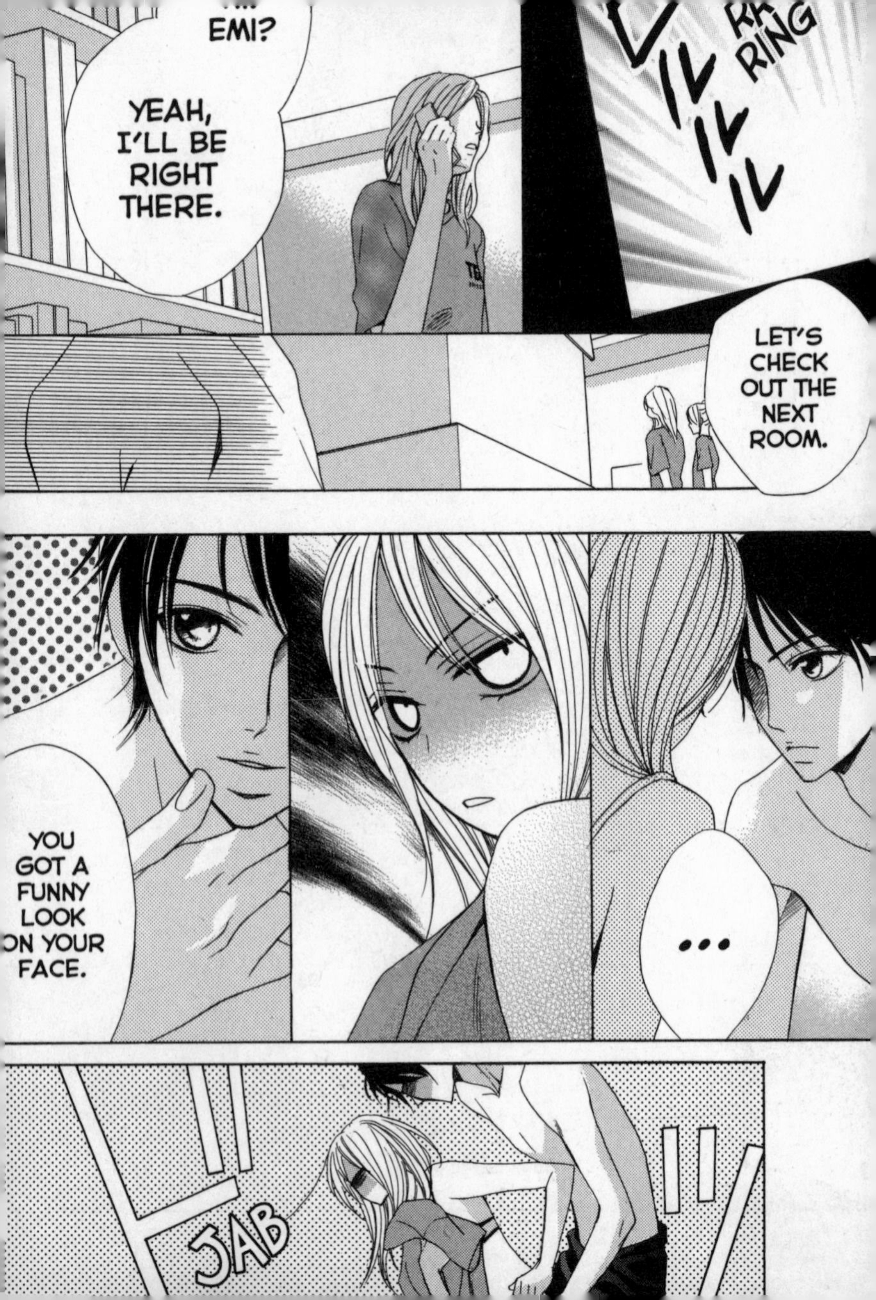
RING
EMI?
YEAH, I'LL BE RIGHT THERE.
LET'S CHECK OUT THE NEXT ROOM.
...
YOU GOT A FUNNY LOOK ON YOUR FACE.
JAB

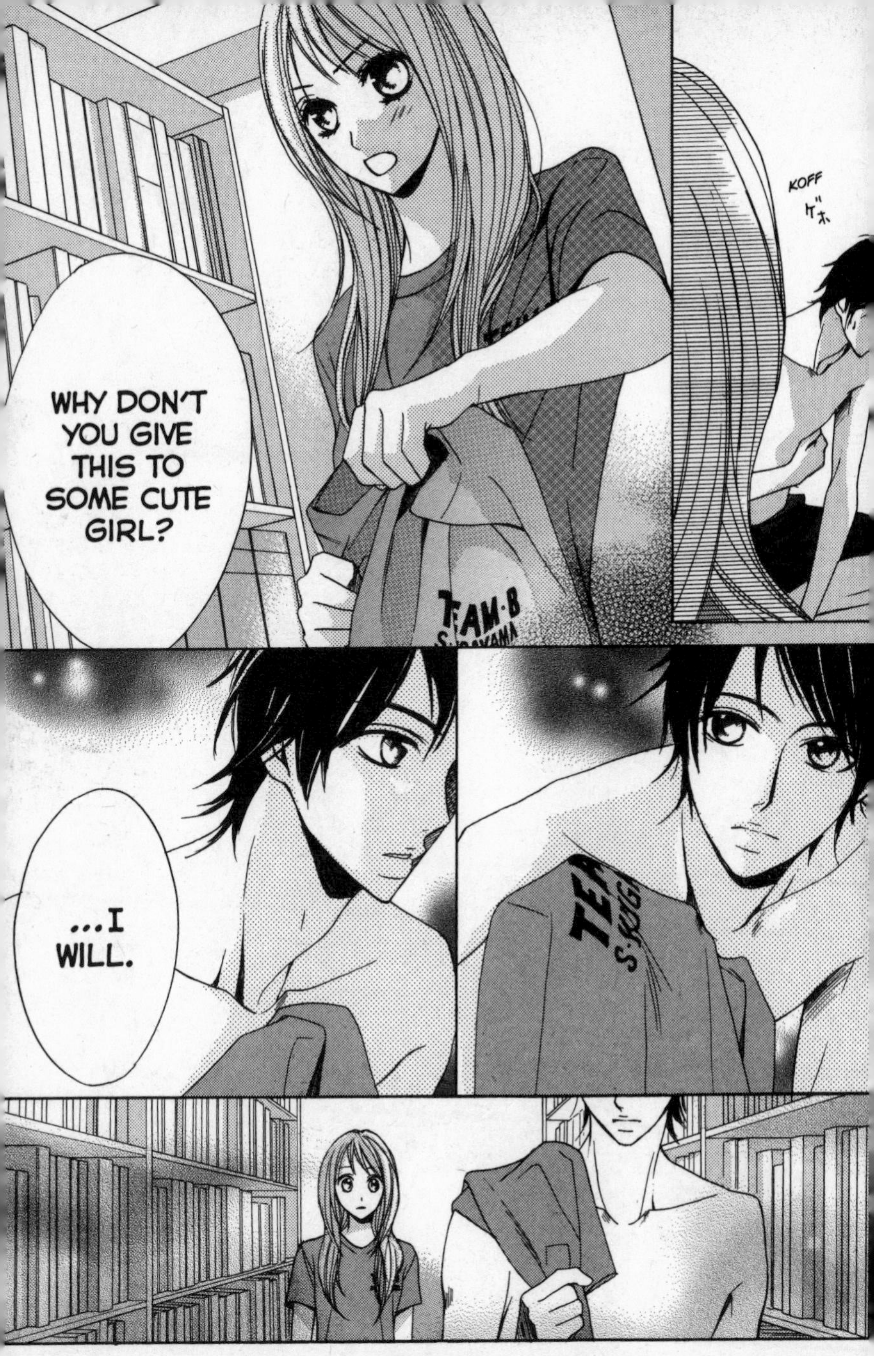
KOFF
ゲホ
WHY DON'T YOU GIVE THIS TO SOME CUTE GIRL?
...I WILL.

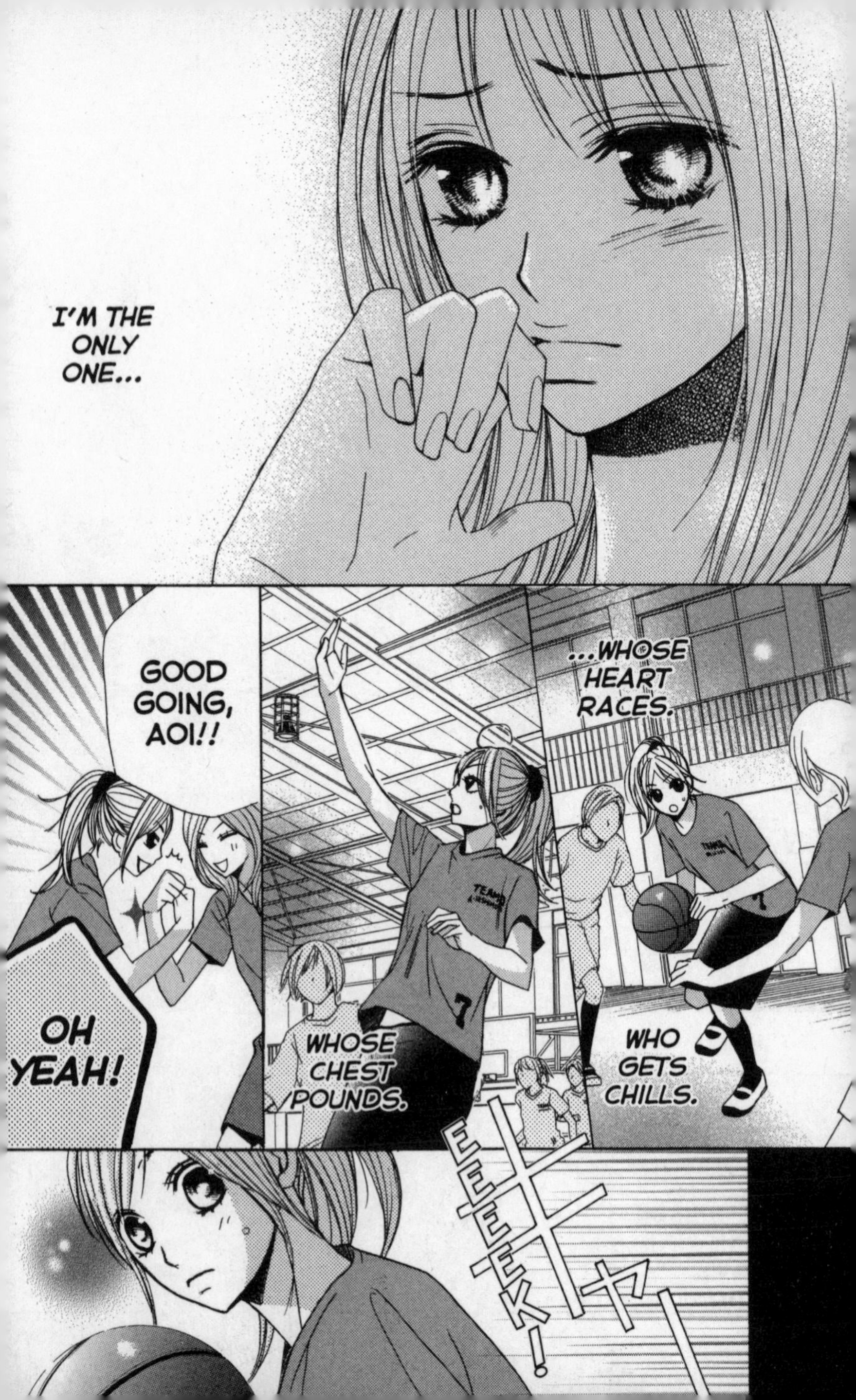
I'M THE ONLY ONE...
...WHOSE HEART RACES.
WHO GETS CHILLS.
WHOSE CHEST POUNDS.
GOOD GOING, AOI!!
OH YEAH!
EEEEEK!

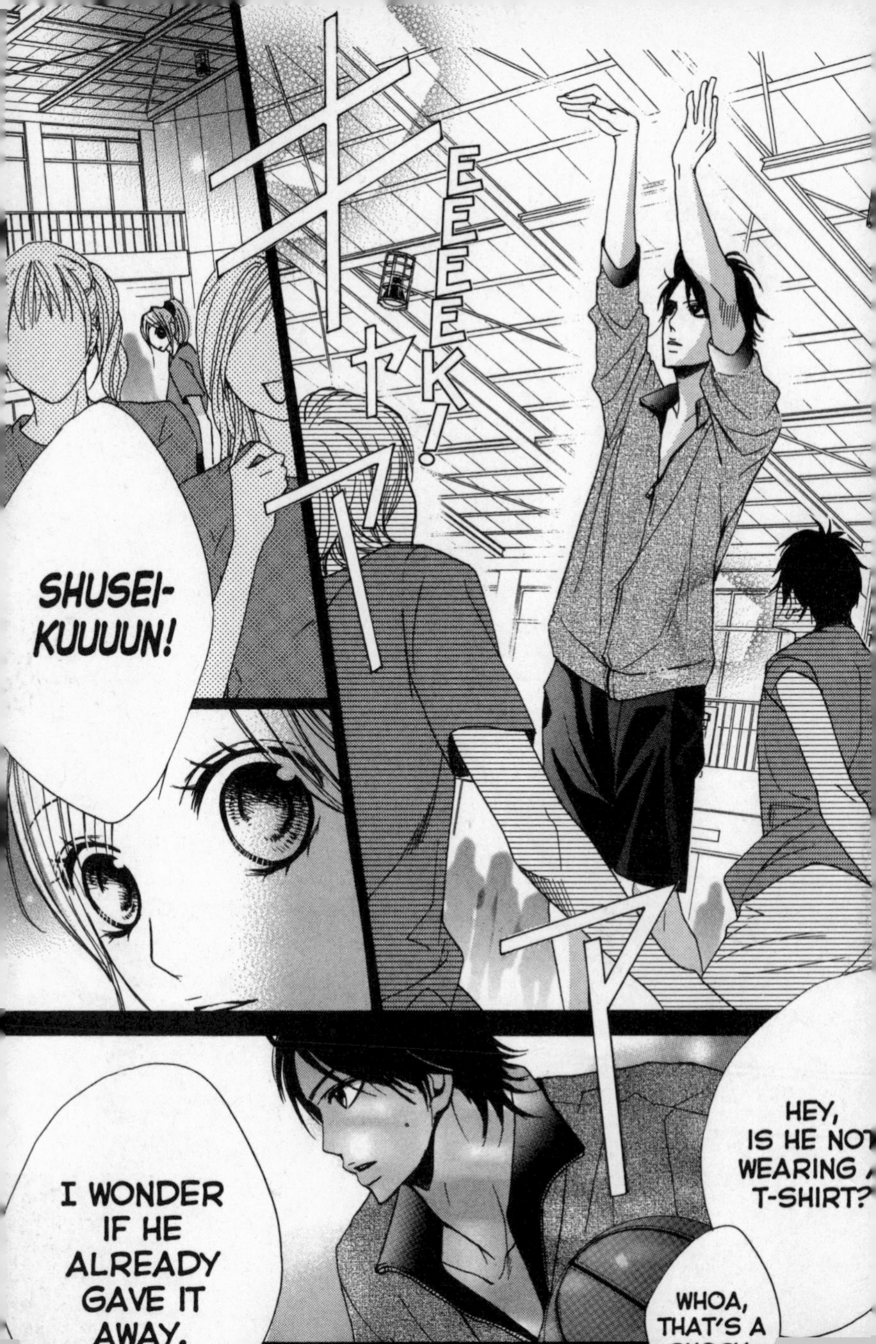
EEEEK!
SHUSEI-KUUUUN!
HEY, IS HE NOT WEARING T-SHIRT?
WHOA, THAT'S A SHOCK.
I WONDER IF HE ALREADY GAVE IT AWAY.

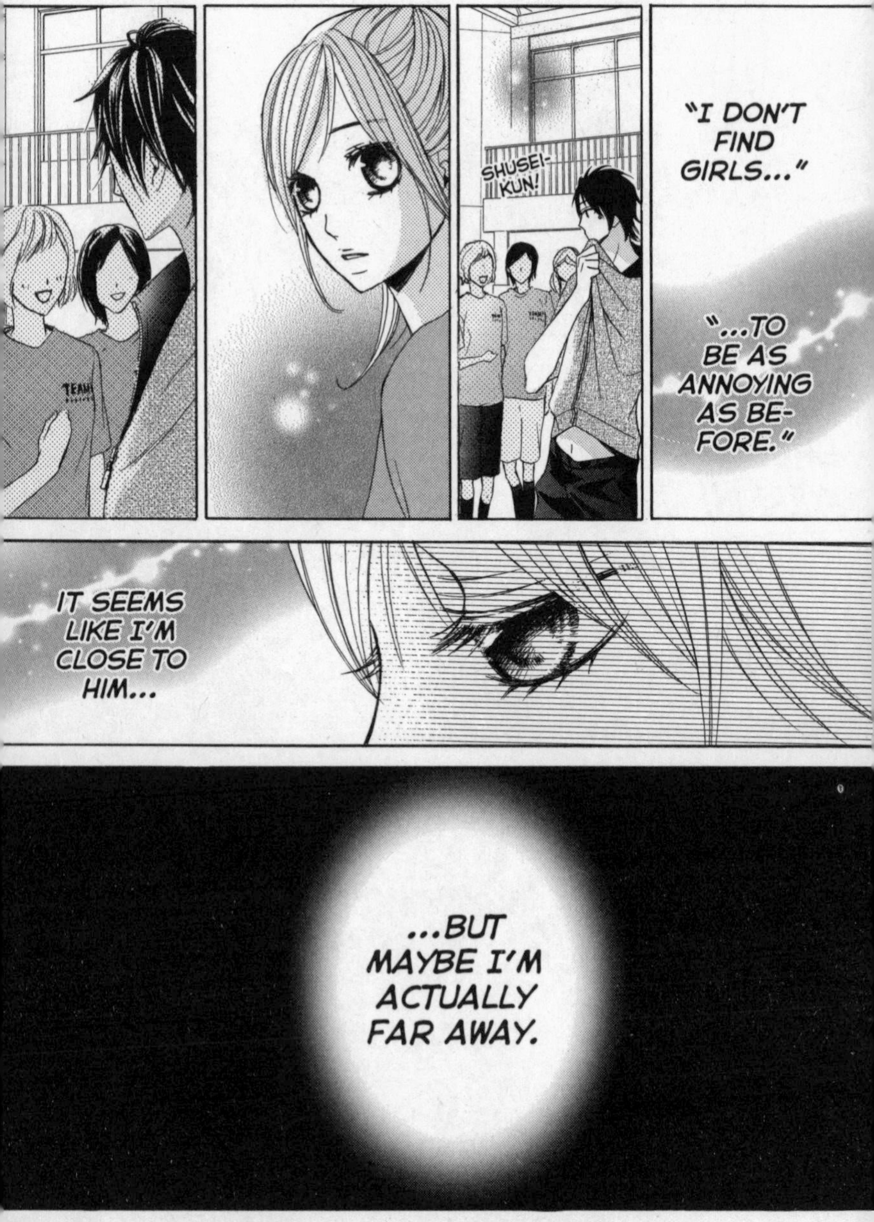
"I DON'T FIND GIRLS..."
"...TO BE AS ANNOYING AS BEFORE."
SHUSEI-KUN!
IT SEEMS LIKE I'M CLOSE TO HIM...
...BUT MAYBE I'M ACTUALLY FAR AWAY.

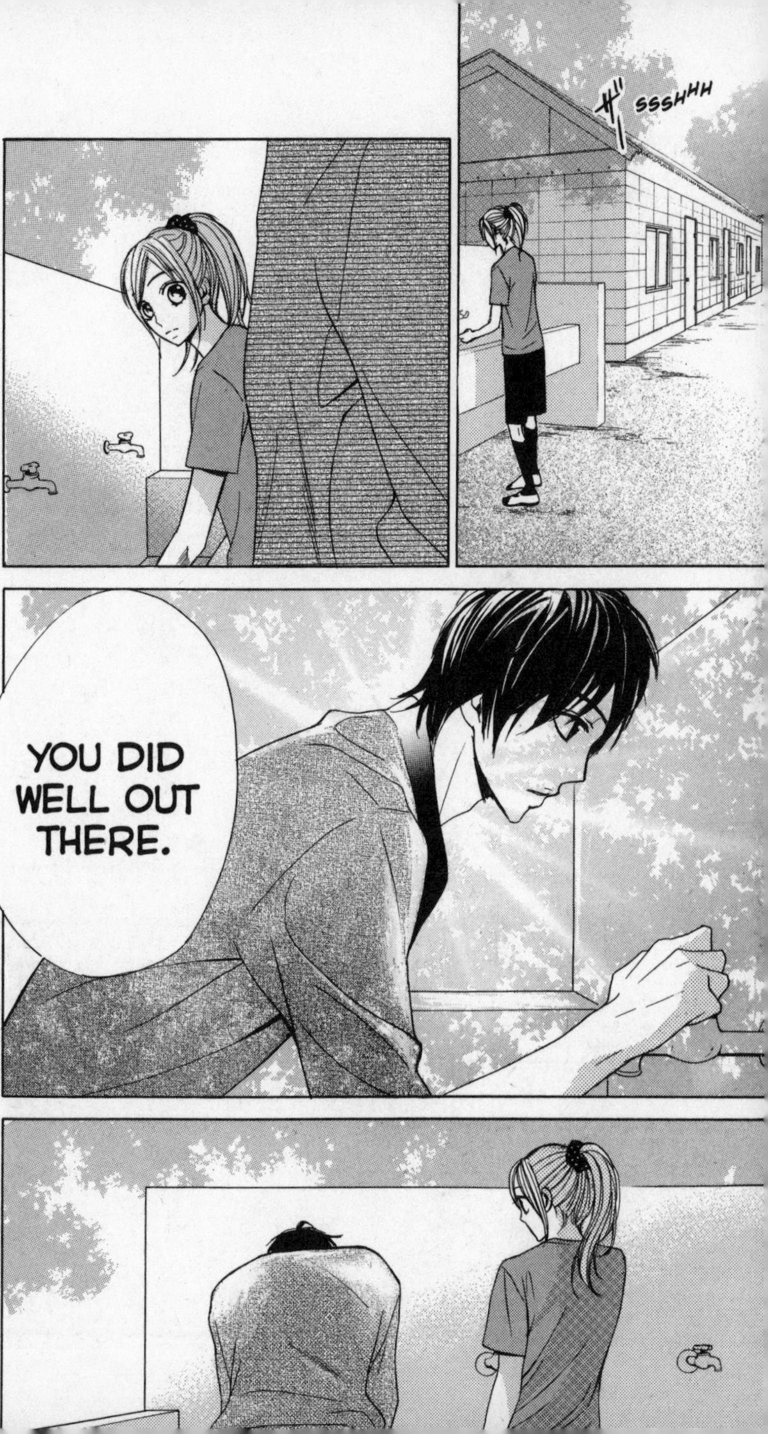
ザ
SSSHHH
YOU DID WELL OUT THERE.

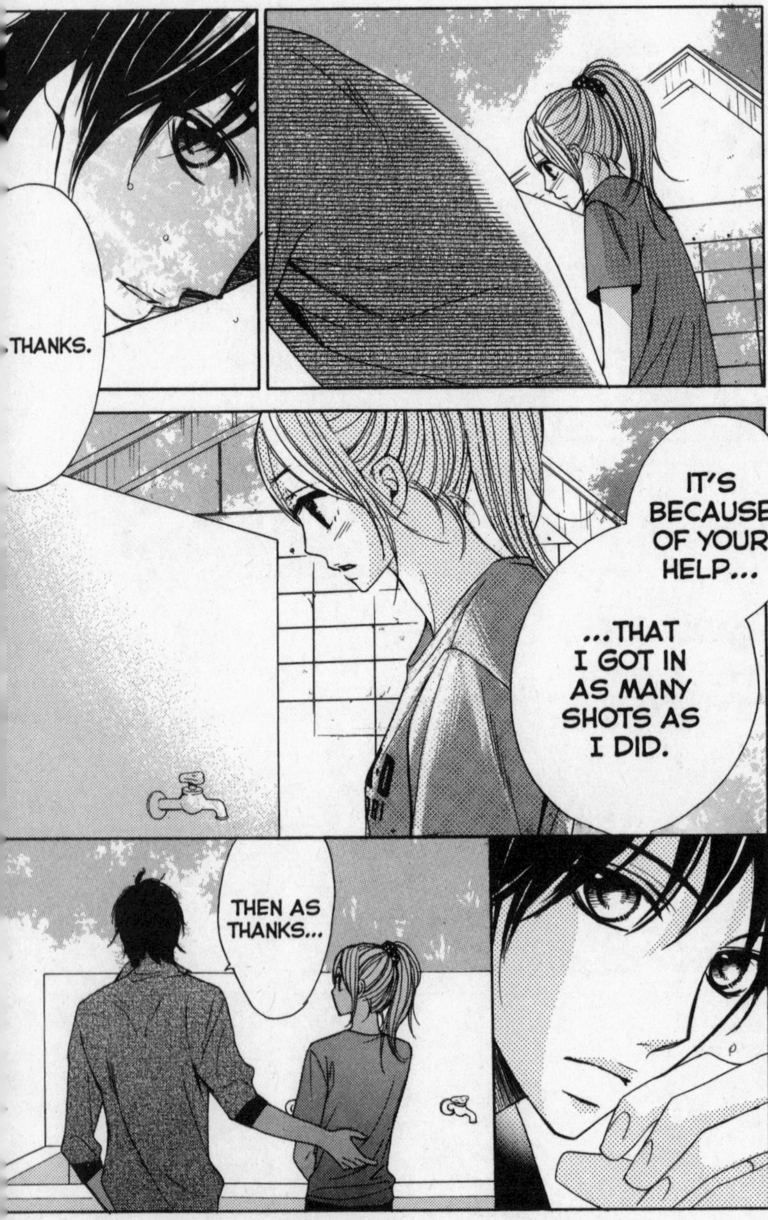

THANKS.
IT'S BECAUSE OF YOUR HELP...
...THAT I GOT IN AS MANY SHOTS AS I DID.
THEN AS THANKS...

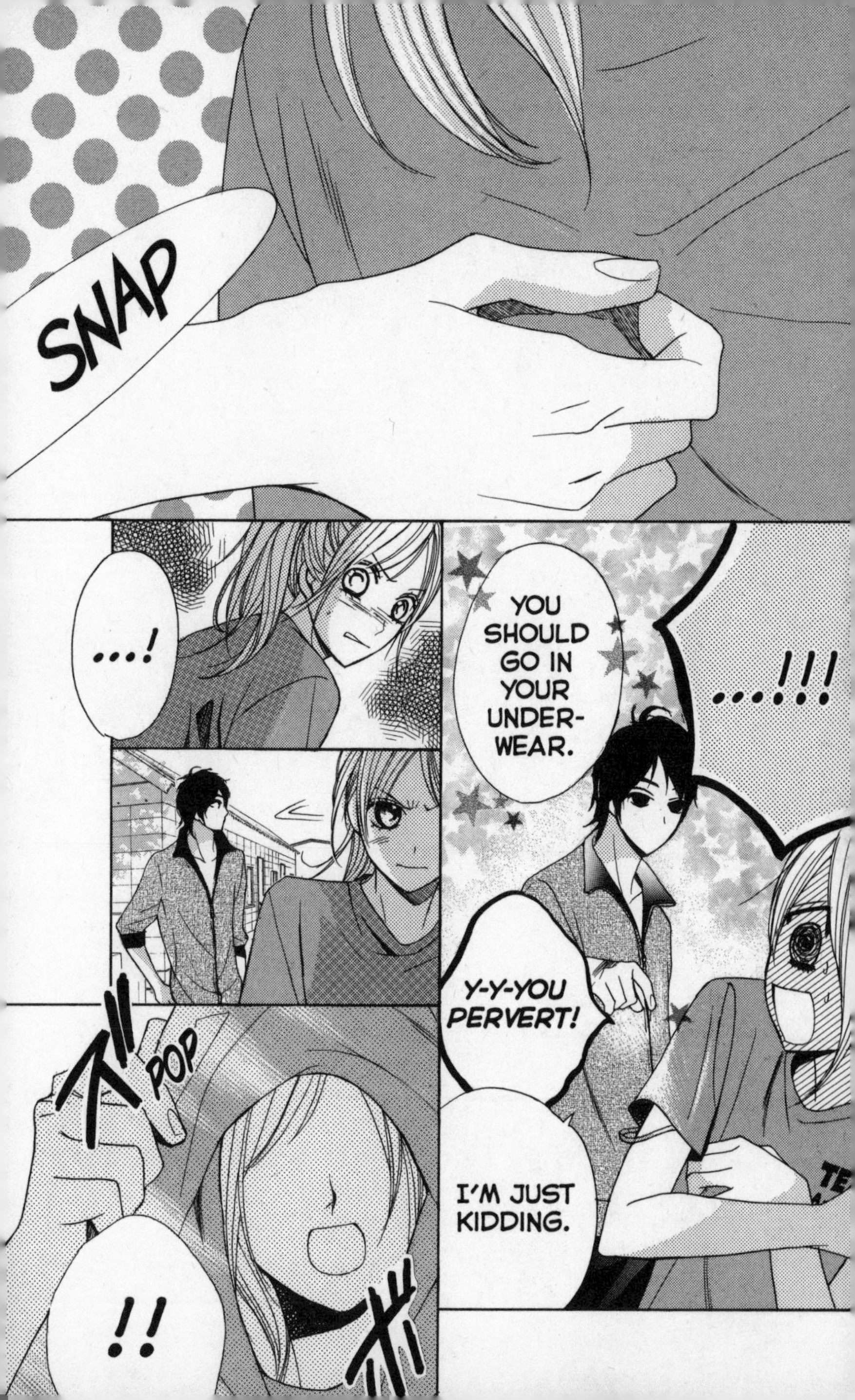
SNAP
YOU SHOULD GO IN YOUR UNDER-WEAR.
...!!!
Y-Y-YOU PERVERT!
I'M JUST KIDDING.
...!
POP
!!

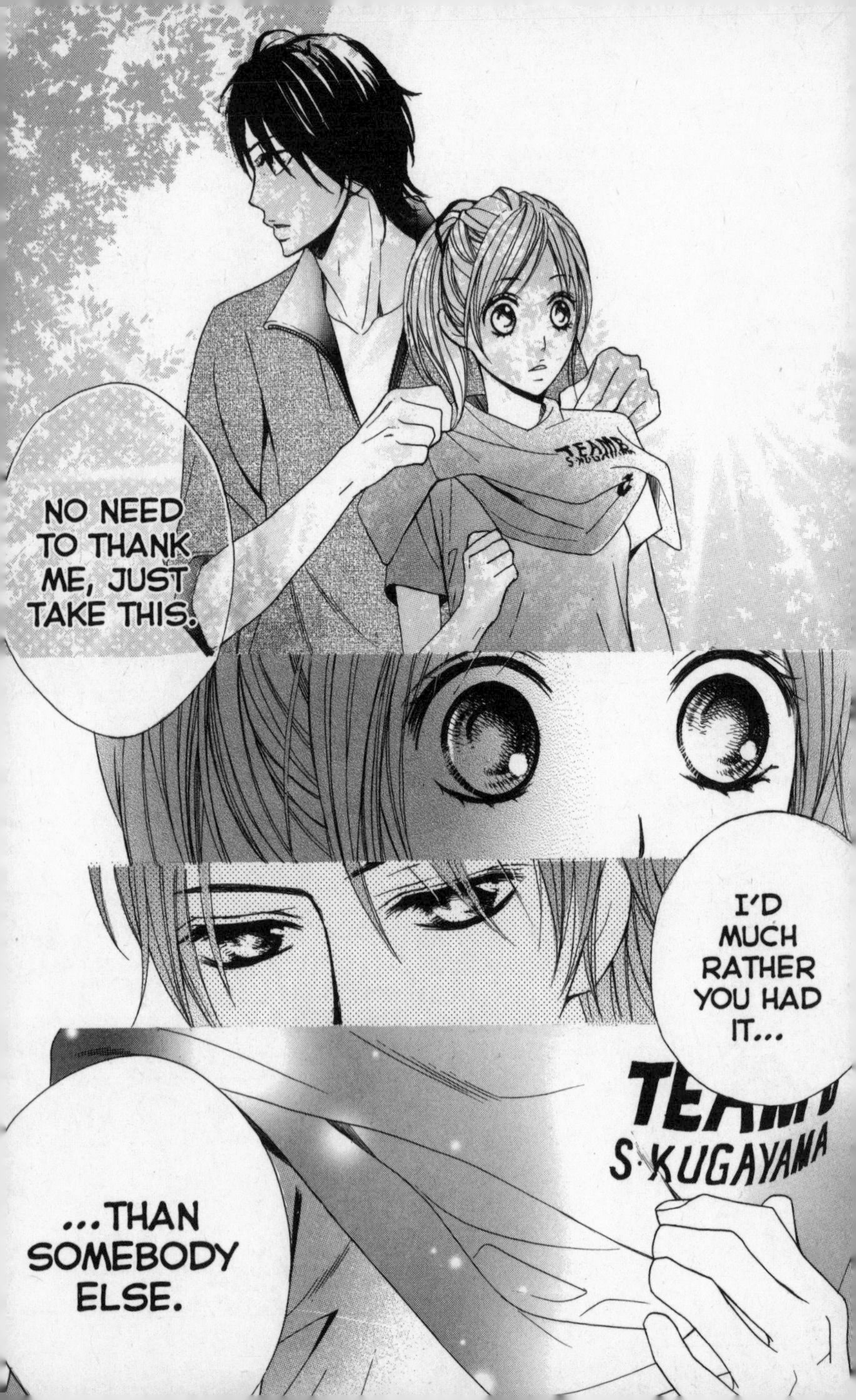
NO NEED TO THANK ME, JUST TAKE THIS.
TEAM B
S·KUGAYAMA
I'D MUCH RATHER YOU HAD IT...
...THAN SOMEBODY ELSE.
TEAM B
S·KUGAYAMA

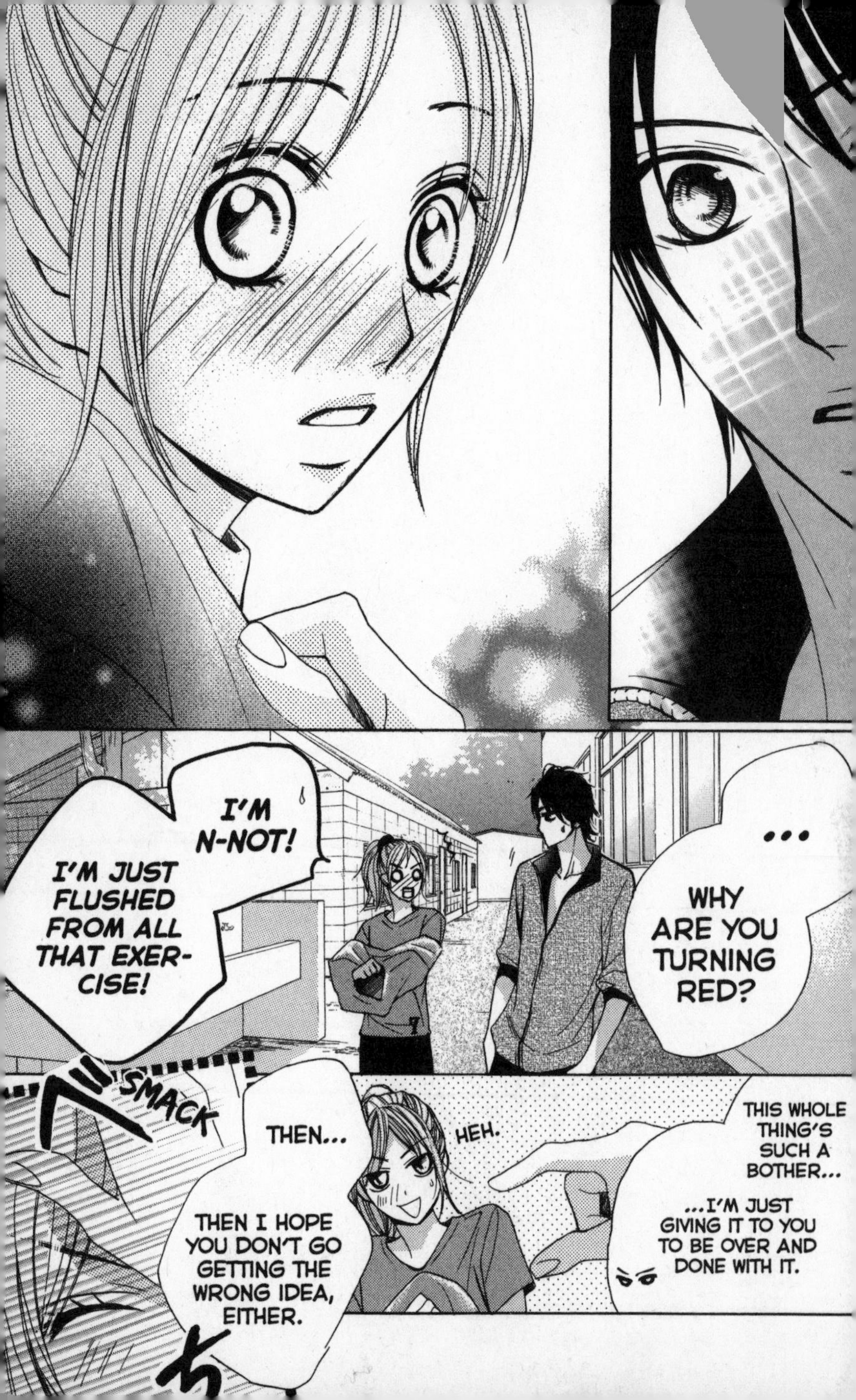
...
WHY ARE YOU TURNING RED?
I'M N-NOT!
I'M JUST FLUSHED FROM ALL THAT EXER-CISE!
THIS WHOLE THING'S SUCH A BOTHER...
...I'M JUST GIVING IT TO YOU TO BE OVER AND DONE WITH IT.
HEH.
SMACK
THEN...
THEN I HOPE YOU DON'T GO GETTING THE WRONG IDEA, EITHER.

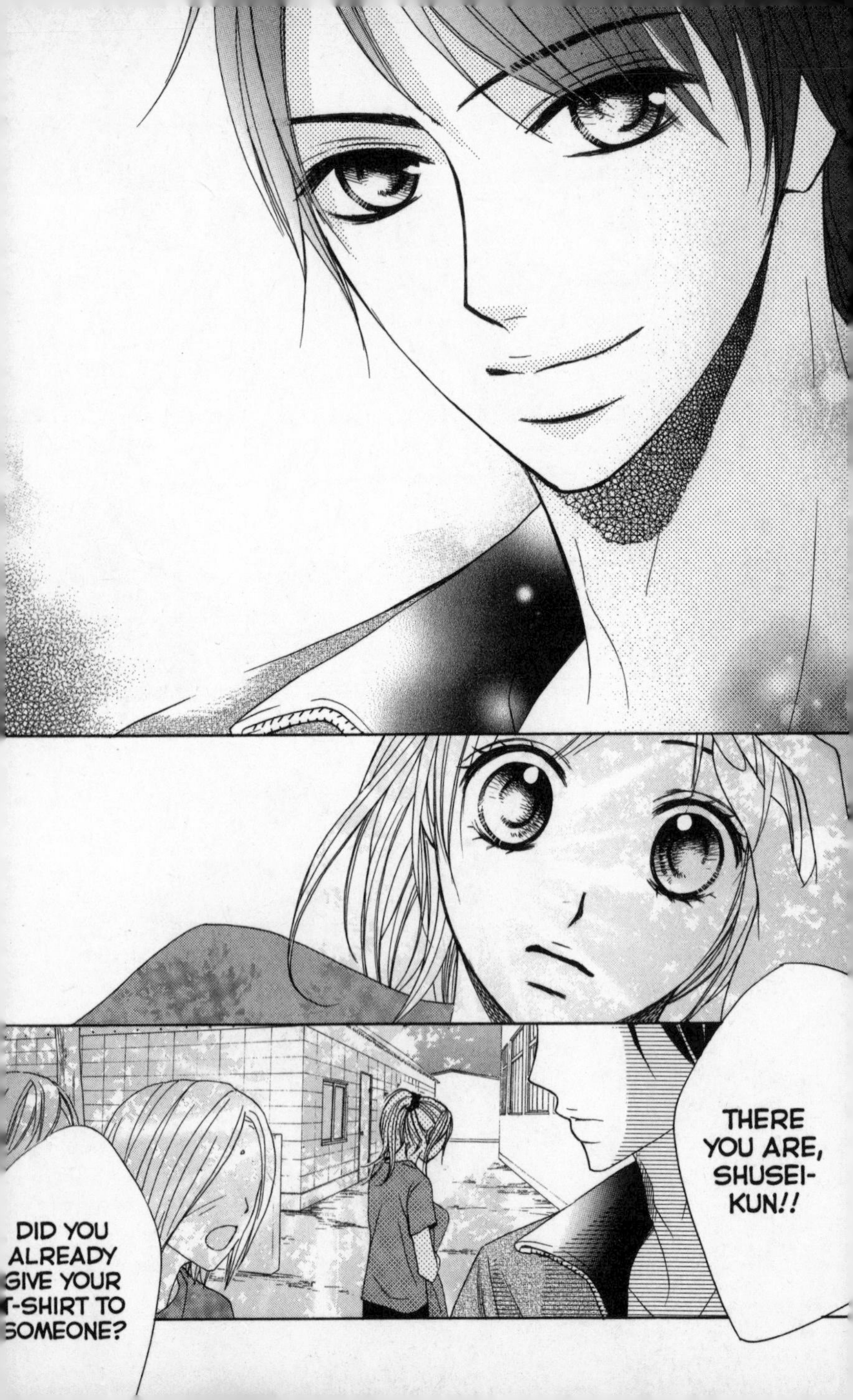
THERE YOU ARE, SHUSEI-KUN!!
DID YOU ALREADY GIVE YOUR T-SHIRT TO SOMEONE?

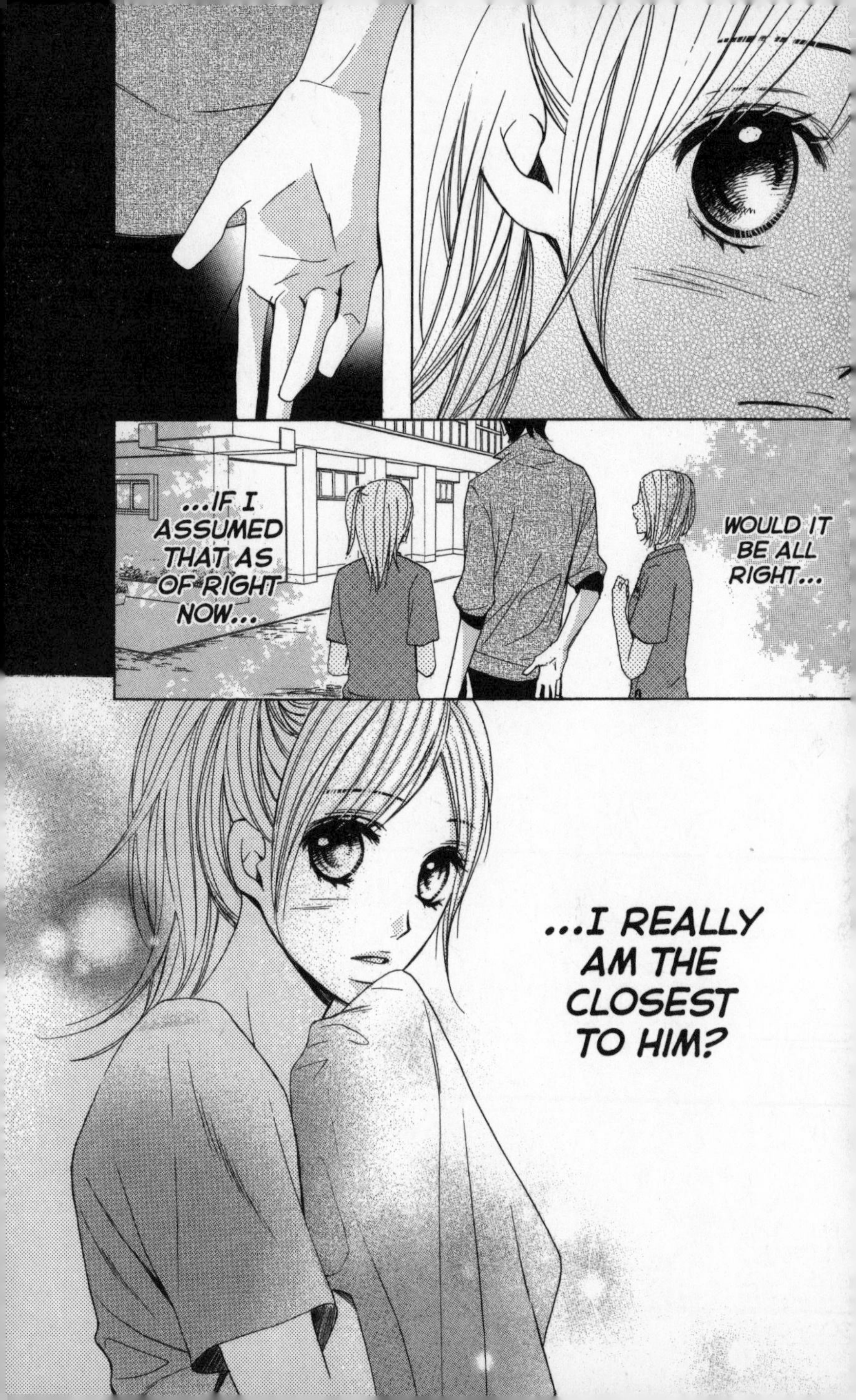
WOULD IT BE ALL RIGHT...
...IF I ASSUMED THAT AS OF RIGHT NOW...
...I REALLY AM THE CLOSEST TO HIM?

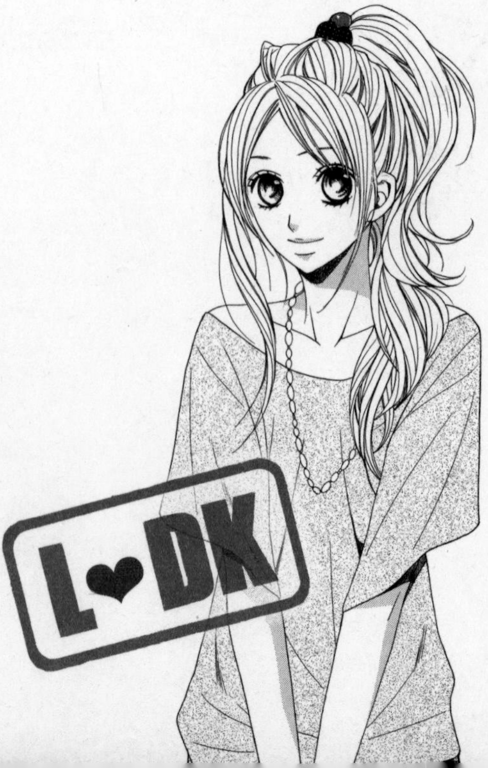
L♥DK

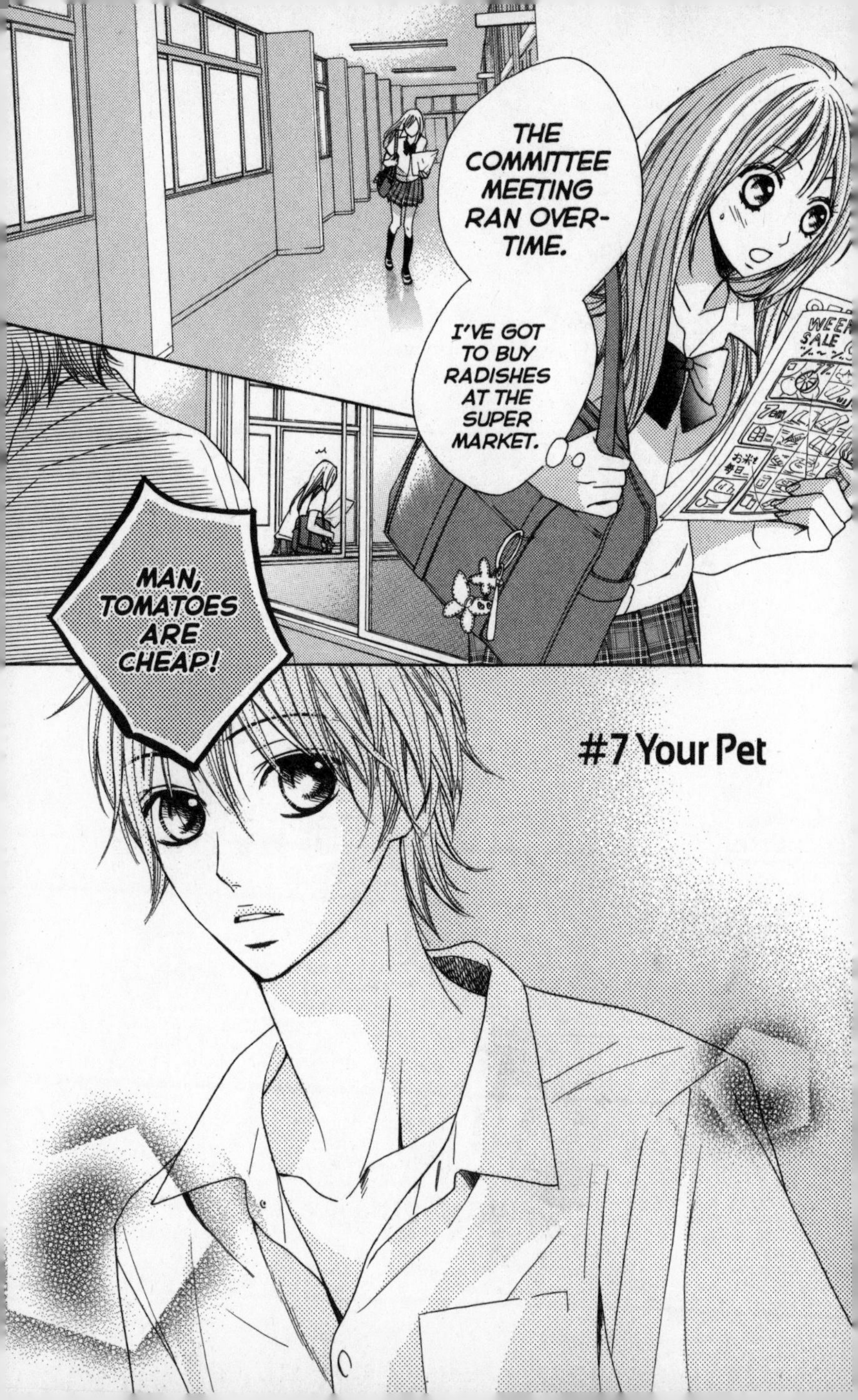
THE COMMITTEE MEETING RAN OVER-TIME.
I'VE GOT TO BUY RADISHES AT THE SUPER MARKET.
MAN, TOMATOES ARE CHEAP!
#7 Your Pet

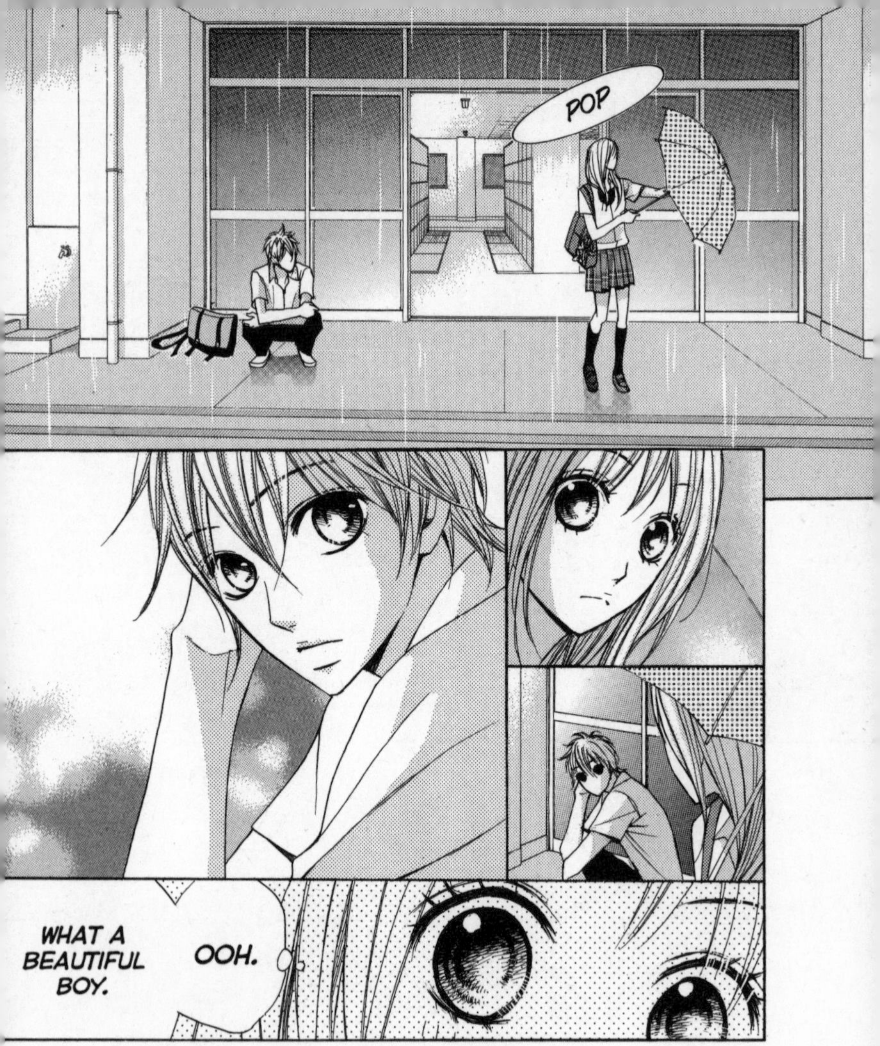
POP
OOH.
WHAT A BEAUTIFUL BOY.

L♥DK

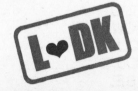

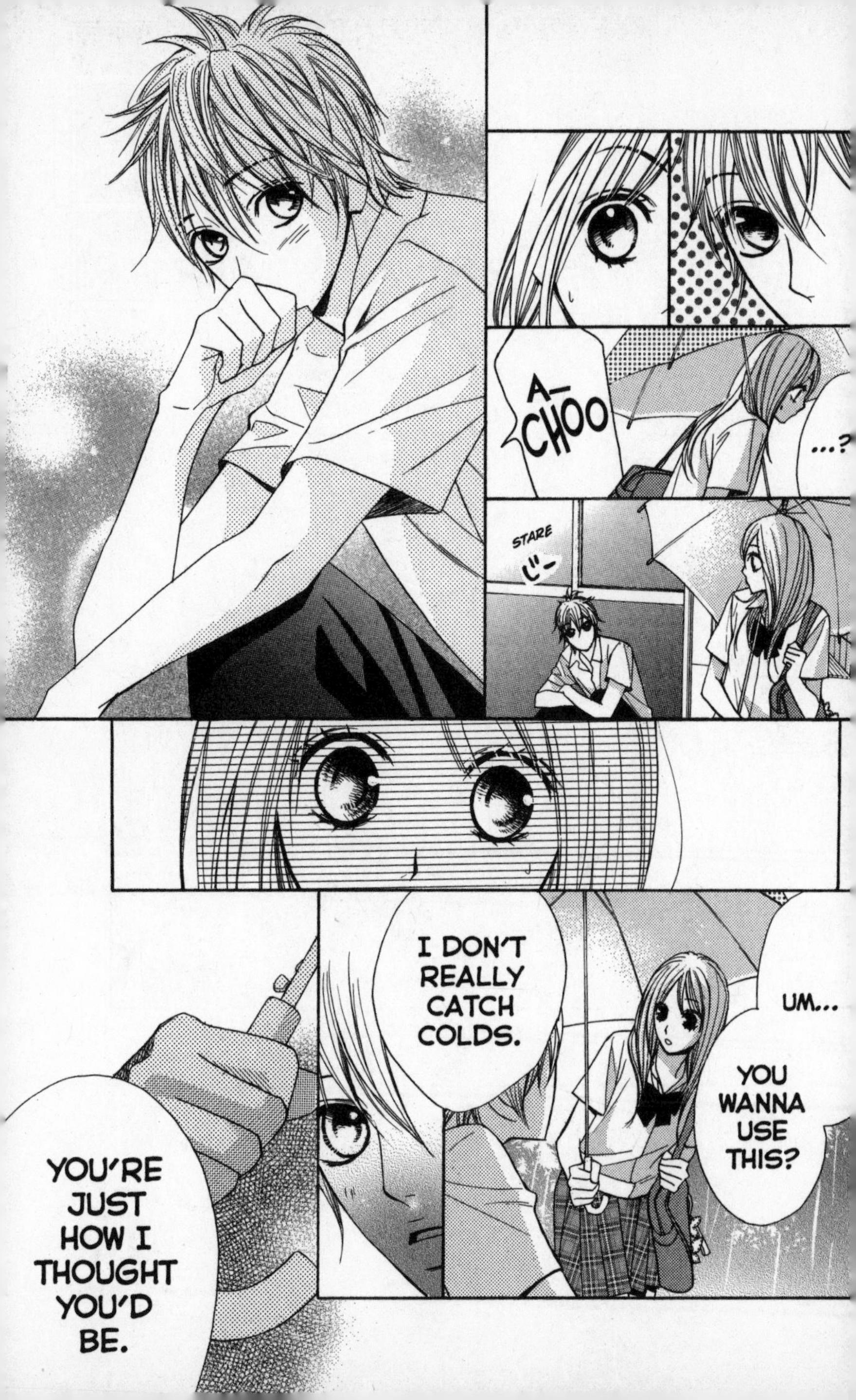
A-CHOO
...?
STARE
じー
UM...
YOU WANNA USE THIS?
I DON'T REALLY CATCH COLDS.
YOU'RE JUST HOW I THOUGHT YOU'D BE.

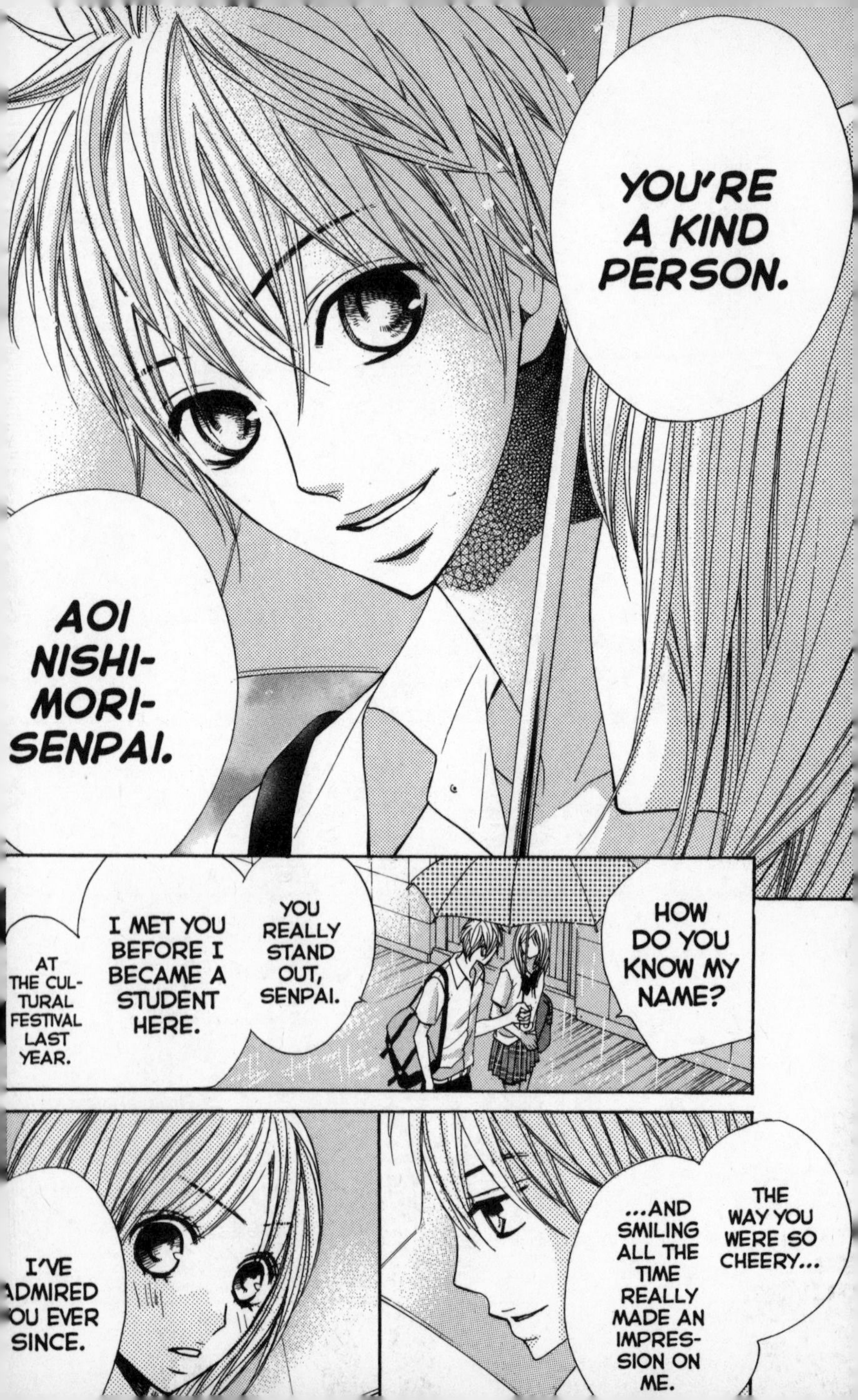
YOU'RE A KIND PERSON.
AOI NISHI-MORI-SENPAI.
HOW DO YOU KNOW MY NAME?
YOU REALLY STAND OUT, SENPAI.
I MET YOU BEFORE I BECAME A STUDENT HERE.
AT THE CUL-TURAL FESTIVAL LAST YEAR.
THE WAY YOU WERE SO CHEERY...
...AND SMILING ALL THE TIME REALLY MADE AN IMPRES-SION ON ME.
I'VE DMIRED OU EVER SINCE.

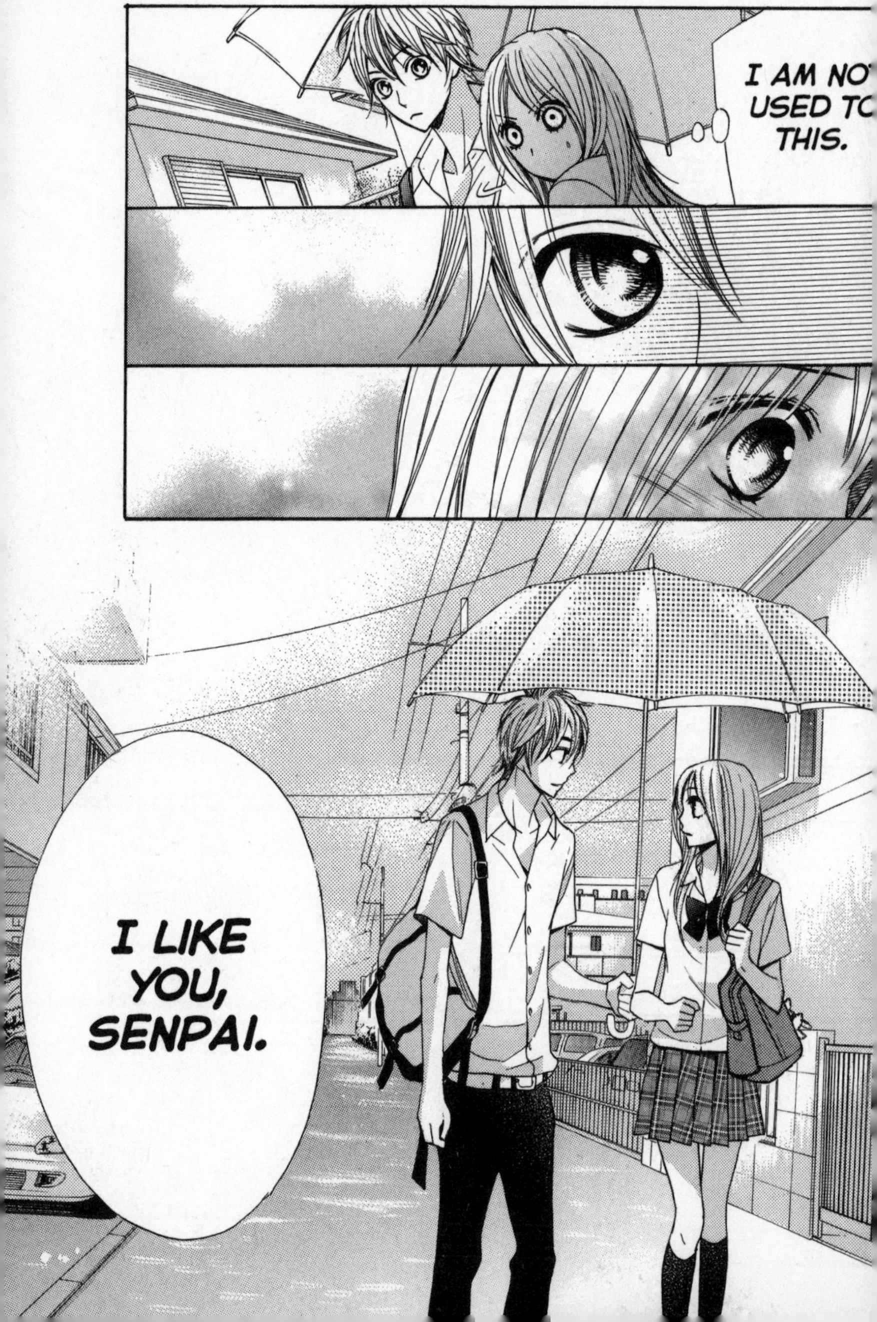
I AM NOT USED TO THIS.
I LIKE YOU, SENPAI.

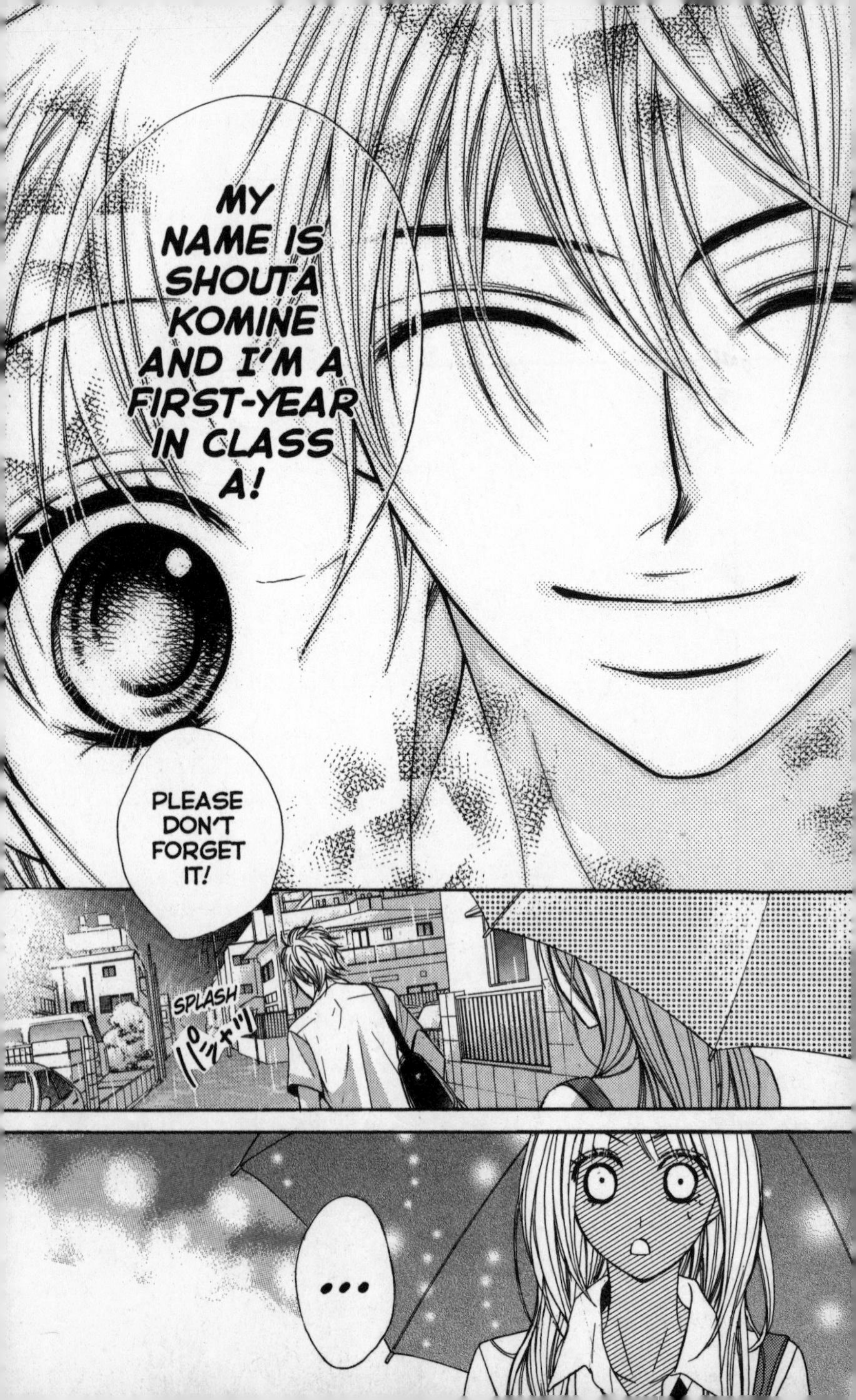
MY NAME IS SHOUTA KOMINE AND I'M A FIRST-YEAR IN CLASS A!
PLEASE DON'T FORGET IT!
SPLASH
パシャッ
...

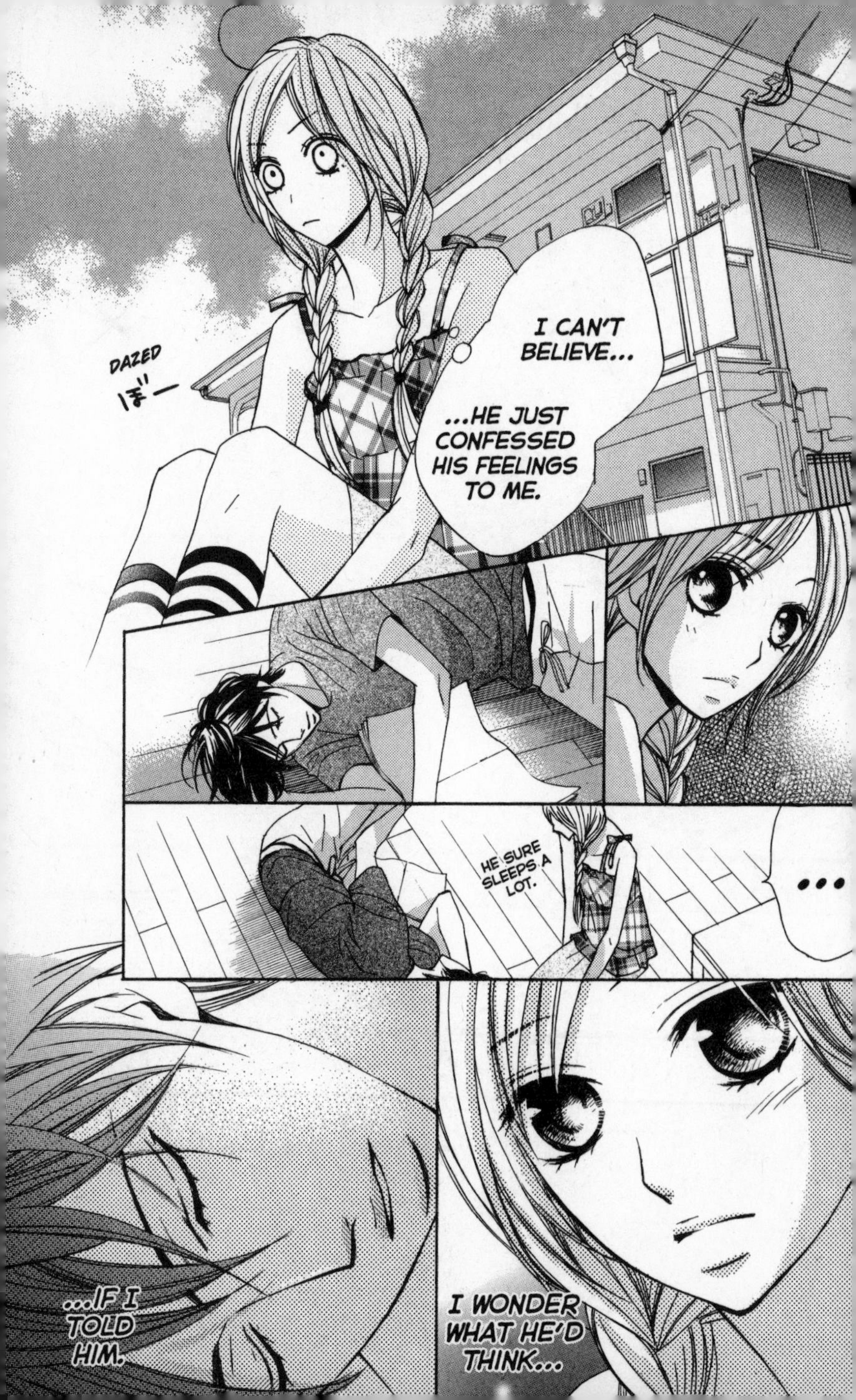
I CAN'T BELIEVE...
...HE JUST CONFESSED HIS FEELINGS TO ME.
DAZED
ぼー
...
HE SURE SLEEPS A LOT.
I WONDER WHAT HE'D THINK...
...IF I TOLD HIM.

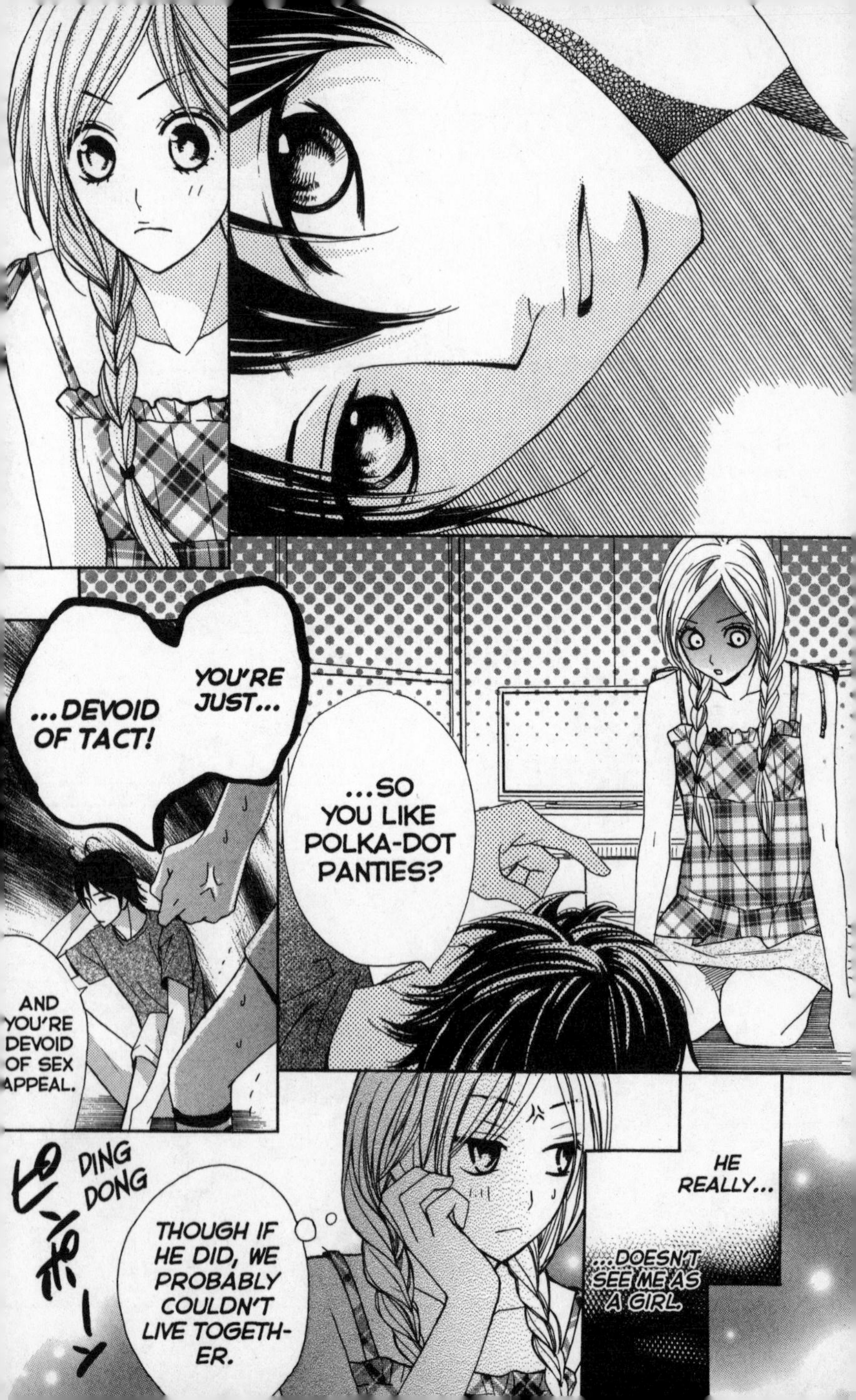
...SO YOU LIKE POLKA-DOT PANTIES?
YOU'RE JUST...
...DEVOID OF TACT!
AND YOU'RE DEVOID OF SEX APPEAL.
HE REALLY...
...DOESN'T SEE ME AS A GIRL.
THOUGH IF HE DID, WE PROBABLY COULDN'T LIVE TOGETH-ER.
ピンポーン
DING DONG

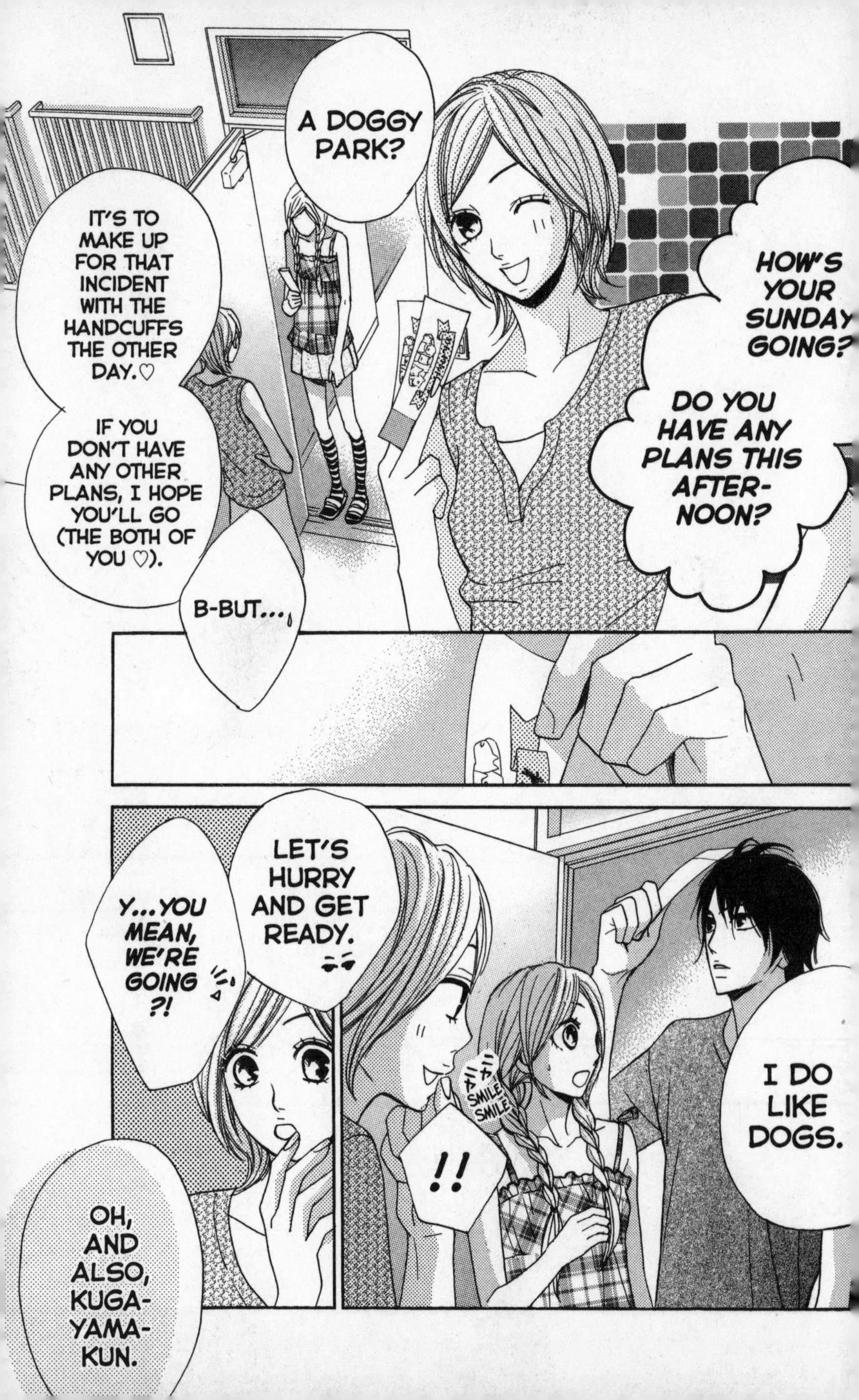
HOW'S YOUR SUNDAY GOING?
DO YOU HAVE ANY PLANS THIS AFTER-NOON?
A DOGGY PARK?
IT'S TO MAKE UP FOR THAT INCIDENT WITH THE HANDCUFFS THE OTHER DAY.♡
IF YOU DON'T HAVE ANY OTHER PLANS, I HOPE YOU'LL GO (THE BOTH OF YOU ♡).
B-BUT...
I DO LIKE DOGS.
!!
SMILE SMILE
LET'S HURRY AND GET READY.
Y...YOU MEAN, WE'RE GOING?!
OH, AND ALSO, KUGA-YAMA-KUN.

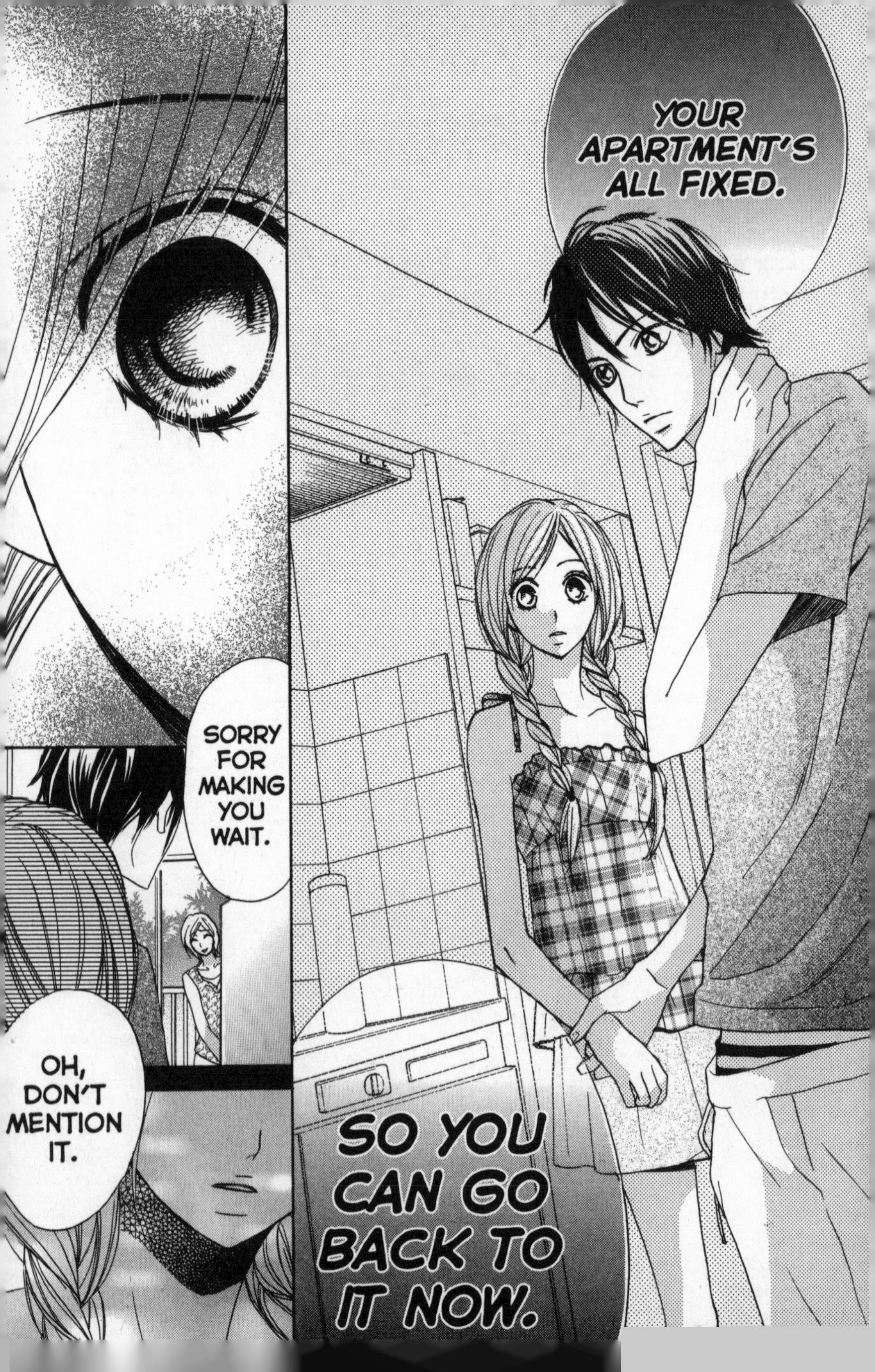
YOUR APARTMENT'S ALL FIXED.
SO YOU CAN GO BACK TO IT NOW.
SORRY FOR MAKING YOU WAIT.
OH, DON'T MENTION IT.

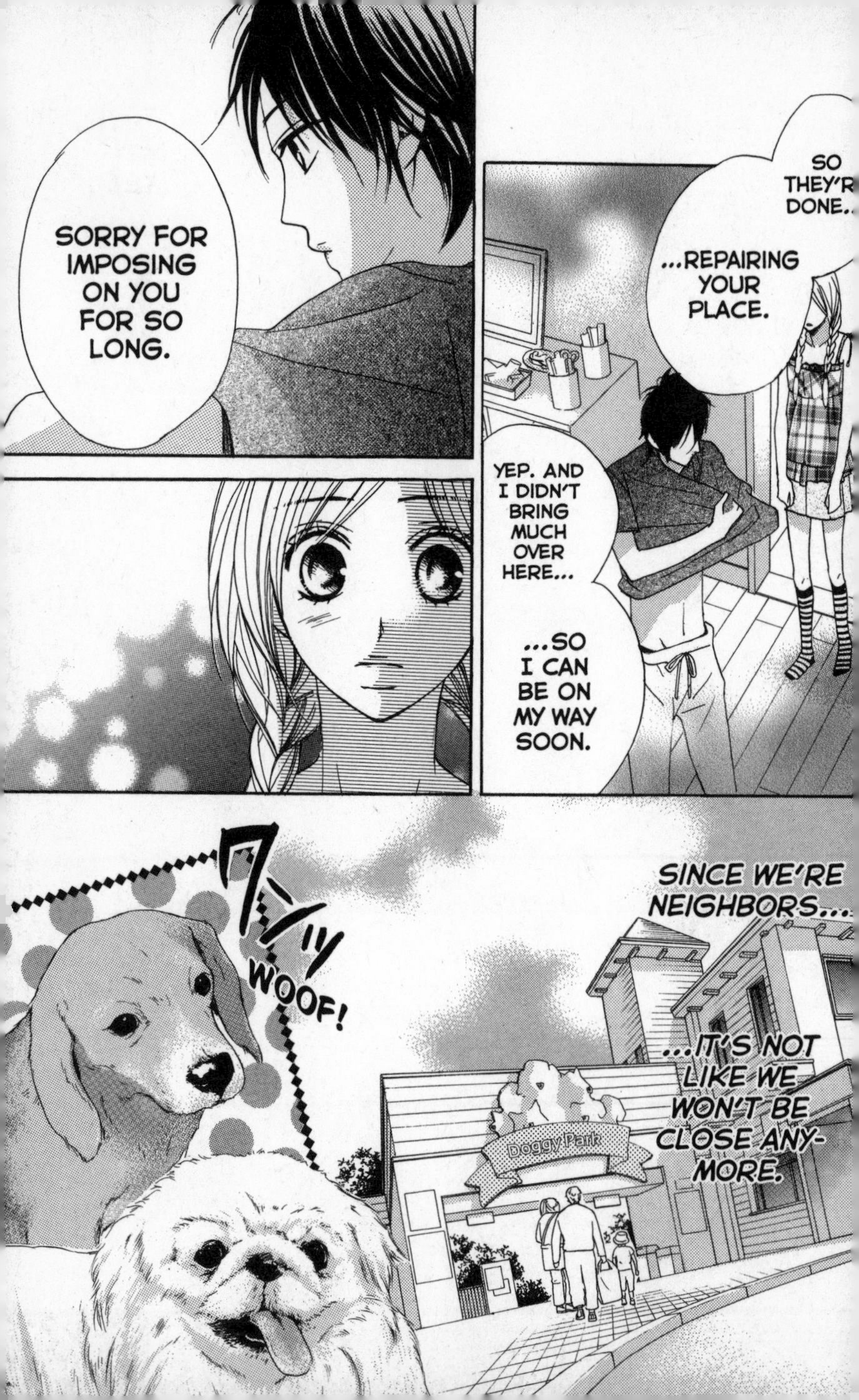
SO THEY'R DONE..
...REPAIRING YOUR PLACE.
YEP. AND I DIDN'T BRING MUCH OVER HERE...
...SO I CAN BE ON MY WAY SOON.
SORRY FOR IMPOSING ON YOU FOR SO LONG.
SINCE WE'RE NEIGHBORS....
...IT'S NOT LIKE WE WON'T BE CLOSE ANY-MORE.
ワンッ
WOOF!
Doggy Park

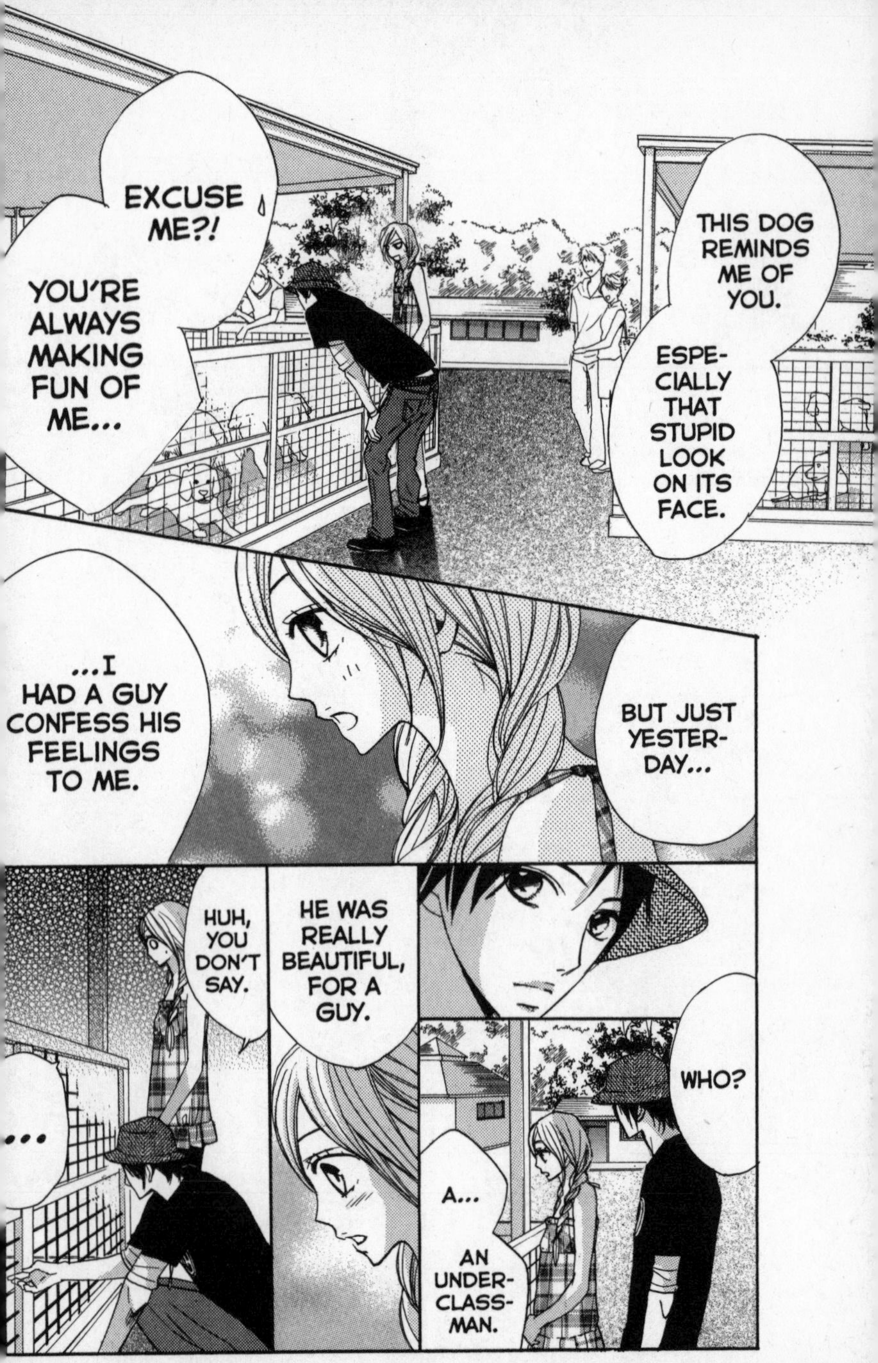
THIS DOG REMINDS ME OF YOU.
ESPECIALLY THAT STUPID LOOK ON ITS FACE.
EXCUSE ME?!
YOU'RE ALWAYS MAKING FUN OF ME...
BUT JUST YESTERDAY...
...I HAD A GUY CONFESS HIS FEELINGS TO ME.
WHO?
A...
AN UNDERCLASSMAN.
HE WAS REALLY BEAUTIFUL, FOR A GUY.
HUH, YOU DON'T SAY.
...

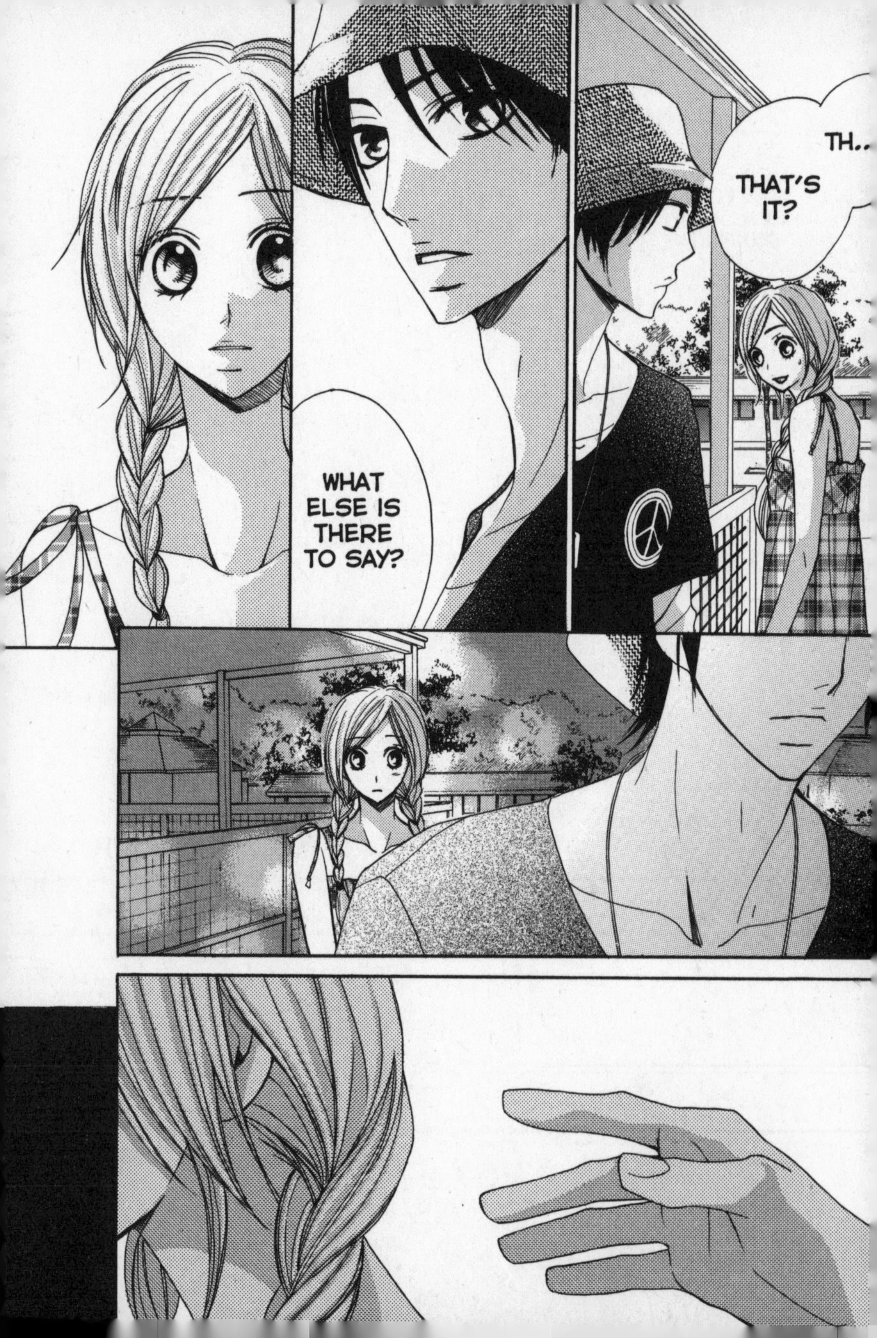
TH...
THAT'S IT?
WHAT ELSE IS THERE TO SAY?

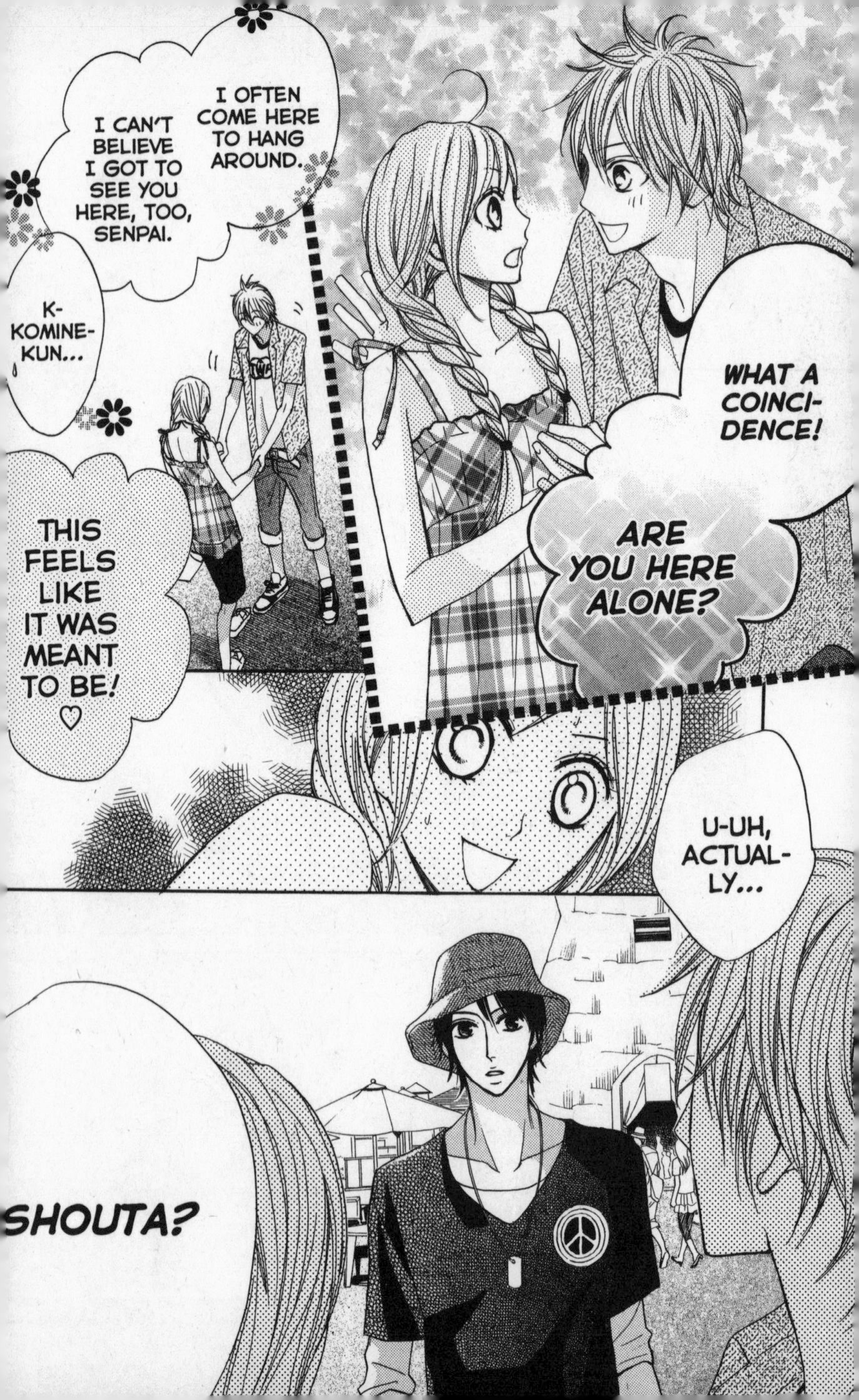
WHAT A COINCI-DENCE!
ARE YOU HERE ALONE?
I OFTEN COME HERE TO HANG AROUND.
I CAN'T BELIEVE I GOT TO SEE YOU HERE, TOO, SENPAI.
K-KOMINE-KUN...
THIS FEELS LIKE IT WAS MEANT TO BE! ♡
U-UH, ACTUAL-LY...
SHOUTA?

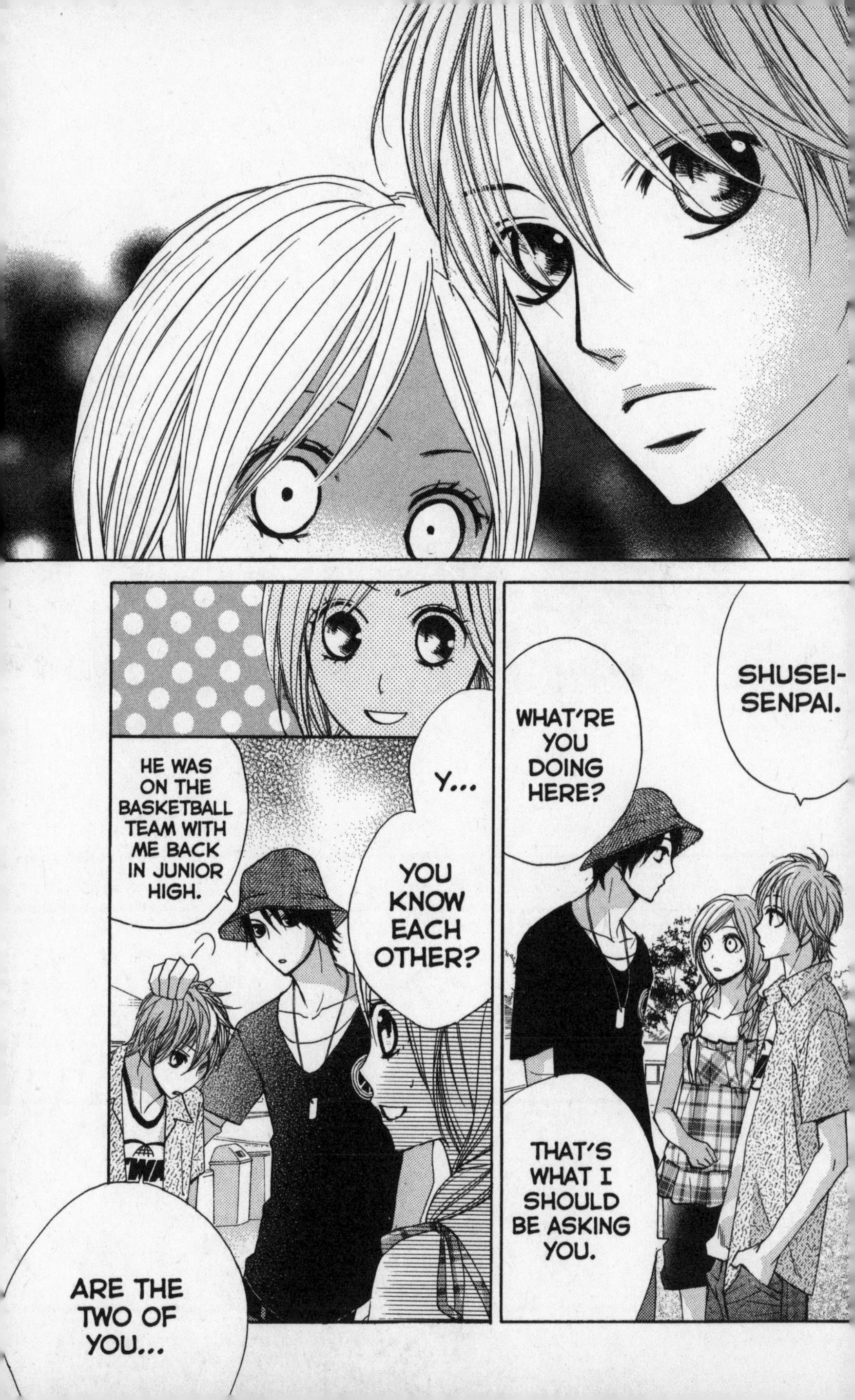
SHUSEI-SENPAI.
WHAT'RE YOU DOING HERE?
THAT'S WHAT I SHOULD BE ASKING YOU.
Y...
YOU KNOW EACH OTHER?
HE WAS ON THE BASKETBALL TEAM WITH ME BACK IN JUNIOR HIGH.
ARE THE TWO OF YOU...

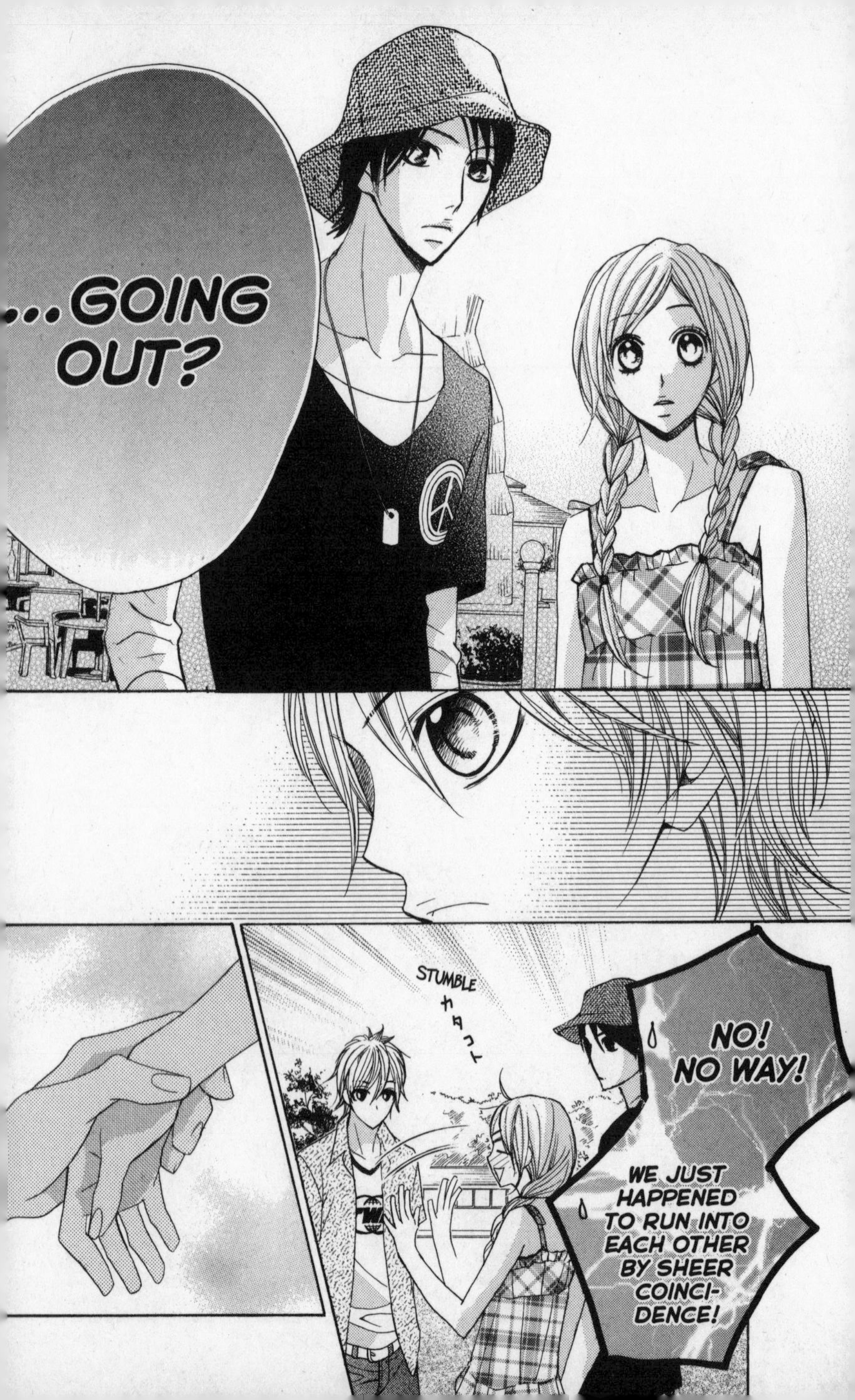
...GOING OUT?
STUMBLE
カタコト
NO! NO WAY!
WE JUST HAPPENED TO RUN INTO EACH OTHER BY SHEER COINCI-DENCE!

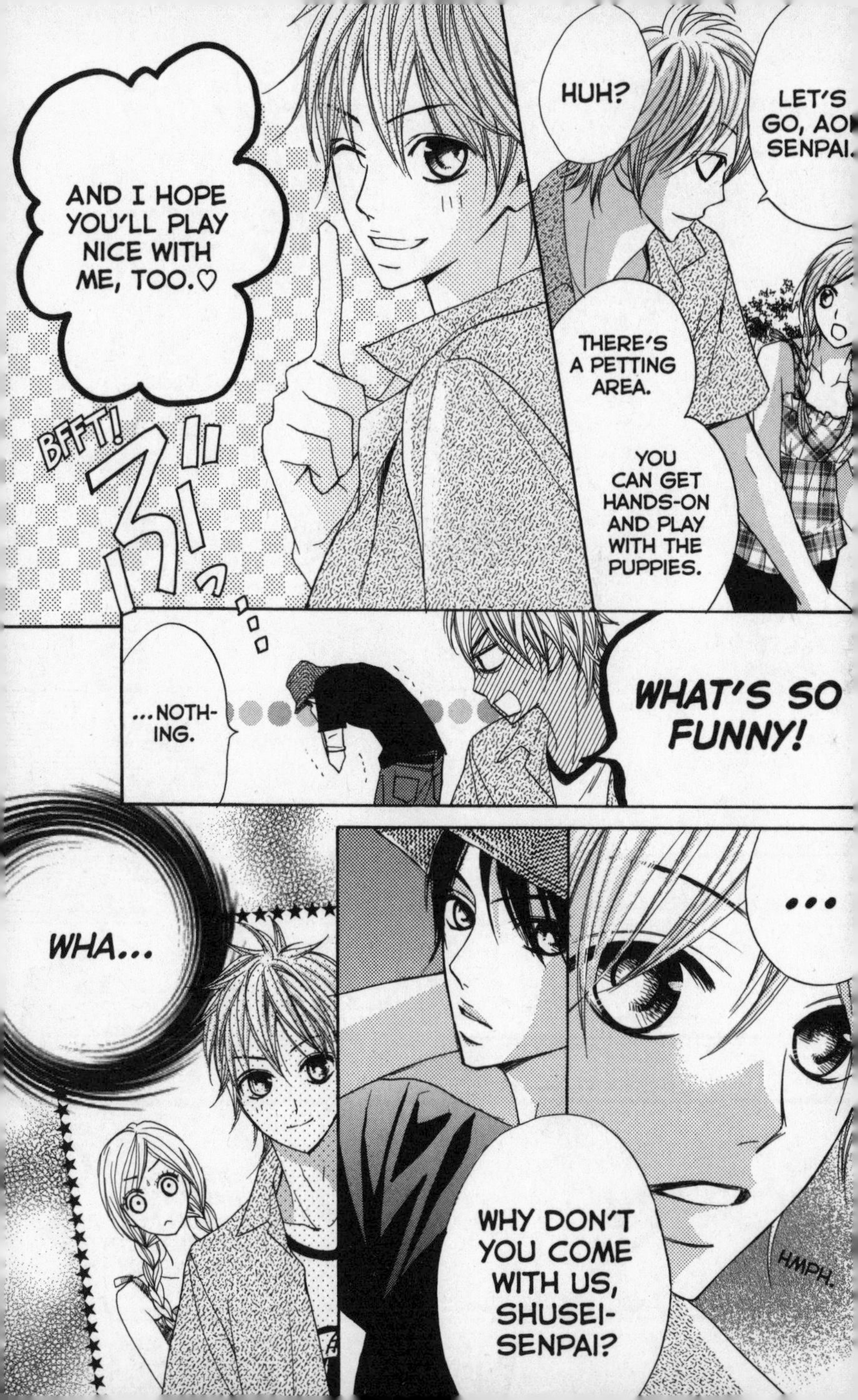
LET'S GO, AOI SENPAI.
HUH?
THERE'S A PETTING AREA.
YOU CAN GET HANDS-ON AND PLAY WITH THE PUPPIES.
AND I HOPE YOU'LL PLAY NICE WITH ME, TOO.♡
BFFT!
WHAT'S SO FUNNY!
...NOTH-ING.
...
HMPH.
WHY DON'T YOU COME WITH US, SHUSEI-SENPAI?
WHA...

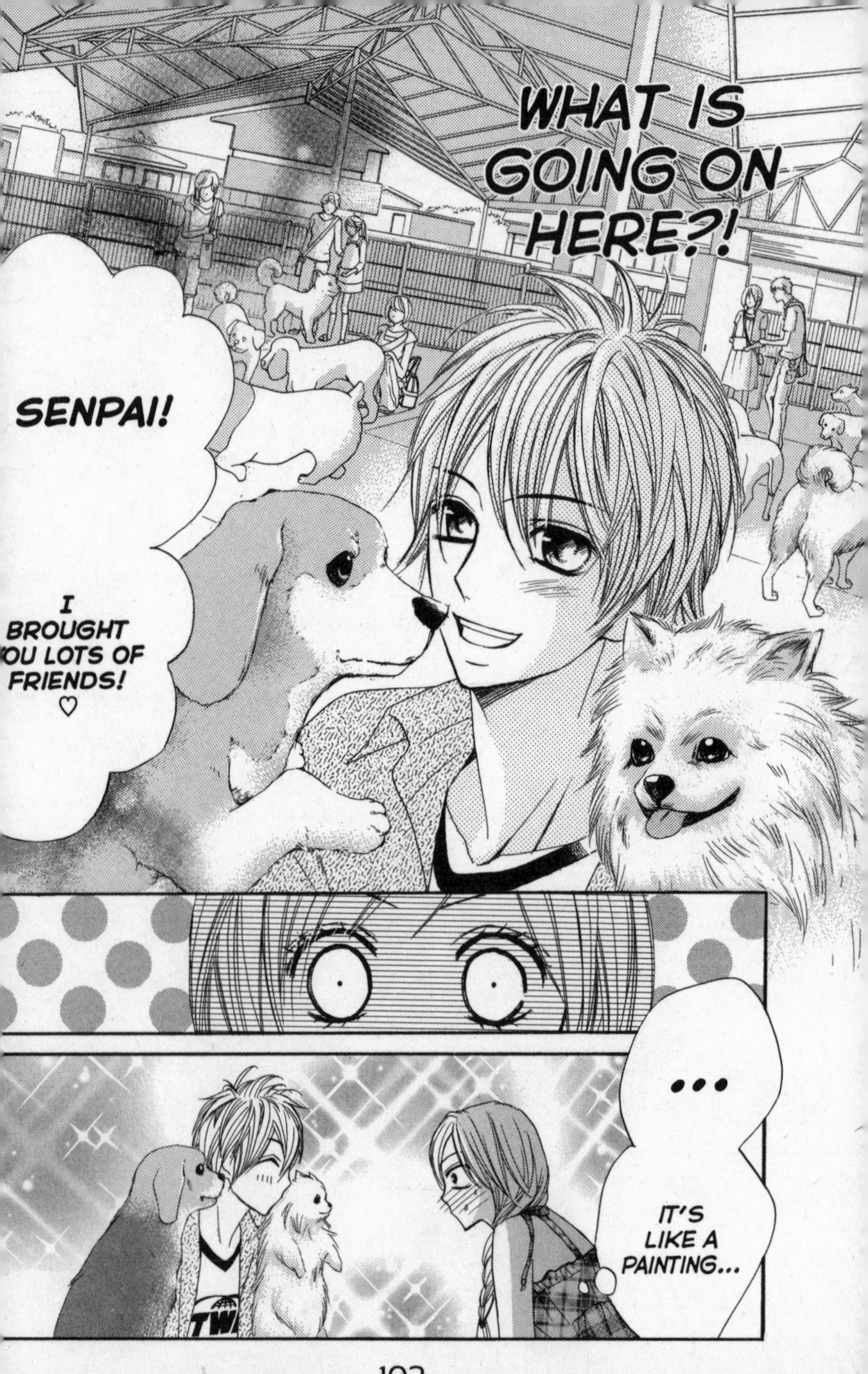

WHAT IS GOING ON HERE?!
SENPAI!
I BROUGHT YOU LOTS OF FRIENDS! ♡
...
IT'S LIKE A PAINTING...

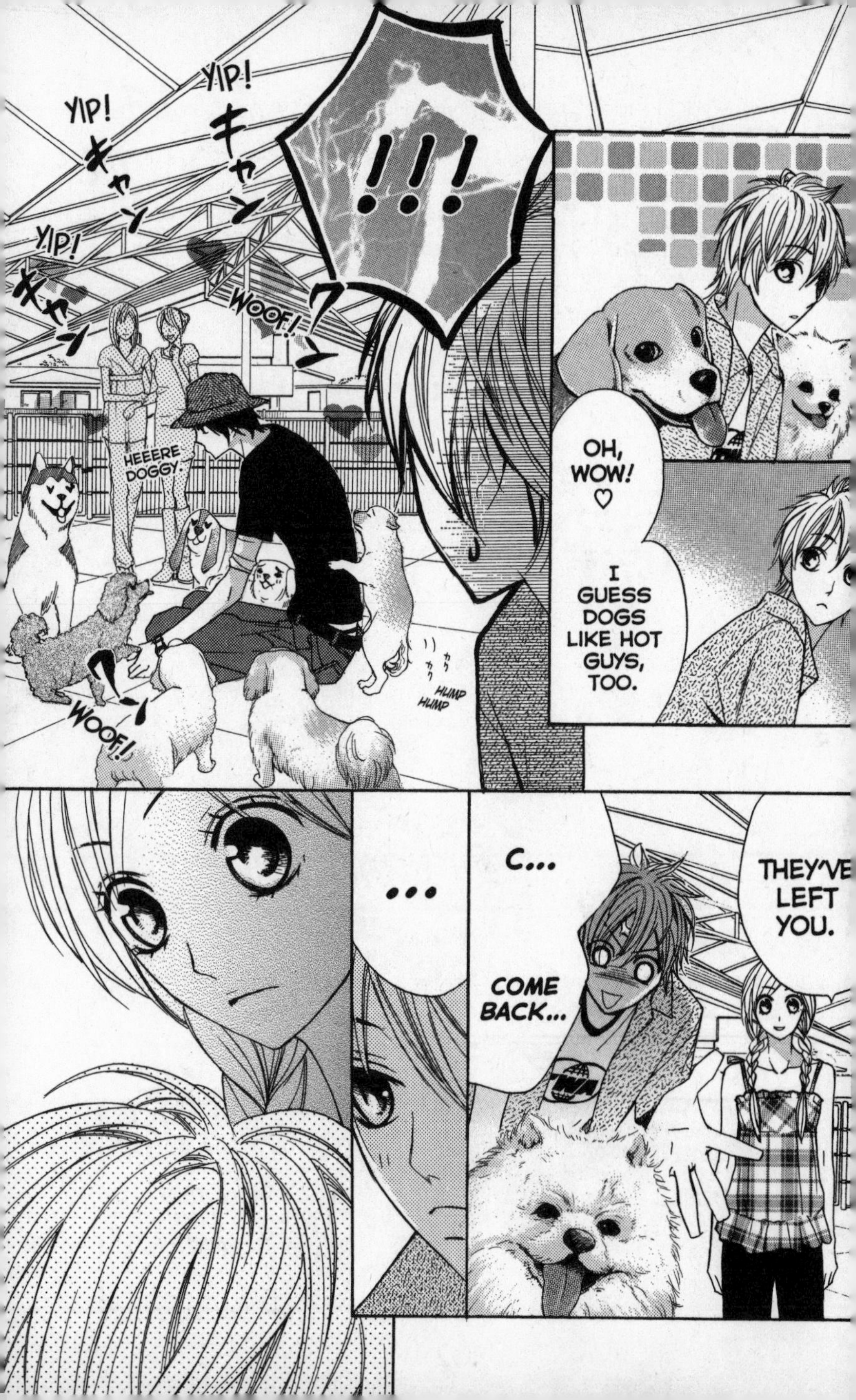
OH, WOW! ♡
I GUESS DOGS LIKE HOT GUYS, TOO.
!!!
YIP!
キャン
YIP!
キャン
YIP!
キャン
WOOF!
HEEERE DOGGY.
HUMP HUMP
WOOF!
THEY'VE LEFT YOU.
C...
COME BACK...
...

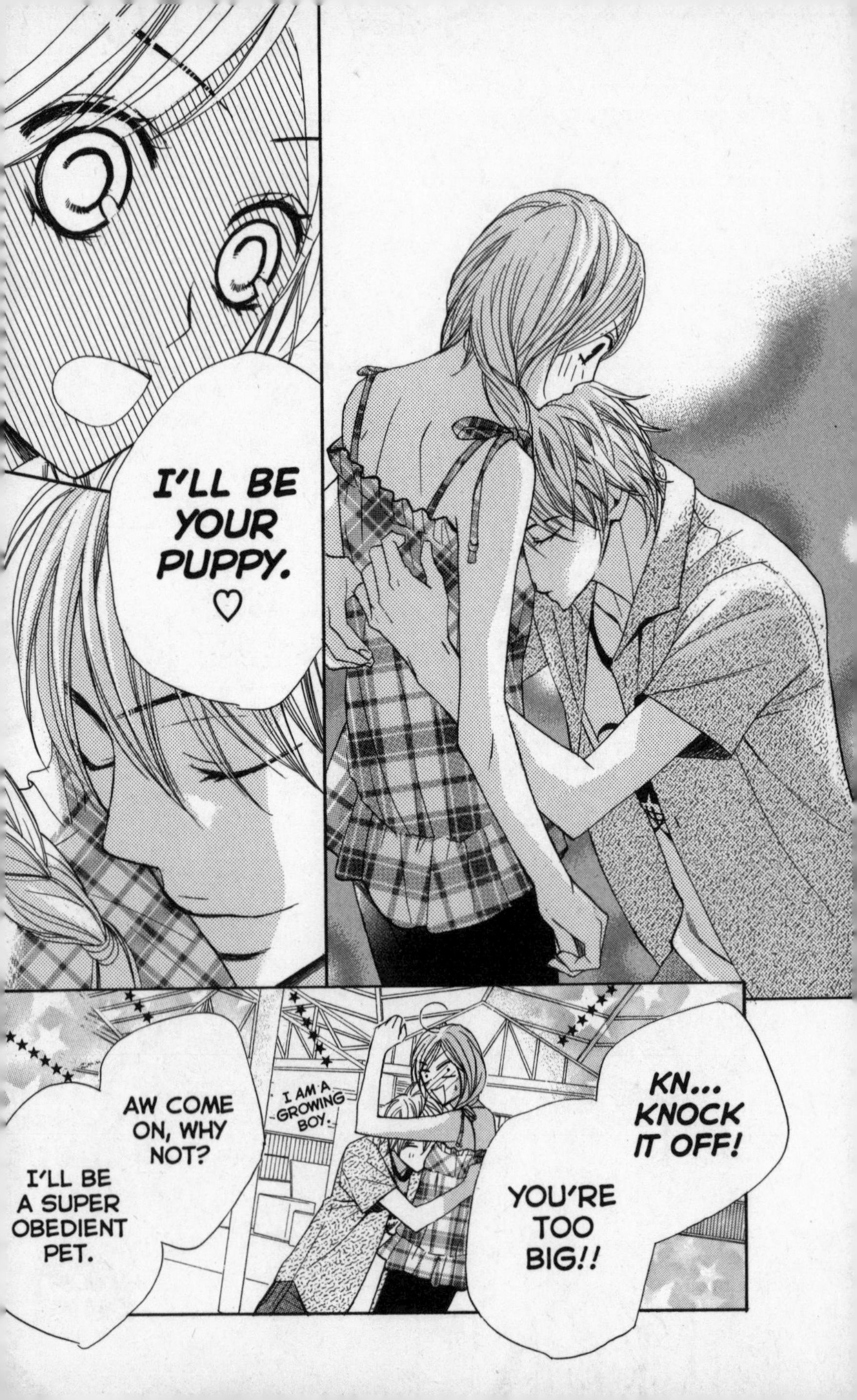
I'LL BE YOUR PUPPY. ♡
KN... KNOCK IT OFF!
YOU'RE TOO BIG!!
I AM A GROWING BOY.
AW COME ON, WHY NOT?
I'LL BE A SUPER OBEDIENT PET.

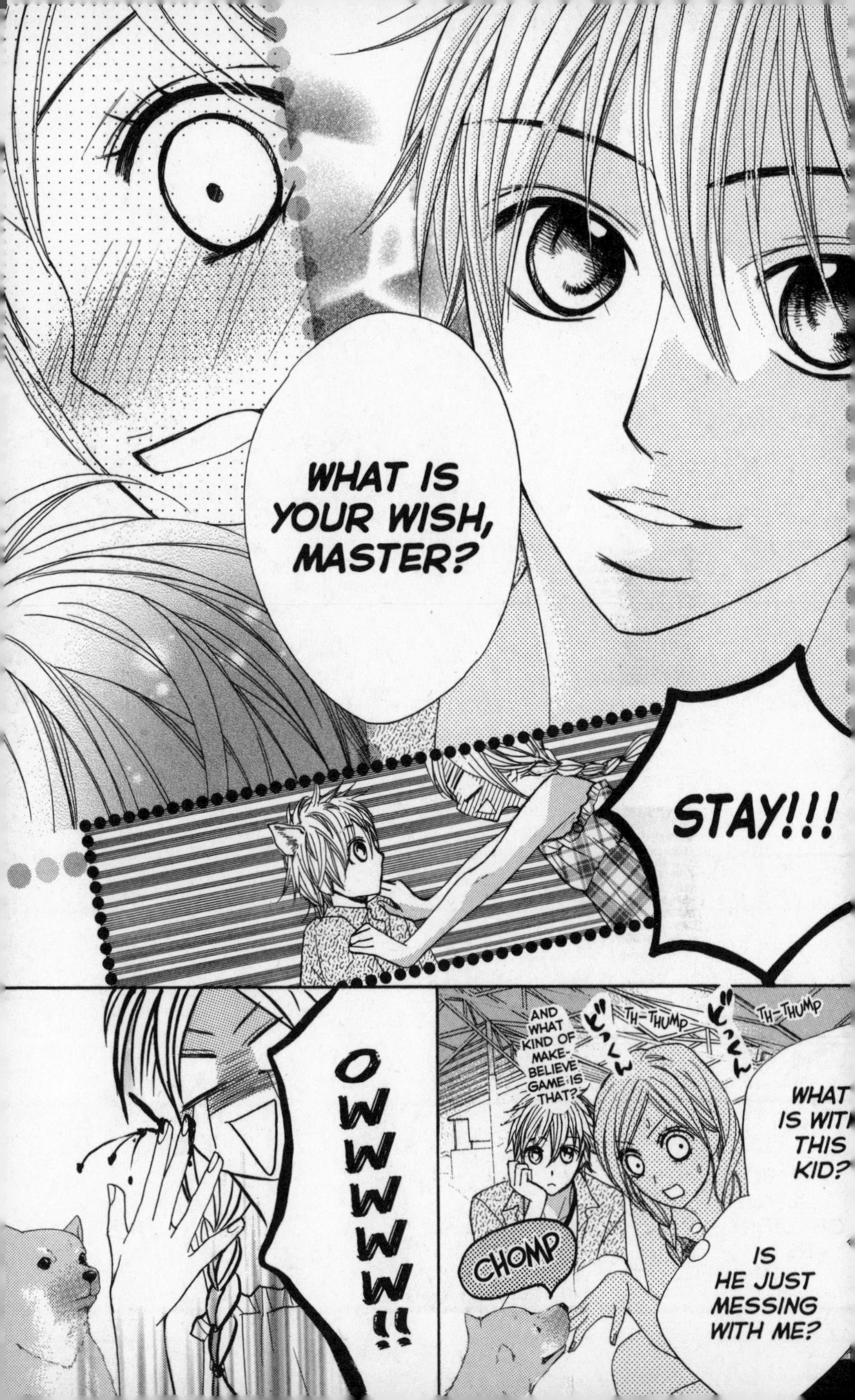
WHAT IS YOUR WISH, MASTER?
STAY!!!
WHAT IS WIT THIS KID?
TH-THUMP
TH-THUMP
AND WHAT KIND OF MAKE-BELIEVE GAME IS THAT?
IS HE JUST MESSING WITH ME?
CHOMP
OWWWWWW!!

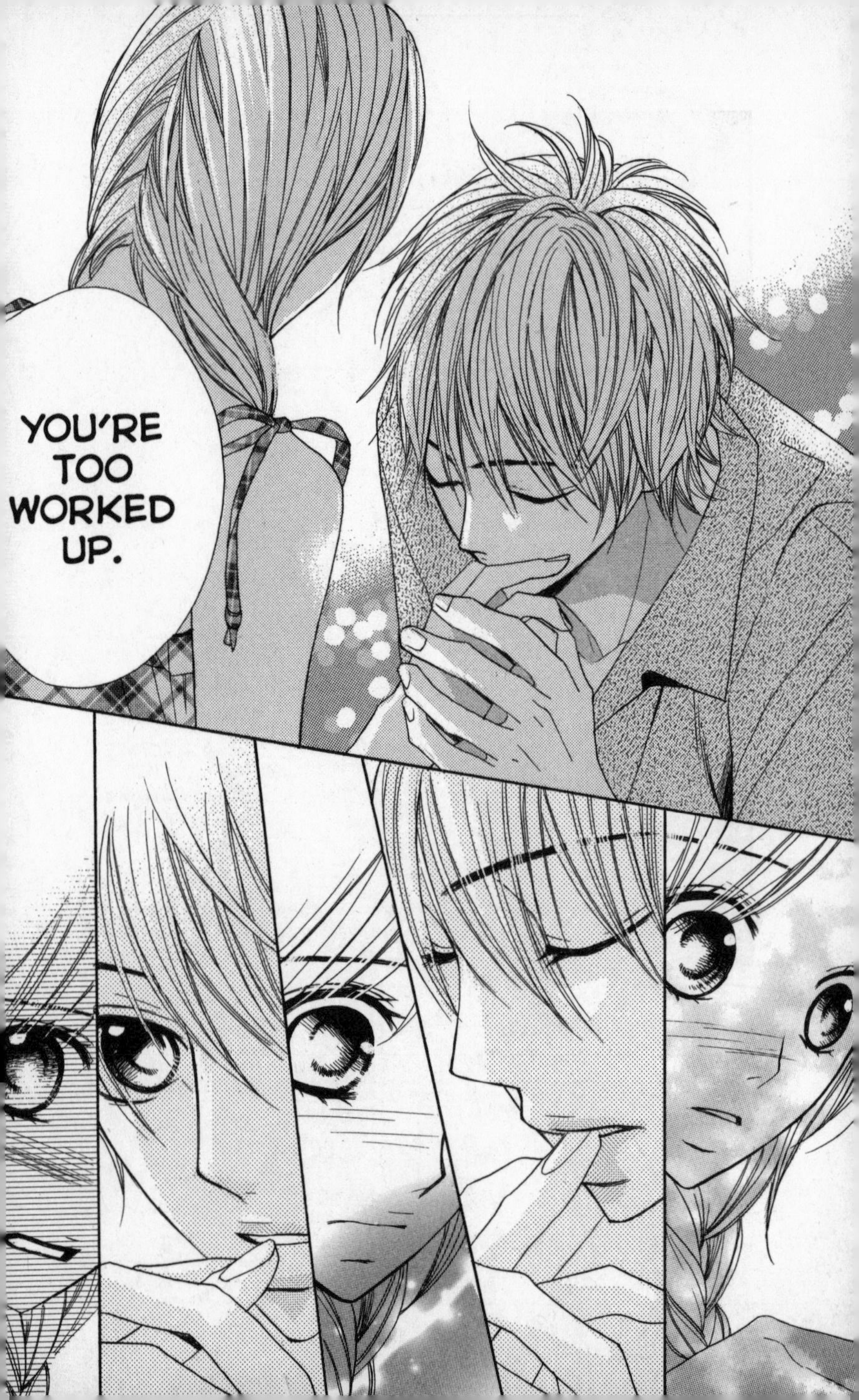
YOU'RE TOO WORKED UP.

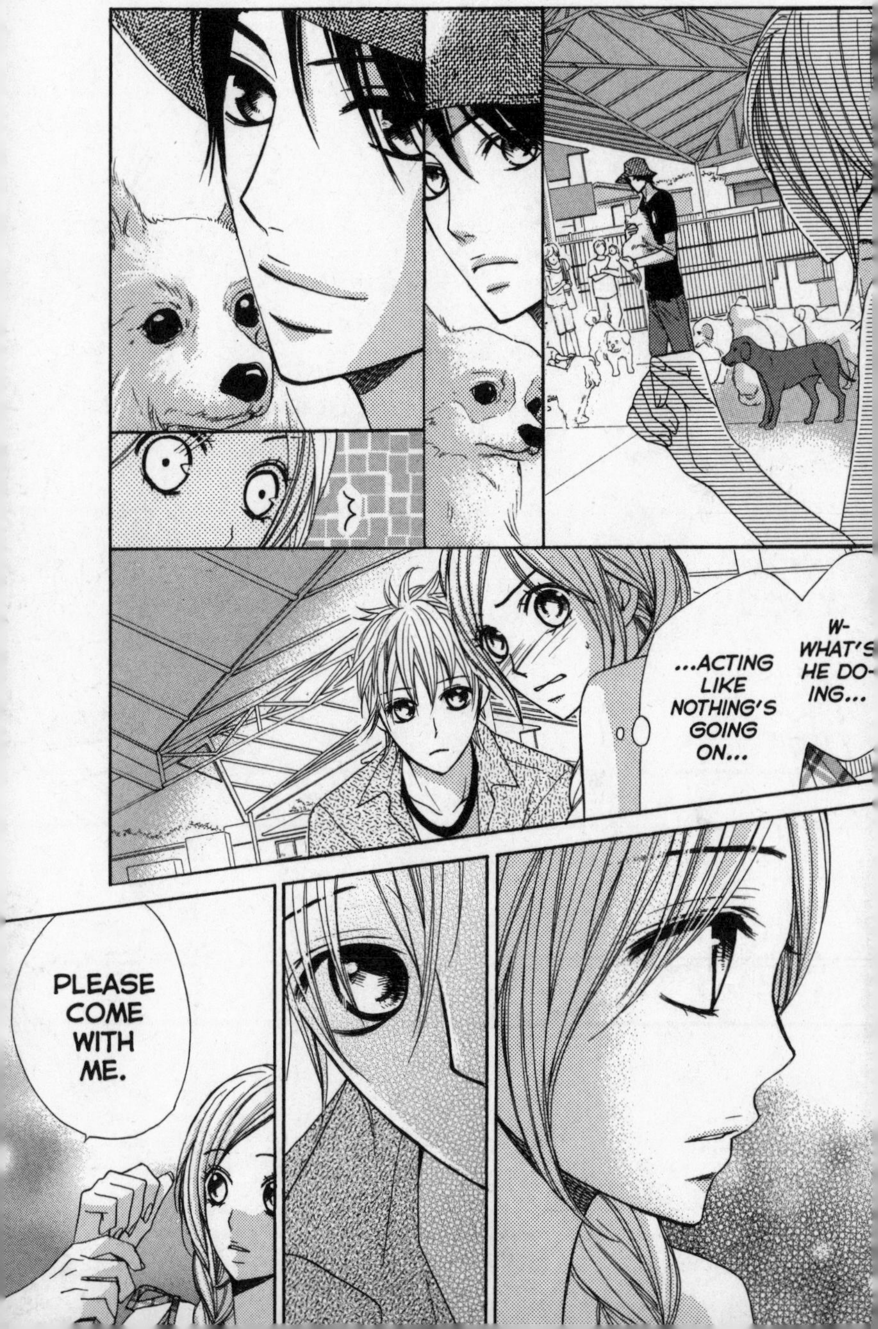
W-WHAT'S HE DO-ING...
...ACTING LIKE NOTHING'S GOING ON...
PLEASE COME WITH ME.

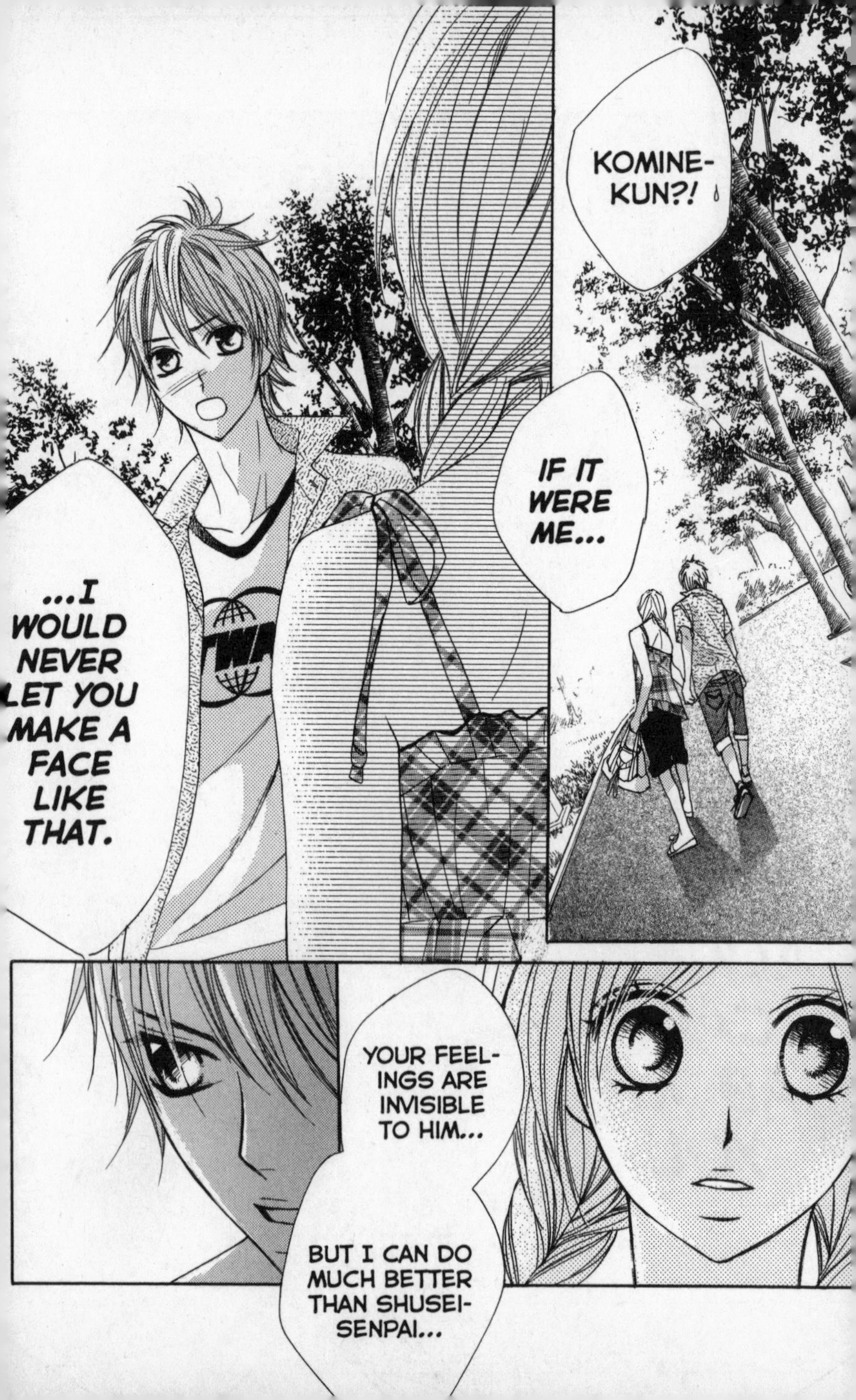
KOMINE-KUN?!
IF IT WERE ME...
...I WOULD NEVER LET YOU MAKE A FACE LIKE THAT.
YOUR FEEL-INGS ARE INVISIBLE TO HIM...
BUT I CAN DO MUCH BETTER THAN SHUSEI-SENPAI...

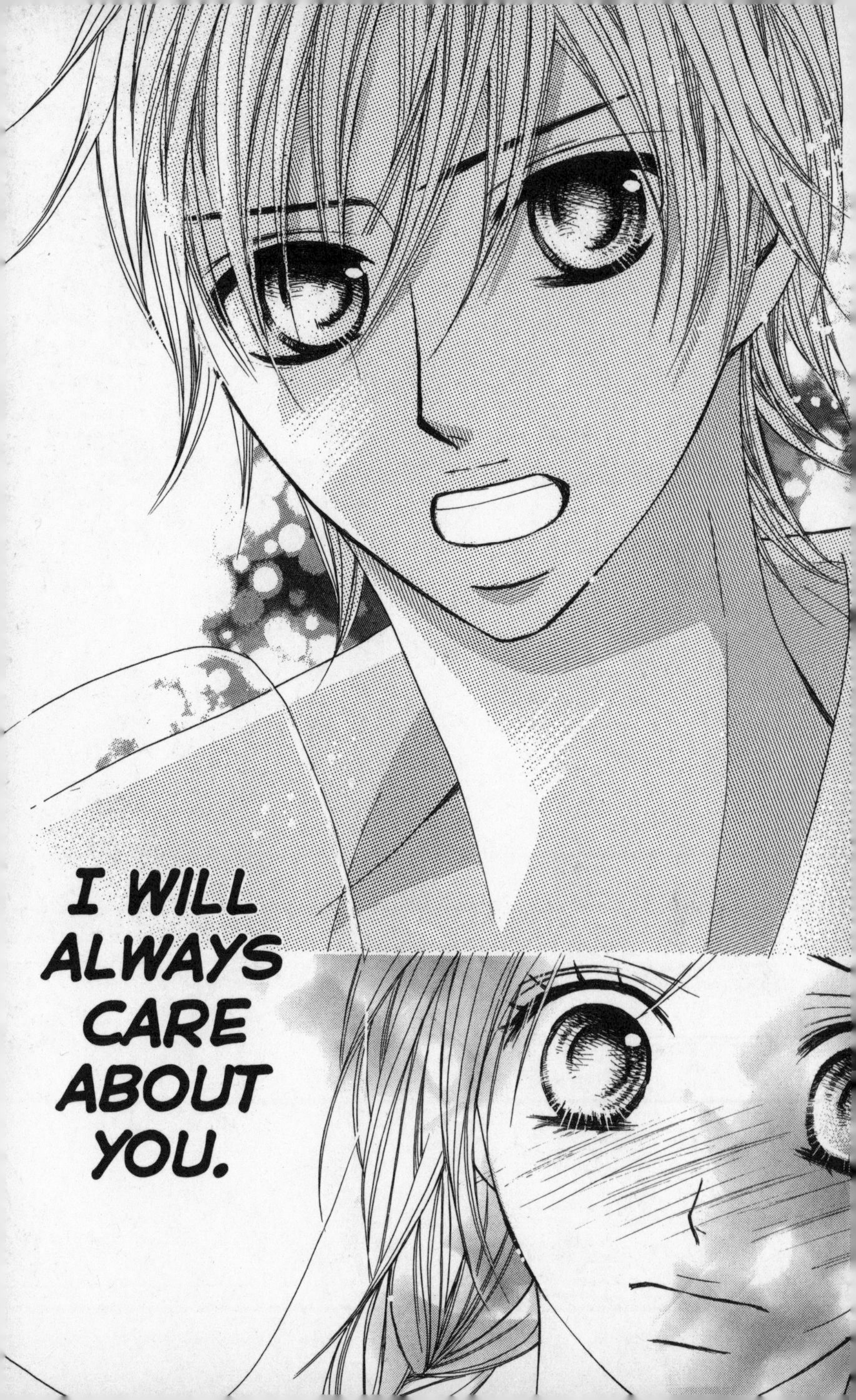
I WILL ALWAYS CARE ABOUT YOU.

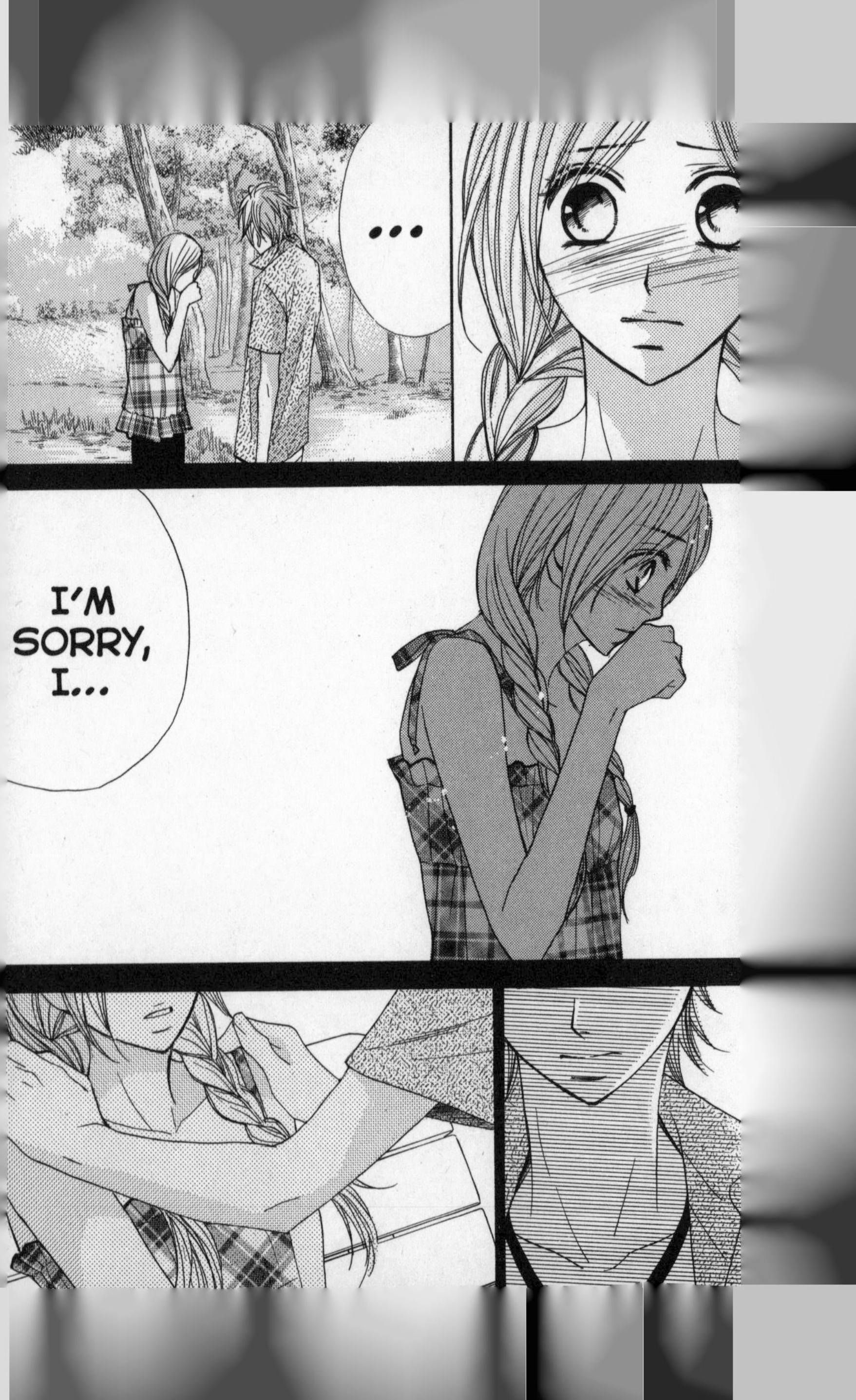
...
I'M SORRY, I...

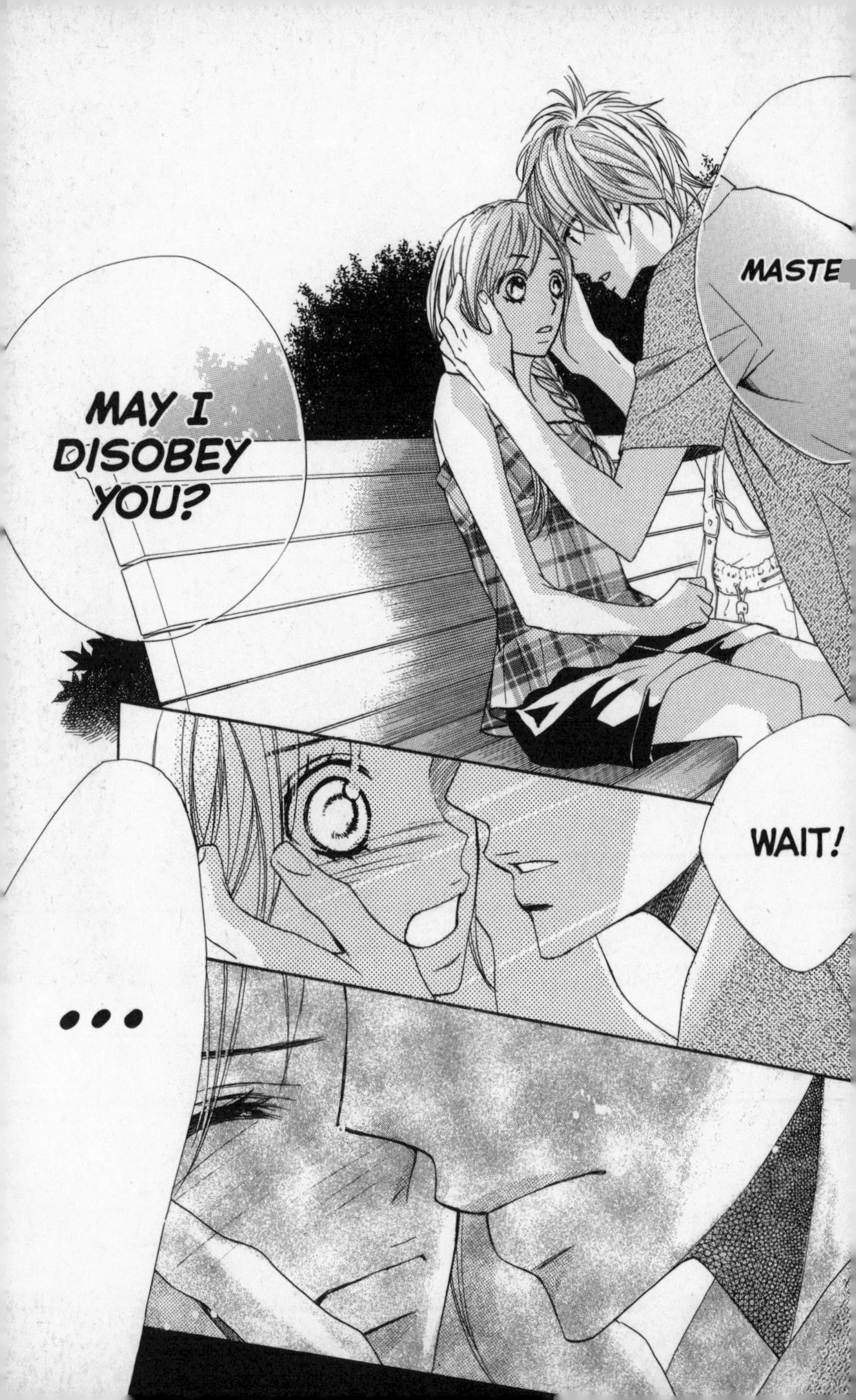
MASTE
MAY I DISOBEY YOU?
WAIT!
...

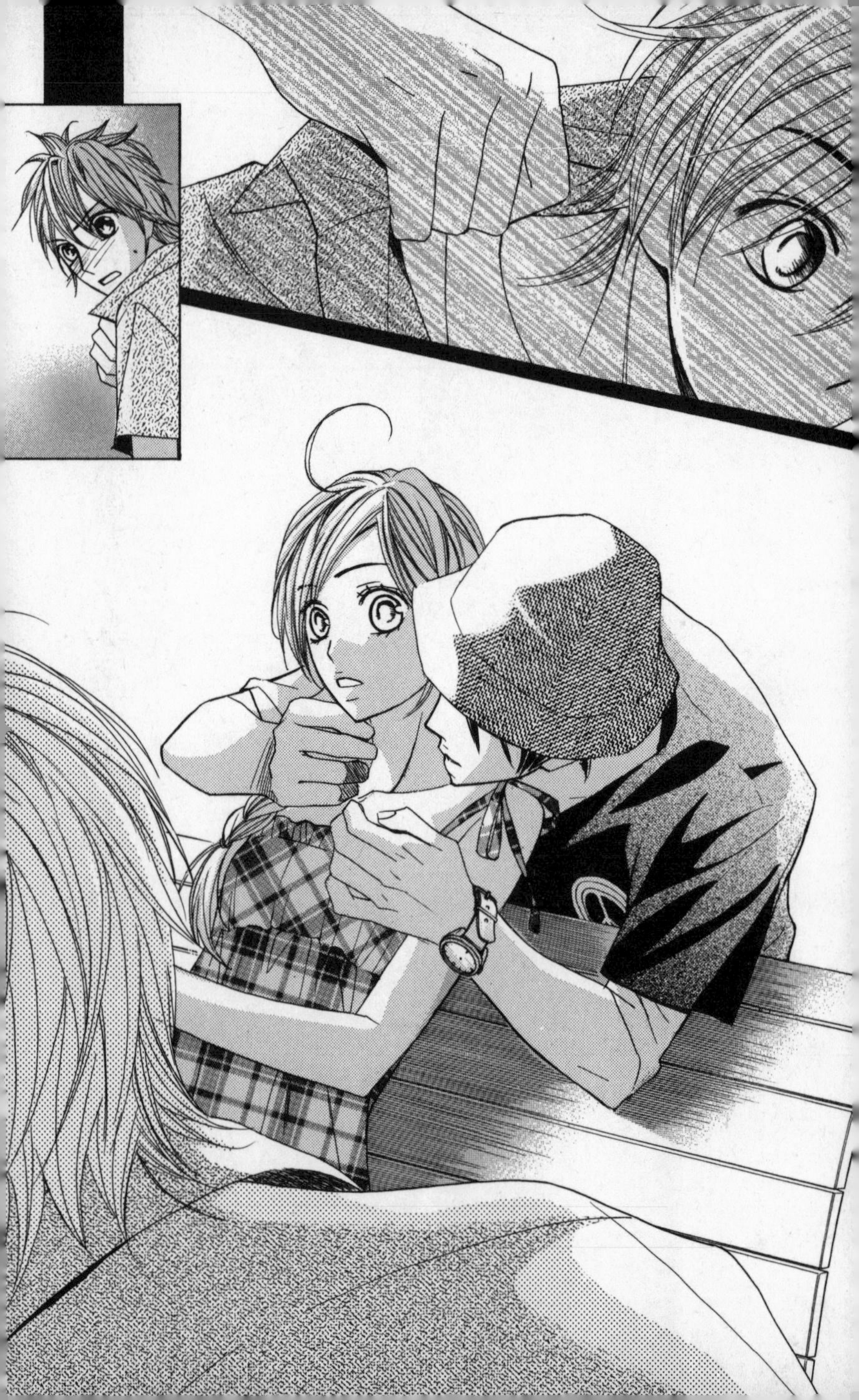

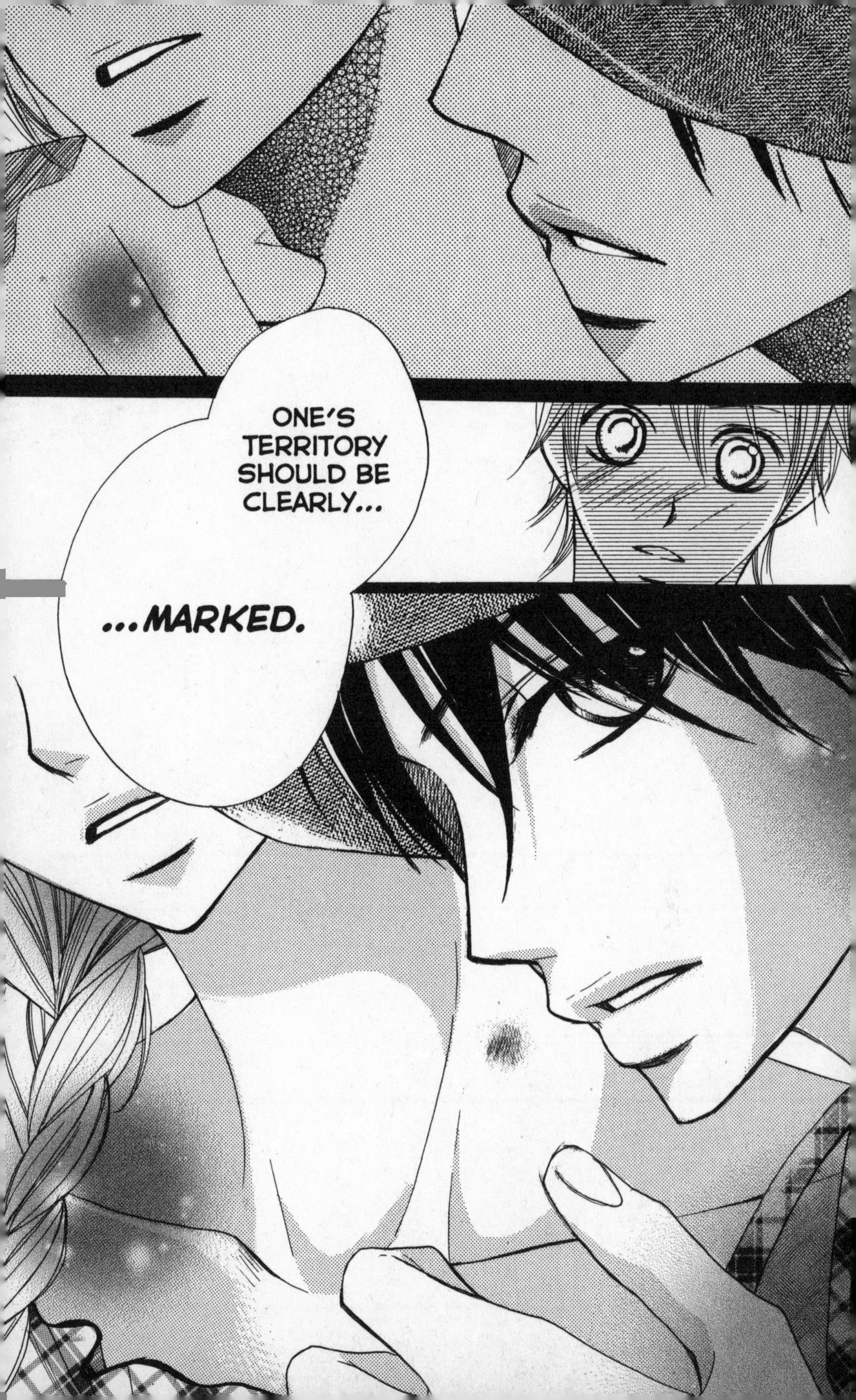
ONE'S TERRITORY SHOULD BE CLEARLY...
...MARKED.

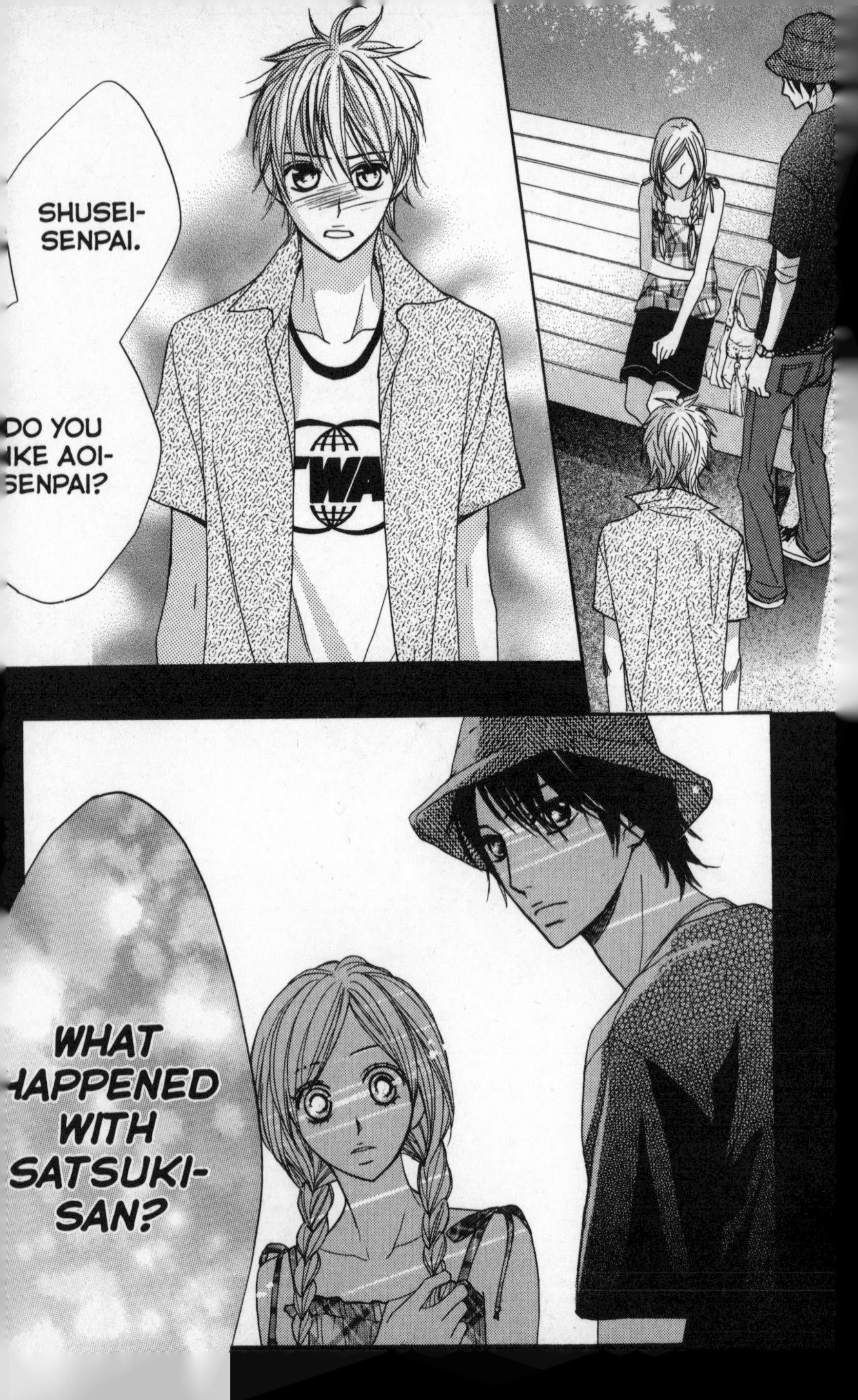
SHUSEI-SENPAI.
DO YOU IKE AOI-SENPAI?
WHAT HAPPENED WITH SATSUKI-SAN?

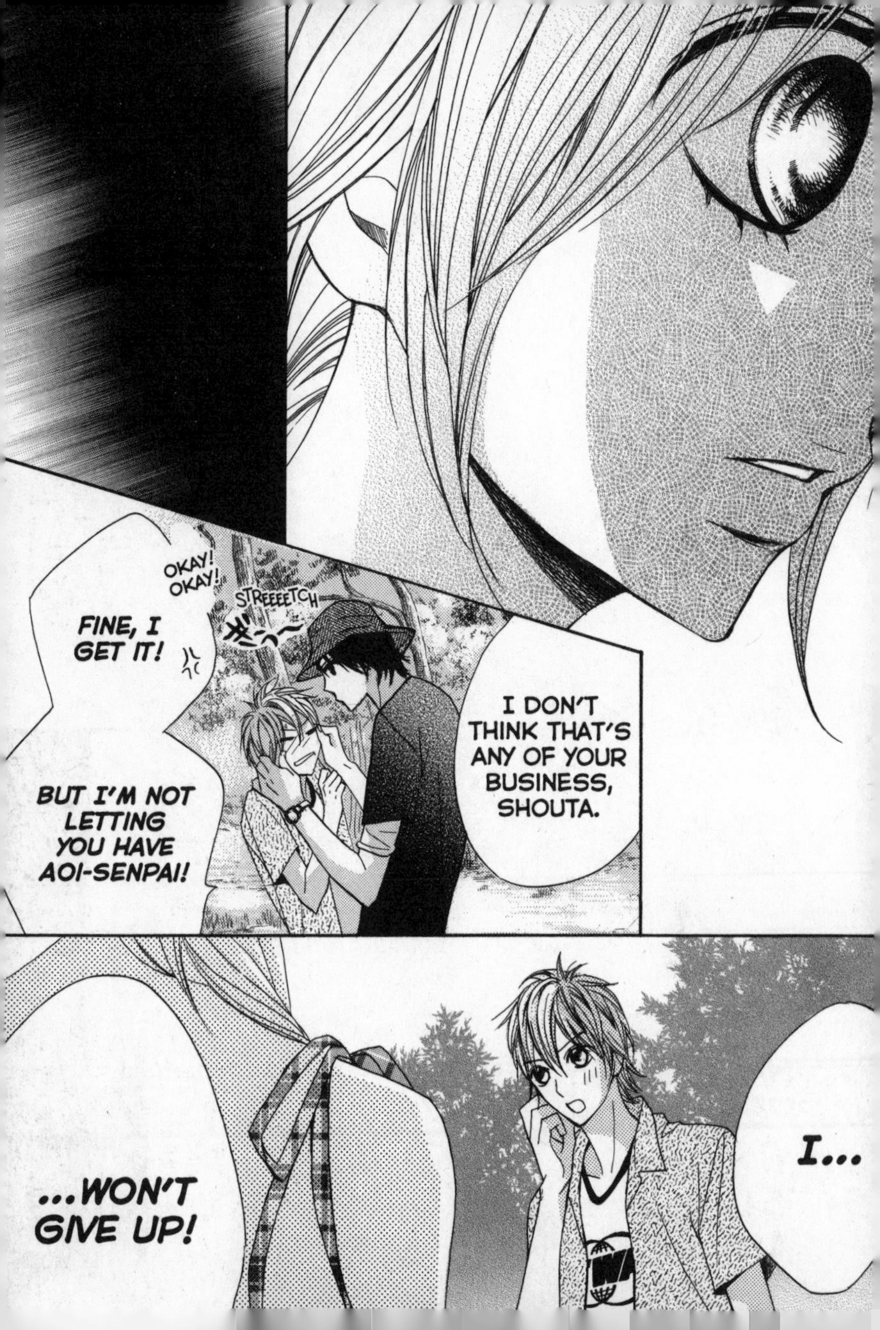
I DON'T THINK THAT'S ANY OF YOUR BUSINESS, SHOUTA.
OKAY! OKAY!
STREEEEETCH
FINE, I GET IT!
BUT I'M NOT LETTING YOU HAVE AOI-SENPAI!
I...
...WON'T GIVE UP!

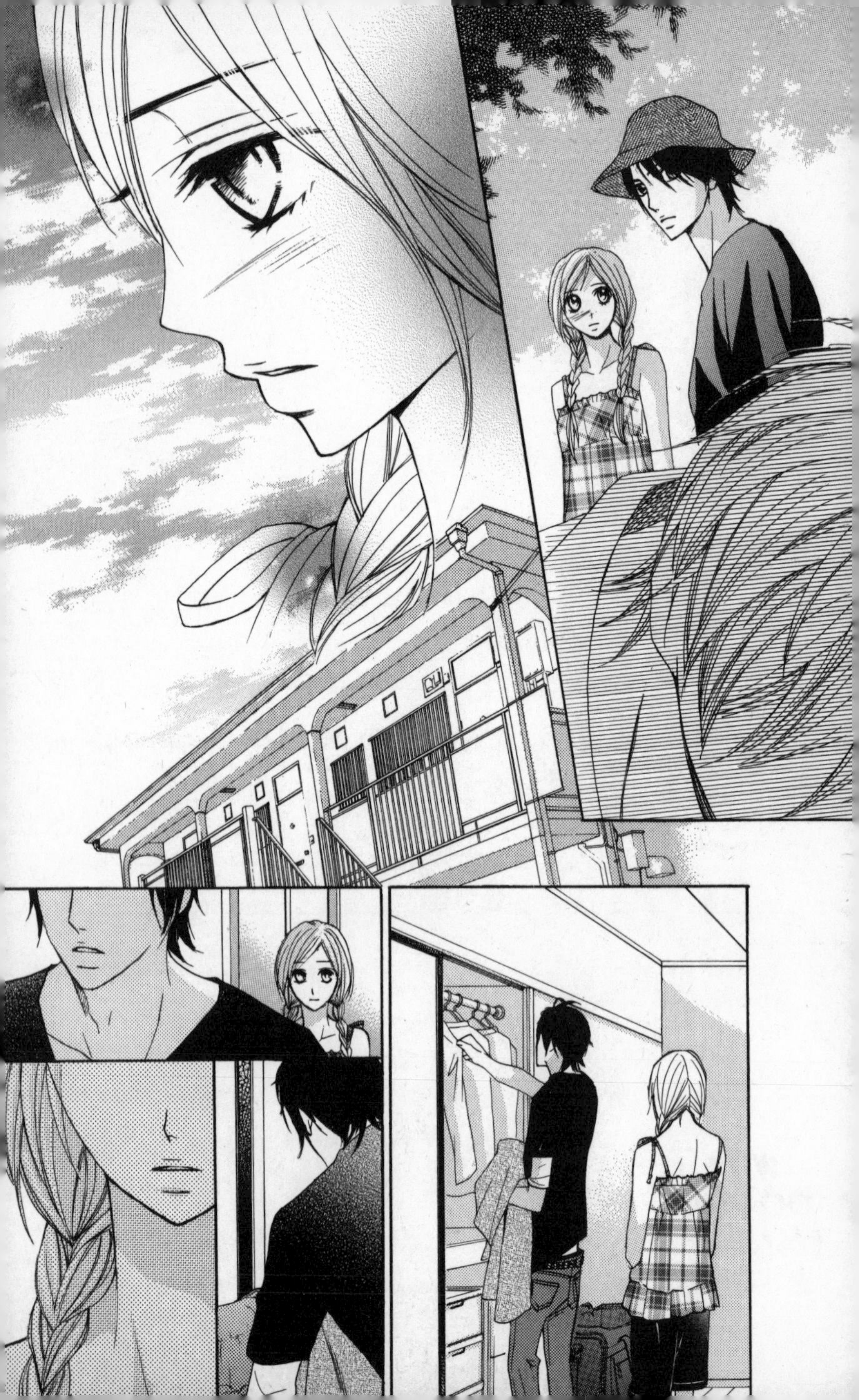

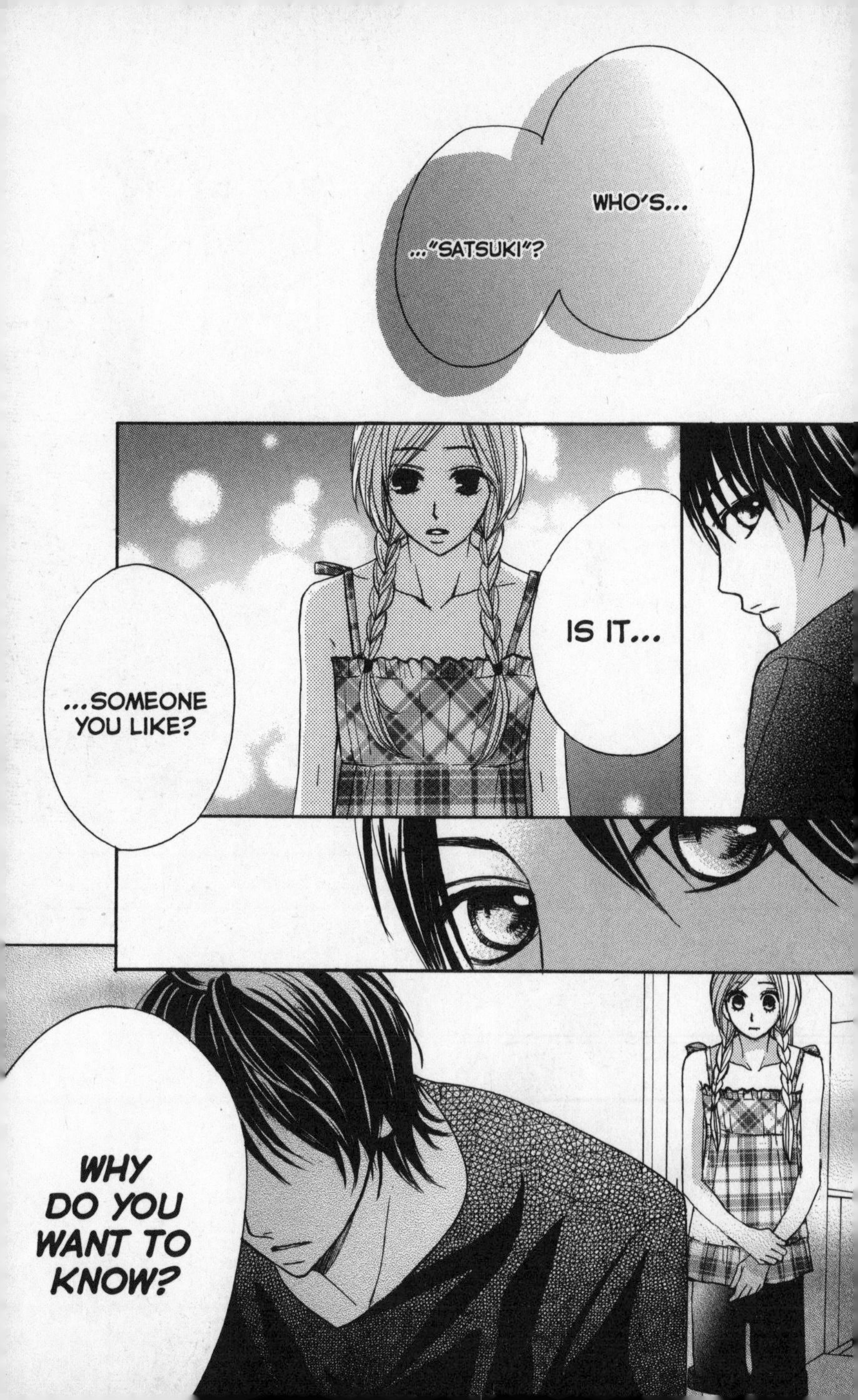
WHO'S...
..."SATSUKI"?
IS IT...
...SOMEONE YOU LIKE?
WHY DO YOU WANT TO KNOW?

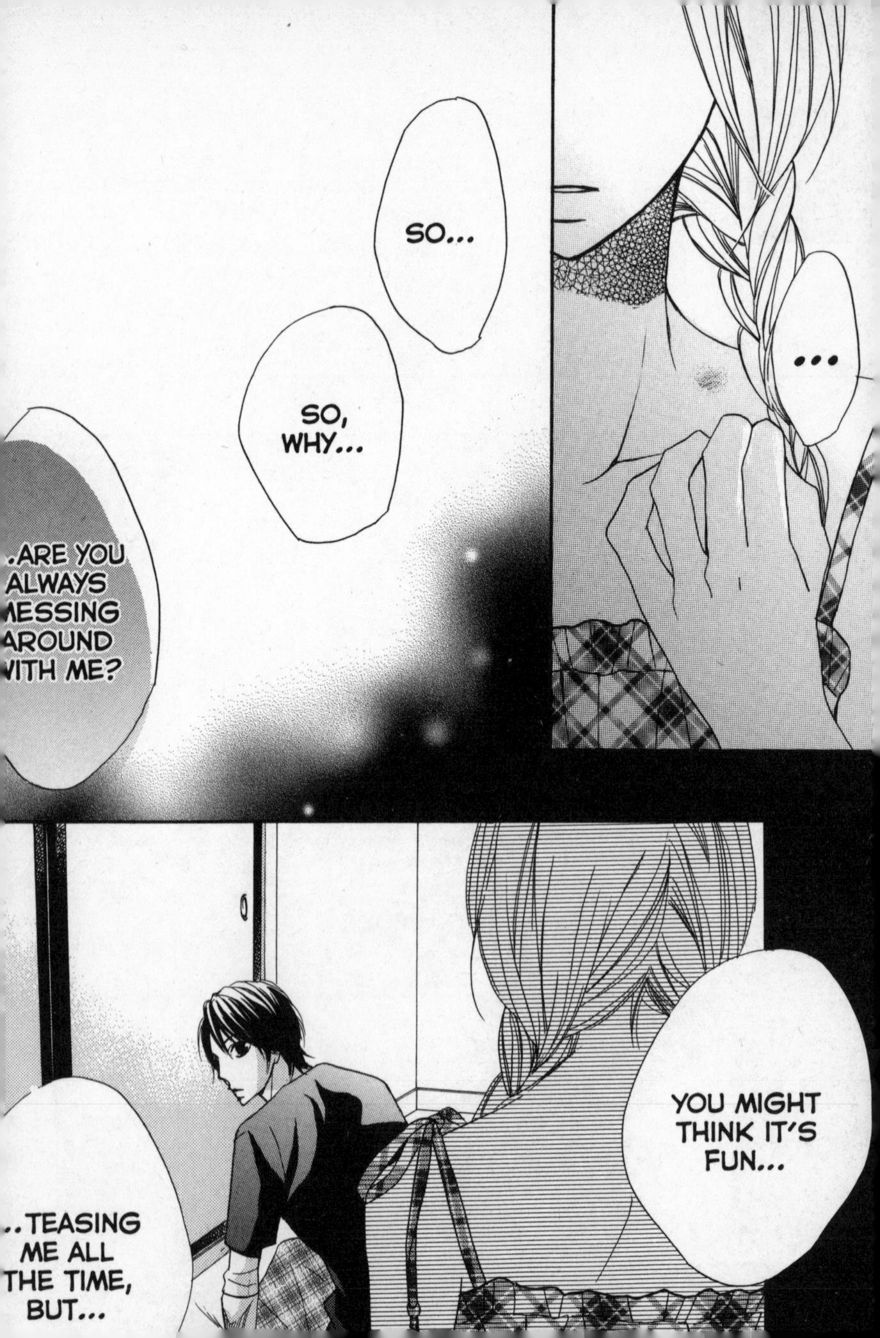
...
SO...
SO, WHY...
..ARE YOU ALWAYS MESSING AROUND WITH ME?
YOU MIGHT THINK IT'S FUN...
..TEASING ME ALL THE TIME, BUT...

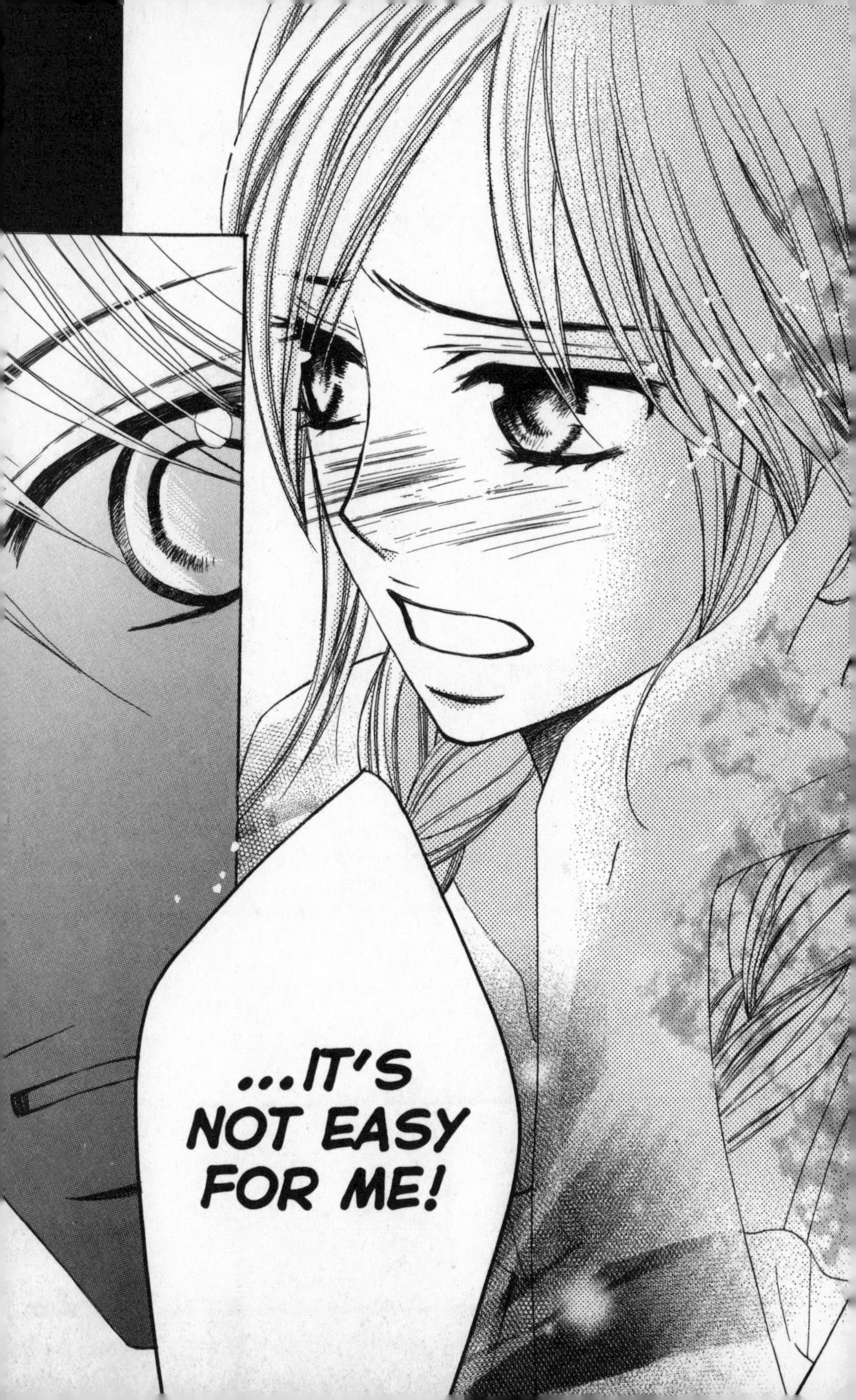
...IT'S NOT EASY FOR ME!

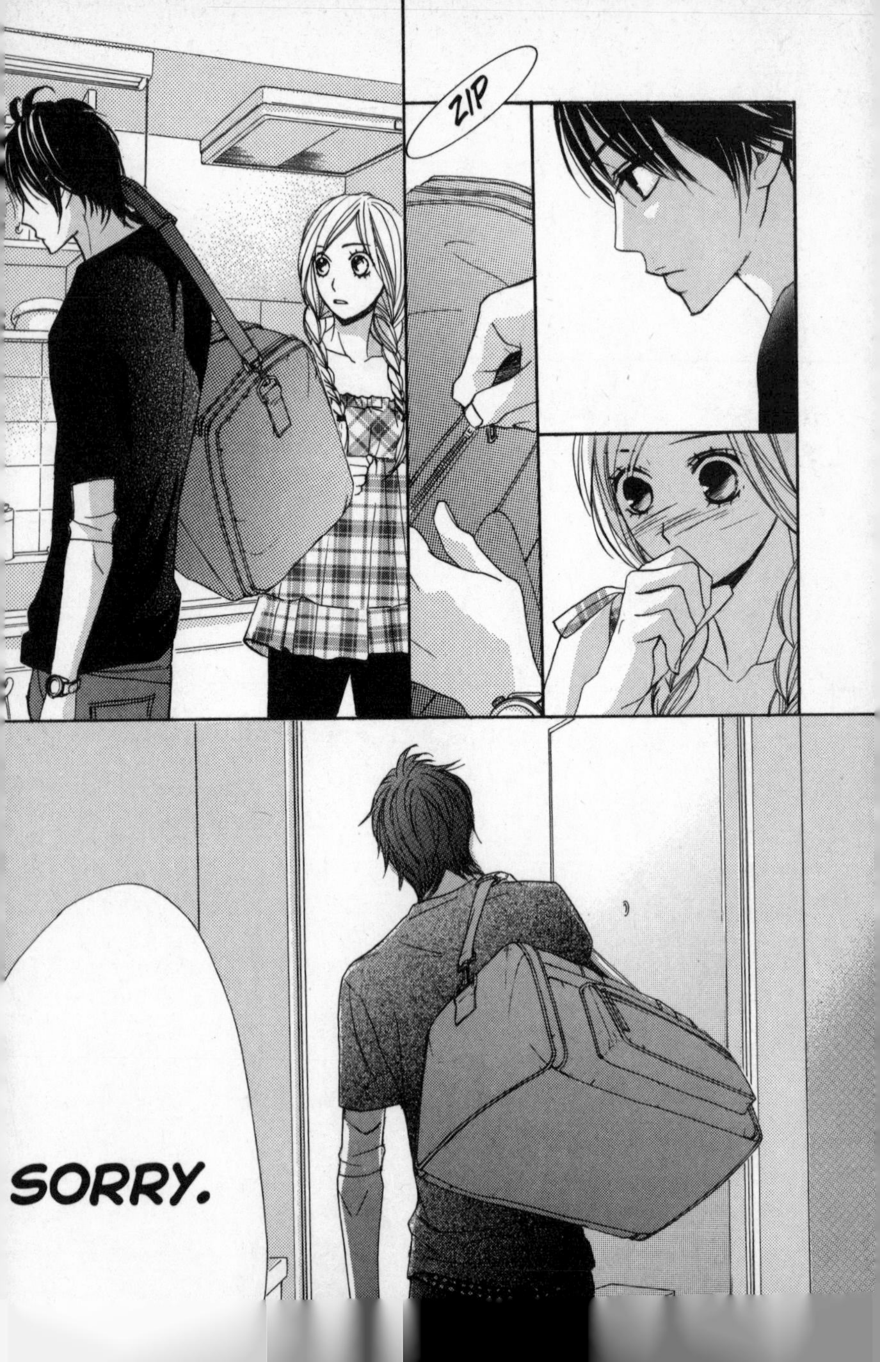
ZIP
SORRY.

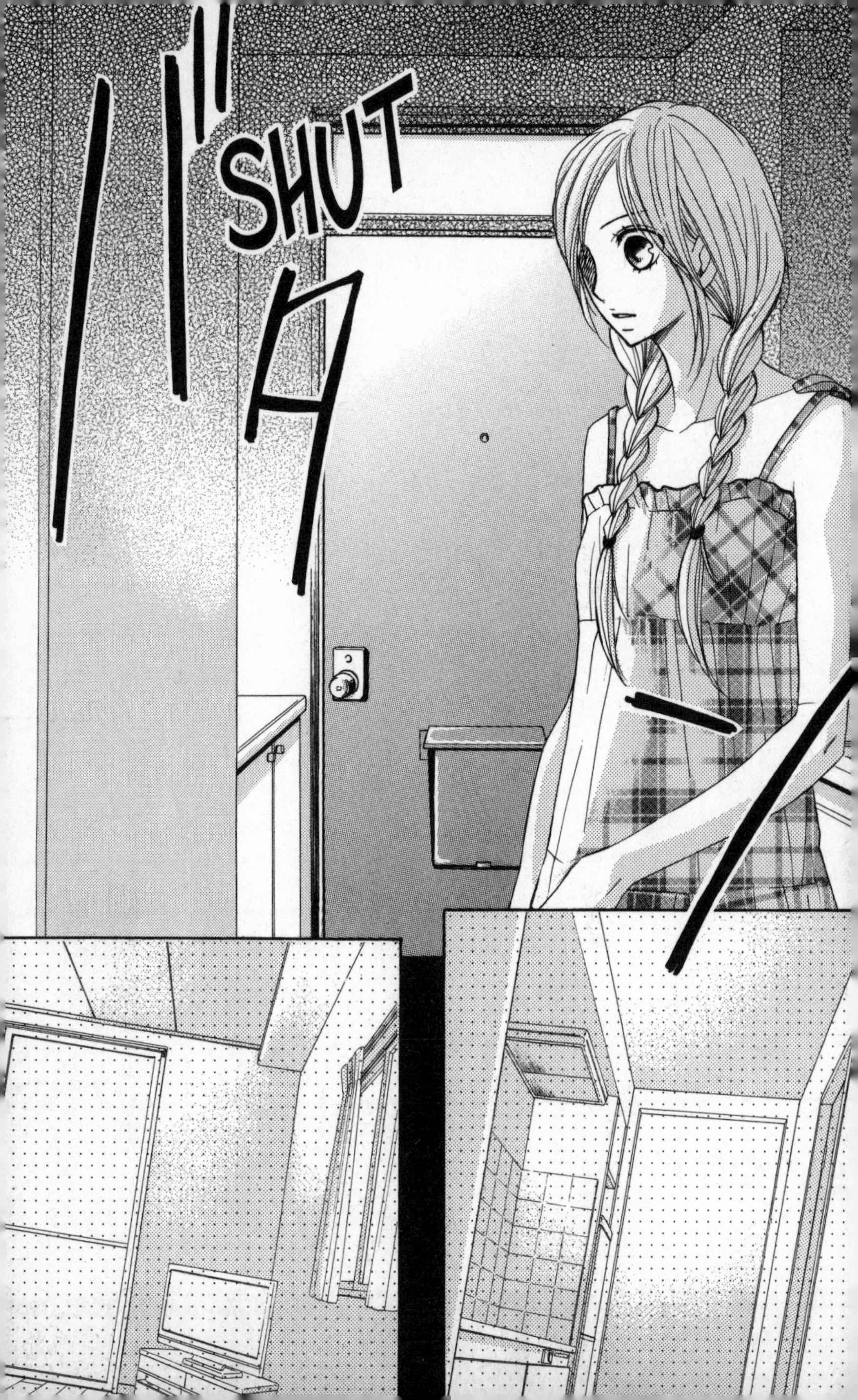
SHUT

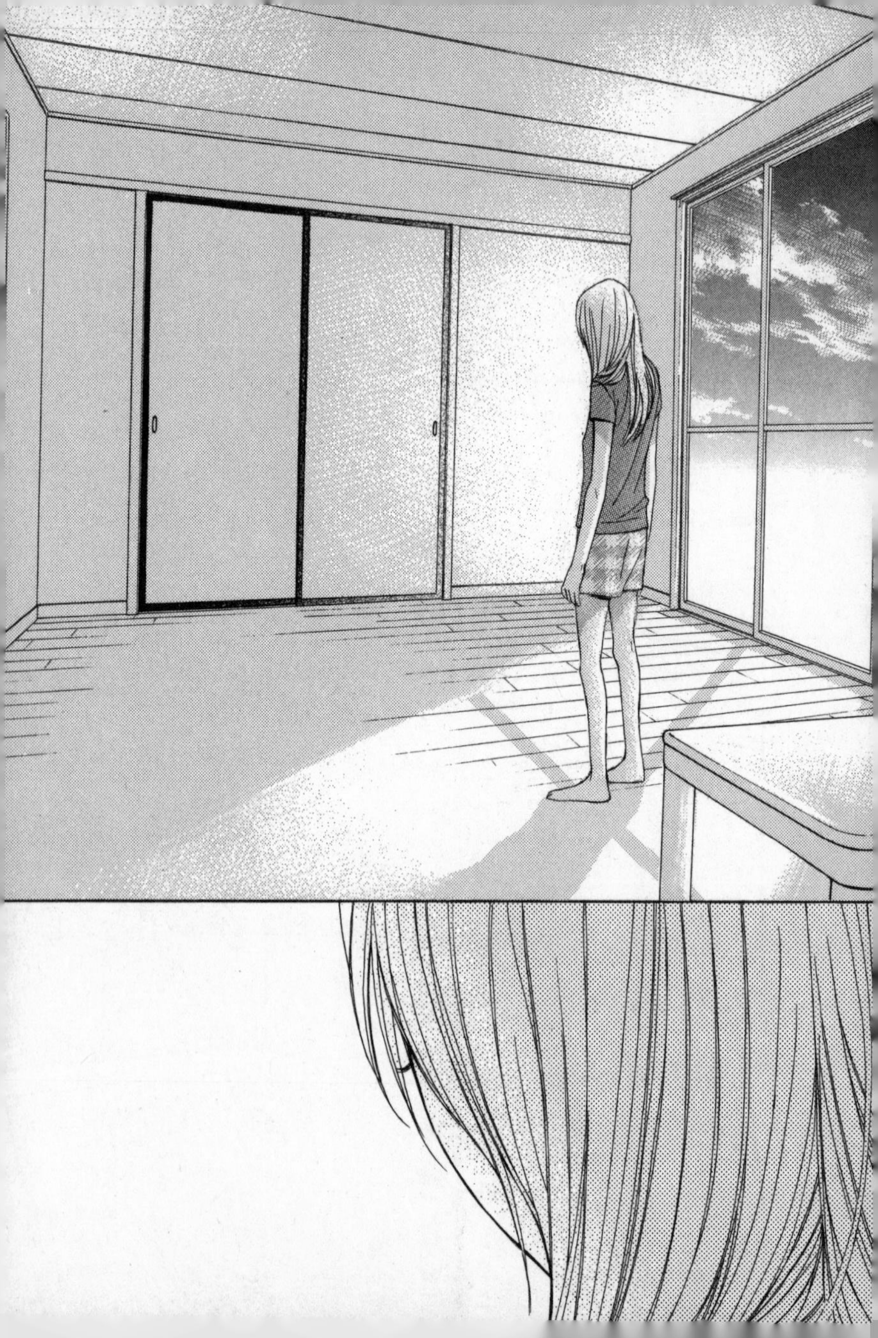

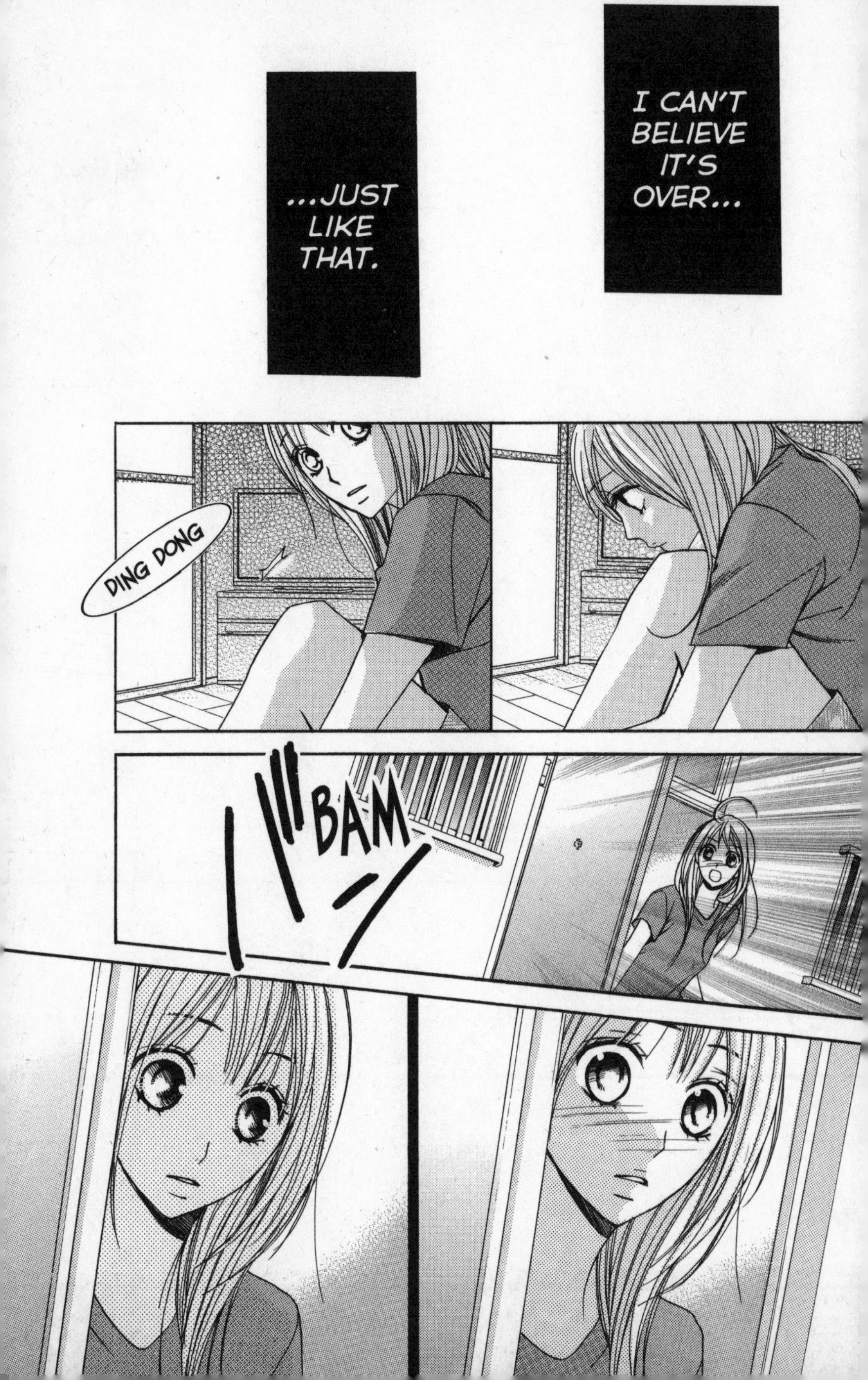
I CAN'T BELIEVE IT'S OVER...
...JUST LIKE THAT.
DING DONG
BAM

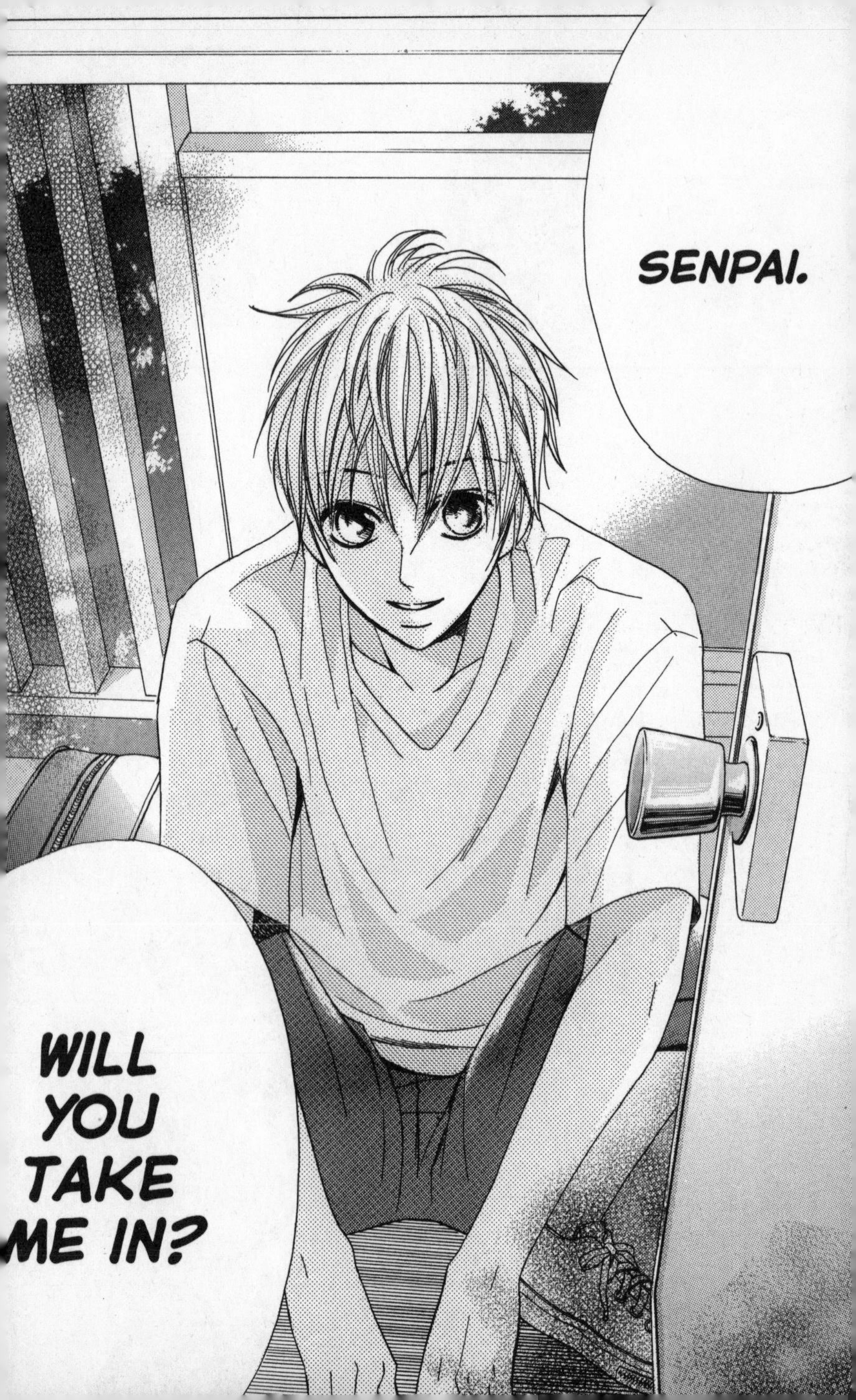
SENPAI.
WILL YOU TAKE ME IN?

#8 Realized Feelings

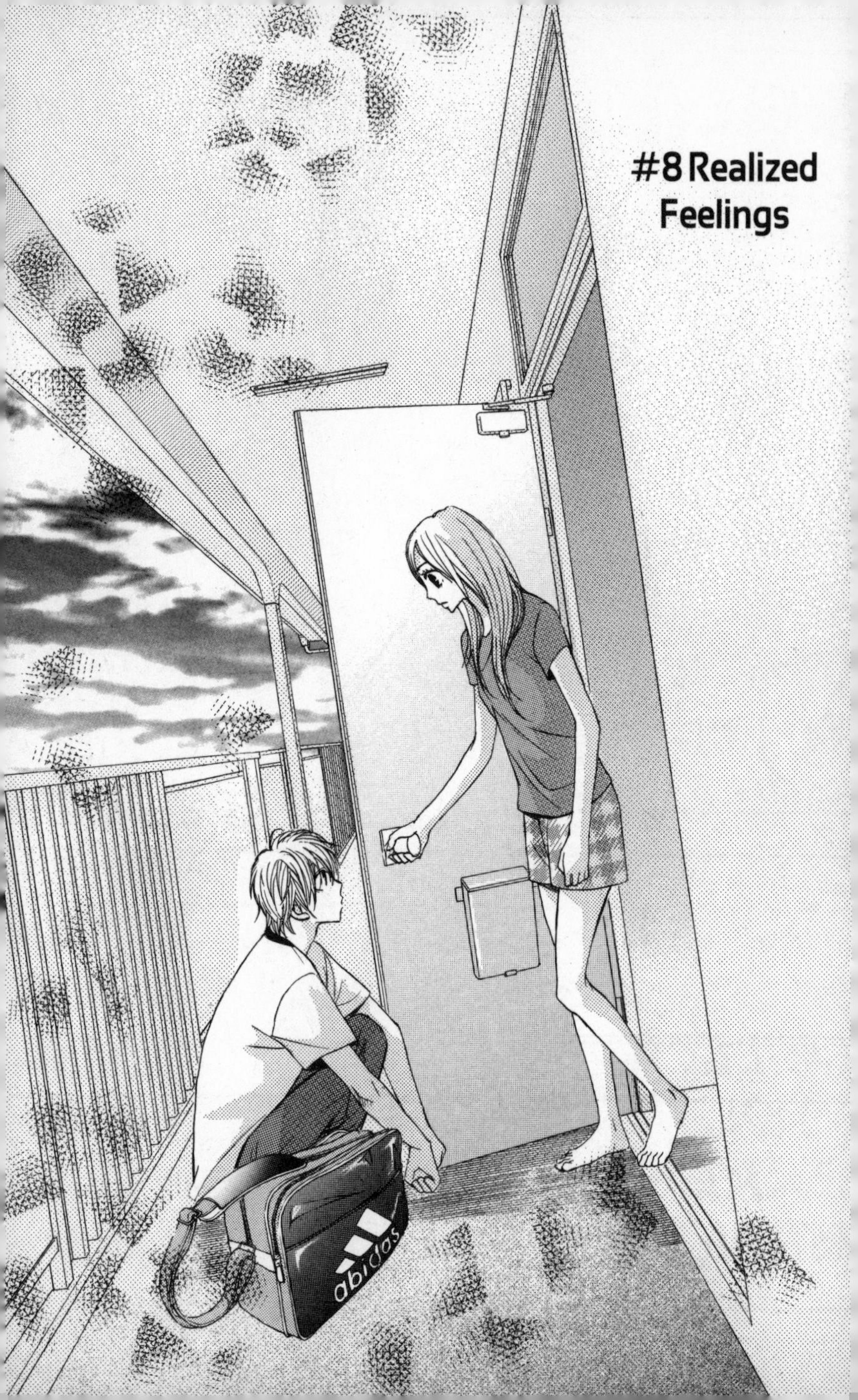
abidas

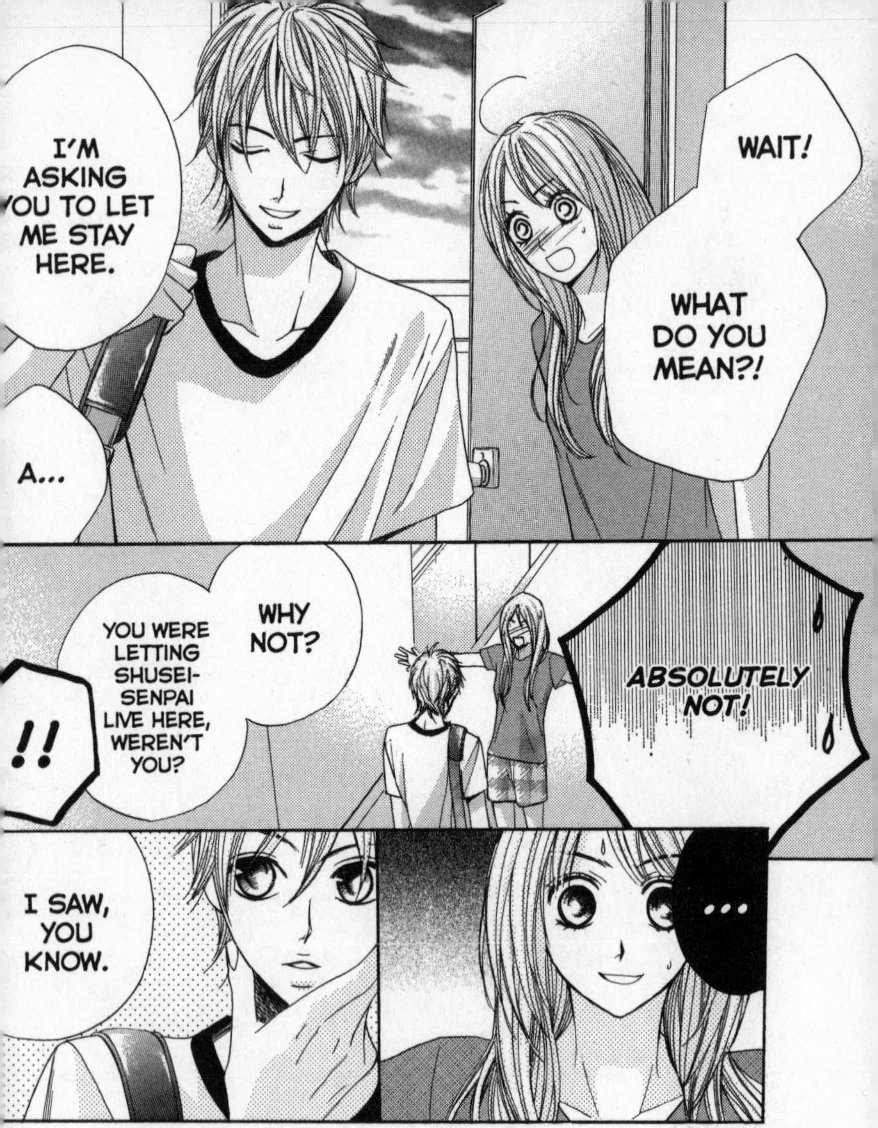
WAIT!
WHAT DO YOU MEAN?!
I'M ASKING YOU TO LET ME STAY HERE.
A...
ABSOLUTELY NOT!
WHY NOT?
YOU WERE LETTING SHUSEI-SENPAI LIVE HERE, WEREN'T YOU?
!!
...
I SAW, YOU KNOW.

L♥DK

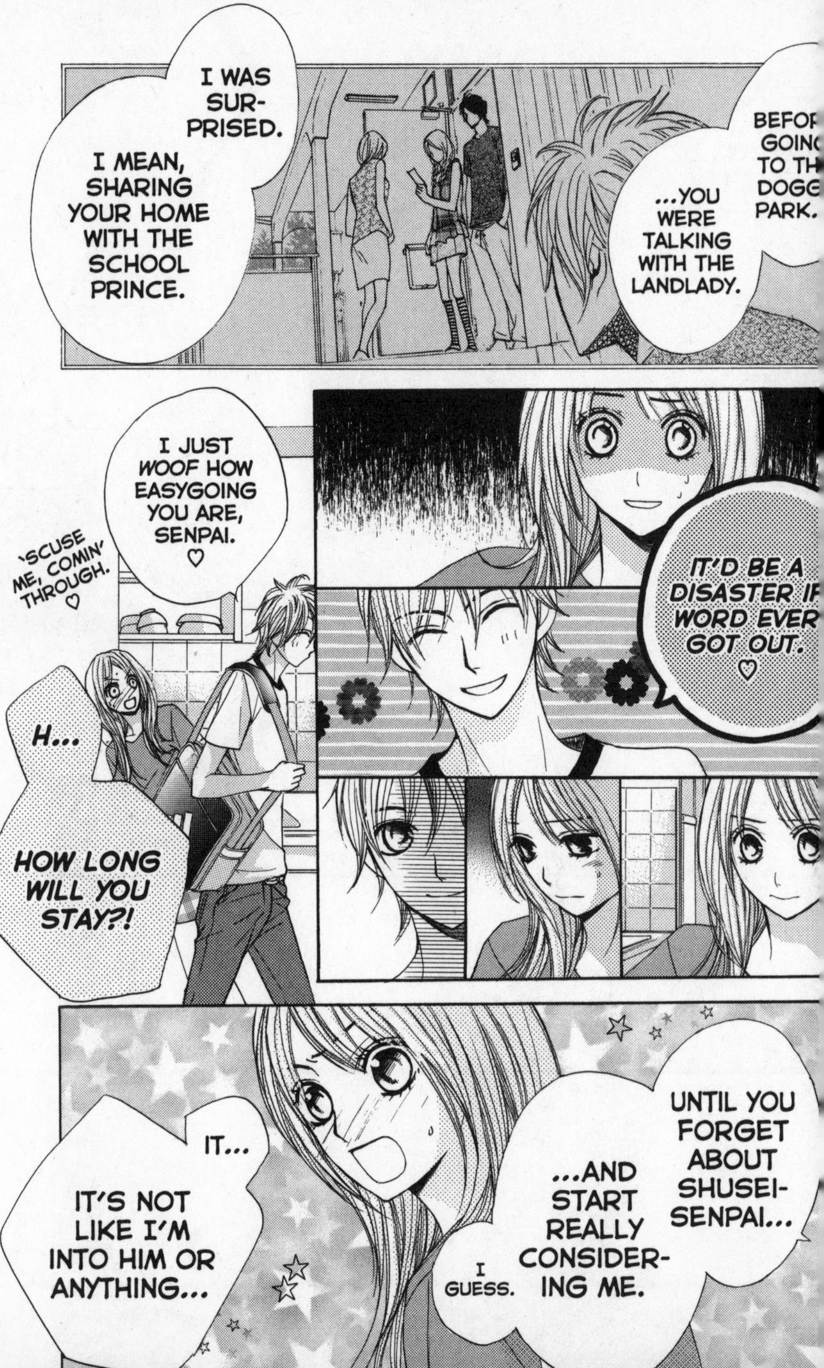
BEFOR GOIN TO TH DOGG PARK.
...YOU WERE TALKING WITH THE LANDLADY.
I WAS SUR-PRISED.
I MEAN, SHARING YOUR HOME WITH THE SCHOOL PRINCE.
IT'D BE A DISASTER I WORD EVER GOT OUT. ♡
I JUST *WOOF* HOW EASYGOING YOU ARE, SENPAI. ♡
'SCUSE ME, COMIN' THROUGH. ♡
H...
HOW LONG WILL YOU STAY?!
UNTIL YOU FORGET ABOUT SHUSEI-SENPAI...
...AND START REALLY CONSIDER-ING ME.
I GUESS.
IT...
IT'S NOT LIKE I'M INTO HIM OR ANYTHING...

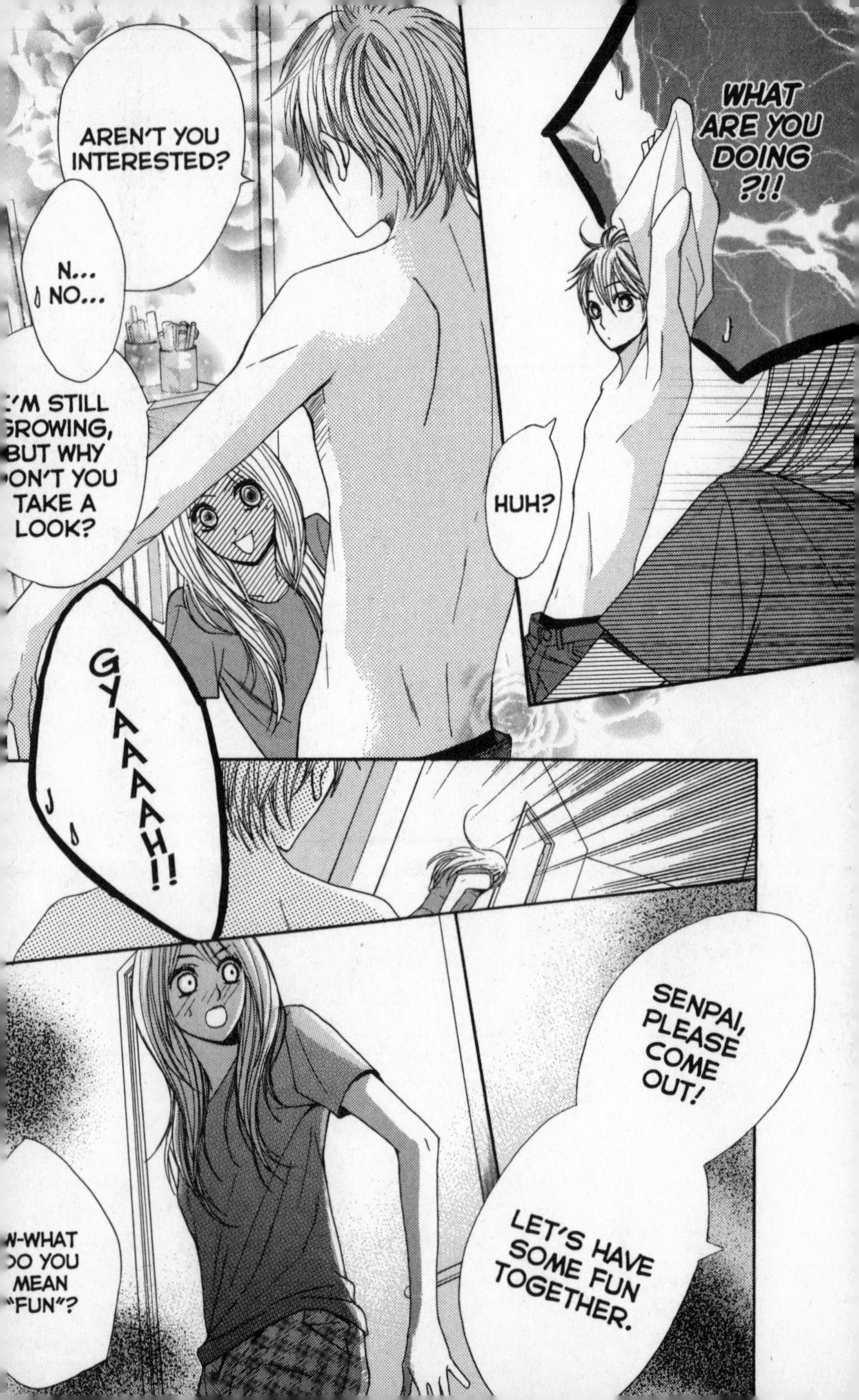
WHAT ARE YOU DOING ?!!
HUH?
AREN'T YOU INTERESTED?
N... NO...
'M STILL ROWING, BUT WHY ON'T YOU TAKE A LOOK?
GYAAAAH!!
SENPAI, PLEASE COME OUT!
LET'S HAVE SOME FUN TOGETHER.
-WHAT O YOU MEAN "FUN"?

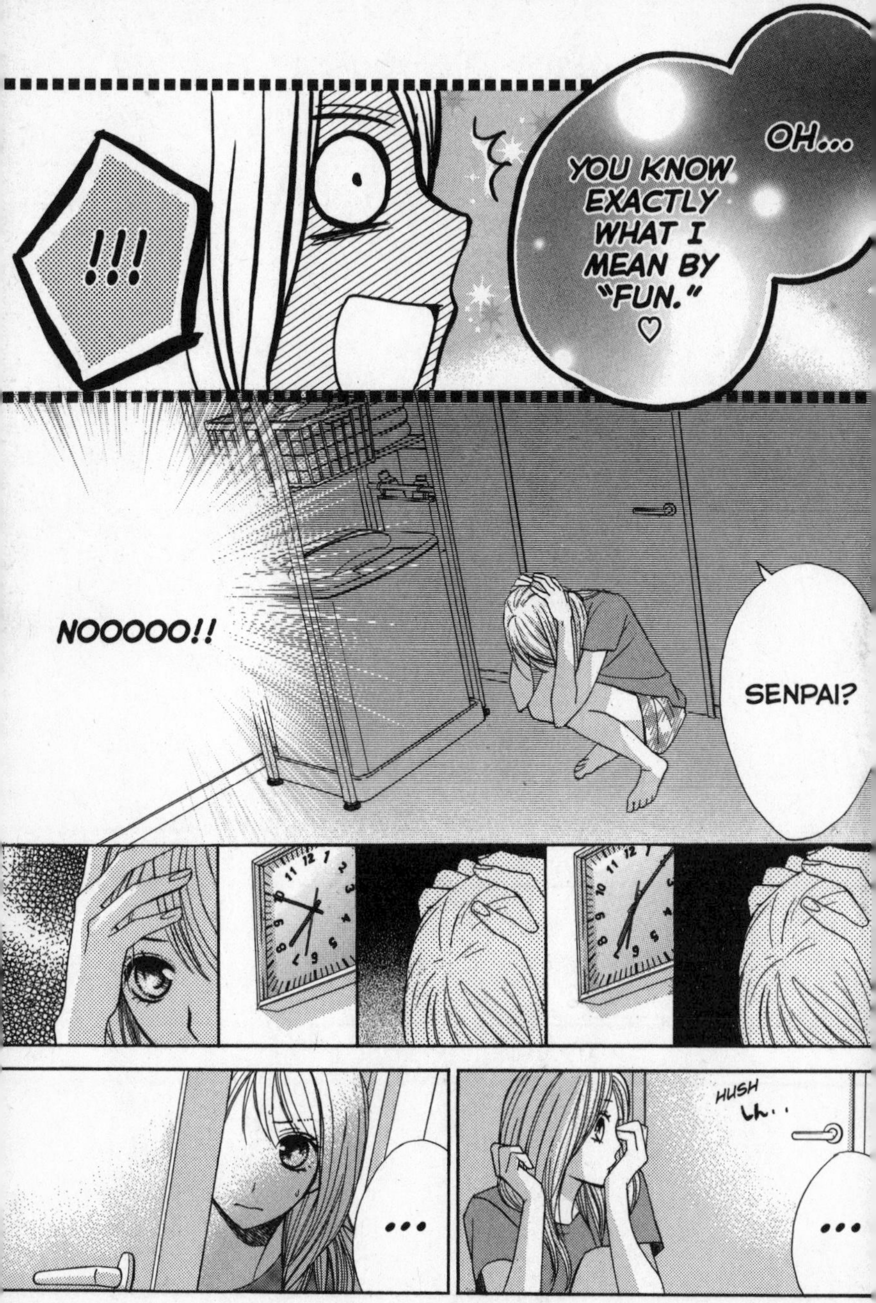
OH... YOU KNOW EXACTLY WHAT I MEAN BY "FUN." ♡
!!!
SENPAI?
NOOOOO!!
HUSH
しん..
...
...

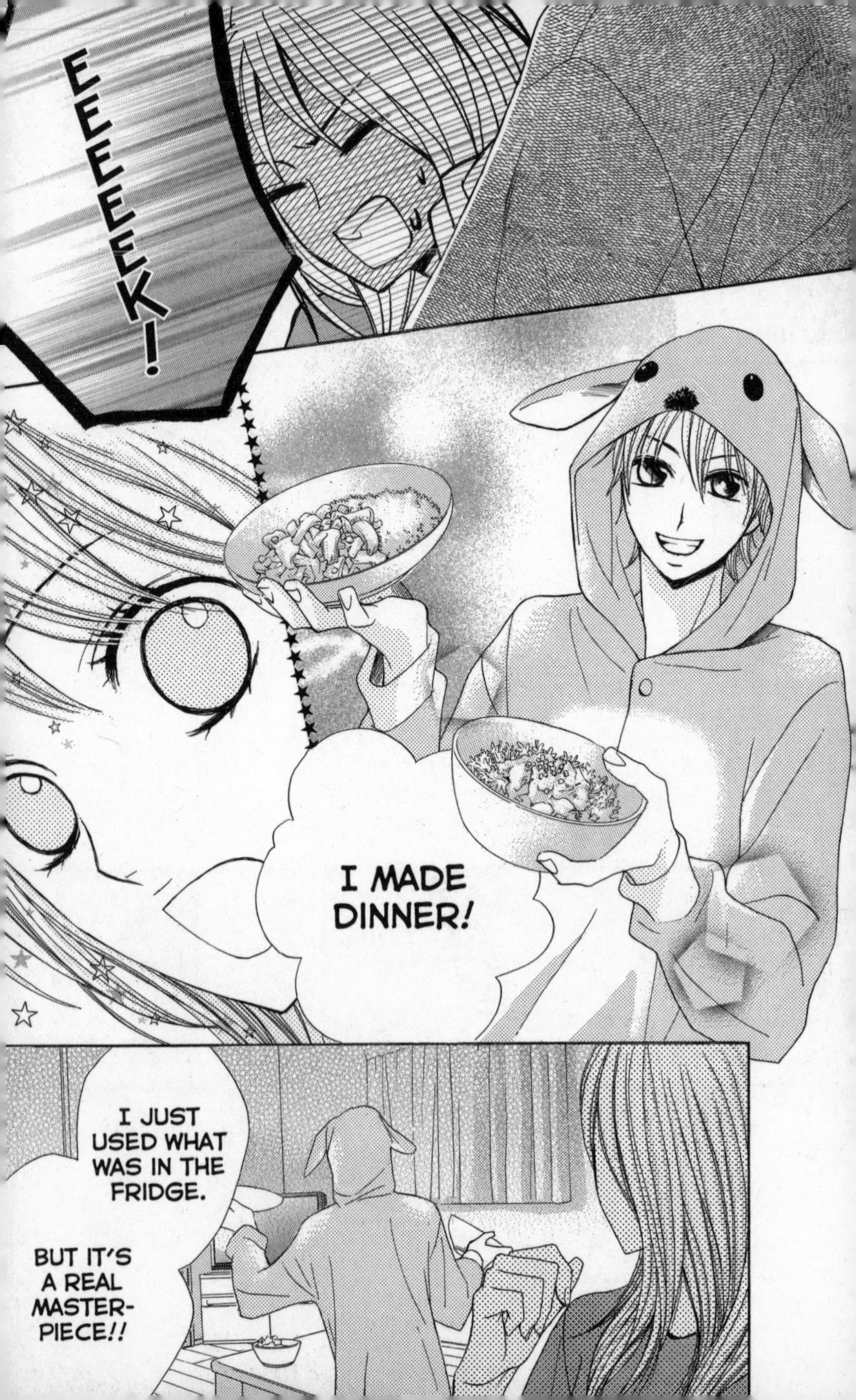
EEEEEEK!
I MADE DINNER!
I JUST USED WHAT WAS IN THE FRIDGE.
BUT IT'S A REAL MASTER-PIECE!!

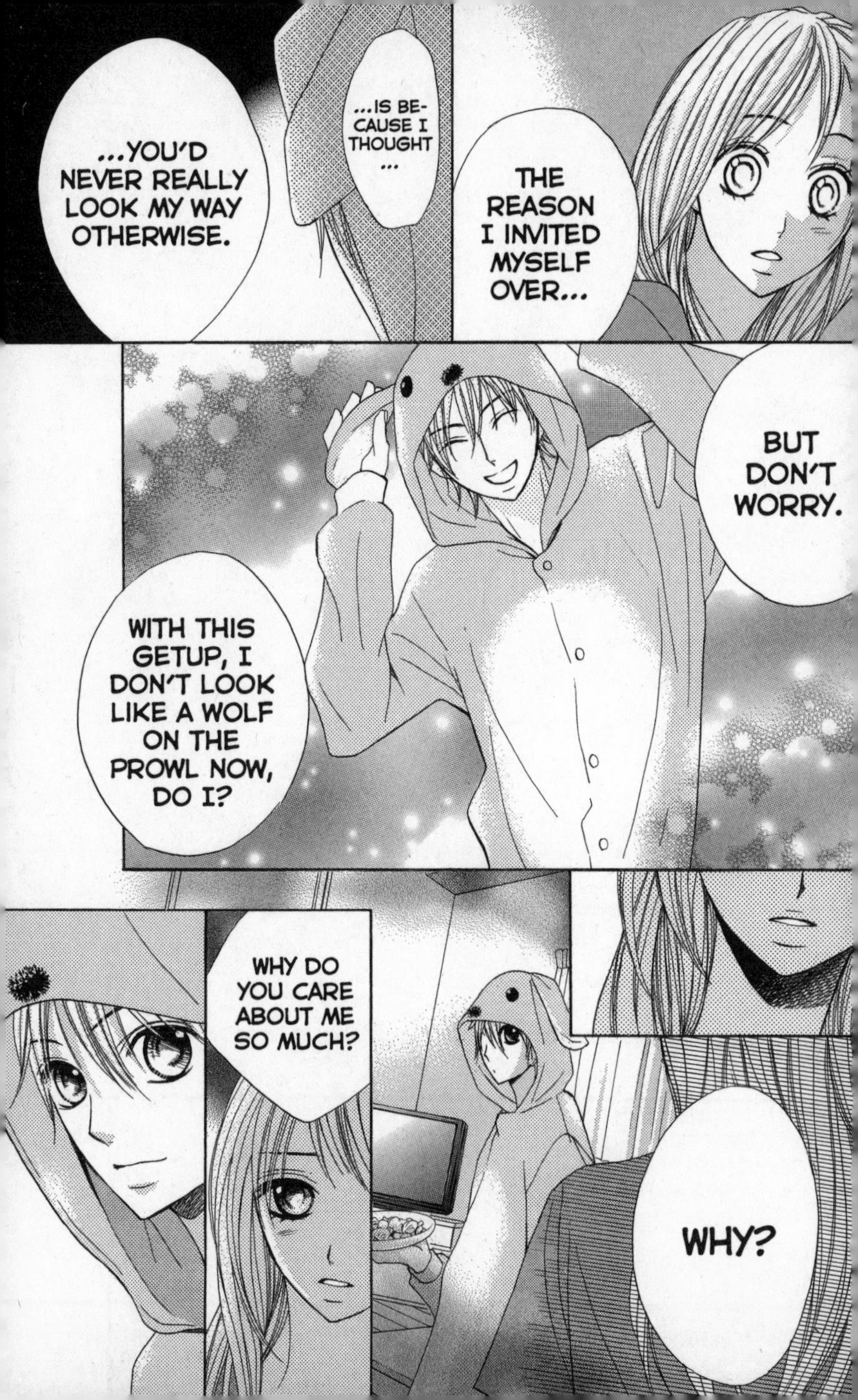
THE REASON I INVITED MYSELF OVER...
...IS BE-CAUSE I THOUGHT...
...YOU'D NEVER REALLY LOOK MY WAY OTHERWISE.
BUT DON'T WORRY.
WITH THIS GETUP, I DON'T LOOK LIKE A WOLF ON THE PROWL NOW, DO I?
WHY?
WHY DO YOU CARE ABOUT ME SO MUCH?

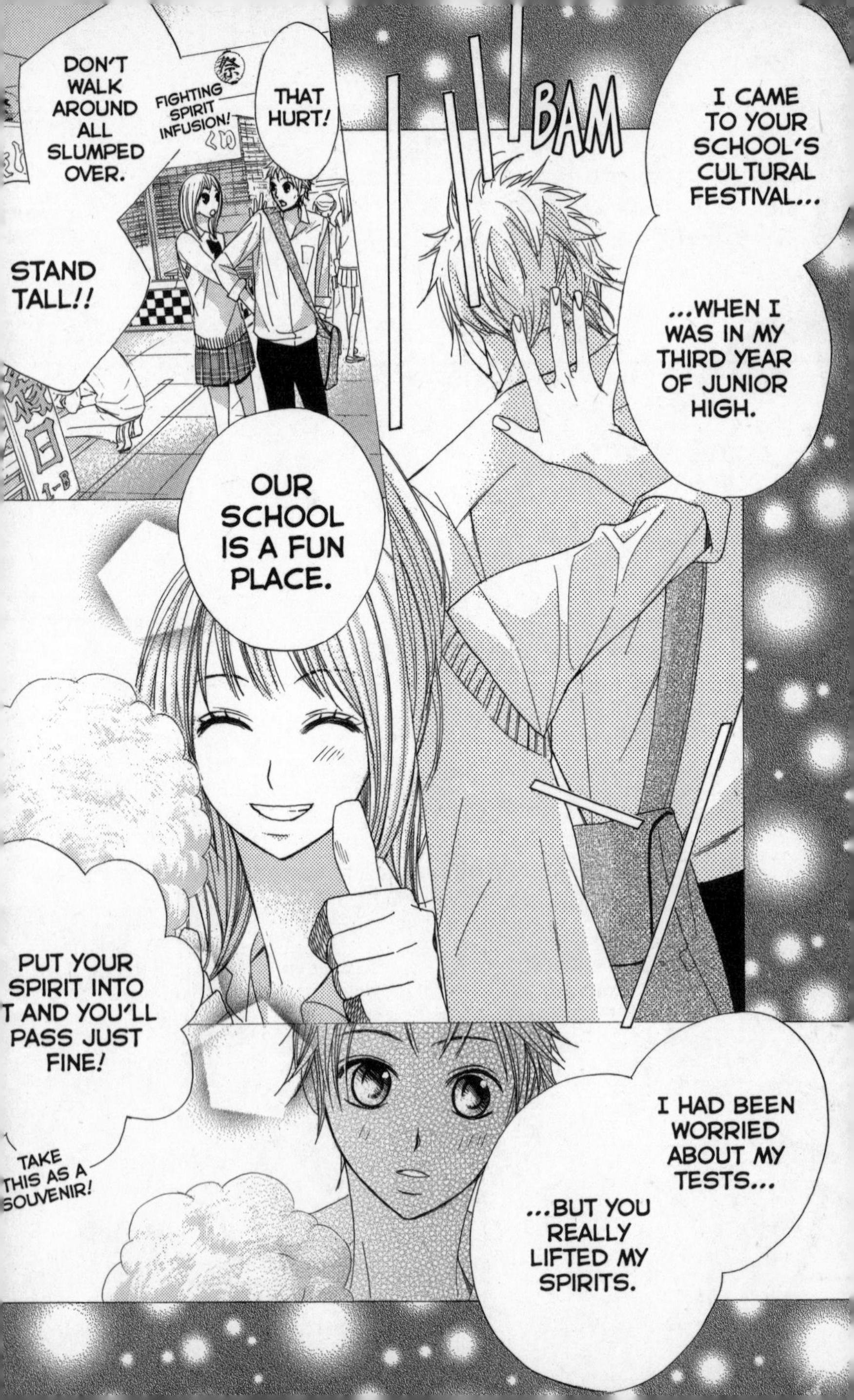
BAM
I CAME TO YOUR SCHOOL'S CULTURAL FESTIVAL...
...WHEN I WAS IN MY THIRD YEAR OF JUNIOR HIGH.
THAT HURT!
FIGHTING SPIRIT INFUSION!
DON'T WALK AROUND ALL SLUMPED OVER.
STAND TALL!!
OUR SCHOOL IS A FUN PLACE.
PUT YOUR SPIRIT INTO T AND YOU'LL PASS JUST FINE!
TAKE THIS AS A SOUVENIR!
I HAD BEEN WORRIED ABOUT MY TESTS...
...BUT YOU REALLY LIFTED MY SPIRITS.

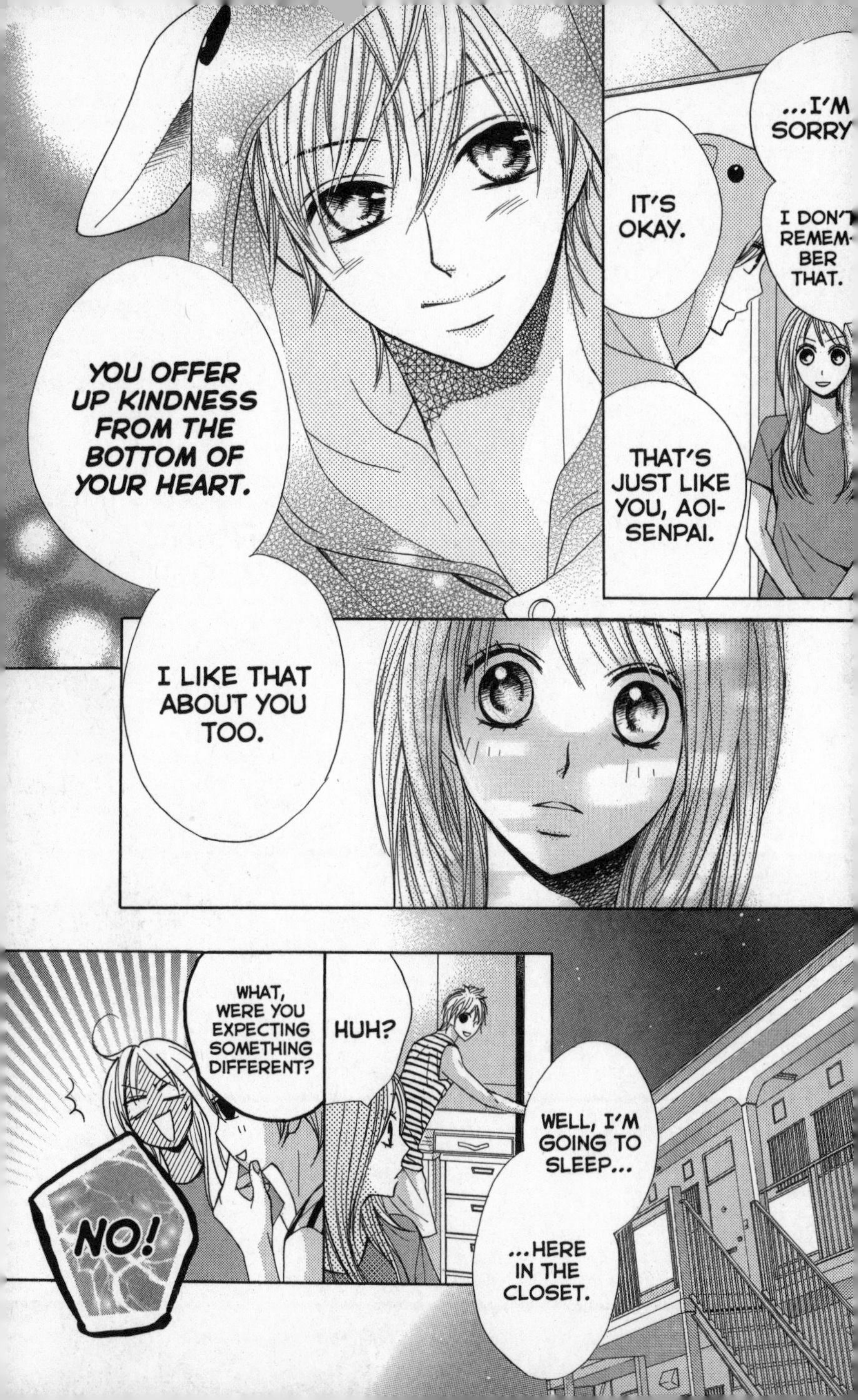
...I'M SORRY
I DON'T REMEMBER THAT.
IT'S OKAY.
THAT'S JUST LIKE YOU, AOI-SENPAI.
YOU OFFER UP KINDNESS FROM THE BOTTOM OF YOUR HEART.
I LIKE THAT ABOUT YOU TOO.
WELL, I'M GOING TO SLEEP...
...HERE IN THE CLOSET.
HUH?
WHAT, WERE YOU EXPECTING SOMETHING DIFFERENT?
NO!

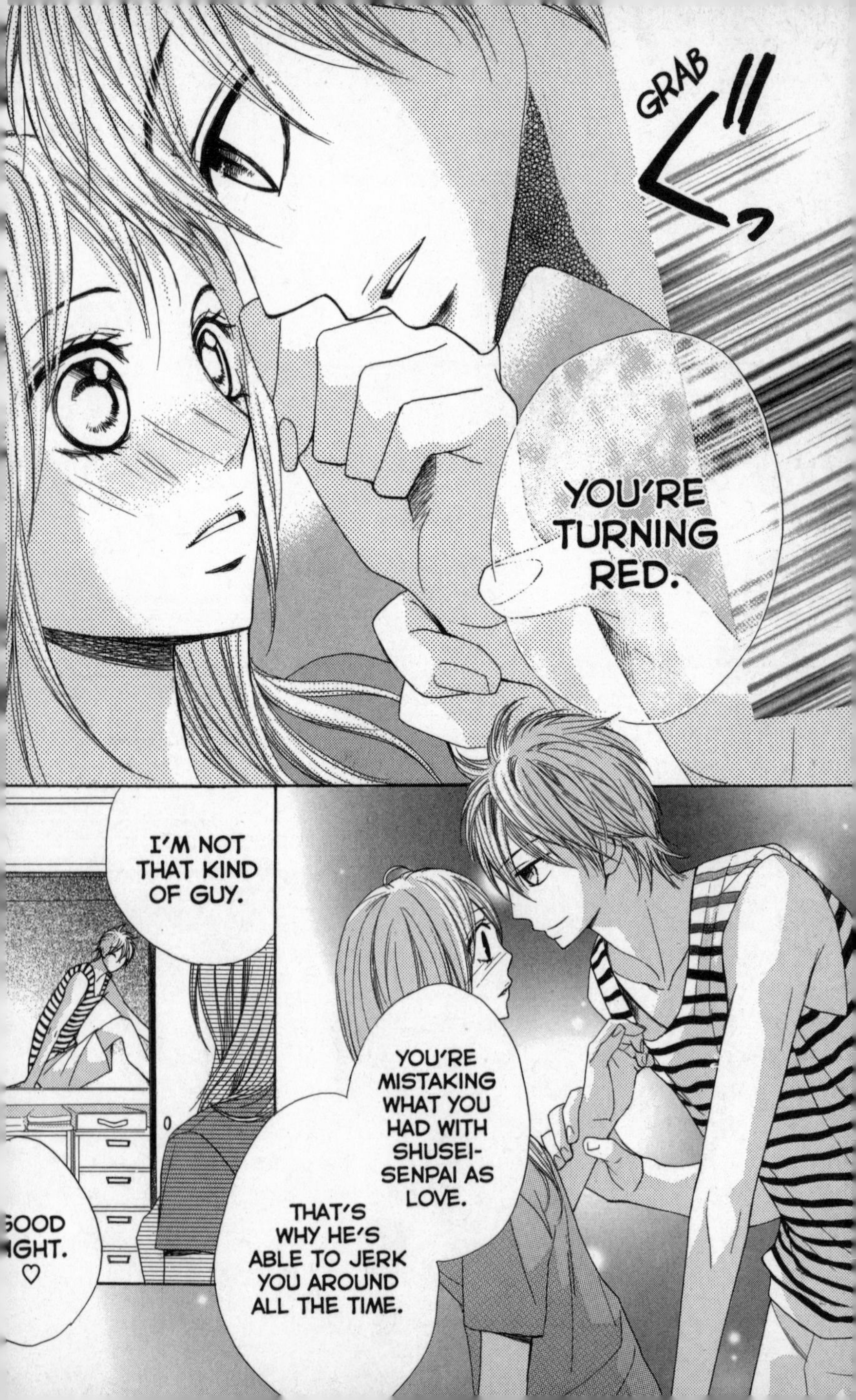
GRAB
YOU'RE TURNING RED.
YOU'RE MISTAKING WHAT YOU HAD WITH SHUSEI-SENPAI AS LOVE.
THAT'S WHY HE'S ABLE TO JERK YOU AROUND ALL THE TIME.
I'M NOT THAT KIND OF GUY.
GOOD IGHT. ♡

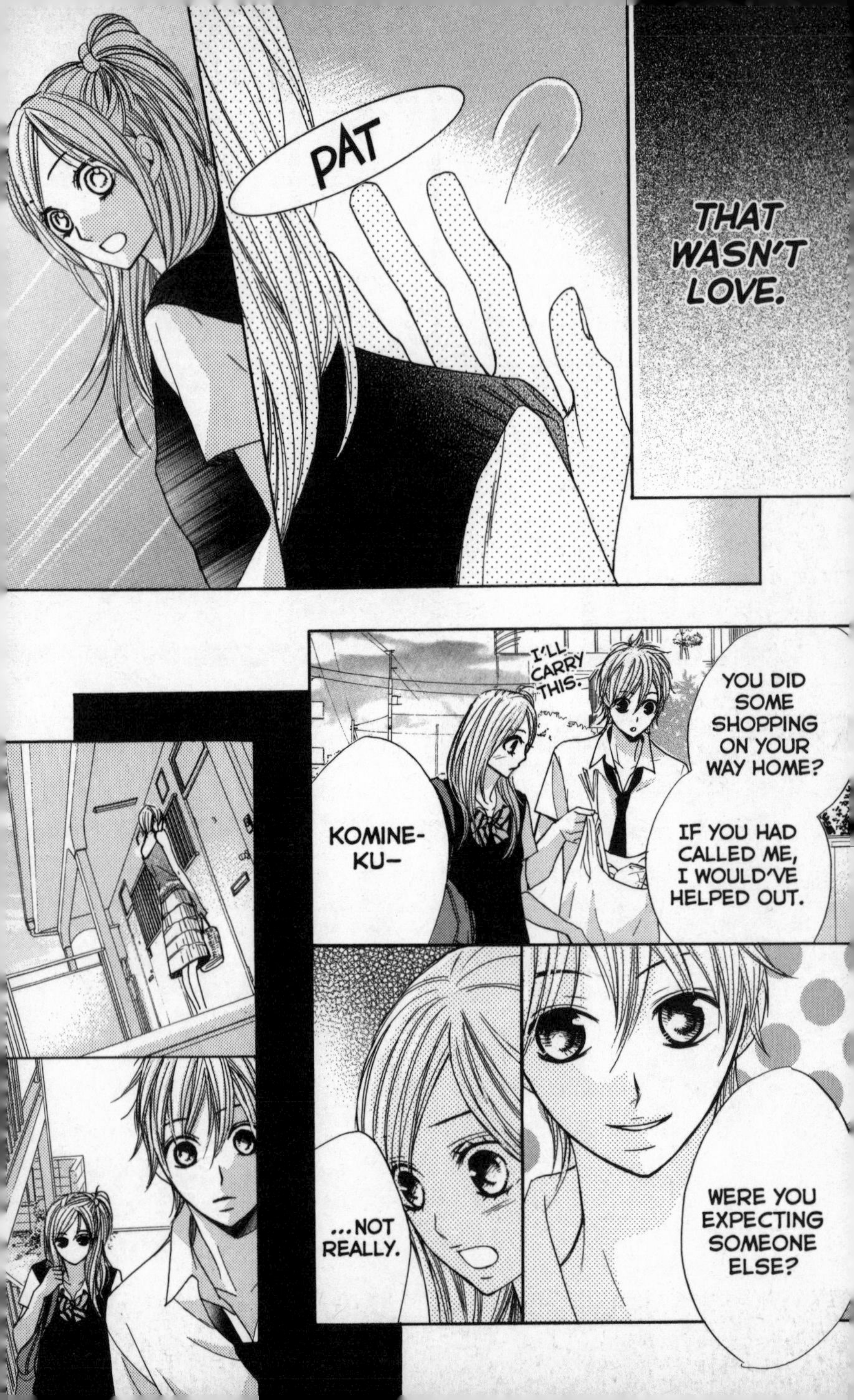
THAT WASN'T LOVE.
PAT
YOU DID SOME SHOPPING ON YOUR WAY HOME?
I'LL CARRY THIS.
IF YOU HAD CALLED ME, I WOULD'VE HELPED OUT.
KOMINE-KU-
WERE YOU EXPECTING SOMEONE ELSE?
...NOT REALLY.

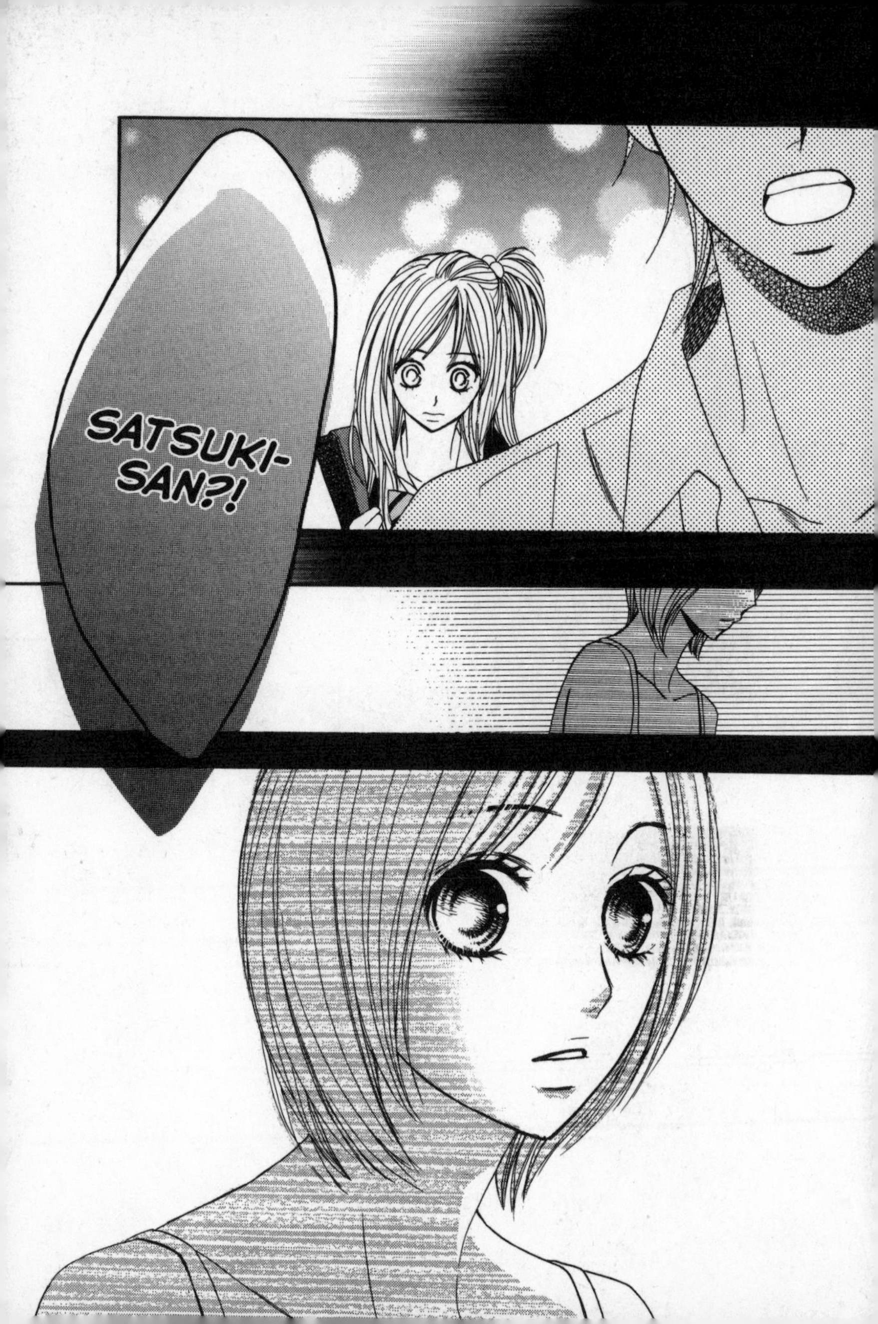
SATSUKI-SAN?!

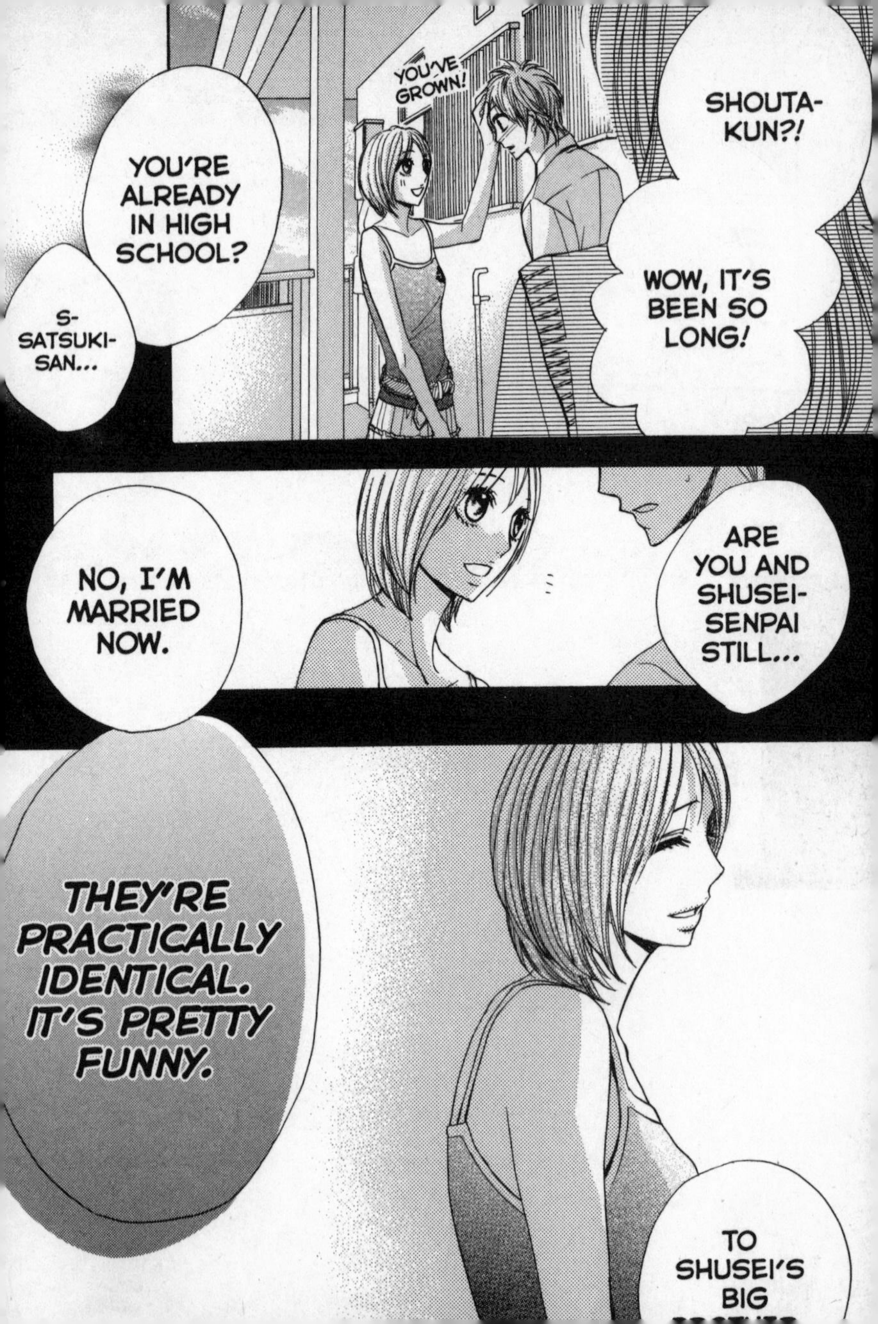
SHOUTA-KUN?!
WOW, IT'S BEEN SO LONG!
YOU'VE GROWN!
YOU'RE ALREADY IN HIGH SCHOOL?
S-SATSUKI-SAN...
ARE YOU AND SHUSEI-SENPAI STILL...
NO, I'M MARRIED NOW.
TO SHUSEI'S BIG
THEY'RE PRACTICALLY IDENTICAL. IT'S PRETTY FUNNY.

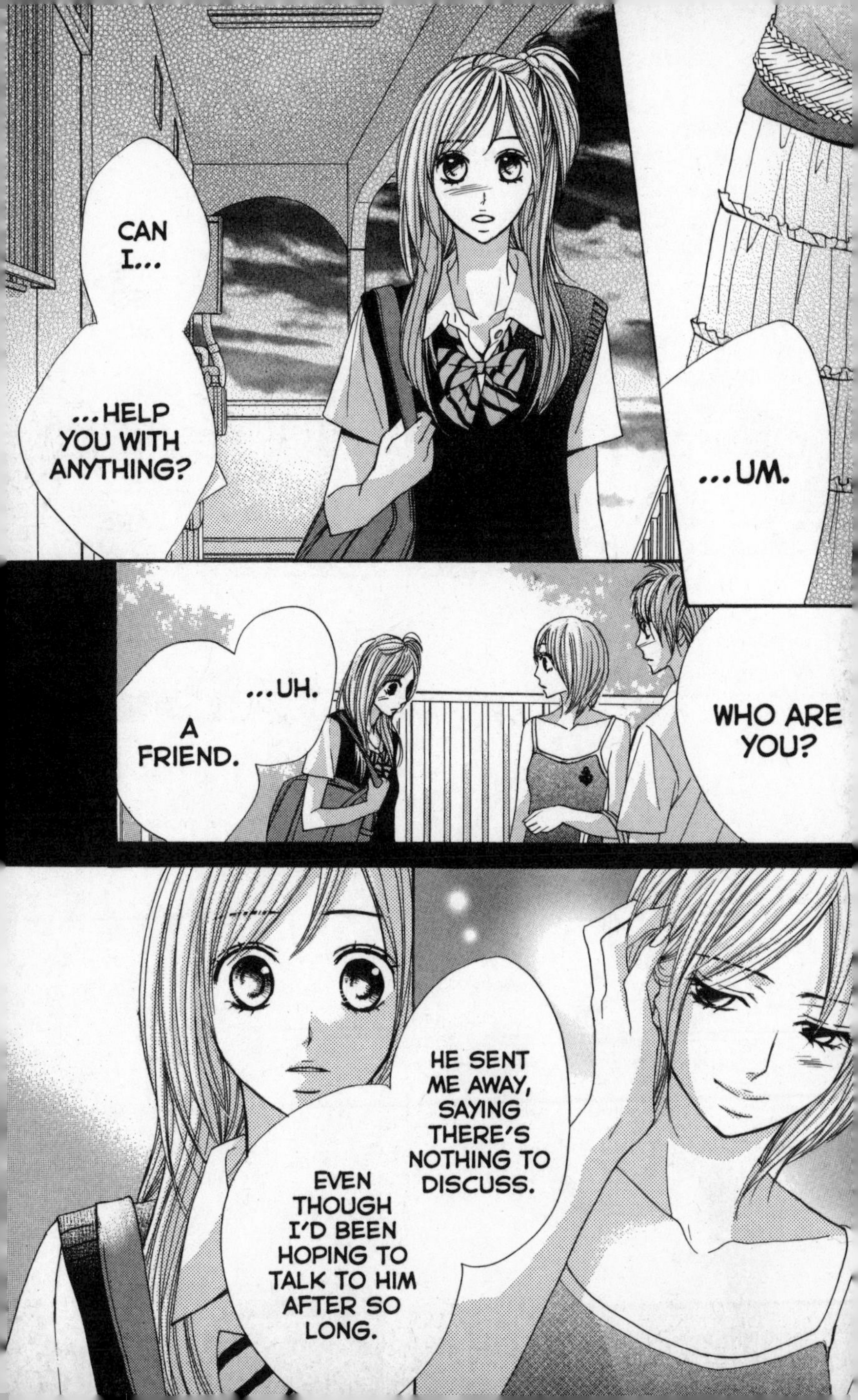
...UM.
CAN I...
...HELP YOU WITH ANYTHING?
WHO ARE YOU?
...UH.
A FRIEND.
HE SENT ME AWAY, SAYING THERE'S NOTHING TO DISCUSS.
EVEN THOUGH I'D BEEN HOPING TO TALK TO HIM AFTER SO LONG.

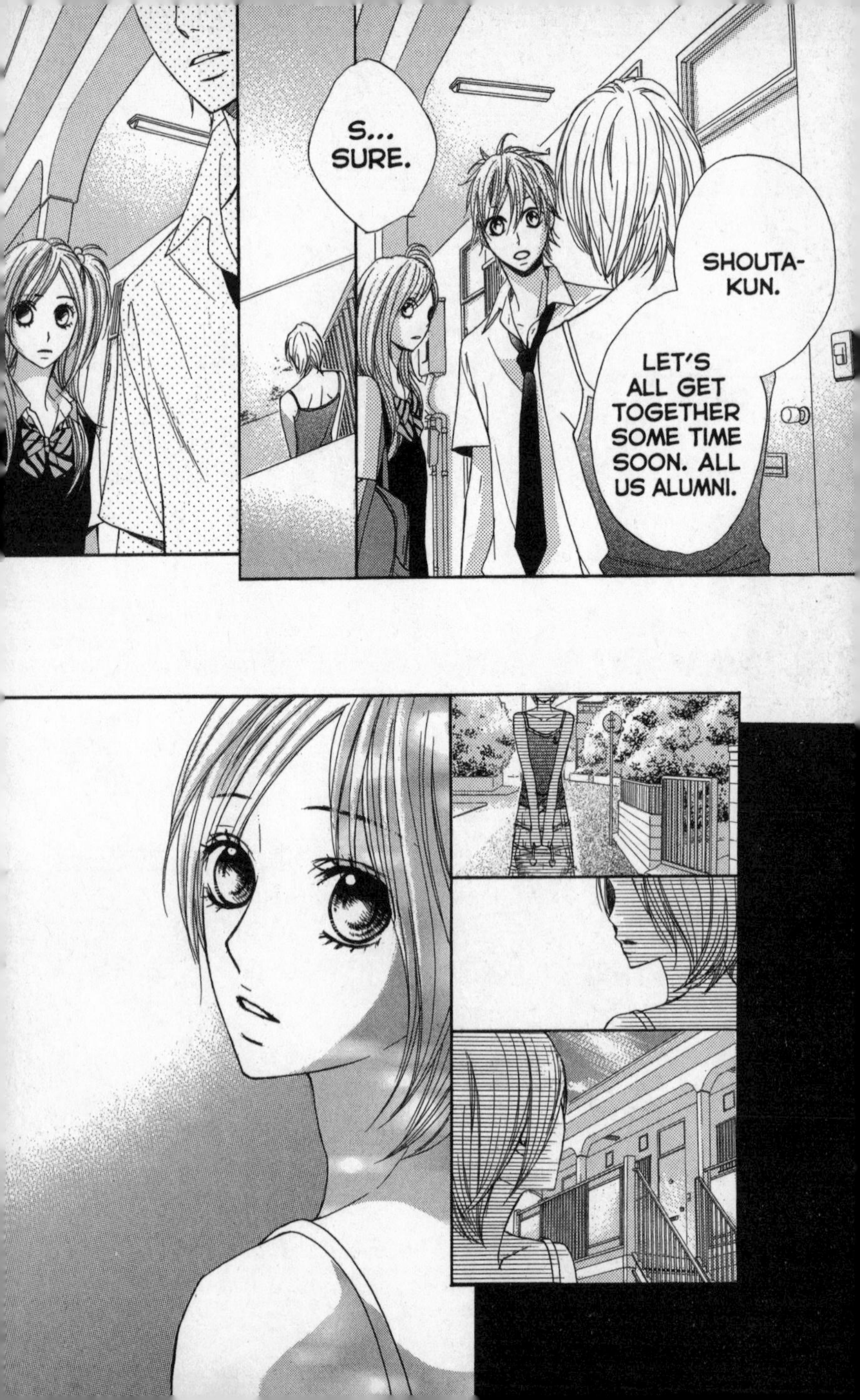
SHOUTA-KUN.
LET'S ALL GET TOGETHER SOME TIME SOON. ALL US ALUMNI.
S... SURE.

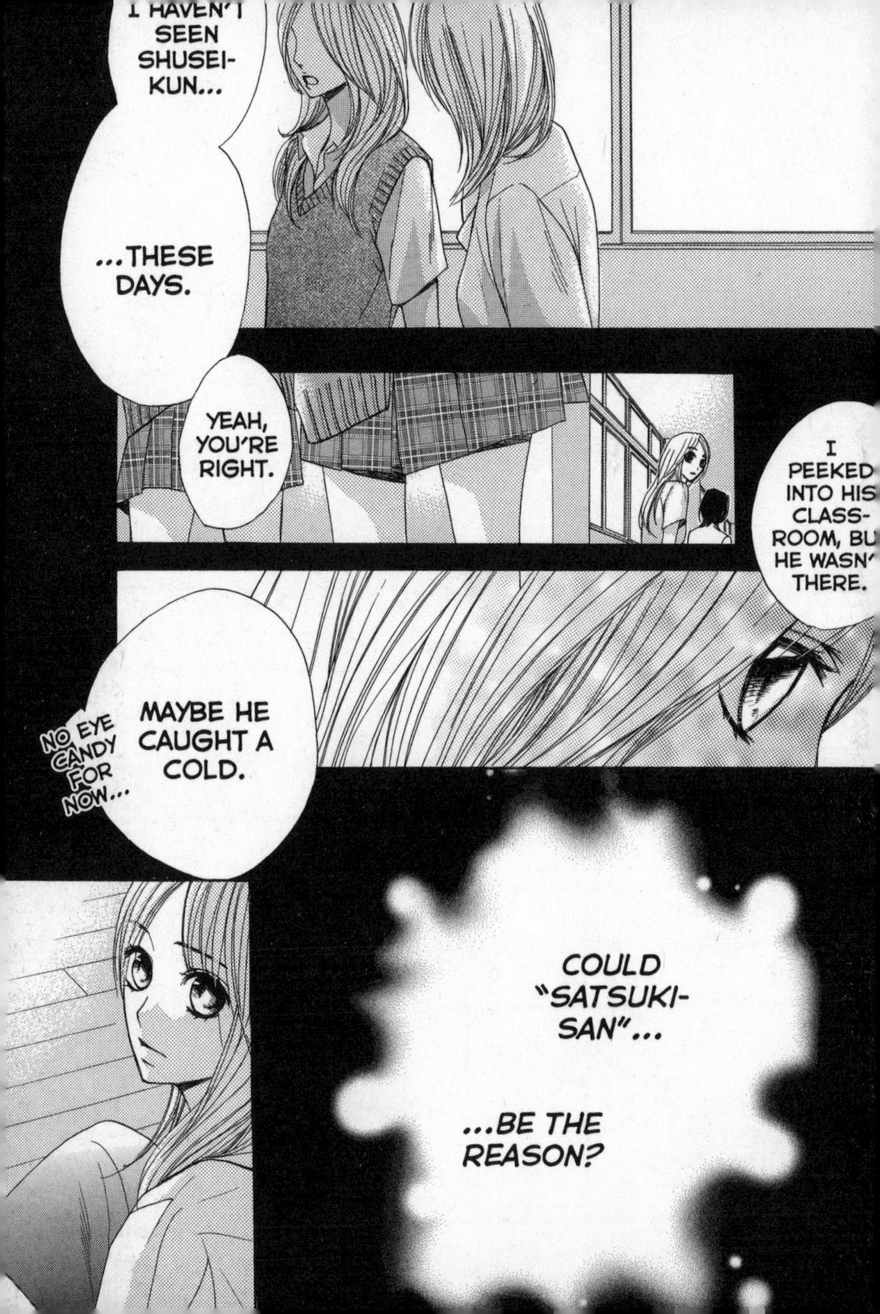
I HAVEN'T SEEN SHUSEI-KUN...
...THESE DAYS.
I PEEKED INTO HIS CLASS-ROOM, BU HE WASN' THERE.
YEAH, YOU'RE RIGHT.
MAYBE HE CAUGHT A COLD.
NO EYE CANDY FOR NOW...
COULD "SATSUKI-SAN"...
...BE THE REASON?

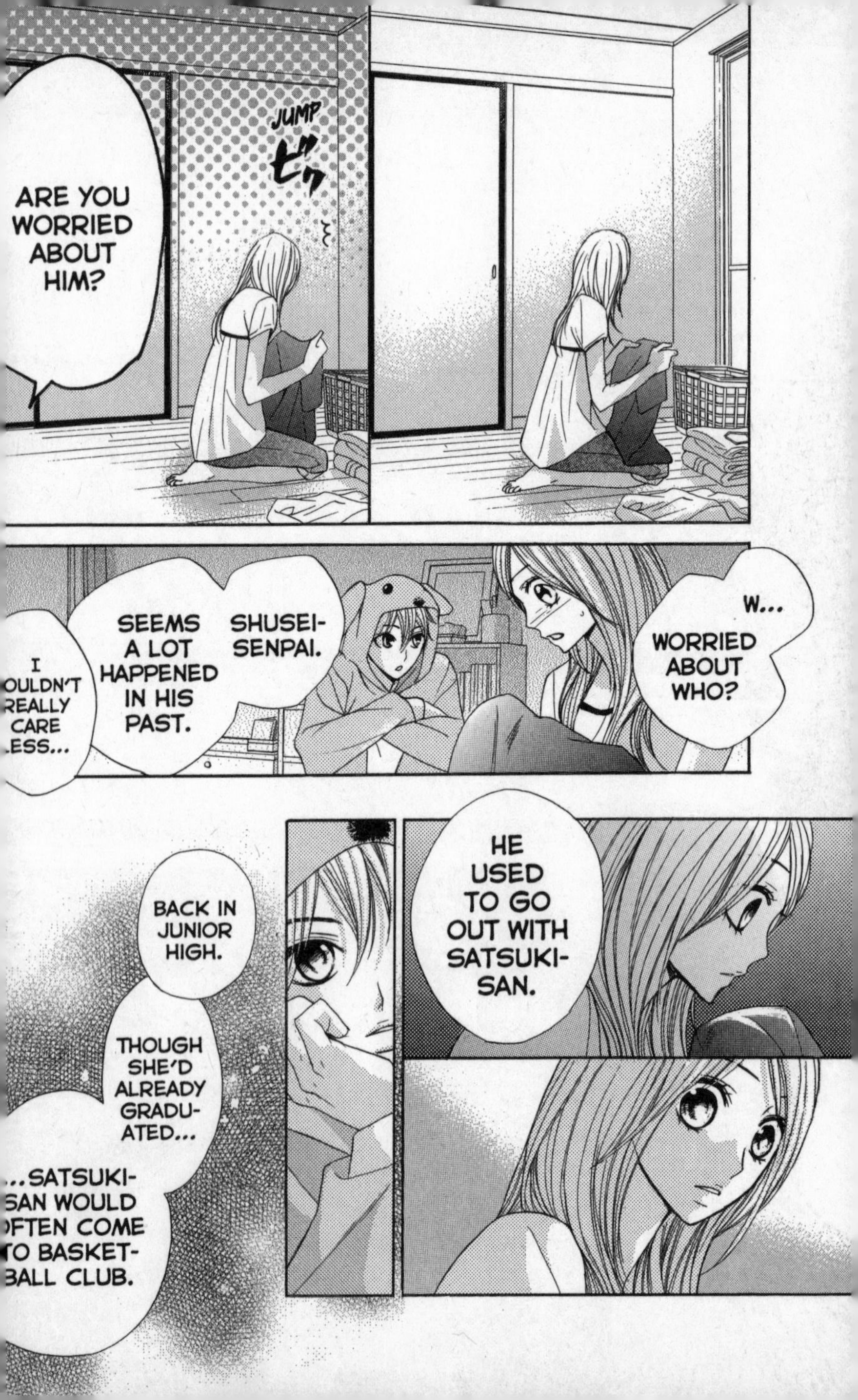
JUMP
ARE YOU WORRIED ABOUT HIM?
W... WORRIED ABOUT WHO?
SHUSEI-SENPAI.
SEEMS A LOT HAPPENED IN HIS PAST.
I OULDN'T REALLY CARE LESS...
HE USED TO GO OUT WITH SATSUKI-SAN.
BACK IN JUNIOR HIGH.
THOUGH SHE'D ALREADY GRADUATED...
...SATSUKI-SAN WOULD FTEN COME TO BASKET-BALL CLUB.

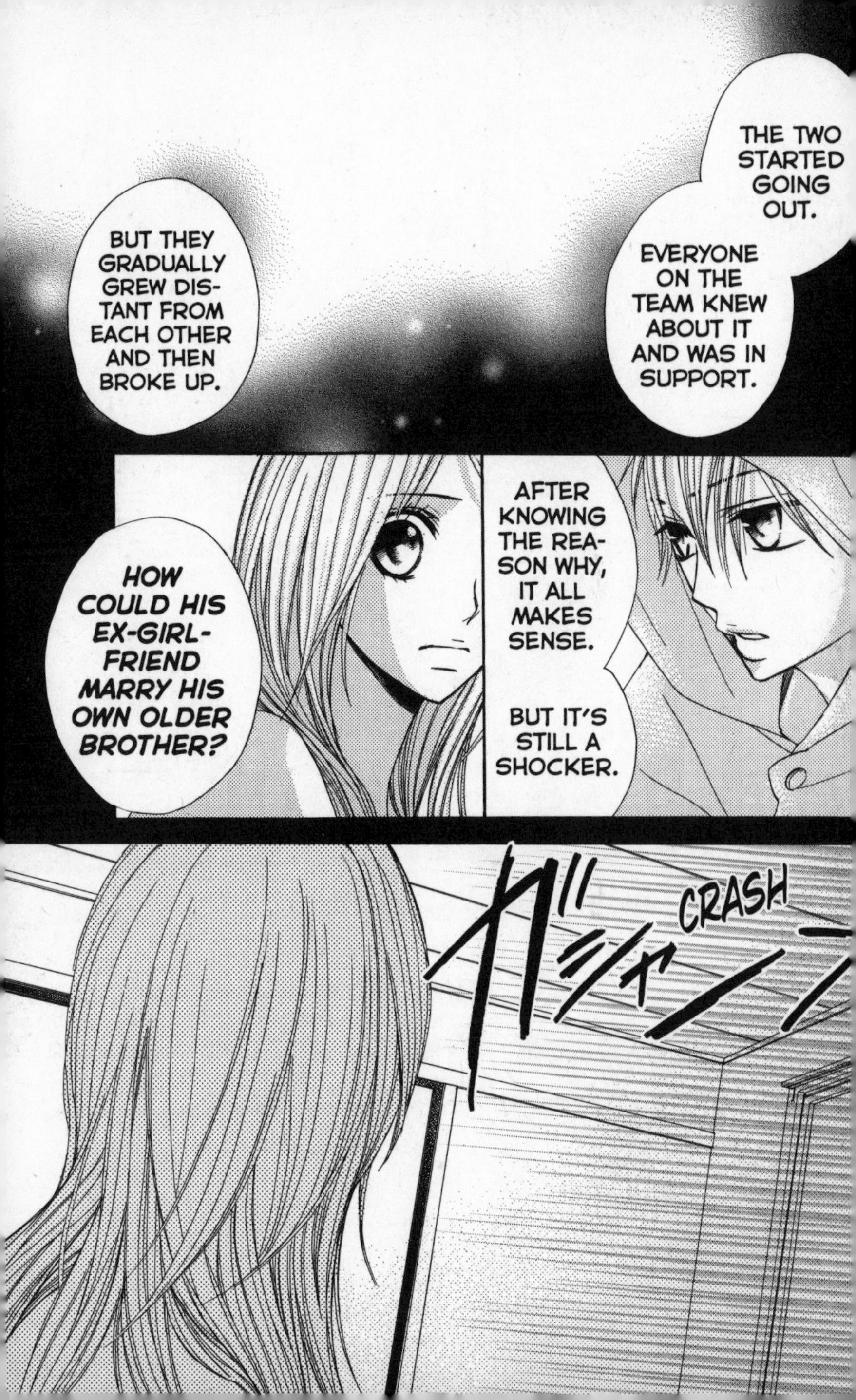
THE TWO STARTED GOING OUT.
EVERYONE ON THE TEAM KNEW ABOUT IT AND WAS IN SUPPORT.
BUT THEY GRADUALLY GREW DIS-TANT FROM EACH OTHER AND THEN BROKE UP.
AFTER KNOWING THE REA-SON WHY, IT ALL MAKES SENSE.
BUT IT'S STILL A SHOCKER.
HOW COULD HIS EX-GIRL-FRIEND MARRY HIS OWN OLDER BROTHER?
CRASH

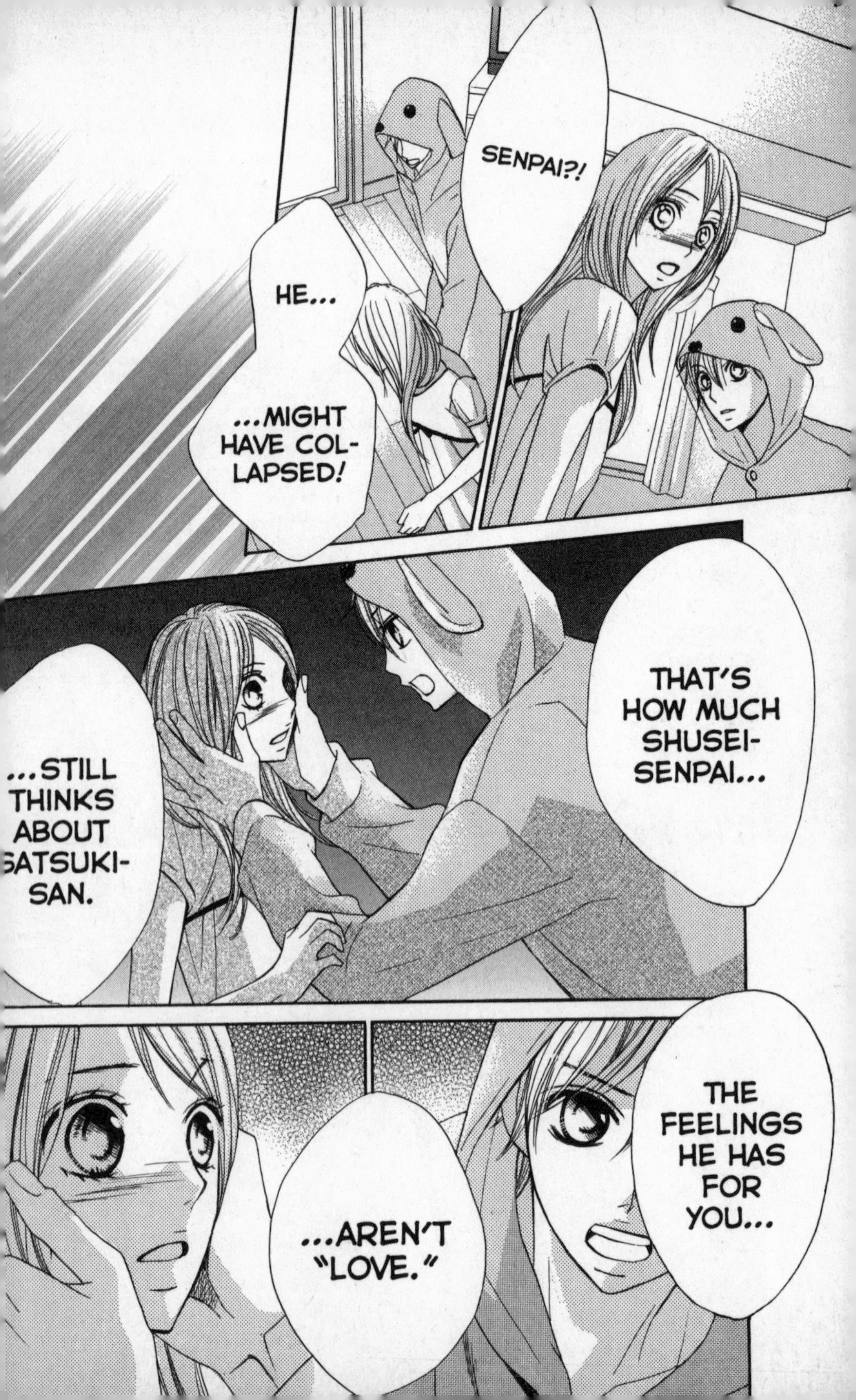
SENPAI?!
HE...
...MIGHT HAVE COL-LAPSED!
THAT'S HOW MUCH SHUSEI-SENPAI...
...STILL THINKS ABOUT SATSUKI-SAN.
THE FEELINGS HE HAS FOR YOU...
...AREN'T "LOVE."

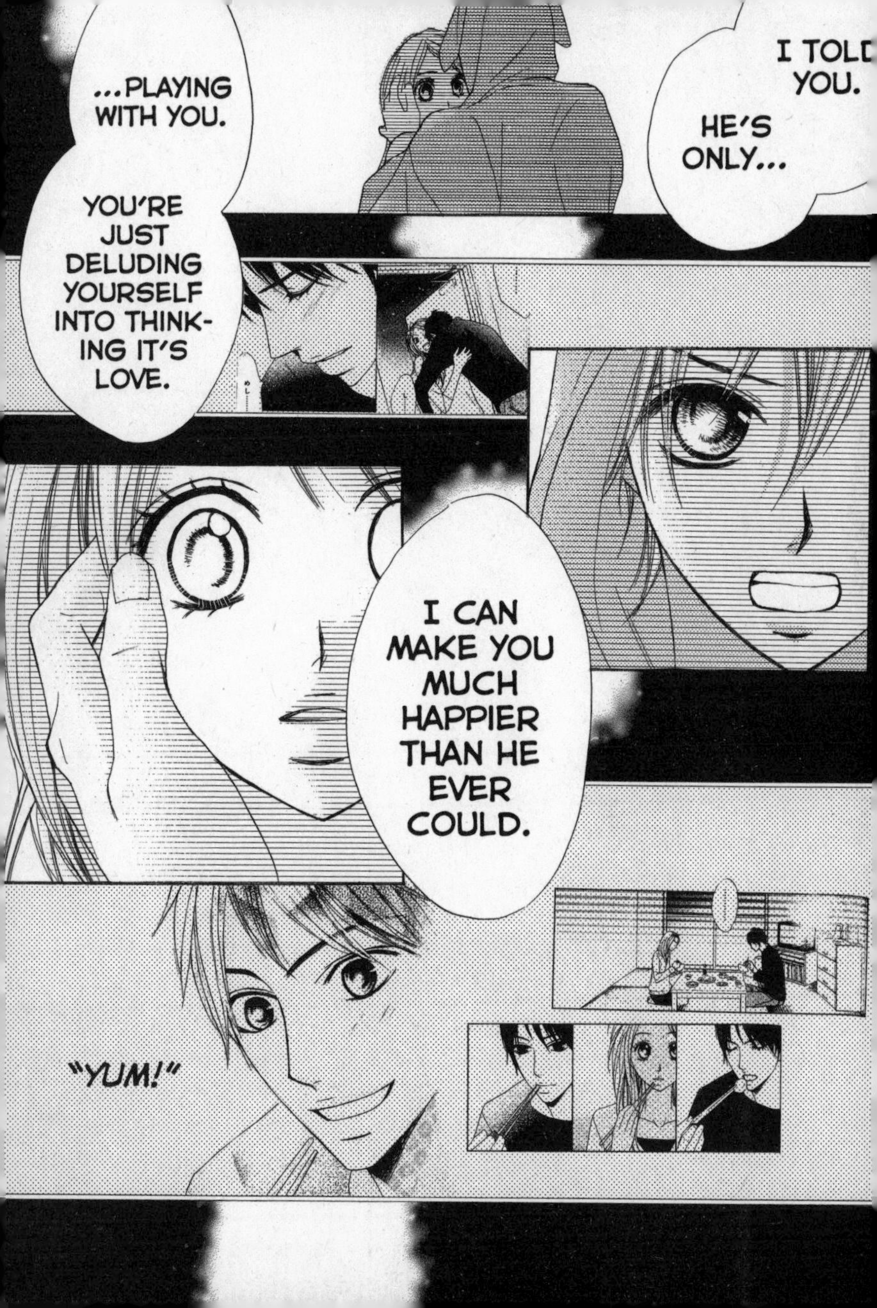
I TOLD YOU.
HE'S ONLY...
...PLAYING WITH YOU.
YOU'RE JUST DELUDING YOURSELF INTO THINKING IT'S LOVE.
I CAN MAKE YOU MUCH HAPPIER THAN HE EVER COULD.
"YUM!"

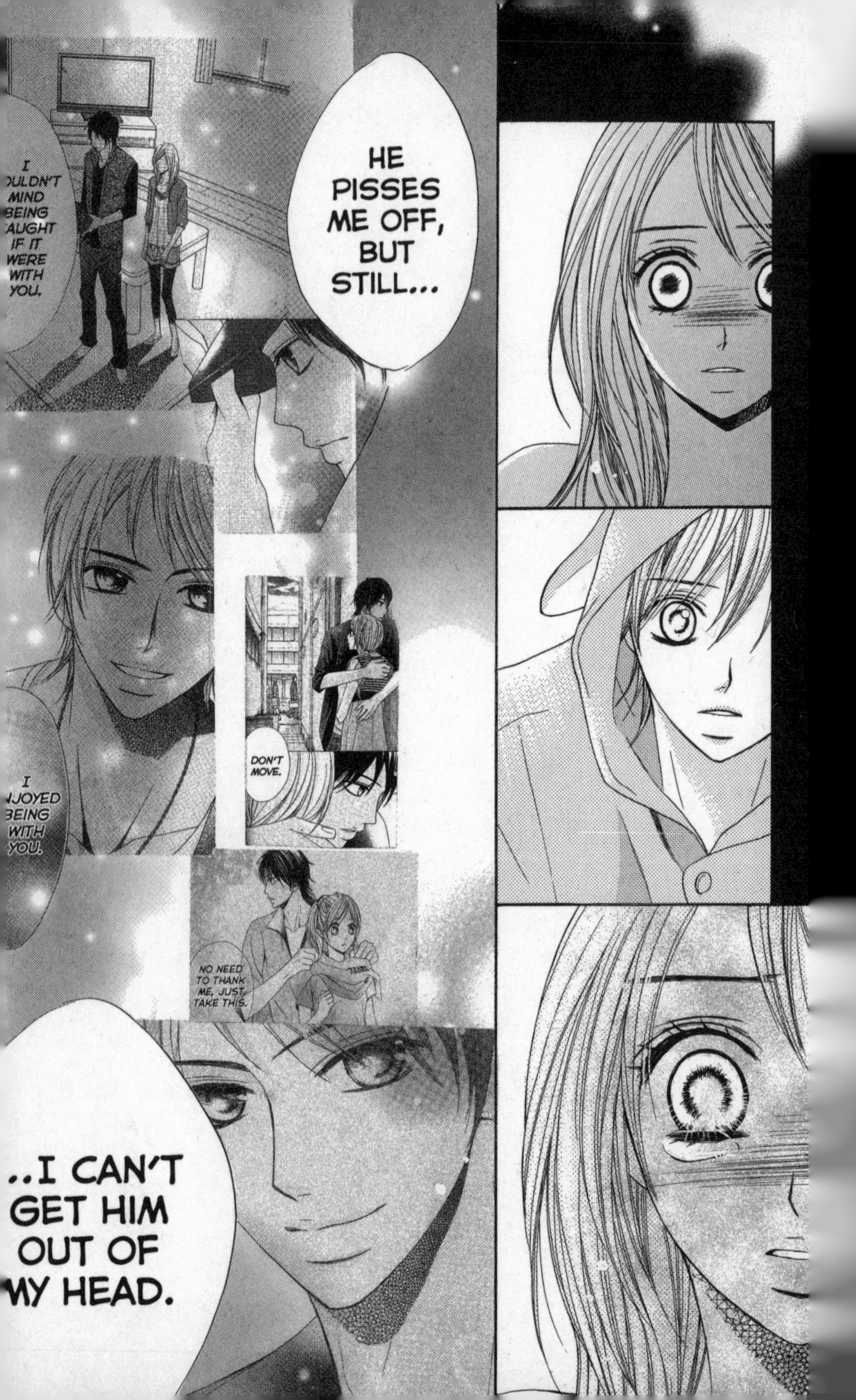
HE PISSES ME OFF, BUT STILL...
I OULDN'T MIND BEING AUGHT IF IT WERE WITH YOU.
DON'T MOVE.
I NJOYED BEING WITH YOU.
NO NEED TO THANK ME, JUST TAKE THIS.
..I CAN'T GET HIM OUT OF MY HEAD.

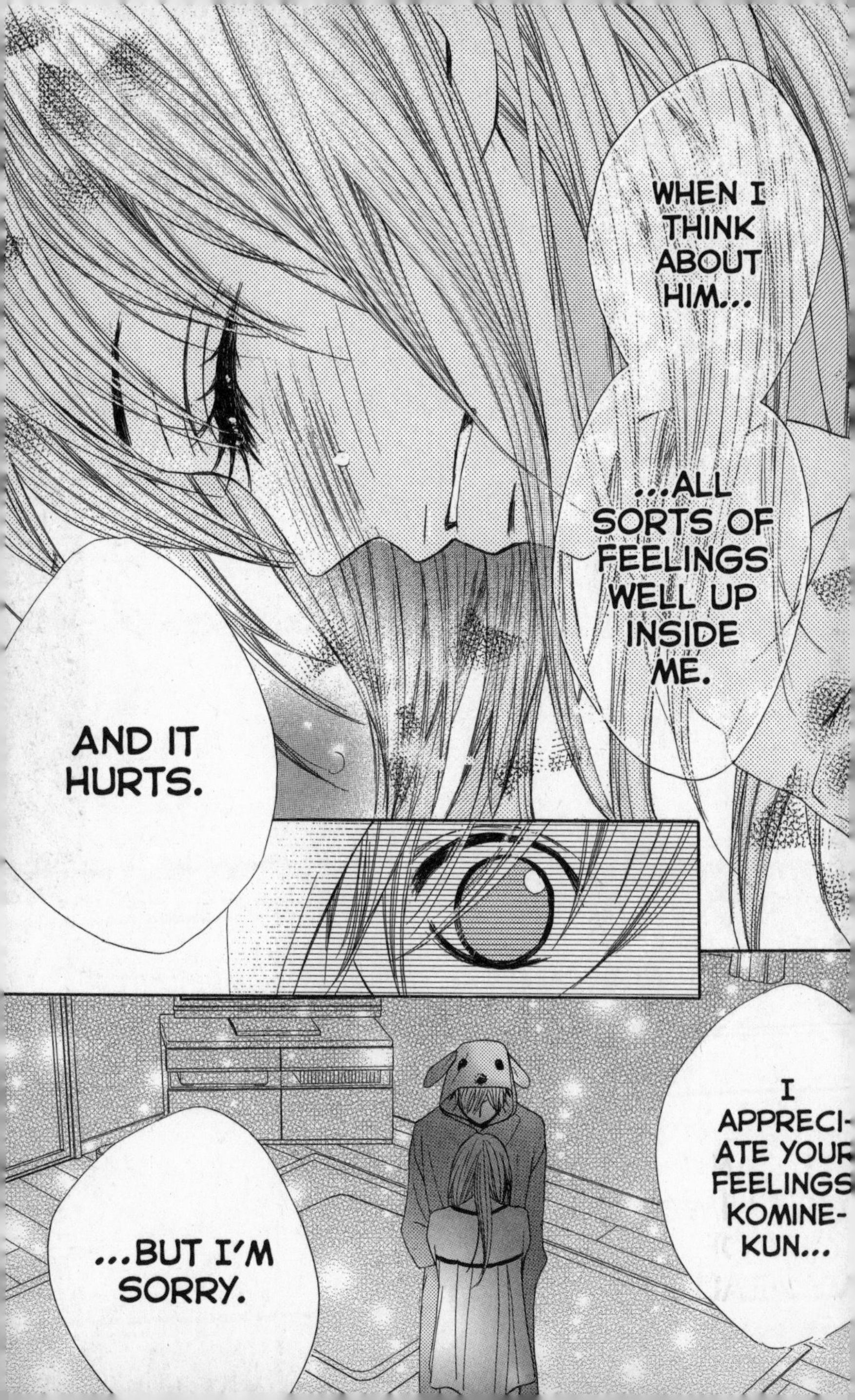
WHEN I THINK ABOUT HIM...
...ALL SORTS OF FEELINGS WELL UP INSIDE ME.
AND IT HURTS.
I APPRECIATE YOUR FEELINGS KOMINE-KUN...
...BUT I'M SORRY.

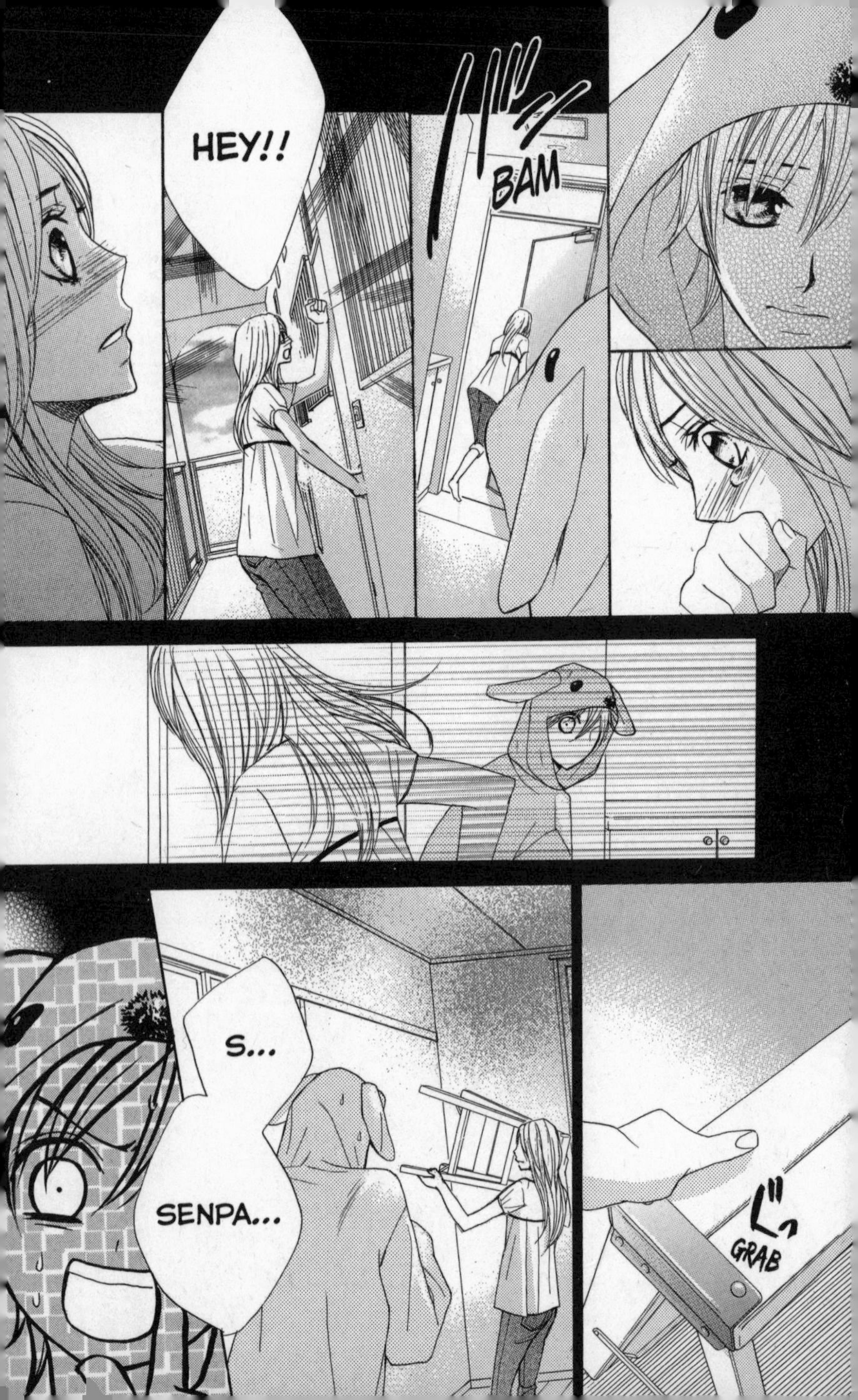
BAM
HEY!!
じっ GRAB
S...
SENPA...

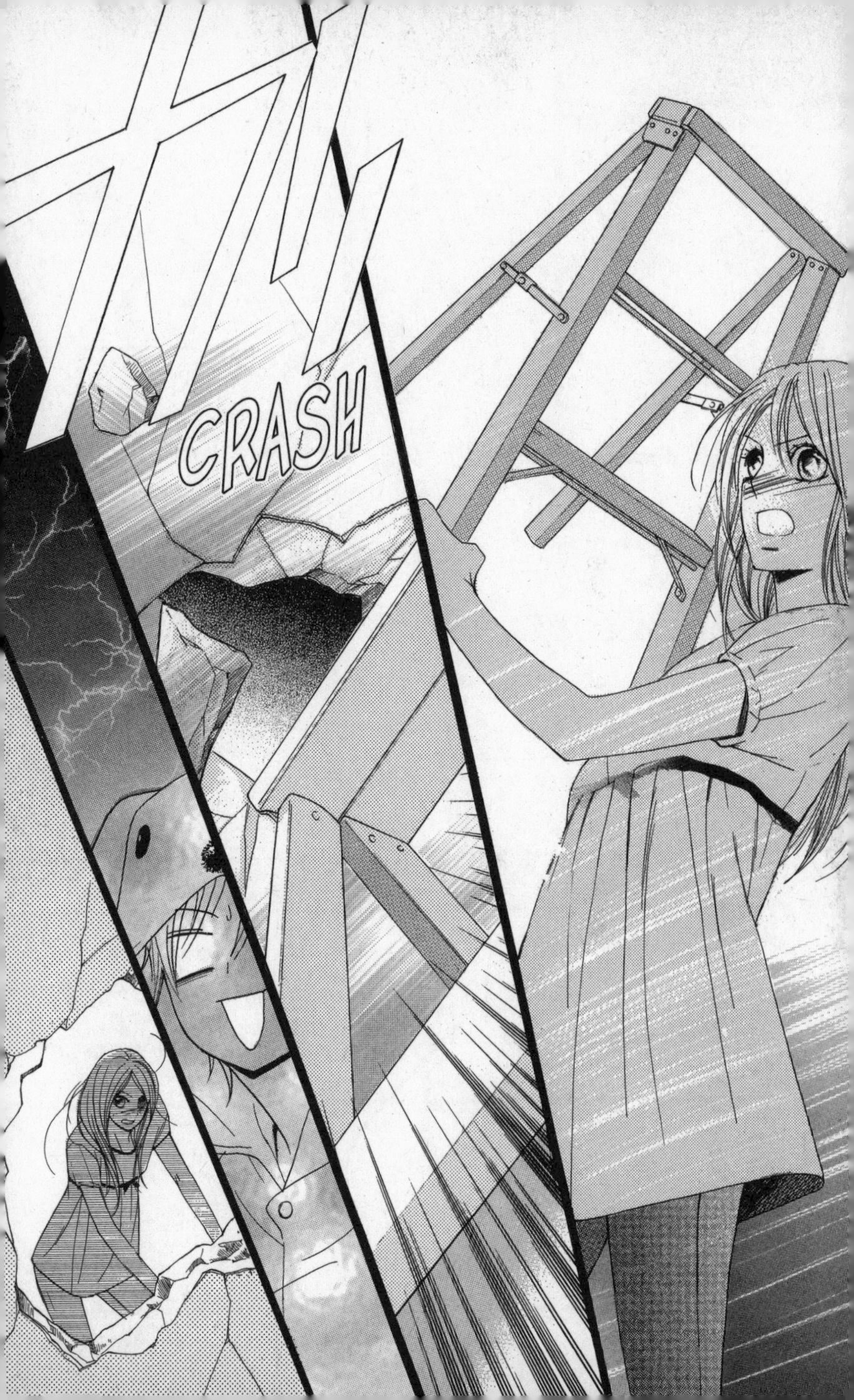
CRASH

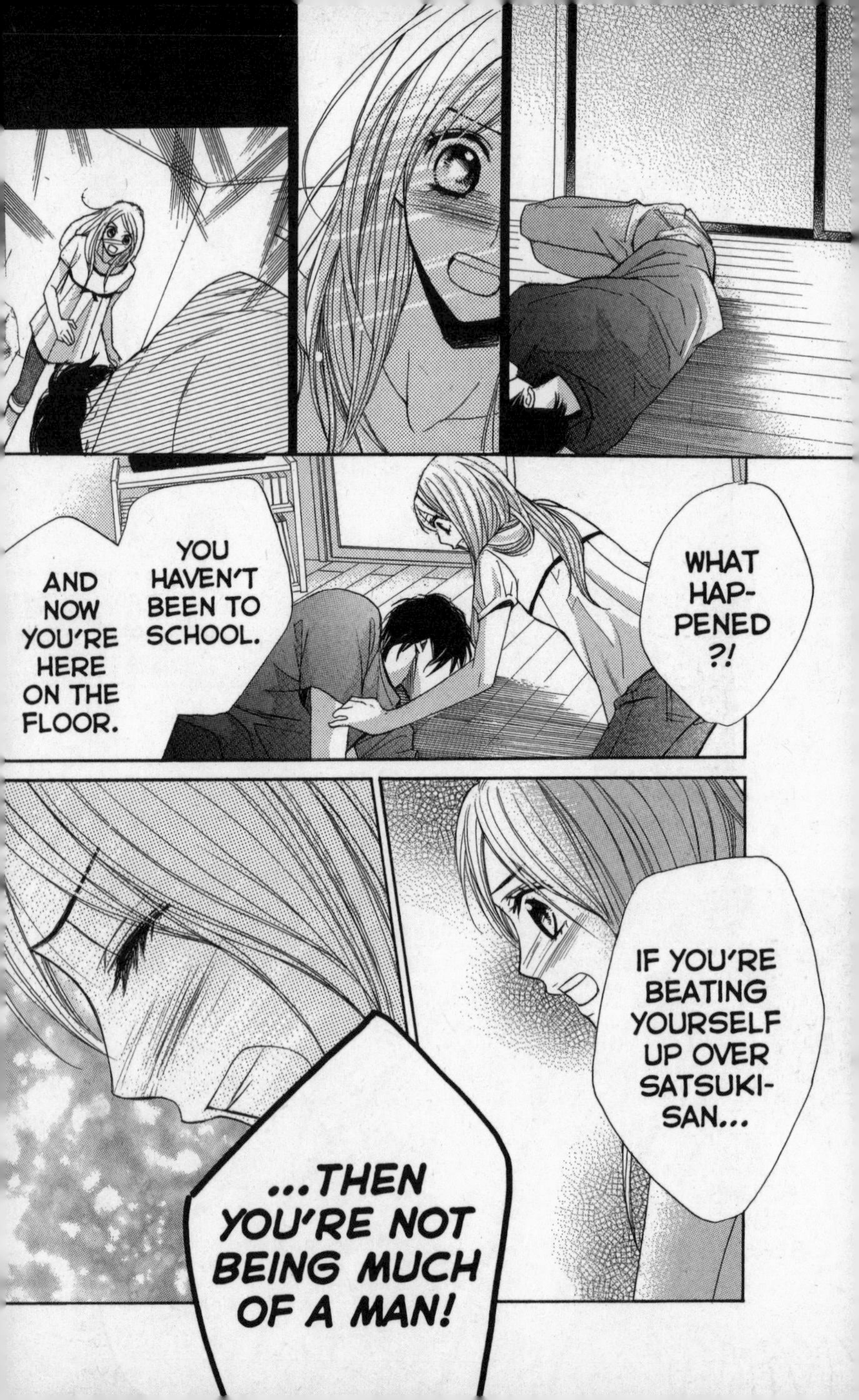
WHAT HAP-PENED?!
YOU HAVEN'T BEEN TO SCHOOL.
AND NOW YOU'RE HERE ON THE FLOOR.
IF YOU'RE BEATING YOURSELF UP OVER SATSUKI-SAN...
...THEN YOU'RE NOT BEING MUCH OF A MAN!

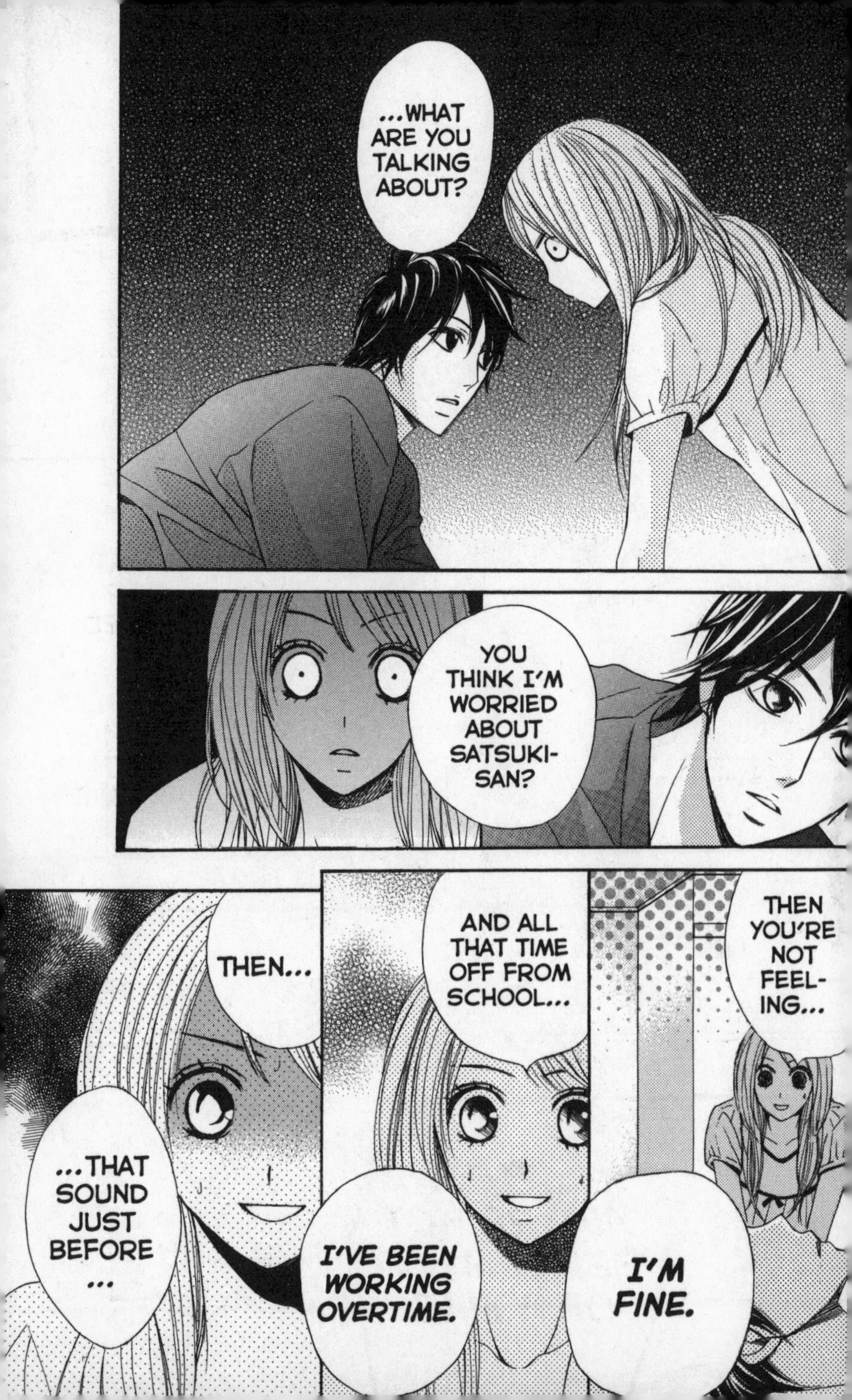
...WHAT ARE YOU TALKING ABOUT?
YOU THINK I'M WORRIED ABOUT SATSUKI-SAN?
THEN YOU'RE NOT FEEL-ING...
I'M FINE.
AND ALL THAT TIME OFF FROM SCHOOL...
I'VE BEEN WORKING OVERTIME.
THEN...
...THAT SOUND JUST BEFORE ...

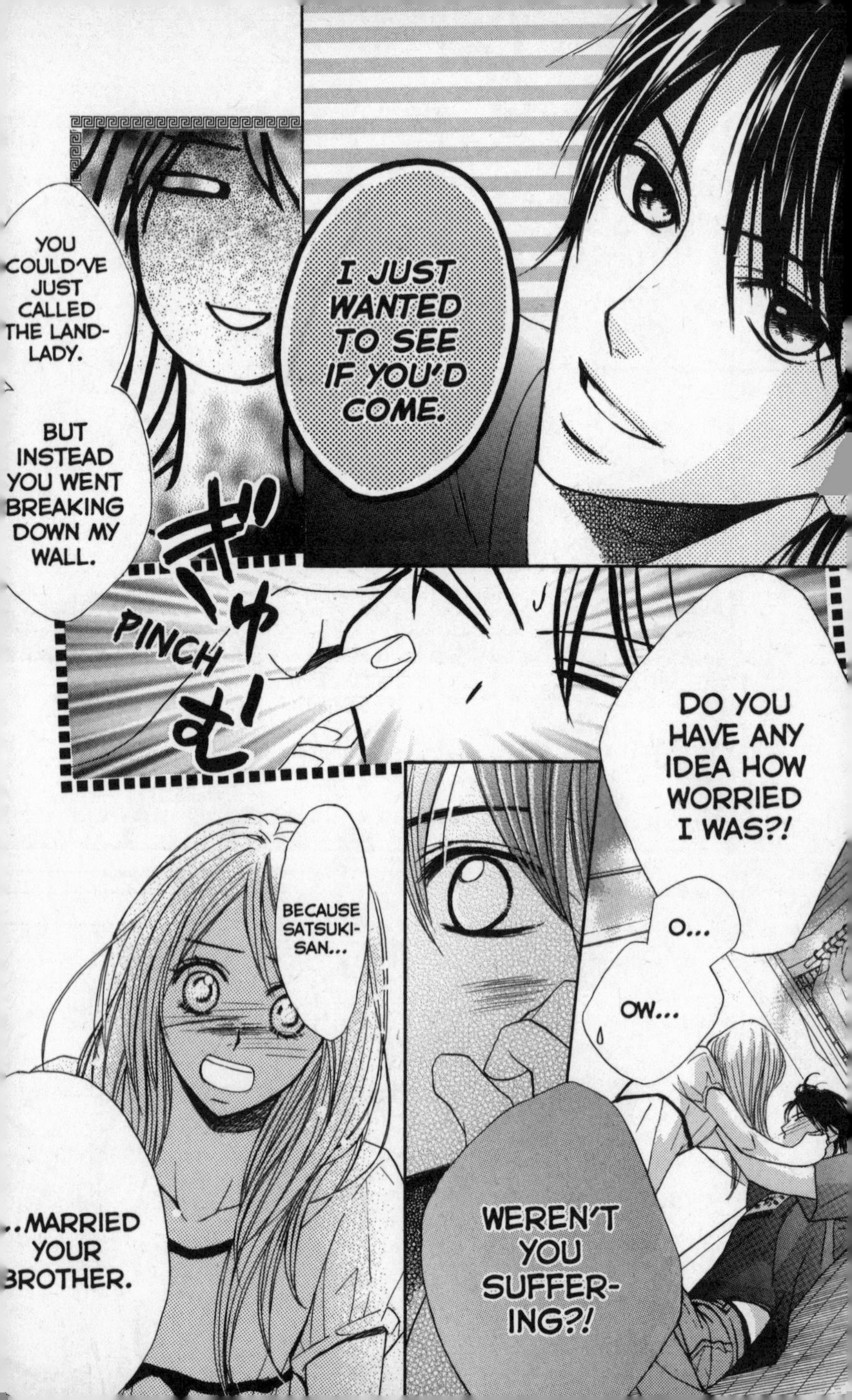
I JUST WANTED TO SEE IF YOU'D COME.
YOU COULD'VE JUST CALLED THE LAND-LADY.
BUT INSTEAD YOU WENT BREAKING DOWN MY WALL.
ぎゅーむ
PINCH
DO YOU HAVE ANY IDEA HOW WORRIED I WAS?!
O...
OW...
WEREN'T YOU SUFFER-ING?!
BECAUSE SATSUKI-SAN...
..MARRIED YOUR BROTHER.

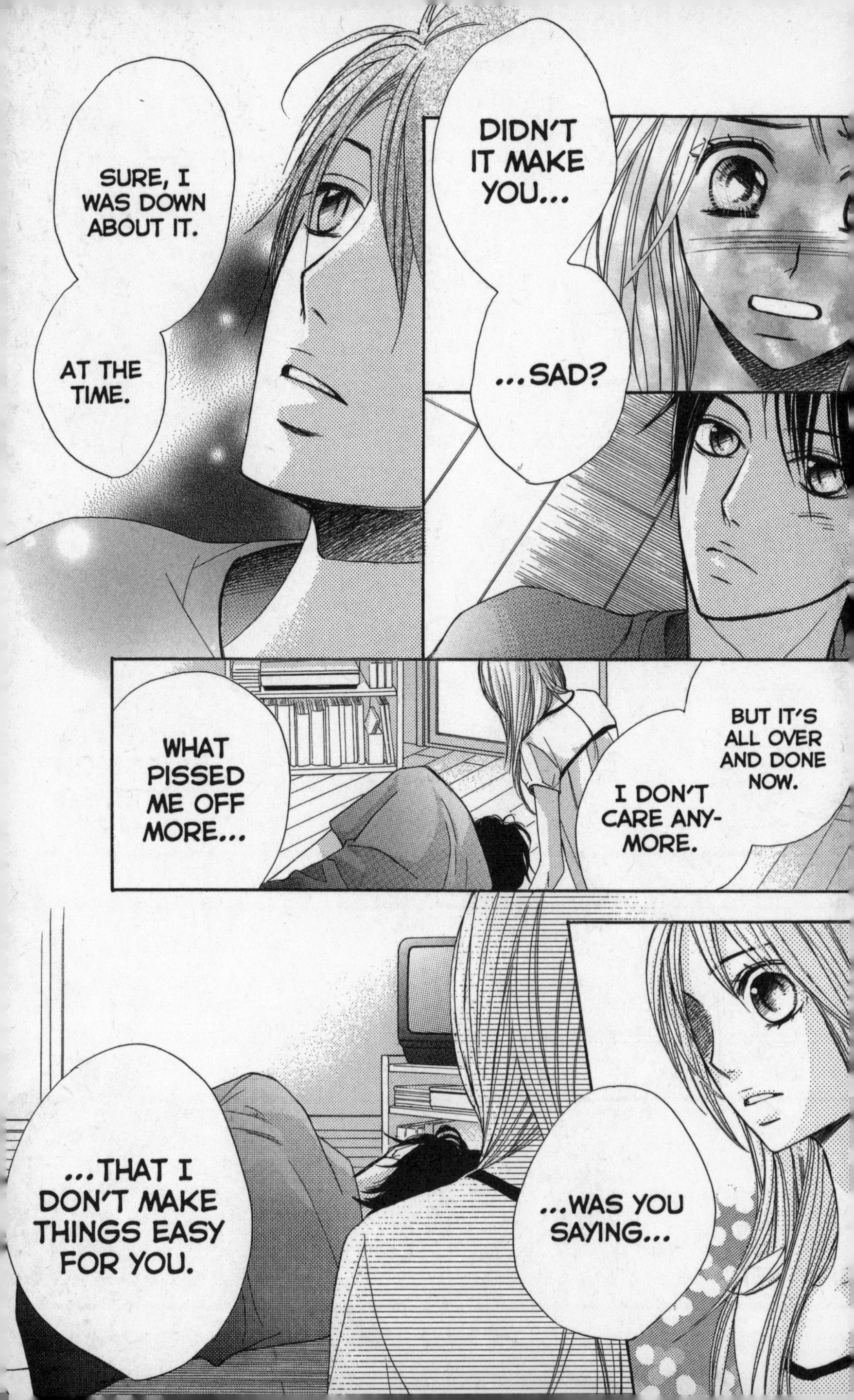
DIDN'T IT MAKE YOU...
...SAD?
SURE, I WAS DOWN ABOUT IT.
AT THE TIME.
BUT IT'S ALL OVER AND DONE NOW.
I DON'T CARE ANY-MORE.
WHAT PISSED ME OFF MORE...
...WAS YOU SAYING...
...THAT I DON'T MAKE THINGS EASY FOR YOU.

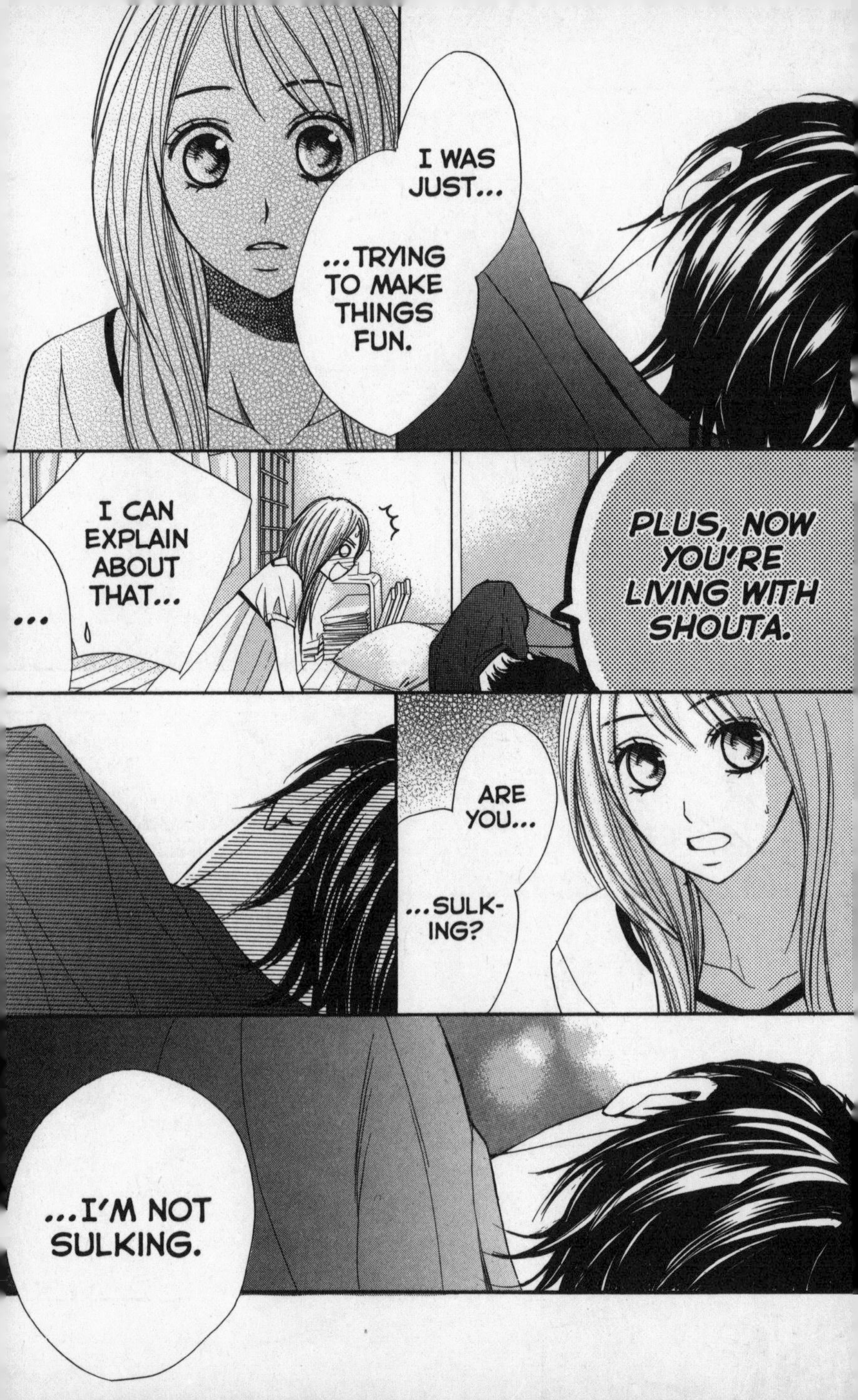
I WAS JUST...
...TRYING TO MAKE THINGS FUN.
PLUS, NOW YOU'RE LIVING WITH SHOUTA.
I CAN EXPLAIN ABOUT THAT...
...
ARE YOU...
...SULK-ING?
...I'M NOT SULKING.

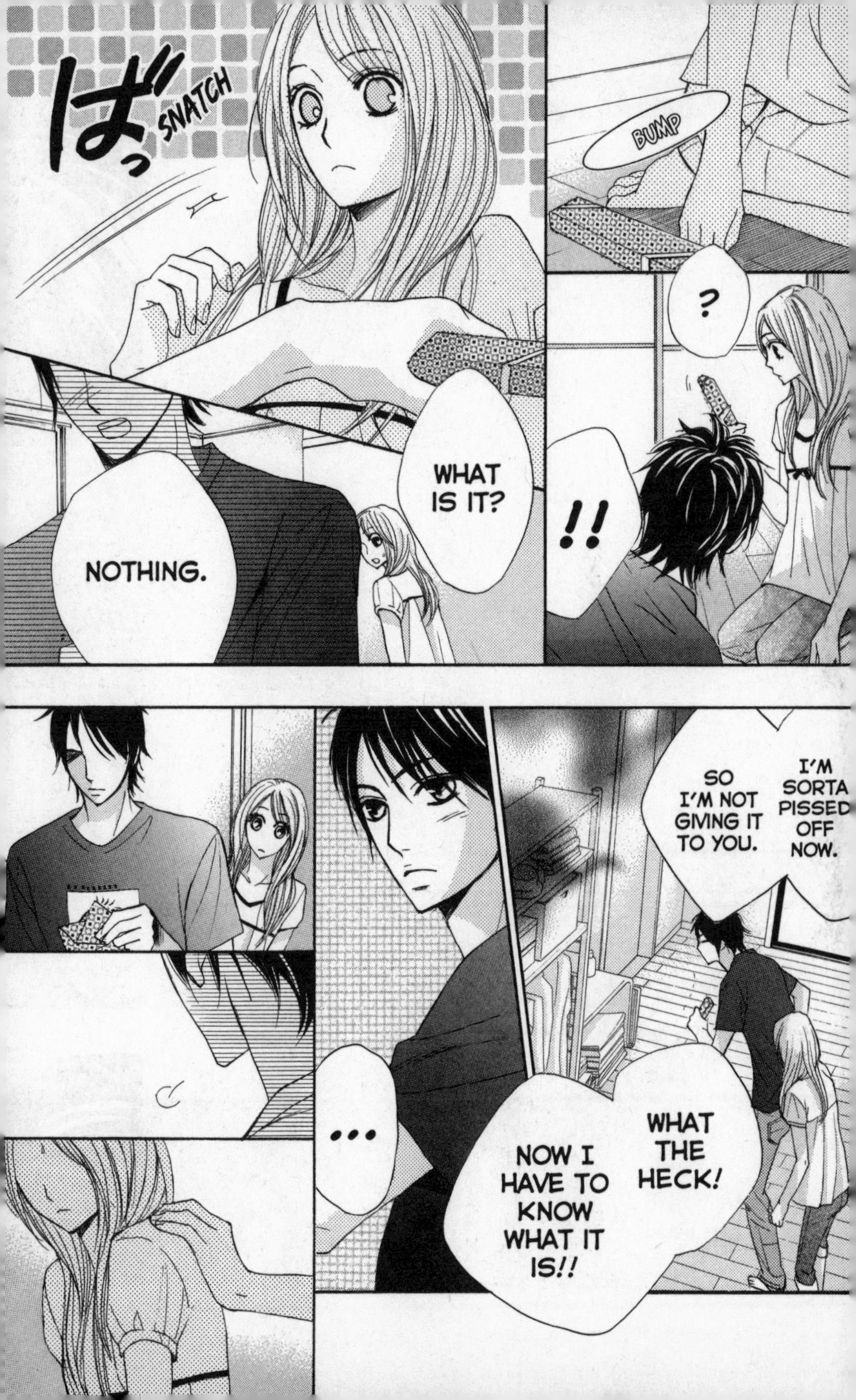
BUMP
?
!!
ばっ
SNATCH
WHAT IS IT?
NOTHING.
I'M SORTA PISSED OFF NOW.
SO I'M NOT GIVING IT TO YOU.
WHAT THE HECK!
NOW I HAVE TO KNOW WHAT IT IS!!
...

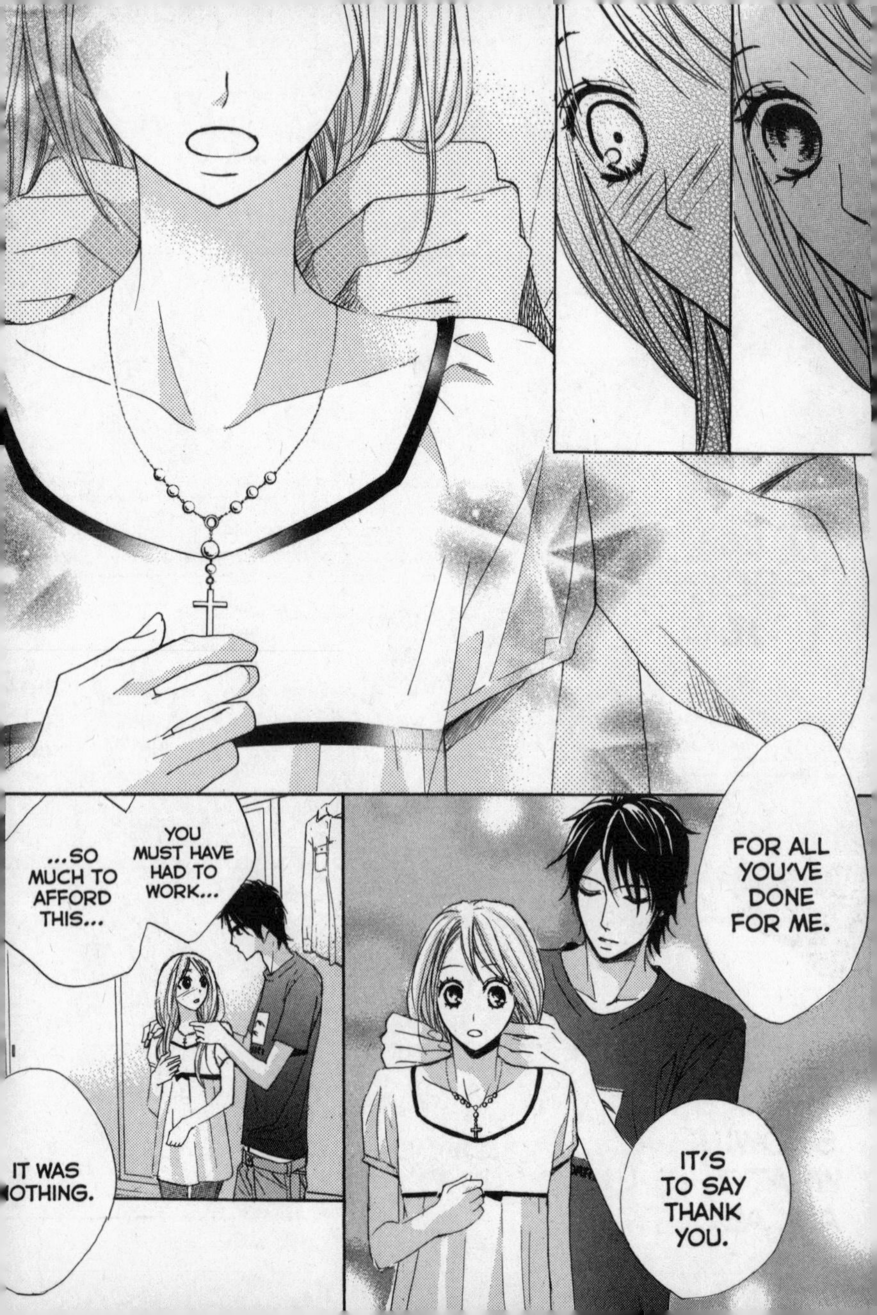
FOR ALL YOU'VE DONE FOR ME.
IT'S TO SAY THANK YOU.
YOU MUST HAVE HAD TO WORK...
...SO MUCH TO AFFORD THIS...
IT WAS OTHING.

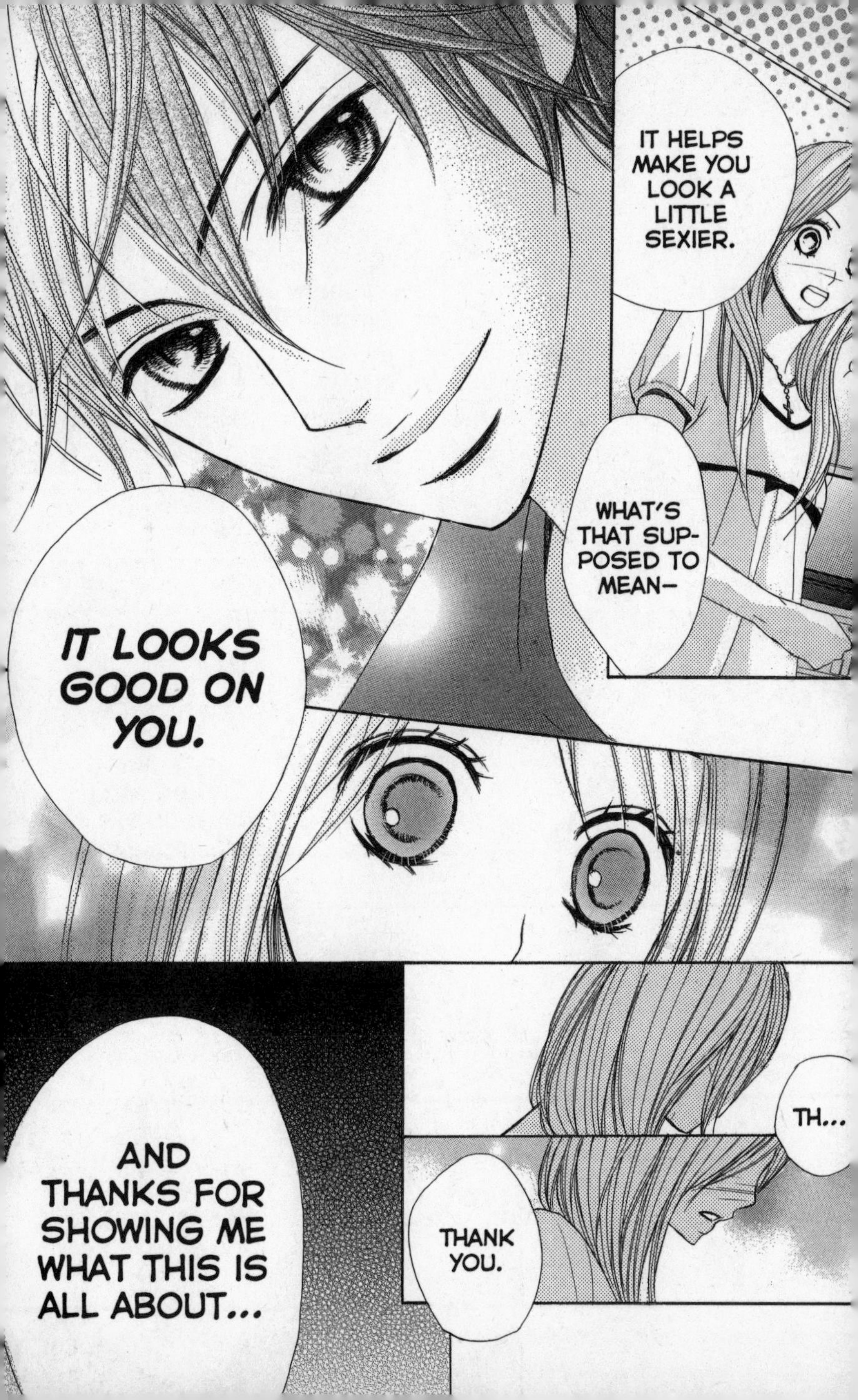
IT HELPS MAKE YOU LOOK A LITTLE SEXIER.
WHAT'S THAT SUP-POSED TO MEAN—
IT LOOKS GOOD ON YOU.
TH...
THANK YOU.
AND THANKS FOR SHOWING ME WHAT THIS IS ALL ABOUT...

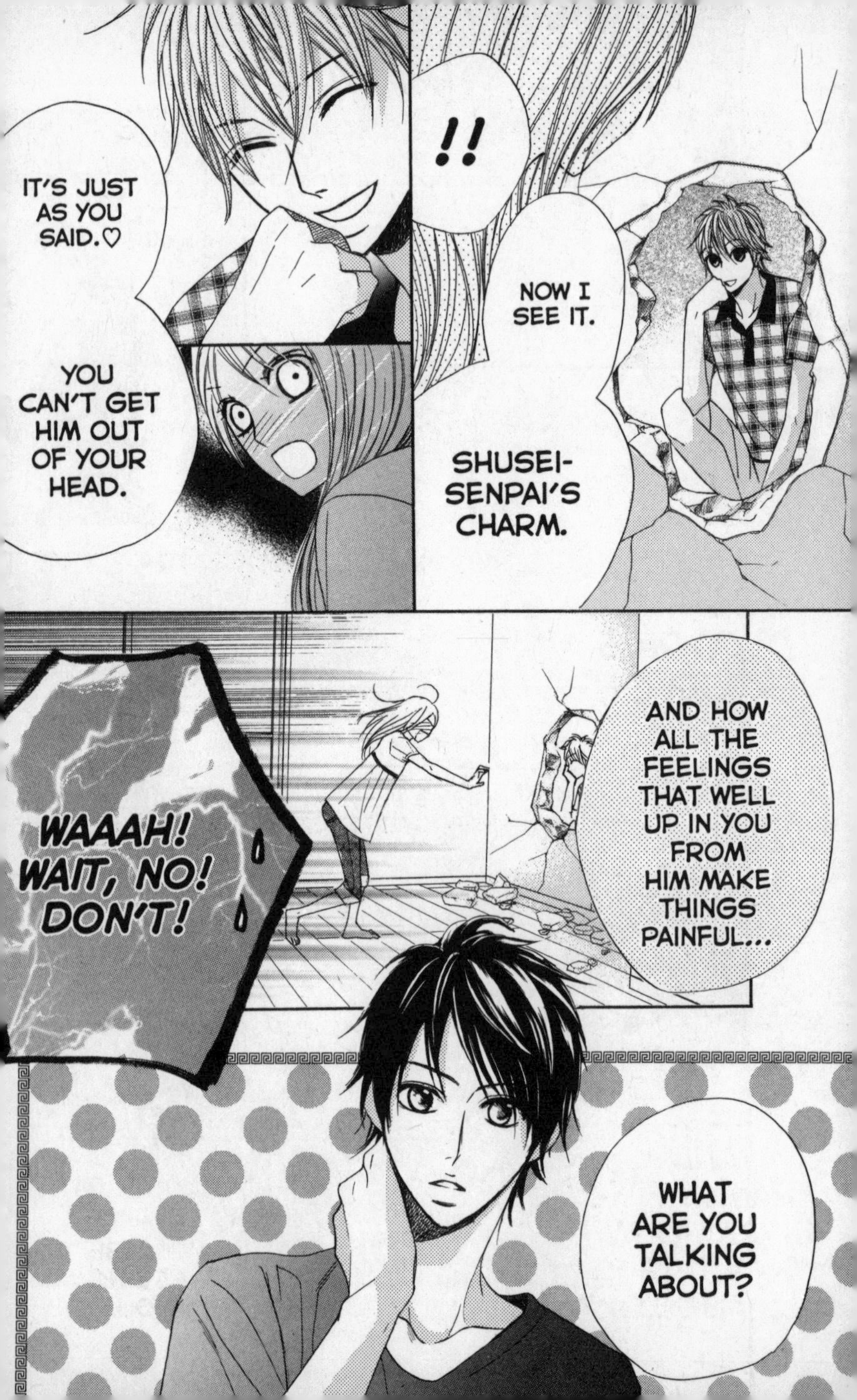
!!
NOW I SEE IT.
SHUSEI-SENPAI'S CHARM.
IT'S JUST AS YOU SAID.♡
YOU CAN'T GET HIM OUT OF YOUR HEAD.
AND HOW ALL THE FEELINGS THAT WELL UP IN YOU FROM HIM MAKE THINGS PAINFUL...
WAAAH! WAIT, NO! DON'T!
WHAT ARE YOU TALKING ABOUT?

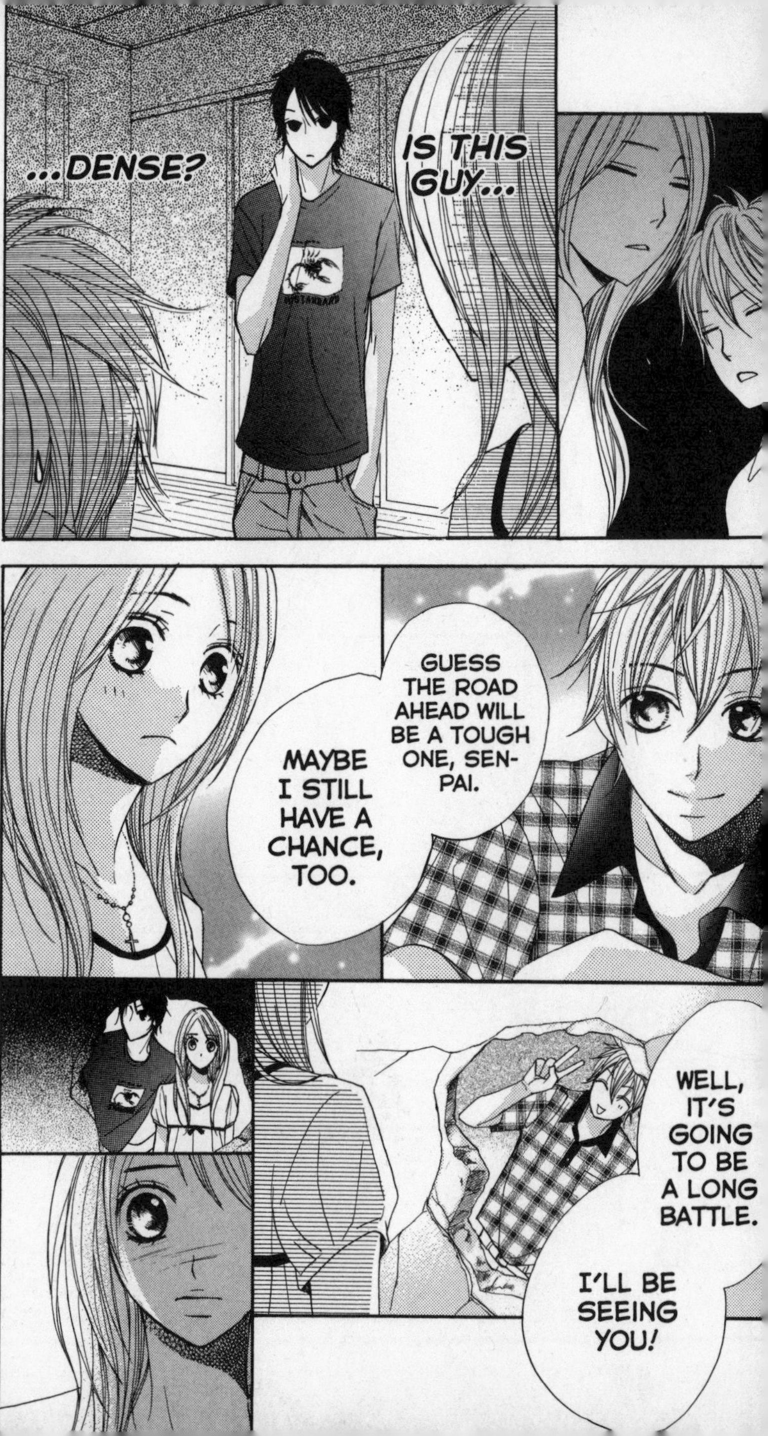
IS THIS GUY...
...DENSE?
GUESS THE ROAD AHEAD WILL BE A TOUGH ONE, SEN-PAI.
MAYBE I STILL HAVE A CHANCE, TOO.
WELL, IT'S GOING TO BE A LONG BATTLE.
I'LL BE SEEING YOU!

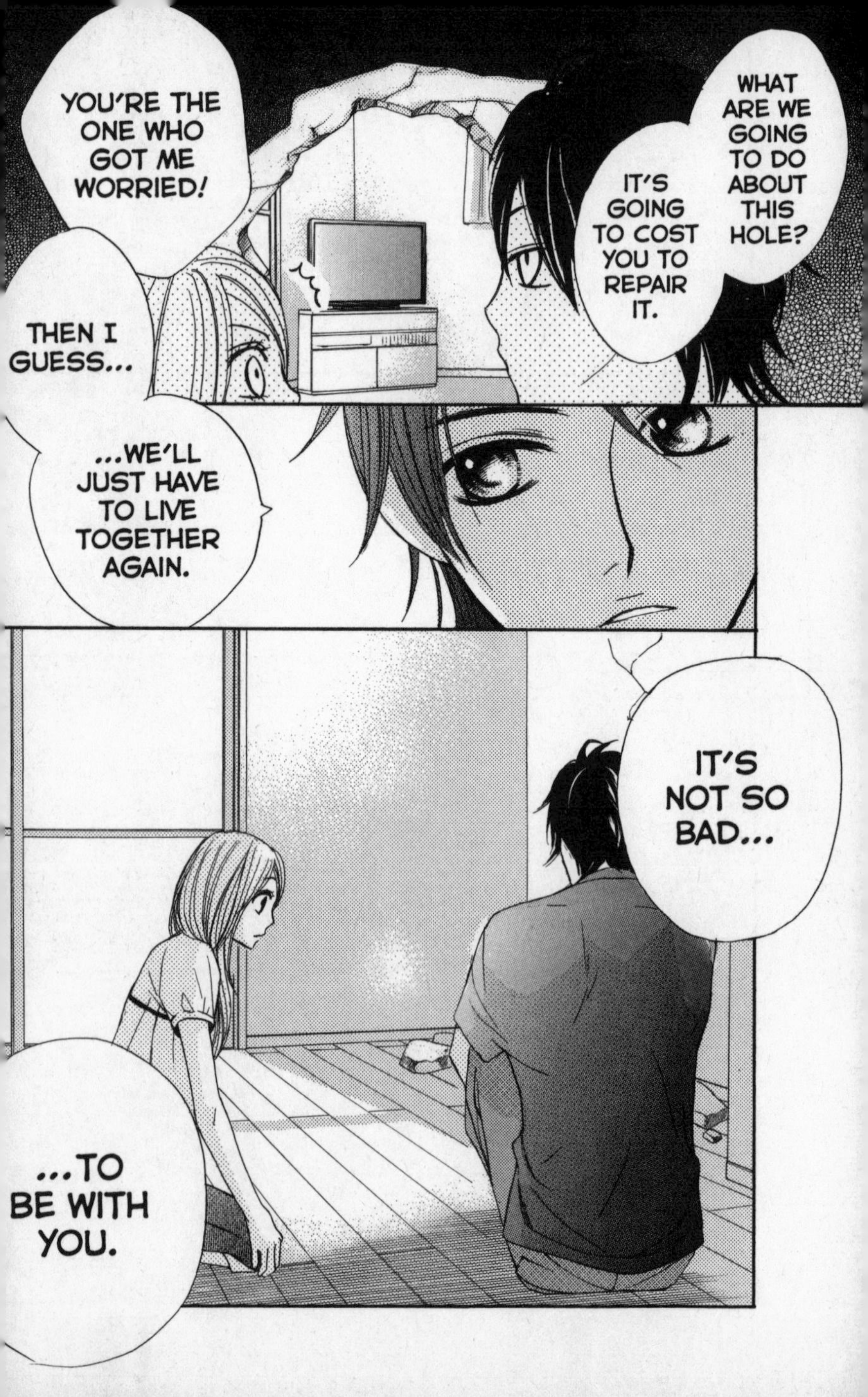
WHAT ARE WE GOING TO DO ABOUT THIS HOLE?
IT'S GOING TO COST YOU TO REPAIR IT.
YOU'RE THE ONE WHO GOT ME WORRIED!
THEN I GUESS...
...WE'LL JUST HAVE TO LIVE TOGETHER AGAIN.
IT'S NOT SO BAD...
...TO BE WITH YOU.

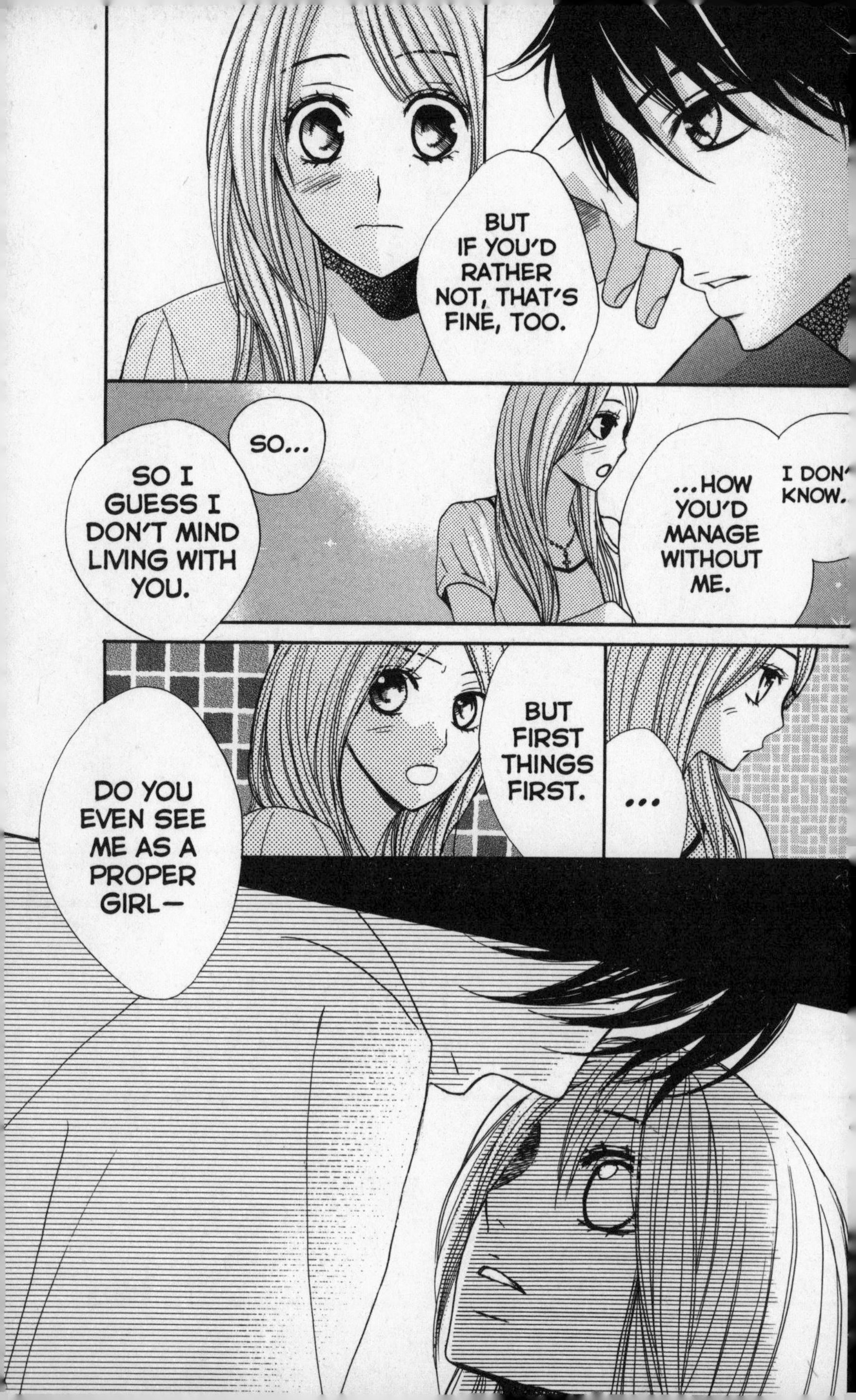
BUT IF YOU'D RATHER NOT, THAT'S FINE, TOO.
I DON' KNOW.
...HOW YOU'D MANAGE WITHOUT ME.
SO...
SO I GUESS I DON'T MIND LIVING WITH YOU.
...
BUT FIRST THINGS FIRST.
DO YOU EVEN SEE ME AS A PROPER GIRL—

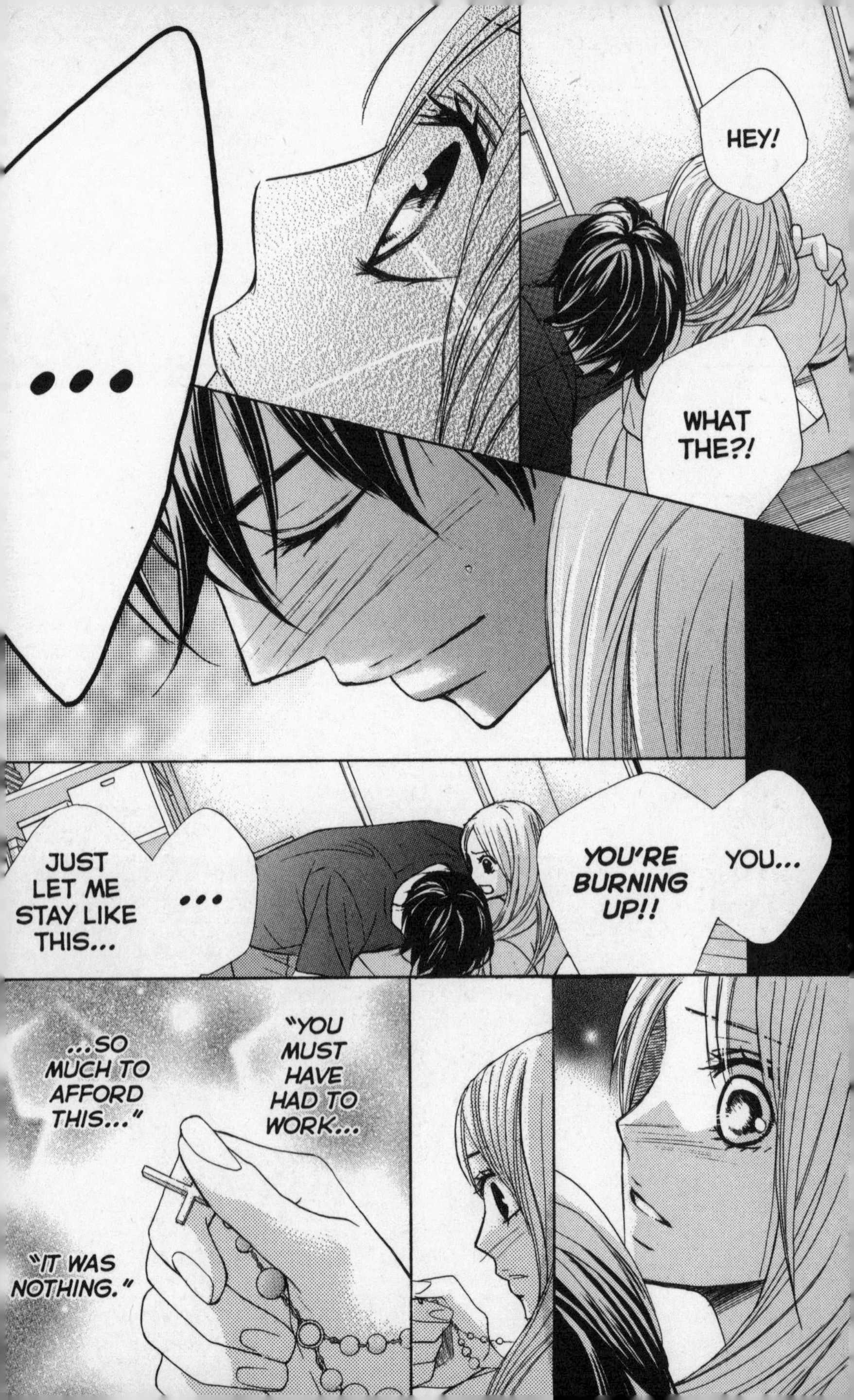
HEY!
WHAT THE?!
...
YOU...
YOU'RE BURNING UP!!
...
JUST LET ME STAY LIKE THIS...
"YOU MUST HAVE HAD TO WORK...
...SO MUCH TO AFFORD THIS..."
"IT WAS NOTHING."

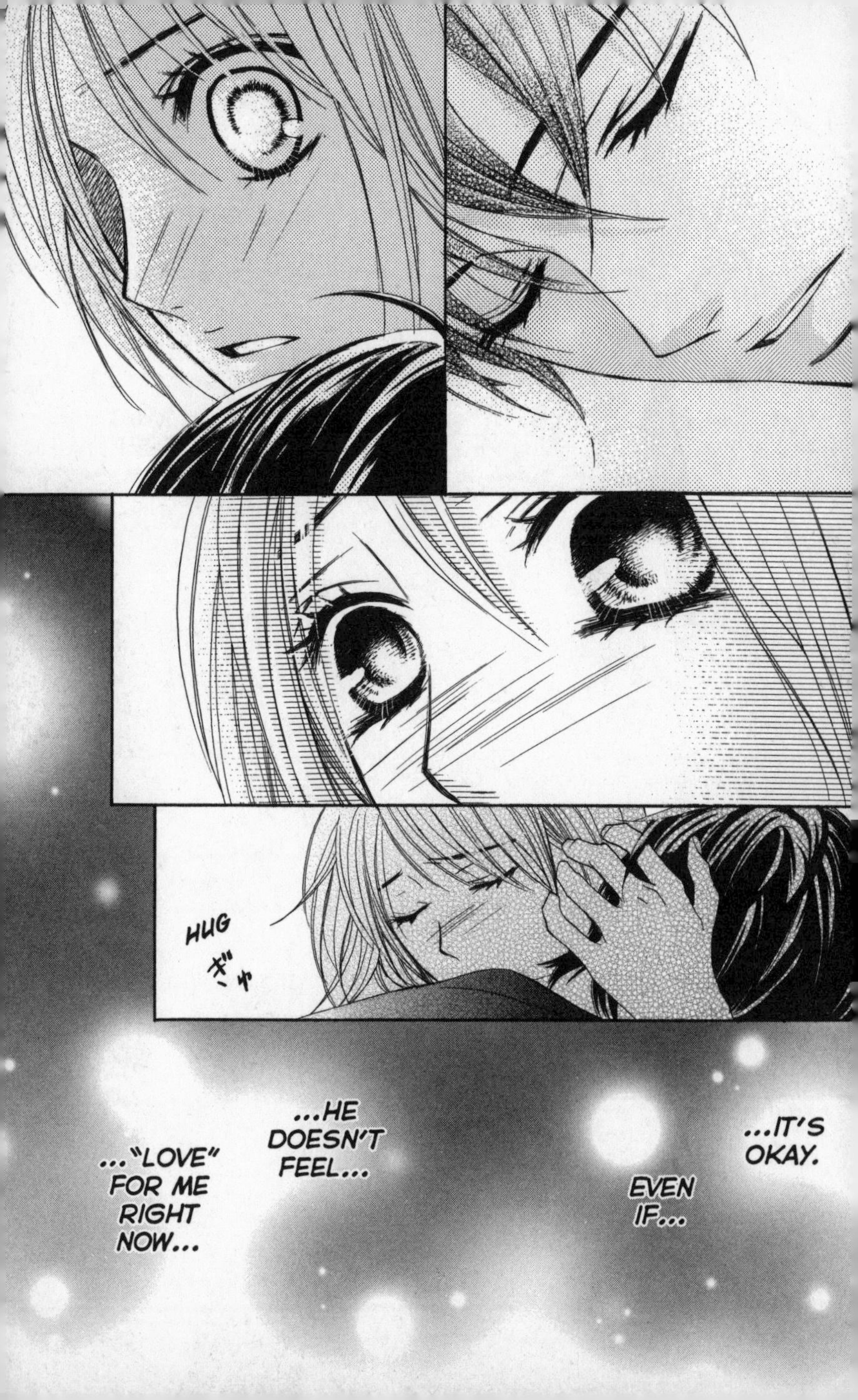
HUG
ぎゅ
...IT'S OKAY.
EVEN IF...
...HE DOESN'T FEEL...
..."LOVE" FOR ME RIGHT NOW...

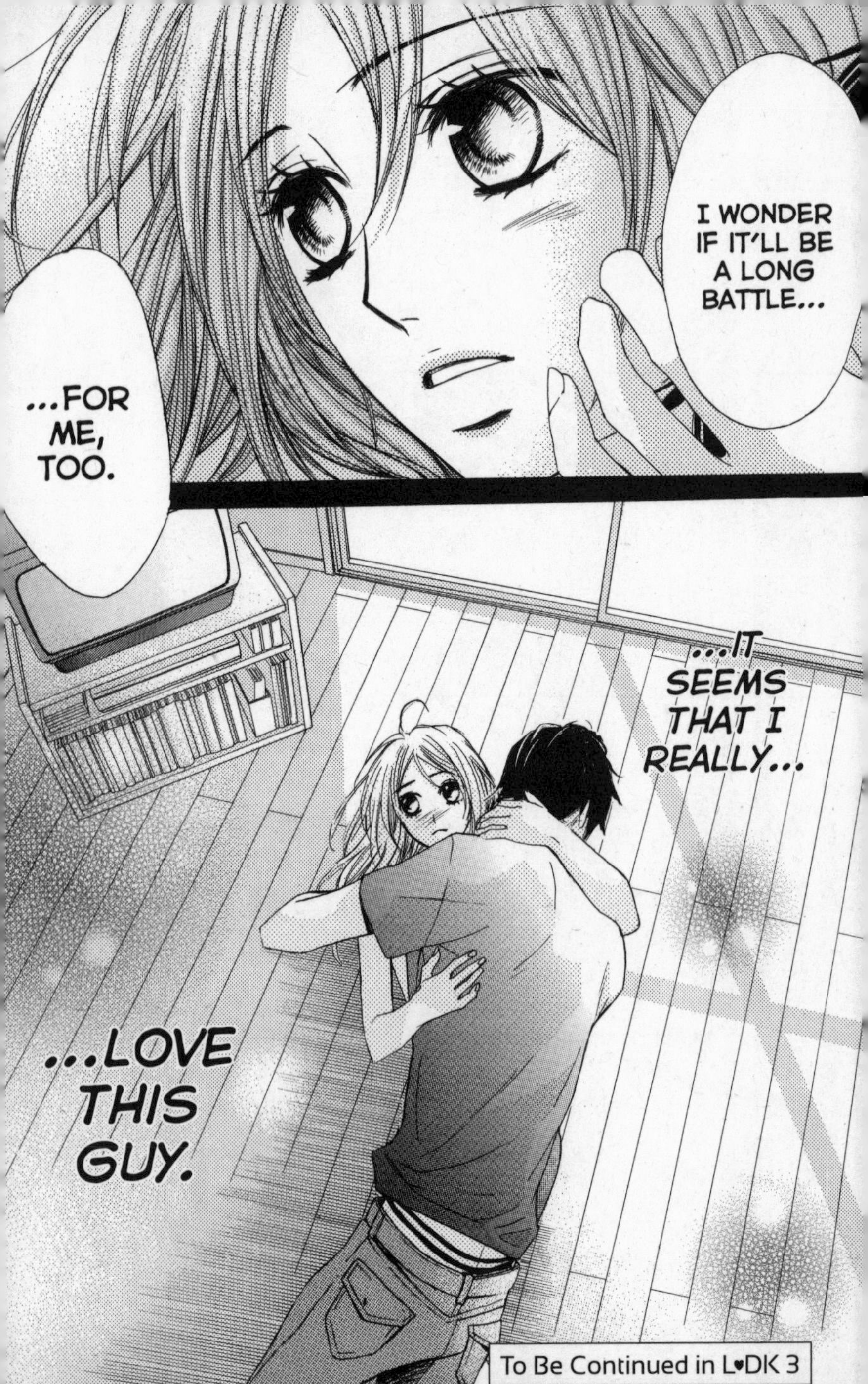
I WONDER IF IT'LL BE A LONG BATTLE...
...FOR ME, TOO.
...IT SEEMS THAT I REALLY...
...LOVE THIS GUY.
To Be Continued in L♥DK 3

L♥DK

Hello, how are you all doing? This is Ayu Watanabe. Thank you very much for picking up Volume 2 of L♥DK. I'm glad we got to meet again. Heh heh heh...

Really though, I can't believe how little of 2009 we have left. Before I knew it, summer had already passed me by. It still feels like I'm back in March, though. Ugh, I can't win. I haven't updated my wardrobe this year at all! Now I'm three seasons behind the fashion! I guess you could call it being frugal!! I really do like to dress myself up and go out every once in a while, though. After all, I am a ♦girl♦ ♥ This is where you're supposed to laugh. But anyway, I'm always just barely getting by in my life so the idea of even going out for a whole day is impossible... That's why I owe so much to my friends who never give up on me and are always watching out for me. I really would like to cherish my friends. These feelings run deep.

Being a bona fide shut-in, when I have any free time, I enjoy listening to the radio and playing on my♦DS♦. I truly live an indoor life. A game I'm really into these days is "Dragon Quest 9." The worldview of Dragon Quest really relaxes me. Right before I go to bed, I work hard on leveling up, and before I know it, I've fallen asleep. It's a great sleeping aid.

Also, as usual, I buy and try out café au lait whenever I see it.
I bet I could do café au lait tastings all day. Anyone care to challenge me to it? Sorry for my constant ramblings. I just never have enough things to talk about. Sorry. But anyway, I'm already jumping right into volume 3 of "L♥DK"!! Thank you, everyone! There are already two chapters in the magazine, so please do check it out. ♥ I'm really going to work hard to keep straight and narrow on my noble path. ♪ Wow, it really is hard to depict ordinary things in a funny light. But I hope to keep making progress. Well then, see you in the next volume!

special thanks

K.Hamano
N.Imai
S.Sato

my family
my friends

M.Morita
M.Horiuchi

AND YOU

Ayu Watanabe
Oct.2009

Translation Notes

Radishes, page 85
Japanese radishes (*daikon* in Japanese) have a greater presence as a main ingredient in Japanese cooking than radishes do in standard American cuisine. This may be one reason why Aoi displays a sense of urgency in buying *daikon* before the market closes.

Cultural festival, page 88
Most Japanese schools hold an annual event called the "cultural festival" during which students display their artistic and creative achievements. These events are typically open to the public, and they are a great opportunity for prospective students to see what the work and atmosphere at the school will be like.

Fighting Spirit Infusion, page 132
This is a phrase that is attributed to perhaps one of the most well-known Japanese wrestlers, Antonio Inoki. When giving speeches or making appearances, Mr. Inoki often gives a performance where he infuses or injects volunteers from the audience with fighting spirit by placing a finger on the volunteer's midsection for a moment and then slapping their face. The volunteer is then invigorated and screams their thanks to Mr. Inoki. In the scene where this is used by Aoi, she is giving Shouta a hard slap on the back to give him fighting spirit so that he can cheer up and pass the entrance exams.

Entrance exams, page 132
In Japan, entrance exams are common for high schools and universities. The tests are often very difficult and much of the last year of junior high school and high school are devoted to studying for entrance exams.

Everyday Essentials, Item 2
Aroma Oils & Diffuser

I choose an oil depending on my
mood. When I'm working, I like to
think I make better progress when
enveloped in a pleasant fragrance,
but sometimes I get so relaxed that it
makes me sleepy instead (Get it
together!).

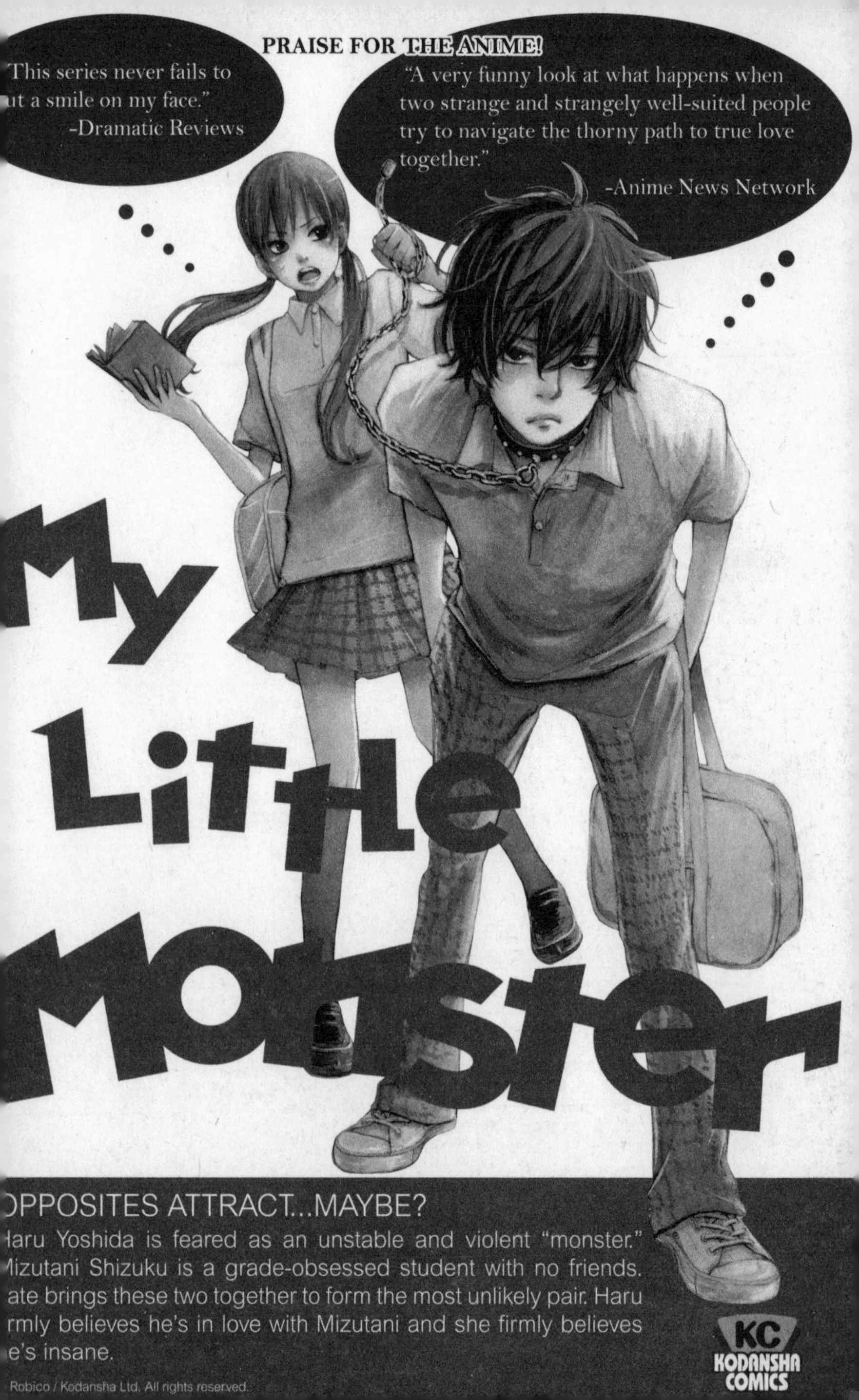
PRAISE FOR THE ANIME!
This series never fails to ut a smile on my face." -Dramatic Reviews
"A very funny look at what happens when two strange and strangely well-suited people try to navigate the thorny path to true love together." -Anime News Network
My Little Monster
)PPOSITES ATTRACT...MAYBE?
laru Yoshida is feared as an unstable and violent "monster." lizutani Shizuku is a grade-obsessed student with no friends. ate brings these two together to form the most unlikely pair. Haru rmly believes he's in love with Mizutani and she firmly believes e's insane.
KC KODANSHA COMICS
Robico / Kodansha Ltd. All rights reserved.

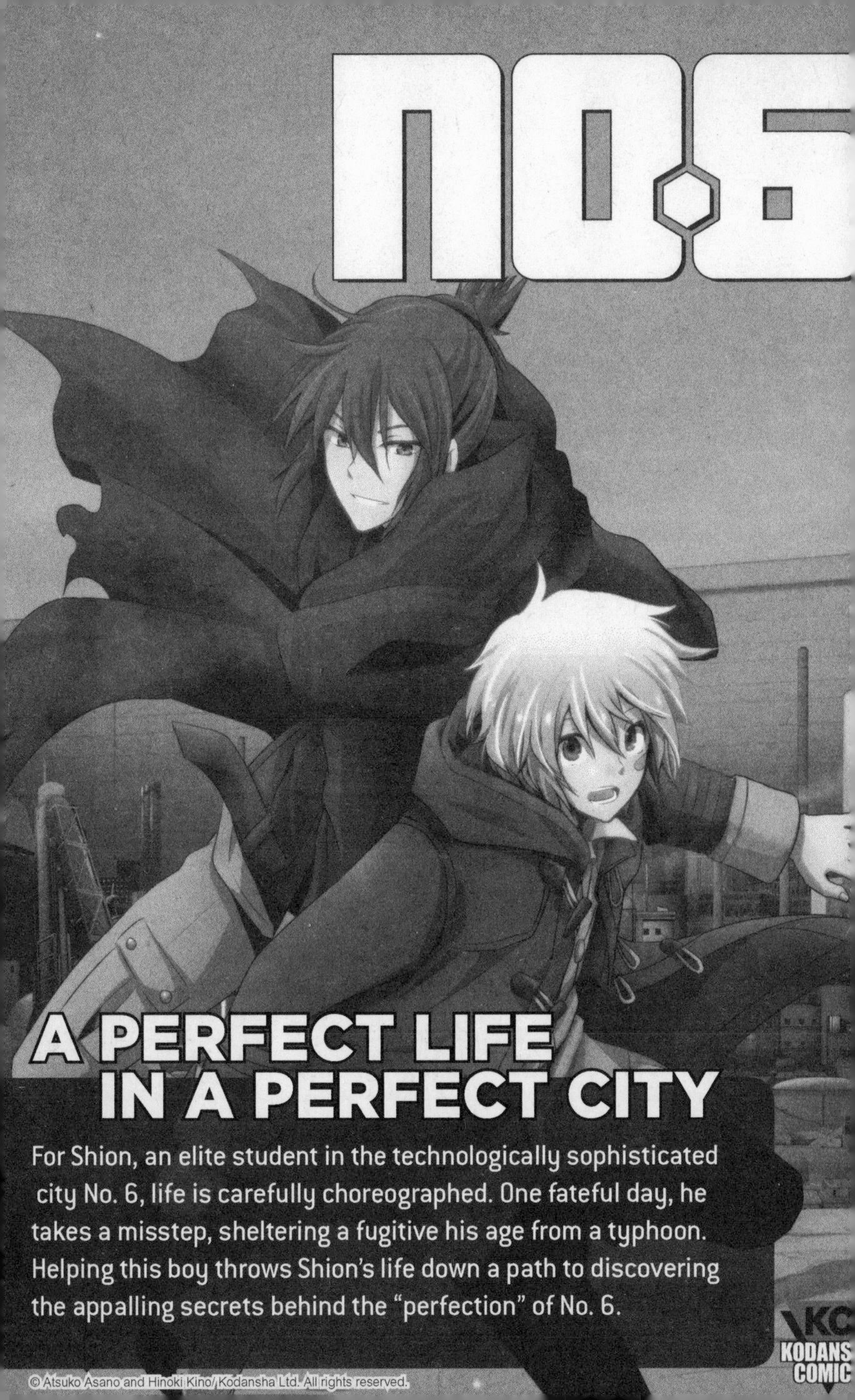
NO.6
A PERFECT LIFE IN A PERFECT CITY
For Shion, an elite student in the technologically sophisticated city No. 6, life is carefully choreographed. One fateful day, he takes a misstep, sheltering a fugitive his age from a typhoon. Helping this boy throws Shion's life down a path to discovering the appalling secrets behind the "perfection" of No. 6.
KC
KODANSHA COMIC
© Atsuko Asano and Hinoki Kino/Kodansha Ltd. All rights reserved.

Praise for the anime:

"The show provides a pleasant window on the highs and lows of young love with two young people who are first timers at the real thing."

-The Fandom Post

"Always it is smarter, more poetic, more touching, just plain better than you think it is going to be."

-Anime News Network

Say I Love You.

Mei Tachibana has no friends — and says she doesn't need them!

But everything changes when she accidentally roundhouse kicks the most popular boy in school! However, Yamato Kurosawa isn't angry in the slightest— in fact, he thinks his ordinary life could use an unusual girl like Mei. But winning Mei's trust will be a tough task. How long will she refuse to say, "I love you"?

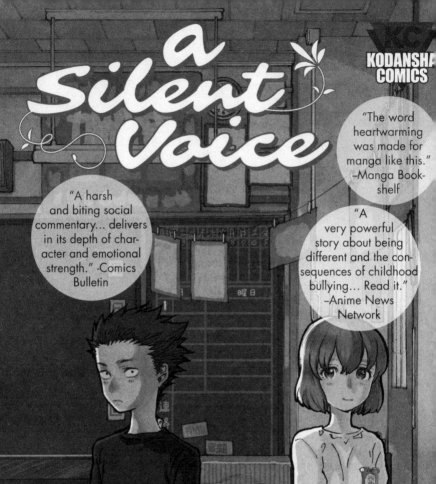

a Silent Voice

"The word heartwarming was made for manga like this."
–Manga Bookshelf

"A harsh and biting social commentary... delivers in its depth of character and emotional strength." -Comics Bulletin

"A very powerful story about being different and the consequences of childhood bullying... Read it."
–Anime News Network

Shoya is a bully. When Shoko, a girl who can't hear, enters his elementary school class, she becomes their favorite target, and Shoya and his friends goad each other into devising new tortures for her. But the children's cruelty goes too far. Shoko is forced to leave the school, and Shoya ends up shouldering all the blame. Six years later, the two meet again. Can Shoya make up for his past mistakes, or is it too late?

Available now in print and digitally!

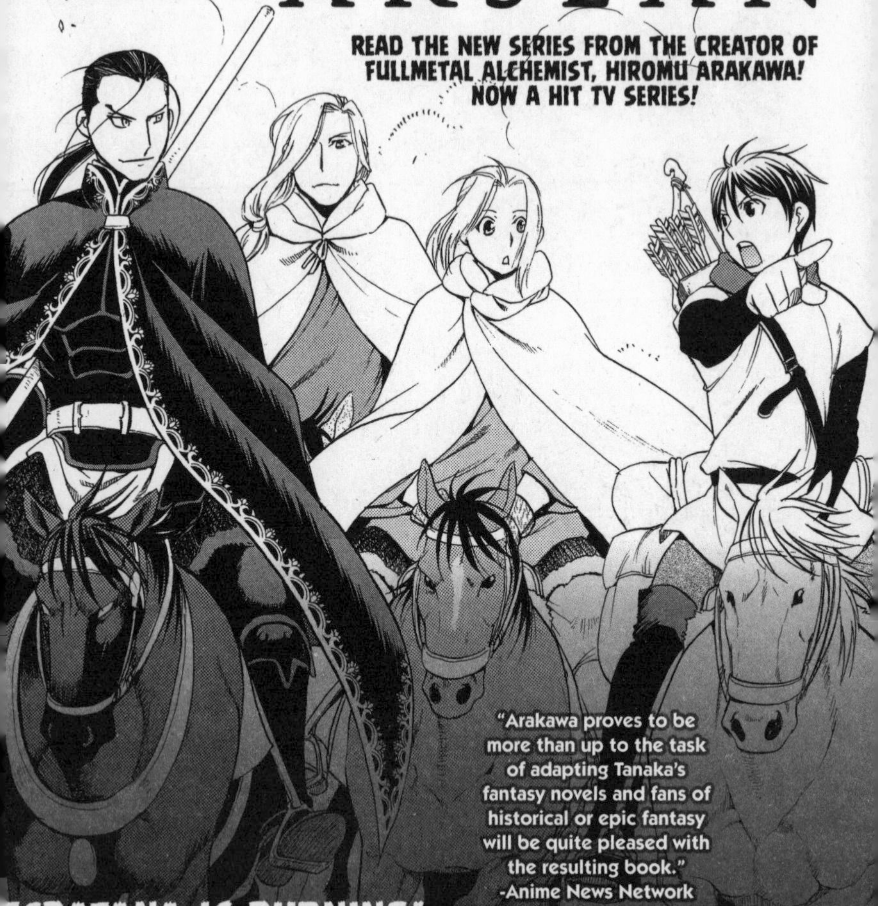

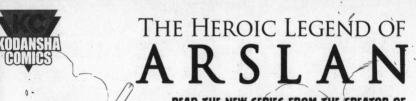

ceya

LDK volume 2 is a work of fiction. Names, characters, places, and incidents are the products of the author's imagination or are used fictitiously. Any resemblance to actual events, locales, or persons, living or dead, is entirely coincidental.

A Kodansha Comics Trade Paperback Original.

Published in the United States by Kodansha Comics, an imprint of Kodansha USA Publishing, LLC, New York.

Publication rights for this English edition arranged through Kodansha Ltd., Tokyo.

First published in Japan in 2009 by Kodansha Ltd., Tokyo, as *L♡DK*, volume 2.

ISBN 978-1-63236-123-3

Printed in the United States of America.

www.kodanshacomics.com

9 8 7 6 5 4 3 2 1

Translator: Christine Dashiell
Lettering: Sara Linsley
Editing: Ajani Oloye
Kodansha Comics Edition Cover Design: Phil Balsman